EUROPEAN

FREE TRADE SYSTEM AND POLICY HANDBOOK

VOLUME 1

INTEGRATION, POLICY, REGULATIONS

International Business Publications, USA
Washington DC, USA

EUROPEAN

FREE TRADE SYSTEM AND POLICY HANDBOOK

VOLUME 1. INTEGRATION, POLICY, REGULATIONS

UPDATED ANNUALLY

We express our sincere appreciation to all EU Central Bank and other government agencies and international organizations which provided information and other materials for this handbook This handbook is based on information obtained free of charge from the European Bank sources and other European financial organizations. No modification to the information have been made

Cover Design: **International Business Publications, USA**

2017 Edition Updated Reprint International Business Publications, USA
ISBN 978-1-5145-2315-5

For additional analytical, business and investment opportunities information,
please contact Global Investment & Business Center, USA
at (703) 370-8082. Fax: (703) 370-8083. E-mail: ibpusa3@gmail.com
Global Business and Investment Info Databank - www.ibpus.com

Printed in the USA

For additional analytical, business and investment opportunities information,
please contact Global Investment & Business Center, USA
at (703) 370-8082. Fax: (703) 370-8083. E-mail: ibpusa3@gmail.com
Global Business and Investment Info Databank - www.ibpus.com

EUROPEAN
FREE TRADE SYSTEM AND POLICY HANDBOOK
VOLUME 1
INTEGRATION, POLICY, REGULATIONS

EUROPEAN UNION STRATEGIC INFORMATION 9

WHAT IS THE EUROPEAN UNION? 9
HOW IS THE EU RUN? 12
A Unique Governing System 12
Governing Institutions 13
Codecision Procedure 13
European Parliament 13
European Council 14
Council of the European Union 14
Agencies and Other Bodies 15
European Commission 15
European Economic and Social Committee 16
Committee of the Regions 16
European Court of Justice (ECJ) 16
Legislation 16
European Court of Auditors (ECA) 17
THE EURO: COMPLETING ECONOMIC UNITY 17
Completing the Changeover 18
Participating in the Euro Area 18
What Does the Euro Mean? 19
The Euro and the Single Market 19
The Euro 20
The Euro and New Member States 20
Competition (Antitrust) 20
Culture 21
Education and Training 21
eEurope 21
Employment and Social Policy 22
Energy 22
Environment 23
Foreign Aid 23
Foreign Policy 24
Human Rights 24
Justice and Home Affairs: Free Movement, Counterterrorism and Internal Security 24
Regional Development 25
Research and Technological Development (R&TD) 26
Telecommunications 27
Trade 27
Transport 27

BUILDING THE NEW EUROPE: THE EU AND ITS NEIGHBORS ... 28
Toward EU Membership ... *28*
Future European Union Enlargement ... *30*
Cyprus, Malta, and Turkey ... *32*
Norway and Switzerland ... *32*
Croatia ... *32*
PHARE, TACIS, CARDS ... *33*
Russia and Its Neighbors ... *33*
Projecting Stability in Southeast Europe ... *34*
Mediterranean and Middle East Countries ... *34*

ECONOMIC, TRADE AND MONETARY UNION OF THE EUROPEAN UNION ... 36

History of the EMU ... *36*
Stage One: 1 July 1990 to 31 December 1993 ... *37*
Stage Two: 1 January 1994 to 31 December 1998 ... *37*
Stage Three: 1 January 1999 and continuing ... *37*

FREE TRADE AREAS IN EUROPE ... 38

EFTA[EDIT] ... 38
CEFTA[EDIT] ... 38
BAFTA[EDIT] ... 38
CISFTA[EDIT] ... 39
EU[EDIT] ... 39
EUROPEAN UNION CUSTOMS UNION[EDIT] ... 39
BALTIC FREE TRADE AREA ... 39
CENTRAL EUROPEAN FREE TRADE AGREEMENT ... 40
MEMBERS ... 40
Membership criteria ... *41*
Current members ... *41*
Original agreement ... *41*
CEFTA 2006 agreement ... *42*
Relations with the EU ... *42*
EUROPEAN UNION FREE TRADE AGREEMENTS ... 42
Free trade agreements in force ... *42*
Pending ... *44*
ACP countries ... *44*
Negotiating ... *44*
Concluded negotiations ... *44*
EU FREE TRADE POLICY WITH REGIONS AND COUNTRIES ... 45
EU Trade Policy and Economic Partnership Agreements ... *45*
Generalised Scheme of Preferences (GSP) ... *45*
West Africa ... *47*
Eastern and Southern Africa (ESA) ... *47*
Caribbean Countries ... *48*
Central Africa ... *50*
Southern African Development Community (SADC) ... *51*
EU and the Southern African Development Community ... *51*
Pacific Countries ... *52*
Andean Community Countries ... *53*
South East Asian Countries ... *54*
Central American Countries ... *55*
Central Asian Countries ... *56*
Mediterranean and North African Countries ... *57*
Gulf Region Countries ... *59*

South American (Mercosur) Countries *60*
South Caucasus Countries *61*
Western Balkans Countries *62*

EU TRADE AND FINANCIAL INTEGRATION **65**

EU FINANCIAL SERVICE POLICY 65
FREQUENTLY ASKED QUESTIONS (FAQS) ON EU FINANCIAL SERVICES POLICY FOR THE NEXT FIVE YEARS 66
LEGISLATION IN FORCE 71
REGULATORY CAPITAL 71
Capital requirements for credit institutions and investment firms *71*
Adoption of the Capital Requirements Directive *72*
European Commission proposal for a new capital requirements framework for banks and investment firms - frequently asked questions *72*
EUROPEAN FREE TRADE ASSOCIATION 77
Political History *78*
Membership history *78*
Current members *78*
General SecretarY *79*
Institutions *79*
EEA-related institutions *79*
Locations *79*
PORTUGAL FUND 79
EFTA in Economic Indicators *79*
Social Indicators *80*
International conventions *80*
EUROPEAN ECONOMIC AREA 81
Membership *81*
Freedoms and obligations *81*
Legislation *81*
Institutions *82*
EEA and Norway Grants *82*
INTERNATIONAL RELATIONSHIPS 82
Free Trade Agreement *82*
Signed agreement 2008, not yet ratified *82*
Signed agreement 2009, not yet ratified *82*
Finalised negotiations 2008 ..... *83*
Currently negotiating agreements *83*
Declarations on Cooperation *83*
Joint workgroups *83*
FUTURE 83

ESTERNAL TRADE AND POLICIES **84**

The rules-based system *84*
A network of agreements *84*
Trade and development *84*
Trade with major partners *85*
TRADE LEGISLATION, REGULATIONS AND POLICY 85
TRADE POLICY FUNDAMENTALS *85*
ACTION PLAN *86*
External dimension *87*
COMMON TRADE POLICY REGIME AND BASIC REGULATIONS FOR EXPORT 88
Exports *88*
Export credit insurance *90*

Dual-use items and technology ... *91*
Export of cultural goods ... *92*
Ban on trade in instruments of torture ... *93*
COMMON TRADE POLICY REGIME AND BASIC REGULATIONS FOR EXPORT IMPORTS ... 95
Common rules for imports ... *95*
Common rules for imports from certain Non-EU Member Countries ... *97*
Community procedure for administering quantitative quotas ... *98*
Products derived from seals ... *100*
COMMERCIAL DEFENCE STRATEGY ... 101
Anti-dumping measures ... *101*
Anti-subsidy measures ... *105*
Protection against trade barriers ... *106*
Protection against subsidies and unfair pricing practices which cause injury in the air transport sector ... *108*
Community statistics ... *110*
EXTERNAL TRADE AND GLOBALISATION ... 112
The Multilateral Trade Framework of the World Trade Organisation (WTO) ... *112*
Adoption of the WTO agreements ... *112*
Aspects relating to trade in goods ... *116*
RULES CONCERNING NON-TARIFF MEASURES ... *118*
CUSTOMS AND TRADE ADMINISTRATION ... *118*
TRADE PROTECTION MEASURES ... *119*
OTHER TRADE-RELATED RULES ... *120*
Aspects relating to trade in services ... *121*
Aspects of intellectual property rights ... *123*
Development ... *125*
Scheme of preferences from 2006 to 2015 - Guidelines ... *125*
A scheme of generalised tariff preferences 2009-2011 ... *125*
Towards an EU Aid for Trade strategy ... *127*
SCHEME OF PREFERENCES FROM 2006 TO 2015 - GUIDELINES ... 130
ASSISTING DEVELOPING COUNTRIES TO BENEFIT FROM TRADE ... 133
FAIR TRADE ... 135
AGRICULTURAL COMMODITIES, DEPENDENCE AND POVERTY ... 136
THE INTERNATIONAL COFFEE AGREEMENT 2007 ... 139
GLOBAL PARTNERSHIP FOR SUSTAINABLE DEVELOPMENT ... 140
INTEGRATION OF THE ENVIRONMENTAL DIMENSION IN DEVELOPING COUNTRIES ... 143
PROMOTING CORPORATE SOCIAL RESPONSIBILITY ... 145
STRATEGY FOR THE CUSTOMS UNION ... 148
Customs 2013 (2008-2013) ... *150*
The contribution of taxation and customs policies to the Lisbon Strategy ... *152*
Enhancing police and customs cooperation in the European Union ... *155*
Customs response to latest trends in counterfeiting and piracy ... *159*
European anti-counterfeiting and anti-piracy plan ... *161*
Money laundering: prevention through customs cooperation ... *162*
EU TRADE AND COMMERCIAL POLICY REGULATIONS ... 164

IMPORTANT OFFICIAL MATERIALS AND REGULATIONS ... 169

MAKING GLOBALISATION WORK FOR EVERYONE: THE EUROPEAN UNION AND WORLD TRADE ... 169
Trade for a better world ... *169*
Role and responsibilities of the European Union ... *169*
Free and fair ... *170*
Doing what you are good at ... *171*
The EU and the World Trade Organisation ... *172*
Forum for the whole world ... *172*

Ensuring countries play by the rules ... *173*
The EU's bilateral trade agreements ... *174*
Doing business with neighbours ... *174*
EU trade: the big players ... *175*
Opening up trade around the world ... *175*
Focus on development ... *176*
EU openness to exports from developing countries ... *177*
Aid and trade together ... *177*
Least developed countries exports to the EU ... *178*
The Doha development agenda: a new era for world trade ... *178*
Priorities for the future ... *179*
Trade-related assistance ... *179*
Taking on board issues of general public concern ... *180*
COMMON RULES FOR IMPORTS REGULATIONS ... 181
TITLE I General principles ... *183*
TITLE II Community information and consultation procedure ... *184*
TITLE III Community investigation procedure ... *184*
TITLE IV Surveillance ... *187*
TITLE V Safeguard measures ... *189*
TITLE VI Final provisions ... *191*
ANNEX I List of particulars to be given in the boxes of the surveillance document ... *192*
COMMON RULES FOR EXPORTS REGULATIONS ... 193
GLOBAL EUROPE EUROPE'S TRADE DEFENCE INSTRUMENTS IN A CHANGING GLOBAL ECONOMY ... 197
PART 1. What is the role of trade defence measures in a global economy? ... *199*
PART 2. Weighing different EU interests in trade defence investigations ... *200*
PART 3. The launching and conduct of trade defence investigations ... *202*
PART 4. The form, timing and duration of trade defence measures ... *204*
PART 5. Transparency in trade defence investigations ... *205*
PART 6. Institutional process ... *206*
GLOBAL EUROPE: A STRONGER PARTNERSHIP TO DELIVER MARKET ACCESS FOR EUROPEAN EXPORTERS 206
1. Introduction ... *206*
2. Market access in a changing global economy ... *207*
3. Proposals for a stronger Partnership to deliver market access ... *209*
4. Conclusion ... *212*
EU AID FOR TRADE STRATEGY ... 214
1. ORIGIN OF THE EU AID FOR TRADE STRATEGY ... *214*
2. OBJECTIVES ... *214*
3. INCREASING THE VOLUME OF EU AID FOR TRADE ... *215*
4. ENHANCING THE QUALITY OF EU AID FOR TRADE ... *217*
5. SPECIFIC ACP ANGLES OF THE PROPOSALS ... *220*
COMMUNITY PROGRAMMES CUSTOMS 2013 AND FISCALIS 2013 ... 222
1. BACKGROUND ... *222*
2. THE PRESENT PROGRAMMES ... *223*
3. POLICY CHALLENGES TO BE ADDRESSED BY THE SUCCESSOR PROGRAMMES ... *225*
4. IMPLEMENTATION CHALLENGES FOR THE SUCCESSOR PROGRAMMES ... *226*
5. BUDGET ... *228*

SUPPLEMENTS ... 230

FREE TRADE AGREEMENTS IN FORCE ... 230
WTO AGREEMENTS ... *230*
The Uruguay Round agreements ... *230*
Uruguay Round ministerial decisions and declarations ... *232*
TRATE AGREEMENTS EUROPE ... *234*
GLOSSARY ... 236

A *236*
B *237*
C *238*
D *244*
E *248*
F *255*
G *258*
H *259*
I *260*
H *263*
J *264*
K *264*
L *264*
M *266*
N *271*
O *273*
P *275*
Q *277*
R *277*
S *281*
T *285*
U *287*
W *287*
X *288*
Y *288*
BASIC TITLES ON EUROPEAN UNION (EU) 288

EUROPEAN UNION STRATEGIC INFORMATION

WHAT IS THE EUROPEAN UNION?

The European Union is a unique, treaty-based, institutional framework that defines and manages economic and political cooperation among its fifteen European member countries. The Union is the latest stage in a process of integration begun in the 1950s by six countries—Belgium, France, Germany, Italy, Luxembourg, and the Netherlands—whose leaders signed the original treaties establishing various forms of European integration.

These treaties gave life to the novel concept that, by creating communities of shared sovereignty in matters of coal and steel production, trade, and nuclear energy, another war in Europe would be unthinkable. While common EU policies have evolved in a number of other sectors since then, the fundamental goal of the Union remains the same: to create an ever-closer union among the peoples of Europe.

History: The Union's Origins

Economic integration was launched in the wake of World War II, as a devastated Western Europe sought to rebuild its economy. On May 9, 1950, French Foreign Minister Robert Schuman announced a plan, conceived by French businessman-turned-advisor, Jean Monnet, that proposed pooling European coal and steel production under a common authority. While contributing to economic recovery, this plan would also control the raw materials of war.

The Schuman Declaration was regarded as the first step toward achieving a united Europe—an ideal that in the past had been pursued only by force. Belgium, the Federal Republic of Germany, Italy, Luxembourg, and the Netherlands accepted the French proposal and signed the European Coal and Steel Community (ECSC) Treaty in Paris on April 18, 1951. The Six set up the ECSC High Authority, to which member governments transferred portions of their sovereign powers. Coal and steel trade among the Six increased by 129 percent over the next five years.

Encouraged by this success, the Six pursued integration in the military and political fields. When these efforts were derailed, European leaders decided to continue the unification of Europe on the economic front alone. A historic meeting in Messina, Italy, in June 1955, launched the negotiation of two treaties to establish:

- A European Economic Community (EEC) to merge separate national markets into a single market that would ensure the free movement of goods, people, capital, and services with a wide range of common economic policies; and

- A European Atomic Energy Community (EAEC or EURATOM) to further the use of nuclear energy for peaceful purposes.

The Six signed the treaties on March 25, 1957, in Rome. Often referred to as the "Rome Treaties," they came into force in January 1958.

Membership: Who can join the EU?

Union membership is open to any European country with a stable democratic government, a good human rights record, a properly functioning market economy, and sound macroeconomic policies. Candidates must also have the capacity to fulfill and to implement existing EU laws and policies (known as the *acquis communautaire*).

Four enlargements have taken place: Denmark, Ireland, and the United Kingdom joined the original six European Community members (Belgium, France, Germany, Italy, Luxembourg, Netherlands) in 1973. Greece joined in 1981, followed by Spain and Portugal in 1986. Austria, Finland, and Sweden acceded to the European Union on January 1, 1995. Norway had also negotiated and signed an accession treaty in 1994, but Norwegian voters narrowly rejected membership in a referendum.

Although it was not officially an enlargement, the five Laender of the former German Democratic Republic entered the Union as part of a united Germany on October 3, 1990. A fifth enlargement of the European Union to more than twenty-five member states is in progress. For more on the latest enlargement, see Chapter Six.

A United States of Europe?

The Union is often compared to the United States, and there are some similarities. Member countries have agreed to pool some of their sovereign powers for the sake of unity, just as American states did to create a federal republic. In the fields where such pooling of national sovereignty has occurred—for example, in trade and agriculture—the Union negotiates directly with the United States and other countries. Twelve member states have also pooled their sovereignty in the area of monetary policy by joining the Economic and Monetary Union. (See Chapter Three).

But there are also many differences. EU member states retain their sovereign powers in such fields as security and defense, although they now can take joint action in certain foreign and security policy areas. The development of a European Security and Defense Policy and Rapid Reaction Force (see Chapter Seven) are important steps in this effort.

While the US federal model continues to inspire the search for political unity, Europe is constructing its own model for unification, ensuring respect for the historical, cultural, and linguistic diversity of the European nations. Following the signing of the Treaty of Nice, European leaders engaged in the "Debate on the Future of the European Union" (http://europa.eu.int/futurum/index_en.htm) to exchange their visions prior to the 2004 EU Intergovernmental Conference (IGC).

The Treaties

The European Union does not yet have a formal constitution. A Constitutional Convention to discuss this issue (http://european-convention.eu.int/Static.asp?lang=EN&Content=Introduction) was organized recently. Instead, the European Union was built by means of a series of treaties that represent binding commitments by the member states signing them. Member states negotiate these treaties through intergovernmental conferences, or "IGCs," that culminate in a summit chaired by the member state holding the Council presidency.

This process began with three separate treaties dating from the 1950s: the European Coal and Steel Community (ECSC), the European Atomic Energy Community (EURATOM) and the European Economic Community (EEC). In 1967, they collectively became known as the European Communities.

The Treaty on European Union, signed in Maastricht, Netherlands, and in effect since November 1993, was a major overhaul of the founding treaties. Maastricht provided a blueprint to achieve Economic and Monetary Union (EMU), further developed the Union's inherent political dimension through the new Common Foreign and Security Policy (CFSP), and expanded cooperation in judicial and policing matters.

It created the "three pillar" European Union that exists today (see below).

Pillar One incorporated the three founding treaties now forming the "European Community" and set out the institutional requirements for EMU. It also provided for expanded Community action in certain areas, such as the environment, research, education, and training.

Pillar Two established the CFSP, which makes it possible for the Union to take joint action in foreign and security affairs.

Pillar Three created the Justice and Home Affairs (JHA) policy, dealing with asylum, immigration, judicial cooperation in civil and criminal matters, and customs and police cooperation against terrorism, drug trafficking, and fraud.

The CFSP and JHA operate by intergovernmental cooperation, rather than by the Community institutions that operate Pillar One. Maastricht also created European citizenship and strengthened the European Parliament's legislative role in certain areas.

The Treaty of Amsterdam

The Treaty of Amsterdam, which took effect in 1999, continued the reforms of the Maastricht Treaty and began to streamline the EU's institutions ahead of the next enlargement. Many institutional questions were postponed to the Intergovernmental Conference launched at the Helsinki European Council Summit in December 1999 and resulting in the Treaty of Nice.

The Amsterdam Treaty strengthened the CFSP and the EU's ability to undertake joint foreign policy actions. More decisions could be reached by qualified majority instead of unanimity, as required by Maastricht, and member states became able to abstain from a vote or an action without impeding the majority. The Union also appointed Javier Solana as High Representative for CFSP and established a new policy unit.

The Treaty of Nice

The Treaty of Nice, signed in Nice, France, in December 2000, entered into force on February 1, 2003. It addressed a number of institutional questions remaining after the Treaty of Amsterdam. Most of the institutional aspects of the Treaty of Nice will not take effect until 2005.

Its most important purpose is to prepare the EU institutions for enlargement to as many as twenty-eight member states. Measures in the Treaty of Nice include:

- Extension of qualified majority voting and reweighting of votes within the Council (see chart in Chapter Two);

- Extending the use of "enhanced cooperation" to allow groups of at least eight member states to proceed with policy initiatives;

- Redistribution of seats within the European Parliament in preparation for new members (see chart in Chapter Two); and
- Reconfiguring the College of Commissioners and strengthening the European Commission presidency.

The *Declaration on the Future of the Union,* annexed to the Treaty of Nice, called for a deeper and wider debate about the future of Europe and the structure of the European Union. The "European Convention" and the "Debate on the Future of the European Union" have provided the groundwork for the 2004 Intergovernmental Conference (IGC) to consider:

- More clearly defining the competences of the Union and its member states, based on the principle of subsidiarity;
- Measures to simplify the treaties;
- The role of national parliaments in the European construction; and
- The legal status of the *Charter of Fundamental Rights.*

Looking Ahead

Through the search for "ever closer union," the European Union has consolidated economic prosperity and democracy in Western Europe and helped bring stability to Central and Eastern Europe. Increasingly, the EU must deal with the challenges of globalization in the twenty-first century. The Treaty of Nice and the 2004 IGC are important developments, but they should be seen in this broad, evolutionary context.

HOW IS THE EU RUN?

A UNIQUE GOVERNING SYSTEM

As the treaties summarized in Chapter One indicate, the EU system is inherently evolutionary, adapting to changing political and economic circumstances.

Unlike the United States, the EU is founded on international treaties among sovereign nations rather than a constitution. (A Constitutional Convention to discuss this issue was organized recently.) The power to enact laws that are directly binding on all EU citizens throughout the EU territory also distinguishes the Union from international organizations. This governing system differs from all previous national and international models.

In areas falling under Pillar One of the EU (as described in Chapter One), member states have relinquished part of their national sovereignty to the EU institutions. This has led to descriptions of the Union as a supranational entity, with many decisions made and final authority residing at the EU level. In these areas the member states work together, in their collective interest, through the EU institutions to administer their sovereign powers jointly.

Under Pillars Two and Three, member states have agreed to cooperate but retain much more discretion over their participation, including the right to veto certain measures. Here the EU has been described as an intergovernmental entity, with EU policies administered largely by the member states themselves, rather than through the EU institutions.

The Union also operates according to the principle of "subsidiarity"—or devolution, as it is known in the US, which characterizes most federal systems. Under this principle, the Union is granted jurisdiction only over those policies that cannot be handled effectively at the national or lower levels of government.

GOVERNING INSTITUTIONS

The European Union is governed by five institutions: European Parliament, Council of the European Union, European Commission, European Court of Justice, and European Court of Auditors. In addition, the heads of state and government and the Commission president meet at least twice a year in European Council (see below) summits to provide overall strategy and political direction. The European Central Bank is responsible for monetary policy and managing the euro in the Economic and Monetary Union.

These institutions embody the supranational and intergovernmental aspects of the EU.

CODECISION PROCEDURE

The Maastricht Treaty gave the European Parliament the power of "codecision" with the Council in a limited number of areas such as research, health, and culture. It left the Council with the last say on a significant number of other policies but still substantially increased the Parliament's power. Before Maastricht, the Parliament could amend the Council's draft legislation (the so-called cooperation procedure), offer its opinion through the "consultation" procedure, or withhold its "assent" to Council decisions in certain areas (residence rights, the structural and cohesion funds, treaties of accession, and others).

The Amsterdam Treaty increased Parliament's responsibilities by making the codecision procedure the general rule, furthered by the Treaty of Nice. If the Council and Parliament cannot agree, a special Conciliation Committee is formed. Even if the Committee agrees to a joint text, Parliament may still reject the proposed act by an absolute majority of its members.

The "cooperation" procedure will survive only within the confines of Economic and Monetary Union. The "assent" procedure will be required in cases such as applications for membership of the Union and certain major international agreements.

For more on changes made by the Treaty of Nice, please consult Memo/03/23.

For additional information on EU decision-making, please see the description and chart on the Europa website under "Institutions" (http://europa.eu.int/institutions/decision-making/index_en.htm) and/or a similar section on the Council of Ministers website (http://ue.eu.int/codec/en/index.htm).

EUROPEAN PARLIAMENT

The European Parliament (EP) comprises 626 members, directly elected in EU-wide elections for five-year terms. The president of the Parliament is elected for a two-and-a-half year term. Though they are elected on a national basis, members of the European Parliament (MEPs) form political rather than national groups based on party affiliation.

The legislative role of the European Parliament has been strengthened over the years. Although the EP cannot enact laws like national parliaments, the Maastricht Treaty provided for a codecision procedure that empowers Parliament to veto legislation in certain policy areas and to confer with the Council in a "conciliation committee" to iron out differences in their respective drafts of legislation. The Amsterdam Treaty extended the number of policy areas in which Parliament can exercise these powers. The Treaty of Nice also extended the codecision powers of the Parliament and, for the first time, established a statute for political parties at the European level. It also increased (with the next Parliamentary term) the maximum number of seats to 732 and modified their distribution to make room for the elected representatives of future new members

The Parliament acts as the EU's public forum. It can question the Commission and the Council; amend or reject the EU budget; and dismiss the entire Commission through a vote of censure, a power it has never used. However, pressure from the Parliament led to a critical report and the Commission's collective resignation in March 1999. Parliament now also has the power to confirm a newly appointed Commission and to hold hearings on individual Commissioners. It cannot reject individual nominees, only the full Commission. Since Maastricht, Parliament has an appointed ombudsman to address allegations of maladministration in EU institutions and agencies. The Parliament holds plenary sessions in Strasbourg and Brussels. Its twenty committees, which prepare the work for plenary meetings, and its political groups usually meet in Brussels.

EUROPEAN COUNCIL

The European Council brings together heads of state and government and the president of the Commission. It meets at least twice a year at the end of each EU member state's six-month presidency. The Single European Act (SEA) of 1986 formalized the European Council, which was not foreseen in the original EC treaties. The Nice European Council decided that, from 2002 on, one European Council meeting per presidency would be held in Brussels. Following the accession of ten new member states in 2004, all European Council meetings are held there, reinforcing its status as "the capital of Europe."

COUNCIL OF THE EUROPEAN UNION

The Council of the European Union enacts EU laws, acting on proposals submitted by the Commission.

Comprising ministers from each member state, the Council strikes a balance between national and Union interests. Different ministers participate in the Council according to the subject under discussion. Agricultural ministers, for instance, discuss farm prices in the Agriculture Council, and economic and finance ministers discuss monetary affairs in the ECOFIN Council.

The ministers for foreign affairs provide overall coordination in the General Affairs and External Relations Council (GAERC). They are also responsible for foreign policy in the framework of the Common Foreign and Security Policy. Each government acts as president of the Council for six months in rotation. The Council is assisted by a Committee of Permanent Representatives (COREPER), comprising member state officials holding ambassadorial rank, and a secretariat with a staff of about 2,000.

The Council makes most decisions by qualified majority vote (QMV), with the Treaty of Nice extending QMV to twenty-nine new policy areas. With the Treaty of Nice, QMV requires support by a majority of member states, representing at least 62 percent of the EU population. The voting threshold for QMV also rose with Nice from 71.3 percent for fifteen members—eventually to become 73.9 percent in an EU of twenty-seven members

Unanimity is still required for areas like amendments to the treaties, taxation, the launch of a new common policy, or the admission of a new member state.

In the area of CFSP, the Amsterdam Treaty provided that as many as one-third of member states could "constructively abstain" from a decision while allowing the others to act together on behalf of the EU. Member states that "constructively abstain" were not able to take any action that impeded the decision made by the majority. Amsterdam also provided for qualified majority voting in implementing basic political decisions.

The Treaty of Nice made the procedure of "enhanced cooperation" among member states even more flexible. A minimum of eight member states may choose to cooperate in certain areas, provided that participation is open to all and they do not infringe upon the rights of other member states.

AGENCIES AND OTHER BODIES

- ***Committee of European Securities Regulators* (CESR)** (Paris, France)
- ***Community Plant Variety Office* (CPVO)** (Angers, France).
- ***European Agency for Reconstruction* (EAR)** (Thessaloniki, Greece).
- ***European Agency for Safety and Health at Work* (OSHA)** *(*Bilbao, Spain).
- ***European Agency for the Evaluation of Medicinal Products* (EMEA)** (London, UK).
- ***European Aviation Safety Agency* (EASA)** (Brussels, Belgium).
- ***European Center for the Development of Vocational Training* (CEDEFOP)** (Thessaloniki, Greece).
- ***European Environment Agency* (EEA)** (Copenhagen, Denmark)—a repository of environmental data.
- ***European Food Safety Authority (EFSA)*** (Brussels, Belgium)
- ***European Foundation for the Improvement of Living and Working Conditions* (E.FOUND)** *(*Dublin, Ireland).
- ***European Judicial Network* (EUROJUST – EJN)** (Brussels, Belgium).
- ***European Maritime Safety Agency* (EMSA)** (Brussels, Belgium).
- ***European Monitoring Center for Drugs and Drug Addiction (*EMCDDA*)*** (Lisbon, Portugal).
- ***European Monitoring Center on Racism and Xenophobia (*EUMC*)*** (Vienna, Austria).
- ***European Police Office* (EUROPOL*)*** (The Hague, The Netherlands)—for police coordination among EU member states.
- ***European Training Foundation* (ETF)** (Turin, Italy).
- ***European Union Institute for Security Studies (EUISS)*** (Paris, France).
- ***European Union Satellite Centre (EUSC)*** (Madrid, Spain).
- ***The Food and Veterinary Office* (FVO)** (Dunsany, Ireland).
- ***Humanitarian Aid Office* (ECHO)** (Brussels, Belguim)
- ***Office of Harmonization in the Internal Market* (OHIM)** (Alicante, Spain)—trademarks and designs.
- ***Translation Center for the Bodies of the European Union* (CDT)** (Luxembourg).

EUROPEAN COMMISSION

The Commission is the policy engine. It proposes legislation, is responsible for administration, and ensures that the provisions of the treaties and the decisions of the institutions are properly implemented. It has investigative powers and can take legal action against persons, companies, or member states that violate EU rules. It manages the budget and represents the Union in international trade negotiations and other issues within its jurisdiction.

The twenty commissioners are appointed for five-year terms in line with the European Parliament, which approves the appointment of the Commission as a body. The commissioners act in the Union's interest, independently of the national governments that nominated them. Each is assigned one or more policy areas and is assisted by a small cabinet or team of aides. The Commission's administrative staff, based mainly in Brussels, numbers more than 22,000, divided among more than thirty "Directorates-General" and other administrative services. Given the number of EU official languages (accommodating all member state principal languages), more than 8 percent of the Commission staff are translators and interpreters.

Under the Treaty of Nice, the composition of the College of Commissioners was altered and the powers of the Commission president strengthened. The five largest states gave up their right to name a second commissioner as of 2005, and new member states name one commissioner until the EU reaches twenty-seven members. At that point, the total number of commissioners will be set at a lower number, with appointments made by rotation among member states in a manner to be determined by a unanimous Council vote. The president will be selected by the European Council according to the qualified majority voting procedure, rather than by unanimity as pre-Nice. He or she will have greater control of the structure and allocation of responsibilities within the College of Commissioners and can request a commissioner's resignation. Up to two vice presidents are appointed from among the commissioners.

EUROPEAN ECONOMIC AND SOCIAL COMMITTEE

The European Economic and Social Committee (ESC) was established by the EEC Treaty to fulfill a role as an advisory institution. It is based in Brussels and consists of representatives of labor, employers, agriculture, consumers, and professional associations.

COMMITTEE OF THE REGIONS

The Committee of the Regions (COR) was also established as a consultative body by the Maastricht Treaty and is comprised of representatives of regional and local bodies. It is based in Brussels.

EUROPEAN COURT OF JUSTICE (ECJ)

LEGISLATION

Legislation takes different forms, depending on the objectives to be achieved.

Regulations are binding in their entirety, self-executing, directly applicable, and obligatory throughout the EU territory. They can be compared to US federal laws.

Directives are binding in terms of the results to be achieved and are addressed to the member states, which are free to choose the best forms and methods of implementation.

Decisions are binding in their entirety upon those to whom they are addressed—member states and natural and/or legal persons.

Recommendations and **Opinions** are not binding.

The European Court of Justice, sitting in Luxembourg, is the Community's "Supreme Court." It ensures that the treaties are interpreted and applied correctly by other EU institutions and by the member states. The Court comprises one judge from each member state, appointed for renewable terms of six years. Judgments of the Court in the field of EC law are binding on EU institutions, member states, national courts, companies, and private citizens, and they overrule those of national courts.

Since 1989 a Court of First Instance, also consisting of one judge per member state, has assisted the European Court of Justice.

Under the Treaty of Nice, the Court of First Instance became the common law judge for all direct actions (particularly proceedings against a decision: Article 230 of the Treaty Establishing the European Community), action for failure to act (Article 232 of the Treaty Establishing the European Community), action for damages (Article 235 of the Treaty Establishing the European Community), with the exception of those that will be attributed to a specialized chamber and those the statute reserves for the Court of Justice itself.

The Court of Justice retains responsibility for other proceedings (particularly action for failure to fulfill obligations: Article 226 of the Treaty Establishing the European Community), but the statute can entrust to the Court of First Instance categories of proceedings other than those listed in Article 225 of the Treaty Establishing the European Community.

The idea is to maintain within the Court of Justice, as the jurisdictional supreme body of the European Union, disputes concerning essential issues. The Court of Justice, which is responsible for ensuring uniform application of EU law within the European Union, in principle retains competence for investigating questions referred for a preliminary ruling; however, pursuant to Article 225 of the Treaty Establishing the European Community, the statute may entrust to the Court of First Instance the responsibility for preliminary rulings in certain specific matters.

For additional information on the changes in the EU judicial system wrought by the Treaty of Nice, please consult Memo/03/23.

EUROPEAN COURT OF AUDITORS (ECA)

The European Court of Auditors, based in Luxembourg, is responsible for the sound financial management of the EU budget. It has extensive powers to examine the legality of receipts and expenditures.

European Central Bank (ECB)

The European System of Central Banks (ESCB) and the European Central Bank in Frankfurt are responsible for monetary policy and the euro

THE EURO: COMPLETING ECONOMIC UNITY

As of January 1, 2002, the euro is the official legal tender of twelve of the EU countries, replacing their national currencies. Already established as an accounting currency on January 1, 1999, the euro represents the consolidation of European economic integration. With euros in citizens' pockets for use in daily transactions, the euro is a palpable reality and contributes to a broader sense of European identity.

Several decades in the making, the euro required much planning and political commitment to become a reality. The introduction of the euro began the third stage and the final transition to full Economic and Monetary Union (EMU), a process that was launched in 1990 as EU member states prepared for the 1992 single market. Aimed at boosting cross-border business activity, the first stage of EMU lifted restrictions on movements of capital across internal EU borders (July 1, 1990). Stage two, which began in January 1994, set up the European Monetary Institute (EMI) in Frankfurt to pave the way for the European Central Bank (ECB) in the same location.

The euro-zone is roughly comparable in economic weight to the United States. The population of the twelve member states participating in EMU is about 290 million, and the euro-zone accounts for more than 21 percent of world GDP. In 2000, euro-zone exports amounted to 14.7 percent of world exports, with the comparable figure for euro-zone imports at 13 percent. Beyond its economic impact, the euro has substantial political significance and adds to the EU's capabilities as an international actor.

COMPLETING THE CHANGEOVER

As of February 28, 2002, national notes and coins of the twelve member states in the euro-zone were withdrawn permanently and replaced by the euro. This was a huge logistical task with a corresponding impact on EU citizens in participating member states. Preparatory steps taken since January 1, 1999 included:

- Fixing the conversion rate of the participating currencies to the euro irrevocably;
- Having all operations of the European Central Bank in euros;
- Having wholesale financial and capital markets use the euro;
- Denominating all public debt in euros;
- Denominating private bank accounts in euros;
- Making euro-denominated credit cards available and making payments in euros possible on existing credit cards;
- Having public administrations in the euro countries allow companies to use the euro for accounting purposes, tax payments, and in some cases, social security payments;
- Dual pricing (in national currencies and euros) to help the general public adapt to the euro.

PARTICIPATING IN THE EURO AREA

The decisions about which of the then-fifteen member states would participate in the euro were made for the most part on May 2, 1998, at a special meeting of EU leaders in Brussels. The decisions were based on each member state's performance in meeting the economic "convergence criteria" set out in the Maastricht Treaty, including sound management in the areas of public finances, price stability, exchange rates, and interest rates. Following this decision, on January 1, 1999, the euro became the single currency for eleven EU member states: Austria, Belgium, Finland, France, Germany, Italy, Ireland, Luxembourg, the Netherlands, Spain, and Portugal. On January 1, 2001, Greece joined this group after meeting the Maastricht "convergence criteria." New member states join as they meet the criteria.

WHAT DOES THE EURO MEAN?

The euro means stability. Member states participating in EMU are legally bound to continue the fiscal discipline required by the Maastricht Treaty to qualify for EMU. This is the purpose of the Stability and Growth Pact, agreed to by EU heads of state and government in July 1997, under which sanctions can be brought against member states that do not comply with strict guidelines for managing public finances.

The euro consolidates and extends Europe's single market. By removing transaction costs and completely eliminating currency transactions in the euro-zone, trade and investment are greatly facilitated.

The euro creates new opportunities in the financial sector. The market capitalization of stocks traded in a country or region divided by that region's GDP is a common indicator of the importance and size of an equity market. The euro area's ratio of market capitalization to GDP gained significantly in the 1990s. From 1990 to 1995, the ratio hovered around 25 percent and was remarkably lower than that in Japan or the United States. However, by 2000, the overall growth in the euro area's stock market resulted in an increase in this ratio to 89 percent, topping Japan's 68 percent.

The euro is likely to become a major reserve currency. According to some estimates, the euro could account for 25 percent or more of global foreign exchange reserves in the medium term. This should help the EU and the United States share the burden of global financial stability, particularly in the wake of an economic downturn. The European Central Bank moved to reassure world markets following the September 11, 2001, terrorist attacks in the United States, and subsequently cooperated with the US Federal Reserve and other central banks to ensure sufficient liquidity for market and other economic transactions.

Like any other currency in the floating exchange rate system, the dollar to euro exchange rate fluctuates, reflecting perceptions about economic growth prospects. The dollar to euro exchange rate averaged $0.95 in 2002, $0.90 in 2001, and $0.92 for 2000.

THE EURO AND THE SINGLE MARKET

The euro is the logical complement to Europe's single market, which was largely completed in 1992 following the Single European Act (SEA) of 1986. The SEA facilitated the adoption of a package of nearly 300 "internal market" directives set forth in a 1985 Commission White Paper and designed to achieve the "four freedoms": freedom of movement for goods, capital, people, and services among the member countries.

For most commercial purposes, there is now one frontier instead of individual frontiers for each member state; standards, testing, and certification procedures are either uniform or equivalent; and significant economies of scale are attainable in a market of over 370 million consumers—soon a half-billion. The combination of economic liberalization and monetary integration boosts the competitiveness of European companies while making it easier and cheaper for non-EU companies to do business in Europe.

Almost all of the legislation required for completing the 1992 single market has been enacted. However, due to some implementation delays in a small number of areas, the Commission launched an Action Plan to ensure that member states and private sector operators meet their obligations under EU single market rules.

The single market benefits European and foreign companies alike. Special efforts were made to ensure that the program was fully transparent and accessible to American business and the US authorities. Foreign companies, especially from the United States and Japan, positioned themselves to take advantage of the single market. They have increased their direct investment and entered into joint ventures with European partners.

The graphic symbol for the euro (above) looks like an E with two clearly marked, horizontal, parallel lines across it. It was inspired by the Greek letter epsilon, in reference to the cradle of European civilization and to the first letter of the word "Europe." The parallel lines represent the stability of the euro.

The official abbreviation for the euro is "EUR." It has been registered with the International Standards Organization (ISO) and is used for all business, financial, and commercial purposes.

THE EURO

There are seven euro-denominated notes (5, 10, 20, 50, 100, 200, and 500 euro) and eight coins (1, 2, 5, 10, 20, and 50 euro cents and 1 and 2 euro coins). For a short period in early 2002, dual circulation accompanied the gradual withdrawal of the national currency notes and coins. The coins have a common design on one side and a national design on the other.

THE EURO AND NEW MEMBER STATES

Even though accession to the EU entails acceptance of the objective of EMU, compliance with the "convergence criteria" is not a precondition for EU membership. New countries often join the EU before they qualify for EMU membership. Since the "convergence criteria" are signposts of a macroeconomic policy geared to achieving stability, however, all new member states are expected to move toward them on a permanent basis.

COMPETITION (ANTITRUST)

An efficient competition policy has always been at the heart of European integration, and it remains vital to the proper functioning of Europe's single market and for the protection of its consumers. According to Competition Commissioner Mario Monti, *"Competition should lead to lower prices, a wider choice of goods, and technological innovation, all in the interest of the consumer."* EU competition policy has a dual objective. On the one hand, specific treaty provisions outlaw agreements among companies to fix prices, market share, production, investment and to prohibit the abuse of dominant positions. On the other, it places national subsidies (state aids) to individual firms or industrial sectors under the Commission's supervision to prevent distortion of the market.

Since 1989, the Commission has had jurisdiction over larger-scale mergers and takeovers (acquisitions) affecting more than one member state and exceeding certain thresholds. The Commission may punish antitrust violators with heavy fines. The Commission, like the United States Government, is entitled to review mergers between non-EU companies provided the companies' activities have an appreciable impact in the EU (and reach the "turnover" or revenue thresholds specified in the EU's merger regulation).

The EU's July 3, 2001, decision blocking the GE/Honeywell merger is only the first instance, in over 394 merger examinations up to that point involving at least one US company, where the EU blocked a US approved merger. Monti says, *"It would be wrong to present the GE/Honeywell case as a confrontation between US and EU companies."* Complaints considered for the merger examination came from both sides of the Atlantic.

The EU and the US have concluded cooperative competition agreements—a basic agreement in 1991 and in 1998 the "Positive Comity" Agreement. The principle of "positive comity" provides that, when a party is adversely affected by anticompetitive behavior occurring in the territory of the other party, it may request that the other party take action.

CULTURE

One of Europe's greatest assets is its cultural diversity, which will never become an area for harmonization among the member states. The Maastricht Treaty gave the EU a role to play in bringing "the common cultural heritage to the fore" while respecting national and regional diversity. The completion of the single market, however, does require some measures related to creative endeavor, particularly as regards cross-frontier television, copyright, and the free movement of cultural goods and services.

EDUCATION AND TRAINING

Education and training play a central role in building a highly skilled workforce for a more competitive Europe. While responsibility for academic systems and curricula rests with the member states, the EU has two large-scale education programs to promote cooperation among them. Socrates, with a budget of $1.7 billion for 2000-2006, provides for cross-border mobility of students and teachers; promotion of foreign language competence; and mutual recognition of diplomas, periods of study, and other qualifications.

Leonardo, with a budget of $1.06 billion for 2000-2006, aims to improve the quality of vocational training; promote exchanges; and promote wider use of information age resources.

EEUROPE

The EU's eEurope initiative, launched in March 2000, aims to maximize access to the Internet, create a digitally literate Europe, and spark an entrepreneurial culture—all while avoiding a digital divide and reinforcing social inclusion and cohesion. Making the European Union the most competitive and dynamic knowledge-based economy in the world is a major EU priority. The number of EU households connected to the Internet rose from 18.3 percent in March 2000 to 36.1 percent in June 2001 and 40.4% in June 2002.

EMPLOYMENT AND SOCIAL POLICY

Since the 1957 founding of the Union, the standard of living of Europe's citizens has doubled. However, unemployment remained high in some member states as Europe's economies prepared to launch the euro and begin a new enlargement. To pave the way for a more coordinated European strategy, the 1997 Amsterdam Treaty introduced a new chapter on employment that made job creation a formal goal of the Union. European Councils, beginning particularly with Lisbon in March 2000, expanded this goal to encompass specific measures to alleviate unemployment—including preparations for the shift to a digital, knowledge-based economy. According to the EU's *Employment In Europe, 2002 Report,* high-tech and knowledge-intensive sectors have driven job creation. These sectors contributed approximately 90 percent of total job creation between 1995 and 2001. The unemployment rate in the EU fell from 8.2 percent in 2000 to 7.6 percent in 2002.

With the removal of barriers within the Union, the drive to complete the single market was accompanied by social legislation guaranteeing workers a certain standard of health and safety in all member states and facilitating vocational training and retraining. A Social Protocol was added to the Maastricht Treaty which led to legislation on the European Works Councils, equal rights for part-time and full-time workers, and parental leave for men as well as for women. The Social Protocol was incorporated into the Amsterdam Treaty, giving the Union a greater role in social legislation and providing fresh impetus to initiatives in the social policy area.

The March 2000 Lisbon European Council launched an annual meeting on the economy, and it highlighted the essential linkage between Europe's economic strength and its social model: the Lisbon Strategy. Subsequently, the December 2000 Nice Council adopted the Social Policy Agenda (2000-2005), which seeks to modernize the European social model, invest in people, and combat social exclusion (poverty). The agenda includes job creation that profits from the new working environment and the potential of the knowledge-based economy; modern and improved social protection (the social safety net); social inclusion, gender equality, reinforced fundamental rights; and preparations for enlargement.

ENERGY

Although not a full-fledged common policy, the founding treaties provided for certain common activities in the field of energy, such as promoting energy research under the EU's Research and Technological Development (R&TD) policy, and supporting the establishment of a Trans-European Network (TEN) for energy. In recent years, however, security of the EU's energy supply and protection of the environment have become priorities. The Union is working to establish a single energy market as a means to ensure a supply of energy to all consumers at affordable prices, while respecting both the environment and sustainable development. Policies have focused on the liberalization of the electricity and gas markets within the EU and the facilitation of cross-border transit of both these energy sources. Renewable energy resources are playing an important role in the diversification of energy sources and environmental protection.

The Union was instrumental in the creation of the European Energy Charter, which was signed by fifty-one nations in the Netherlands in 1991. The mission of the Energy Charter process is to strive toward open, efficient, sustainable, and secure energy markets and to promote a constructive climate conducive to energy interdependence based on trust among nations.

ENVIRONMENT

The EU's environment policy was officially launched in 1972 and incorporated into the EEC Treaty by the Single European Act (SEA) (1986). The EU has developed a substantial body of environmental law to protect against water, air, and noise pollution and to control risks related to chemicals, biotechnology, and nuclear energy within the Union. These are supplemented by multiannual action programs, the most recent of which—the Sixth Environmental Action Program (2001-2010)—concentrates on four priority areas: climate change, nature and biodiversity, environment and health, and natural resources and waste.

A European Environment Agency (EEA) was set up in 1993 in Copenhagen to provide reliable scientific data and evaluations for those involved in implementing and developing European environment policy. The Agency is open to participation from other European countries.

The EU is an important actor in international initiatives on the environment. It is party to the Montreal Protocol on Ozone Depletion, the Basel Convention on Toxic Waste, and most recently the Kyoto Protocol on Climate Change. The EU continues its ongoing efforts to secure the entry into force of the Kyoto Protocol and to work hard to reach the agreed-upon Kyoto targets. The EU-US June 2001 summit issued a statement reflecting divergent EU-US views: *"We disagree on the Kyoto Protocol and its ratification, but we are determined to work together in all relevant fora to address climate change...."* Climate change negotiators meeting in Bonn in late July 2001 agreed on implementation rules for the Kyoto Protocol and funding for developing countries. In Marrakech in November 2001, the Seventh Conference of the Parties to the Convention on Climate Change ended with an agreement on operational rules to fight climate change.

The European Union and its member and states—being strong advocates of renewable energies and having experienced significant benefits from the setting of targets and timetables—with fifty-one other nations, launched in 2002 the Johannesburg Coalition on Renewable Energy: a "coalition of the like-minded countries on the way forward on Renewable Energies."

Sustainable development, a fundamental objective under the EU treaties, dictates that the economic, social, and environmental effects of all policies should be examined in a coordinated way and considered in decision-making. It means meeting the needs of the present generation without compromising those of future generations. According to the June 2001 Göteborg summit, *"Getting prices right so that they better reflect the true costs to society of different activities would provide a better incentive for consumers and producers in everyday decisions about which goods and services to make or buy."*

FOREIGN AID

The European Union, many of whose member states are former colonial powers, has been active in development cooperation since the beginning. The Cotonou Convention (formerly the Lomé Conventions) with seventy-seven former African, Caribbean, and Pacific colonies is a prime example of the EU's generous aid and trade relationships with developing countries. The goals of EU development policy were formally set out in the Maastricht Treaty. They are: fostering sustainable economic and social development in developing countries; promoting their smooth and gradual integration into the world economy; fighting poverty and HIV/AIDS; and helping to consolidate democracy, the rule of law, and respect for human rights.

Today, the EU has cooperative agreements with most developing countries and is a leading donor of emergency and humanitarian aid (through the Humanitarian Aid Office, ECHO).

FOREIGN POLICY

The Common Foreign and Security Policy (CFSP) was established by the Maastricht Treaty in 1993. For a fuller description, see Chapter Seven.

HUMAN RIGHTS

The Treaty on European Union (Article 6) explicitly affirms the EU's commitment to respect the rule of law and fundamental and human rights as guaranteed by the 1950 European Convention for the Protection of Human Rights and Fundamental Freedoms (Council of Europe).

Death Penalty. All EU member states have banned the death penalty—all adhere to the European Convention for the Protection of Human and Fundamental Rights, which, according to Protocol 6, Article 1, abolishes the death penalty. Nearly all EU applicant countries (not including Turkey) have ratified this Protocol and prohibit the death penalty. The European Union is opposed to the death penalty in all cases and has consistently called for its abolition in countries that condone capital punishment.

External Actions. Respect for human rights and fundamental freedoms is a general objective of the Common Foreign and Security Policy (CFSP). Many of the EU's external agreements include a section on "political dialogue" dealing with the rule of law, democratization, and human rights. The EU publicly condemns human rights violations wherever they occur, appealing to the countries concerned to end such violations and pressuring the authorities in question.

Charter of Fundamental Rights of the European Union. The *Charter* is a basis for continued integration in Europe. It raises the status of rights in the areas of human dignity, freedom, equality, solidarity, citizenship, and justice to the level of fundamental rights for all citizens.

The 2004 Intergovernmental Conference has been charged with determining the ultimate legal status of the *Charter,* which was not originally legally binding. Romano Prodi, President of the European Commission, announced that he would like to see the *Charter* incorporated into the EU's treaties to make it legally binding "as soon as possible." The European Parliament passed resolutions that support the incorporation of the *Charter* into the treaties.

JUSTICE AND HOME AFFAIRS: FREE MOVEMENT, COUNTERTERRORISM AND INTERNAL SECURITY

The Justice and Home Affairs policy (JHA), established by the Maastricht Treaty and strengthened by the Amsterdam Treaty, had as its objective establishing by May 1, 2004 (five years after the Amsterdam Treaty went into effect), the free movement of European citizens and non-EU nationals throughout the EU, while guaranteeing public security by combating all forms of organized crime and terrorism. Home Affairs cooperation focuses mainly on policy toward non-EU countries in matters of asylum and immigration. Justice involves coordinated measures to combat the trafficking of drugs, arms, and human beings; large-scale international fraud; and other international crime.

The European Police Office (EUROPOL) was established as the EU law enforcement organization to handle criminal intelligence. Once the EUROPOL Convention was ratified by all member states, EUROPOL became fully operational in July 1999 and serves essentially as a police coordination center for the collection, analysis, and dissemination of information. EUROPOL deals with an expanding range of criminal issues when two or more member states are affected.

The Amsterdam Treaty helped make the JHA policy more effective by incorporating the Schengen Agreement into the EU framework. Schengen was concluded in 1990 by Belgium, France, Germany, Luxembourg, and the Netherlands to enable them to remove internal border controls on people without compromising public security. All EU member states except the United Kingdom and Ireland have since joined the Schengen area.

In the wake of the September 11, 2001, terrorist attacks, the EU has made the concerted fight against terrorism a top priority. Within ten days of the attack, the EU acted to establish an EU-wide list defining acts of terrorism and their commensurate penalties. Additionally, the EU adopted a European arrest warrant to replace the traditional extradition procedures among member states. This warrant allows wanted persons to be handed over directly from one judicial authority to another. Yet another measure improved EUROPOL's operation and created a special unit dedicated to counterterrorism.

The US and the EU have resolved to work together to combat terrorism. The September 20, 2001, EU-US Ministerial statement declares, *"The nature of our democratic societies makes it imperative to protect our citizens from terrorist acts, while at the same time protecting their individual liberties, due process, and the rule of law. The US and the EU are committed to enhancing security measures, legislation, and enforcement."*

REGIONAL DEVELOPMENT

Reducing the social and economic disparities among the regions has always been an EU objective—one that has new relevance considering EU enlargement toward Central and Eastern Europe (see Chapter Six). A Cohesion Fund was set up by the Maastricht Treaty to reduce economic disparities among the EU and Spain, Greece, Portugal, and Ireland. Cohesion funding for the four eligible EU member states is $16.6 billion for the period 2000-2006.

The four Structural Funds benefit all the member states and consist of three older funds set up in the 1970s—the European Social Fund (ESF), the European Regional Development Fund (ERDF), and the Guidance section of the European Agricultural Guidance and Guarantee Fund

(EAGGF)—plus the newer Financial Instrument for Fisheries Guidance (FIFG). These funds cofinance projects in areas affected by economic distress or industrial decline. Funding for the period 2000-2006 is $179 billion.

ISPA (Instrument for Structural Policies for Pre-Accession Programs) was created to assist the applicant countries in Central and Eastern Europe with investment projects in transport and the environment. For each year during the period 2000-2006, $920 million is budgeted.

RESEARCH AND TECHNOLOGICAL DEVELOPMENT (R&TD)

A real "European area of research" is beginning to take shape on the European continent, fueled in large part by the accomplishments of the Research and Technological Development (R&TD) framework programs that have been in place since the early 1980s. Formally designated by the Maastricht Treaty as the EU's main R&TD instrument, the framework programs set out the Union's principal scientific and technological objectives. These programs aim to promote cooperation among partners in different countries by funding transnational work and promoting coordination among scientific and technological facilities.

The $16.1 billion Sixth Framework Program (2003-2006) constitutes part of the European Research Area initiative and represents a deliberate break with past programs in terms of ambition, scope, and implementing instruments. The goal is to achieve greater focus on questions of European importance and a better integration of research efforts based on an enhanced partnership among European researchers. This latest program also provides for independent research in the nuclear field as well as comparable efforts to be undertaken by the Joint Research Center (JRC).

The Joint Research Center, the EU's scientific and technical research laboratory, is an integral part of the European Commission. It provides the scientific advice and technical know-how to support EU policies. Another framework program supports the JRC's efforts in the areas of food safety and health, environment and sustainable development, technology foresight, metrology, combating fraud, monitoring/prediction of natural disasters, and data security.

The Fifth Framework Program (1998 to 2002) concentrated on research in four main areas: quality of life and living resources; the information society; competitive and sustainable growth; and preserving the ecosystem. The Fifth Framework Program was also open to the then-EU membership candidates.

The original Community's involvement in R&TD was once confined to coal, steel, and nuclear energy. The Single European Act of 1986 provided specific legal powers in this field that has become crucial to the Union's industrial competitiveness. The Union participates in EUREKA, a Europe-wide venture aimed at developing new high-tech products in response to market demand.

The EU also cooperates with its European neighbors, as well as with the United States and Japan, on a variety of other R&TD projects. The EU-US Agreement on Science and Technology

Cooperation was signed in December 1997. An implementation agreement covering scientific co-operation between the US and the EU in the field of environmental research was forged in 2001.

TELECOMMUNICATIONS

A liberalized telecommunications environment is essential for Europe's economic growth and transition to the information society. The European Union fully liberalized telecommunications, voice telephony, and infrastructure on January 1, 1998, and played a key role in the conclusion of the WTO basic telecommunications agreement, which took effect in February 1998. Since the EU's liberalization process began, there has been tremendous growth in new technologies and services, including mobile phones, the Internet, and electronic commerce.

Several key indicators demonstrate impressive progress: more than one-third of the EU population is now using the Internet (40.4 percent). The gap with the US remains, but it is narrowing. Mobile phone use in Europe is growing at an even faster rate. According to the International Telecommunication Union's *2002 World Telecommunication Indicators*, 76 percent of the EU population subscribed to mobile phones, compared to 45.8 percent in the US.

TRADE

EU member states agree to share sovereignty with the Union in matters of external trade. On trade, the European Commission negotiates on behalf of the Union under a mandate agreed to by the member states. When agreement is reached, the Council of Ministers and the European Parliament must give their approval. The European Commission and the Council of the European Union adjust the common customs tariff, guide export policy, and decide on trade protection measures where necessary. The EU has played a leading role within the General Agreement on Tariffs and Trade (GATT) and its successor, the World Trade Organization (WTO).

TRANSPORT

Because of the importance of transport to the free movement of goods, the 1992 single market program introduced market-opening legislation—applicable EU-wide for all modes of transport. Considerable progress has been achieved in the deregulation of road, air, and maritime services; better access to the market; and the application of competition rules. Legislation has been introduced that addresses the needs of the rail sector. A primary objective of transport policy is to establish "sustainable mobility." This means organizing transport so as to make optimum use of energy consumption and transport times, routes, and conditions.

BUILDING THE NEW EUROPE: THE EU AND ITS NEIGHBORS

As new member countries joined in the seventies, eighties, and nineties, the European Union grew from six to fifteen member countries in its first four decades. Looking ahead, the Union expects to grow to nearly thirty member countries in the immediate future and will include more than a half-billion people. For the first time in history, nearly all the people of Europe will be joined in a single Union by free and democratic consent. The European Union is also forging stronger relations with its neighbors to the east, west, and south, whether or not they will eventually join the Union. The goal is to improve prosperity, political stability, security, and respect for democracy, the rule of law, and human rights in the European region as a whole. The final architecture of Europe is not yet set, nor is the European Union the only entity helping to shape the new Europe. But the EU plays a pivotal role in shaping post-cold war Europe. As it continues to deepen and widen, the Union will likely play an ever more prominent role on the continent in the twenty-first century.

TOWARD EU MEMBERSHIP

June 1989: Western Economic Summit (G7) asks European Commission to coordinate all Western aid to develop democracy and market economies in Central and Eastern Europe. Commission also launches PHARE, the world's largest grant program for the region.

December 1991: Europe Agreements (association agreements, paving way to free trade and eventual full EU membership) signed with Poland, Hungary, and Czechoslovakia. Agreements with Bulgaria, Romania, Estonia, Latvia, Lithuania, and Slovenia follow.

December 1992: Separate Europe Agreements signed with Czech Republic and Slovakia, following breakup of Czechoslovakia. This brings to ten the number of EU membership applicants from Central and Eastern Europe (CE 10).

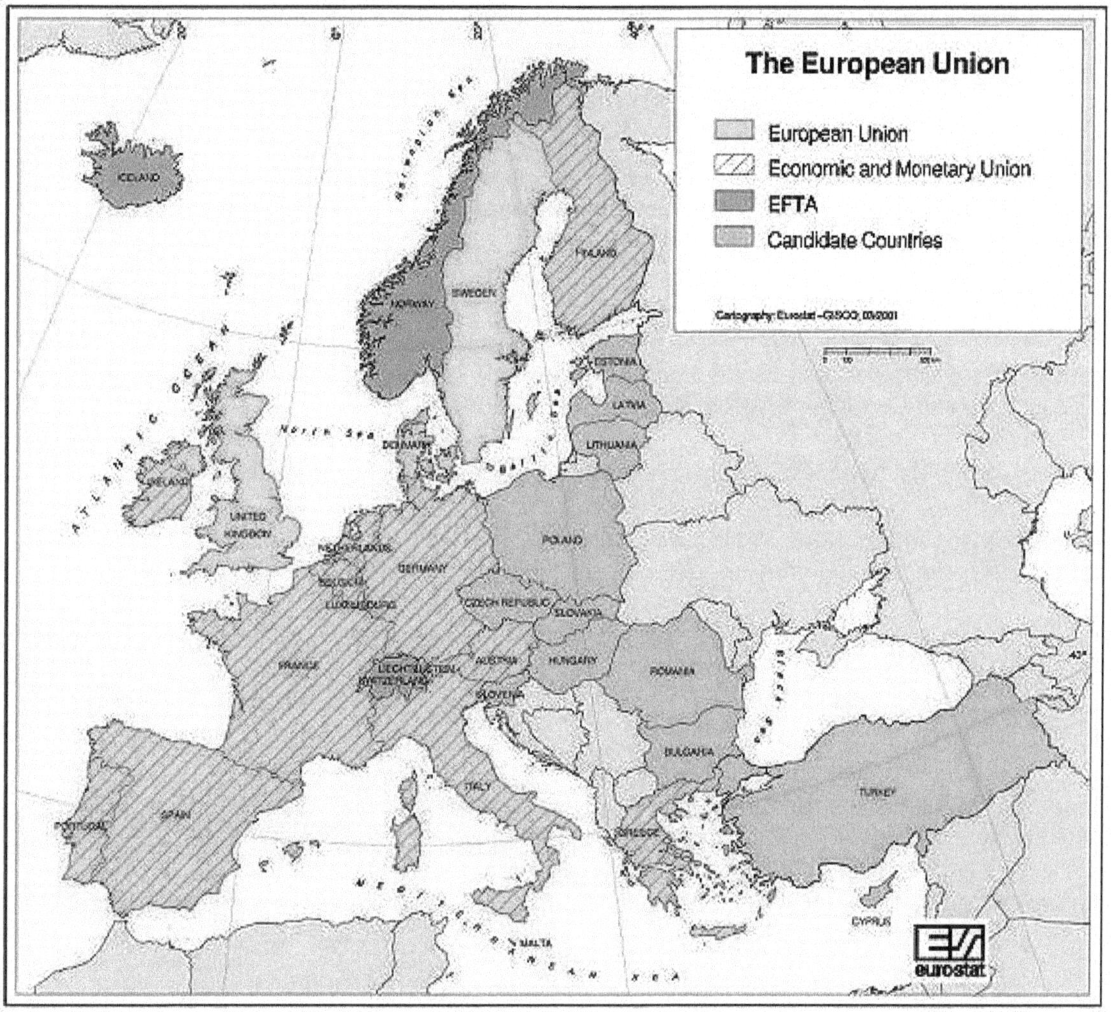

June 1993: Copenhagen summit pledges membership for eligible applicants (demonstrating stable democracy, respect for human rights, rule of law, functioning market economy, readiness for obligations of EU membership).

December 1994: Essen summit adopts "pre-accession strategy" to intensify efforts to prepare CE 10 for membership. Pre-accession package sets up a structured dialogue, improves market access, and directs more PHARE funds to support investment projects.

May 1995: Commission White Paper outlines measures to bring laws, standards, and product certification systems in CE 10 into conformity with EU single market.

July 1997: Commission releases Agenda 2000, with opinions on the readiness of each of the candidates and recommendations for internal EU reforms and expenditures.

December 1997: Luxembourg summit decides on accession strategy based on Agenda 2000, including launching actual negotiations and convening a European conference among all candidate countries on pan-European issues.

March 1998: European conference launched, followed by formal opening of negotiations with five CE countries and Cyprus and accession partnerships for all CE 10.

October 1998: Malta reactivates its membership application, frozen since 1996.

November/December 1998: Publication of first annual reports on progress toward accession by each of the candidate countries; regular reports endorsed by Vienna Council.

March 1999: Berlin Council adopts 2000-2006 funding, including pre-accession and accession-related expenditure.

December 1999: Helsinki summit decides to open negotiations on EU membership with five more CE countries and Malta and to treat Turkey as a candidate on the same terms as others.

December 2000: Treaty of Nice embodies the necessary reforms to EU institutions to prepare for EU enlargement.

June 2001: Göteborg summit declares intention to complete negotiations with a first group of applicants, provided they are ready, in time to allow them to participate as EU members in the June 2004 European Parliament elections.

December 2002: Copenhagen summit declares that Cyprus, Czech Republic, Estonia, Hungary, Latvia, Lithuania, Malta, Poland, Slovak Republic, and Slovenia will become EU members by May 1, 2004.

April 2003: Treaty of Accession for ten new members (above) signed in Athens, Greece.

May 2004: Ten new members join the European Union.

2007: Following the conclusions of the European Council in Brussels and depending on further progress in complying with the membership criteria, the EU hopes to welcome Bulgaria and Romania as members of the European Union.

FUTURE EUROPEAN UNION ENLARGEMENT

In March 1998 the EU opened talks on full membership with six countries: Cyprus, the Czech Republic, Estonia, Hungary, Poland, and Slovenia. Two years later, in February 2000, negotiations began with six other applicant countries: Bulgaria, Latvia, Lithuania, Malta, Romania, and Slovakia. At the Helsinki European Council in December 1999, when this decision was made, it was also decided to grant Turkey full candidate status (see below). Joining a highly integrated Union is inherently complex, and most of the applicant countries were compelled to make far-reaching economic, political, and social adjustments following the end of Communism. Negotiations with each applicant proceed on their own merits and as quickly as possible. As decided by the Copenhagen European Council in December 2002, as of May 1, 2004, the European Union has ten new members: Cyprus, Czech Republic, Estonia, Hungary, Latvia, Lithuania, Malta, Poland, Slovak Republic, and Slovenia. This brings EU membership to twenty-five nations in time for the next elections to the European Parliament in June 2004. The accession treaty, signed in Athens in April 2003, was first to be ratified in each of the ten candidate countries and in each of the then-fifteen EU member states before the ten states became formal EU members in 2004.

US Secretary of State Colin Powell, on the occasion of the signing of the 2003 Treaty of Accession, said: *"The embrace of ten new members attests to the European Union's institutional strength and to its confidence in itself. It also testifies to the essential role the Union plays as a force for democracy, prosperity and a force for stability throughout Europe and well beyond Europe."*

Following the conclusions of the European Council in Brussels and depending on further progress in complying with the membership criteria, the EU hopes to welcome Bulgaria and Romania as members of the European Union in 2007.

Agenda 2000 reinforced the pre-accession strategy under which candidate countries received increased aid, participated in certain EU programs, and adapted to EU procedures in anticipation of membership. EU and member state aid to Central and Eastern Europe alone totaled $85 billion for the period 1990-1999. In today's dollars, this is approximately equivalent to the $13.2 billion in US Marshall Plan aid for the reconstruction of Europe after World War II. This process continues for Bulgaria and Romania, slated for EU membership in 2007—according, again, to the December 2002 Copenhagen European Council. Turkey's accession position has been strengthened.

In July 1997, the Commission completed an exhaustive review of the state of readiness of the applicant countries for full membership, publishing its findings in a three-volume report, known as *Agenda 2000: For a Stronger and Wider Union*. At the time, the Commission concluded that none of the ten Central and East European applicants was ready for full membership under criteria adopted at the 1993 Copenhagen European Council, but five were sufficiently advanced along the path to open negotiations.

In addition, Cyprus (see below) was offered negotiations in this round.

The purpose of Agenda 2000 was twofold: to prepare the candidate countries for membership and to prepare the EU and its institutions for the biggest and most challenging enlargement in its history. After two years of intensive debate, EU leaders meeting in Berlin in March 1999 approved the Agenda 2000 strategy. This included reforms of the Common Agricultural Policy (CAP), the Structural Funds, the EU decision-making procedures, and a financial package totaling $230 billion for the years 2000-2006 for the Central and East European applicants in preparation for the enlargement. Pre-accession financial assistance to Cyprus and Malta extended through 2004.

CYPRUS, MALTA, AND TURKEY

Negotiations with Cyprus for EU membership began in March 1998, along with five countries from Central and Eastern Europe. The European Council had decided in 1995 that the next phase of EU enlargement would include Cyprus and Malta. The EU wanted representatives of both communities in Cyprus to take part in the accession negotiations and hoped that the negotiations would contribute to efforts under United Nations auspices to resolve the dispute dividing the island. However, given the still-divided status of Cyprus at the time, the December 2002 Copenhagen summit stated: *"The European Council has decided that, in the absence of a settlement, the application of the acquis to the northern part of the island shall be suspended, until the Council decides unanimously otherwise, on the basis of a proposal by the Commission. Meanwhile, the Council invites the Commission, in consultation with the government of Cyprus, to consider ways of promoting economic development of the northern part of Cyprus and bringing it closer to the Union."*

Although the EU has decided that Turkey does not yet meet all the criteria for full membership of the Union, it has frequently reaffirmed Turkey's eligibility for EU membership. Turkey applied for full membership in 1987. But the Commission recommended an alternate path, including steadily closer economic relations—a strategy that both sides are implementing. Since 1995, the EU and Turkey have been joined in a customs union that provides for enhanced economic cooperation. Pre-accession financial assistance, comparable to that available to other candidate countries, is being provided to Turkey. In August 1999, following a devastating earthquake in Turkey, the EU responded immediately with humanitarian assistance.

At the December 1999 Helsinki European Council, Turkey was declared a candidate on the same terms as the twelve other then-applicants. An Accession Partnership with Turkey was adopted in March 2001. As a candidate country, Turkey benefits from a pre-accession strategy and partnership with the EU that aims to stimulate and support its political and economic reforms. A closer political dialogue with the Union is sought as well. The timing of Turkey's accession depends upon its progress toward meeting the membership criteria, which are equally stringent for all candidate nations. The December 2002 Copenhagen European Council stated: *"The Union encourages Turkey to pursue energetically its reform process. If the European Council in December 2004, on the basis of a report and a recommendation from the Commission, decides that Turkey fulfils the Copenhagen political criteria, the European Union will open accession negotiations with Turkey without delay."*

NORWAY AND SWITZERLAND

In referenda, Norway decided against EU membership in 1973 and 1994. Switzerland has applied for EU membership in the past, though not actively pursued it. One day perhaps both may reactivate their applications.

CROATIA

On February 21, 2003, Croatia presented its application for EU membership. European Commission President Romano Prodi said at the time: *"This is a powerful signal of hope in future development, stability and growth and for peaceful coexistence throughout the region. It shows that this region, which is an integral part of Europe, is resolved to set behind it forever the dramas and traumas of its recent past. Only once the Balkan countries are members can the Union's enlargement and Europe's reorganisation be considered complete, and only then will the founding fathers' vision of peace and prosperity have come true, perhaps even beyond their wildest dreams."*

PHARE, TACIS, CARDS

PHARE (Originally launched in 1989 as Action Plan for Coordinated Aid to Poland and Hungary for Economic Reconstruction; also means "beacon" in French) is an EU grants program to help the countries of Central and Eastern Europe rejoin the mainstream of European development through membership of the European Union. It acts as a powerful catalyst by unlocking funds for important projects from other donors through studies, capital grants, guarantee schemes, and credit lines. It also invests directly in infrastructure, which will account for more PHARE funds as integration progresses. By 1999, PHARE, the world's largest grant assistance effort for Central and Eastern Europe, committed some $11 billion to programs promoting private sector development; effective food production, processing and distribution; modern energy, transport, and telecommunications infrastructures; nuclear safety and environment; public administration reform; and university education under the TEMPUS (Trans-European Mobility Scheme for University Students) program. For the period 2000-2006, PHARE committed some $10 billion.

TACIS (Technical Assistance to the Commonwealth of Independent States) provides grant finance for the transfer of know-how to twelve countries of the former Soviet Union and Mongolia. It fosters the development of market economies and democratic societies. It is the largest program of its kind operating in the region, and has launched more than 3,000 projects since its inception in 1991. Between 1991 and 2001, TACIS provided $2,624.41 billion in assistance. The TACIS budget for 2000-2006 is $2.9 billion.

CARDS (Community Assistance for Reconstruction, Development, and Stabilization) provides assistance to Albania, Bosnia and Herzegovina, Croatia, the Federal Republic of Yugoslavia, and the Former Yugoslav Republic of Macedonia. It is the successor to OBNOVA (which it repealed) and PHARE for these countries. It establishes a single legal framework for assistance to these countries to help them participate in the stabilization and association process. Program funding for 2000-2006 is $4.3 billion.

RUSSIA AND ITS NEIGHBORS

The EU is forging a network of far-reaching partnerships with countries of the former Soviet Union and is at the forefront of international efforts to support them in carrying out political and economic reforms. Accordingly, the EU has concluded Partnership and Cooperation Agreements (PCAs) with Russia, Armenia, Azerbaijan, Belarus, Georgia, Kazakhstan, Kyrgyz Republic, Moldova, Turkmenistan, Ukraine, and Uzbekistan. All but the two PCAs with Belarus and Turkmenistan have entered into force. (No PCA is envisioned yet with Tajikistan, given its present instability.) These agreements provide for political, economic, and trade relations and lay the basis for cooperation in the social, financial, scientific, technological, and cultural fields. The Partnership and Cooperation Agreement with Russia entered into force in December 1997. The first Cooperation Council under the new agreement was held in January 1998, yielding agreement on a comprehensive work plan for the short and medium terms. Summits with the

Russian Federation are held at approximately six-month intervals, as are meetings of the Cooperation Council.

The PCA with Russia provides for talks on the possibility of free trade as part of the EU's vision of liberalizing trade throughout the continent. Building on the PCA, the European Council adopted a common strategy toward Russia in June 1999, which brings greater focus to the EU's political and economic actions.

The EU is the major trading partner for Russia and most of the newly independent states, accounting for 40 to 50 percent of their global trade. In 2001, EU imports from Russia totaled $42.9 billion, versus $6.3 billion for the US, while EU exports to Russia totaled $25.2 billion, versus $2.7 billion for the US.

The EU continues to support democracy and economic reform in Central and Eastern Europe through PHARE, which is the largest technical assistance program in the region. By 1999, some $11 billion had been committed for projects related to government and private sector reform. For the period 2000-2006, PHARE committed some $10 billion. Since 1991, TACIS has also provided aid to twelve countries of the former Soviet Union, plus Mongolia

PROJECTING STABILITY IN SOUTHEAST EUROPE

As a product of the reconstruction and reconciliation that followed World War II, the EU is a model for Southeast Europe (SEE). For more than a decade, the EU has been helping countries in the region to rebuild their economies and rejoin the mainstream of European development.

Following the September 2000 elections in Yugoslavia, which brought to power a democratically elected coalition with a reform mandate, the EU provided emergency aid for the winter, totaling $184 million, and convened together with the World Bank an international donors conference in June 2001 at which $1.2 billion was pledged for the reconstruction of Yugoslavia.

To promote long-term peace and prosperity in Southeast Europe, the EU is pursuing a two-pronged strategy including: a regional approach aimed at building cooperation among the five former Yugoslav republics plus Albania; and a long-term Stabilization and Association Process, to which the EU committed itself at the Zagreb summit with the countries of the region in November 2000. The EU hopes to draw these countries closer to the EU through Stabilization and Association Agreements (SAA). These aim at developing existing trade ties, reforming political and economic institutions in the SEE countries, and preparing them for eventual EU membership. Croatia applied for EU membership on February 21, 2003. The June 21, 2003, EU Western Balkans Summit participants confirmed the EU intention of extending membership to these nations and resolved to meet periodically to review progress.

MEDITERRANEAN AND MIDDLE EAST COUNTRIES

Euro-Mediterranean Partnership

Algeria
Cyprus*
Egypt
Israel
Jordan
Lebanon
Libya (observer status)
Malta*

Morocco
Palestinian Authority
Syria
Tunisia
Turkey*

*Applicant Countries for EU Membership

ECONOMIC, TRADE AND MONETARY UNION OF THE EUROPEAN UNION

In economics, a monetary union is a situation where several countries have agreed to share a single currency among them. The European **Economic and Monetary Union** (EMU) consists of three stages coordinating economic policy and culminating with the adoption of the euro, the EU's single currency. All member states of the European Union participate in the EMU. Thirteen member states of the European Union have entered the third stage and have adopted the euro as their currency. The United Kingdom, Denmark and Sweden have not accepted the third stage and the three EU members still use their own currency today.

Under the Copenhagen criteria, it is a condition of entry for states acceding to the EU that they be able to fulfil the requirements for monetary union within a given period of time. The 10 new countries that acceded to the European Union in 2004 all intend to join third stage of the EMU in the next ten years, though the precise timing depends on various economic factors. Similarly, those countries who are currently negotiating for entry will also take the euro as their currency in the years following their accession. (See Enlargement of the European Union.)

Prior to adopting the euro, a member state has to have its currency in the European Exchange Rate Mechanism (ERM II) for two years. Cyprus, Denmark, Estonia, Latvia, Lithuania, Malta, and Slovakia are the current participants in the exchange rate mechanism. EMU is sometimes misinterpreted to mean **European Monetary Union**.

HISTORY OF THE EMU

First ideas of an economic and monetary union in Europe were raised well before establishing the European Communities. For example, already in the League of Nations, Gustav Stresemann asked in 1929 for a European currency (Link) against the background of an increased economic division due to a number of new nation states in Europe after WWI.

A first attempt to create an economic and monetary union between the members of the European Communities goes back to an initiative by the European Commission in 1969, which set out the need for "greater co-ordination of economic policies and monetary cooperation"(Barre Report), which was followed by the decision of the Heads of State or Government at their summit meeting in The Hague in 1969 to draw up a plan by stages with a view to creating an economic and monetary union by the end of the 1970s.

On the basis of various previous proposals, an expert group chaired by Luxembourg's Prime Minister and Finance Minister, Pierre Werner, presented in October 1970 the first commonly agreed blueprint to create an economic and monetary union in three stages (Werner plan). The project experienced serious setbacks from the crises arising from the non-convertibility of the US dollar into gold in August 1971 and from rising oil prices in 1972.

The debate on EMU was fully re-launched at the Hanover Summit in June 1988, when an ad hoc committee of the central bank governors of the twelve member states, chaired by the President of the European Commission, Jacques Delors, was asked to propose a new timetable with clear, practical and realistic steps for creating an economic and monetary union.
The Delors report of 1989 set out a plan to introduce the EMU in three stages and it included the creation of institutions like the European System of Central Banks (ESCB), which would become responsible for formulating and implementing monetary policy.

The three stages for the implementation of the EMU were the following:

STAGE ONE: 1 JULY 1990 TO 31 DECEMBER 1993

- On 1 July 1990, exchange controls were abolished, thus capital movements were completely liberalised in the EEC.
- The Treaty of Maastricht in 1992 establishes the completion of the EMU as a formal objective and sets a number of economic convergence criteria, concerning the inflation rate, public finances, interest rates and exchange rate stability.
- The treaty enters into force on the 1 November 1993.

STAGE TWO: 1 JANUARY 1994 TO 31 DECEMBER 1998

- The European Monetary Institute is established as the forerunner of the European Central Bank, with the task of strengthening monetary cooperation between the member states and their national banks, as well as supervising ECU banknotes.
- On 16 December 1995, details such as the name of the new currency (the euro) as well as the duration of the transition periods are decided.
- On 16-17 June 1997, the European Council decides at Amsterdam to adopt the Stability and Growth Pact, designed to ensure budgetary discipline after creation of the euro, and a new exchange rate mechanism (ERM II) is set up to provide stability between the euro and the national currencies of countries that haven't yet entered the eurozone.
- On 3 May 1998, at the European Council in Brussels, the 11 initial countries that will participate in the third stage from 1 January 1999 are selected.
- On 1 June 1998, the European Central Bank (ECB) is created, and in 31 December 1998, the conversion rates between the 11 participating national currencies and the euro are established.

STAGE THREE: 1 JANUARY 1999 AND CONTINUING

- From the start of 1999, the euro is now a real currency, and a single monetary policy is introduced under the authority of the ECB. A three-year transition period begins before the introduction of actual euro notes and coins, but legally the national currencies have already ceased to exist.
- On 1 January 2001, Greece joins the third stage of the EMU.
- The euro notes and coins are finally introduced in January 2002.
- On 1 January 2007, Slovenia joins the third stage of the EMU.

FREE TRADE AREAS IN EUROPE

At present, there are two **free trade areas (FTAs) in Europe** outside of the European Union (EU). The European Free Trade Association (EFTA) was created in 1960 by the outer seven (as a looser alternative to the then-European Communities) but most of its membership has since joined the Communities/EU leaving only four countries still party to it. Following the fall of the Iron Curtain, two FTAs were created in Eastern Europe, the Baltic Free Trade Area (BAFTA) and the Central European Free Trade Agreement (CEFTA), in order to stabilise these countries for membership of the EU. With the 2004 EU enlargement, the original members of both of these have left these agreements and joined the EU.

While BAFTA has ceased to exist, CEFTA has expanded into southern Europe with members from the Western Balkans and Moldova. All of the new CEFTA countries, except for Moldova, are prospective members of the EU and hence EFTA is the only FTA with a long term future, as there are no immediate plans for these countries to change their present status. However, CEFTA may gain new members in the form of countries to the east of the present EU.

EFTA[EDIT]

Main article: European Free Trade Association
The European Free Trade Association (EFTA) was created in 1960 by the outer seven (as a looser alternative to the then-European Communities) but most of its membership has since joined the Communities/EU leaving only four countries (Iceland, Norway, Switzerland and Liechtenstein) still party to the treaty.

CEFTA[EDIT]

Main article: Central European Free Trade Agreement
Following the fall of the Iron Curtain, two FTAs were created in Central Europe, the Baltic Free Trade Area (BAFTA) and the Central European Free Trade Agreement (CEFTA), in order to stabilise these countries for membership of the EU. With the 2004 EU enlargement, the original members of both of these have left these agreements and joined the EU.
CEFTA has expanded into southern Europe with members from the Western Balkans and Moldova. All of the new CEFTA countries, except for Moldova, are prospective members of the EU and hence EFTA is the only FTA with a long term future, as there are no immediate plans for these countries to change their present status. However, CEFTA may gain new members in the form of countries neighbouring the present EU.[1][2]

BAFTA[EDIT]

The Baltic Free Trade Area was a free trade agreement between Estonia, Latvia and Lithuania that existed between 1994 and 2004.
BAFTA was created to help prepare the countries for their accession to the EU. Hence, BAFTA was created more as an initiative of the EU than out of a desire Baltic states to trade between themselves: they were more interested in gaining access to the rest of the European markets.[3]
BAFTA's agreement was signed by the three states on 13 September 1993 and came into force on 1 April 1994. On 1 January 1997 the agreement was extended to cover trade in agricultural produce. On 1 May 2004, all three states joined the European Union, and BAFTA ceased to exist.
BAFTA was part of general co-operation between the three countries, modelled on Nordic co-operation (see Nordic Council). Leaders met regularly and, as well as a free trade area, they formed a common visa area and started military co-operation due to the proximity of Russia.[4]

CISFTA[EDIT]

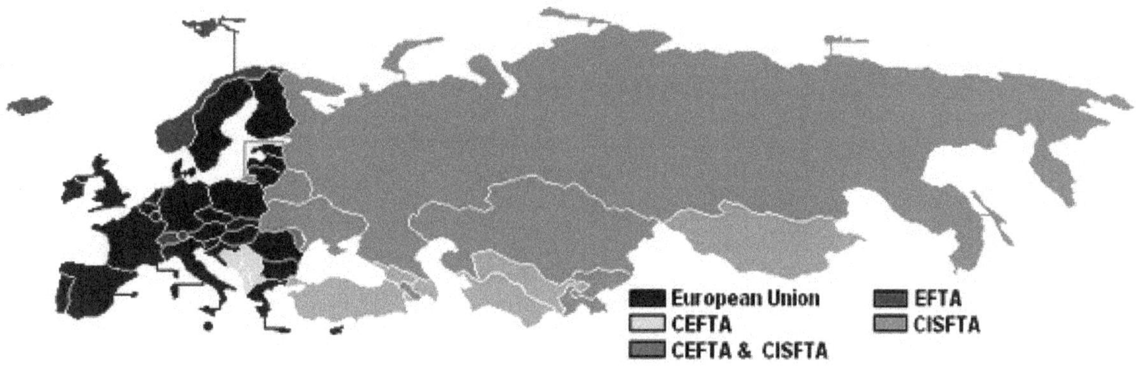

Free trade areas in Europe

The Commonwealth of Independent States had been negotiating a CIS free trade area since 1994 and in 2011 eight countries agreed to create a free trade area. These are; Russia, Ukraine, Belarus, Kazakhstan, Kyrgyzstan, Tajikistan, Armenia and Moldova. Belarus, Kazakhstan and Russia form a customs union.

EU[EDIT]

The European Union (EU) has always operated as more than a free trade area with its predecessor,the European Economic Community (EEC) being founded as a customs union. The EU shares its single market with three EFTA members via the European Economic Area and has a free trade agreement of some level with most other European countries.

EUROPEAN UNION CUSTOMS UNION[EDIT]

Main article: European Union Customs Union

The European Union Customs Union is a customs union which consists of all the Member States of the European Union (EU), Turkey and three European microstates: San Marino, Monaco and Andorra. No customs are levied on goods travelling within the customs union and members of the customs union impose a common external tariff on all goods entering the union. One of the consequences of the customs union is that the European Union has to negotiate as a single entity in international trade deals such as the World Trade Organisation.

BALTIC FREE TRADE AREA

The Baltic Free Trade Area was a free trade agreement between Estonia, Latvia and Lithuania that existed between 1994 and 2004.

BAFTA was created to help prepare the countries for their accession to the European Union (the European Communities before 1993). Hence, BAFTA was created more as an initiative of the Communities than out of a desire Baltic states to trade between themselves: they were more interested in gaining access to the western European markets.

BAFTA's agreement was signed by the three states on 13 September 1993 and came into force on 1 April 1994. On 1 January 1997 the agreement was extended to cover trade in agricultural produce. On 1 May 2004, all three states joined the European Union, and BAFTA ceased to exist.

BAFTA was part of general co-operation between the three countries, modelled on Nordic co-operation (see Nordic Council). Leaders met regularly and, as well as a free trade area, they formed a common visa area and started military co-operation due to the proximity of Russia

CENTRAL EUROPEAN FREE TRADE AGREEMENT

languages	Albanian, Bosnian, Croatian, Macedonian, Montenegrin, Moldovan, and Serbian
Type	Trade agreement
Member states	Albania Bosnia and Herzegovina Croatia Macedonia Moldova Montenegro Serbia UNMIK (Kosovo)
	Establishment
- Signed	21 December 1992
	Area
- Total	309,125 km^2 119,354 sq mi
	Population
- 2007 estimate	30,936,824
- Density	100.07/km^2 259.2/sq mi
GDP (PPP)	2007 (IMF) estimate
- Total	$236.6 billion
- Per capita	7,649
Currency	Albanian Lek, Bosnia and Herzegovina konvertibilna marka, Croatian kuna, Euro, Macedonian denar, Moldovan leu, Serbian dinar (ALL, BAM, HRK, EUR, MKD, MDL, RSD)
Time zone	CET / EET (UTC+1 / +2)
- Summer (DST)	CEST / EEST (UTC+2 / +3)

The **Central European Free Trade Agreement (CEFTA)** is a trade agreement between Non-EU countries in Central and South-Eastern Europe.

MEMBERS

As of 1 May 2007, the parties of the CEFTA agreement are: Albania, Bosnia and Herzegovina, Croatia, Macedonia, Moldova, Montenegro, Serbia and UNMIK
Former parties are Bulgaria, the Czech Republic, Hungary, Poland, Romania, Slovakia and Slovenia. Their CEFTA membership ended when they joined the EU.

Parties of agreement		joined	left
Poland		1992	2004
Hungary		1992	2004
Czechoslovakia	Czech Republic	1992	2004

	Slovakia		2004
Slovenia		1996	2004
Romania		1997	2007
Bulgaria		1999	2007
Croatia		2003	—
Macedonia		2006	—
Albania		2007	—
Bosnia and Herzegovina		2007	—
Moldova		2007	—
Montenegro		2007	—
Serbia		2007	—
Kosovo		2007	—

MEMBERSHIP CRITERIA

Former Poznań Declaration criteria:

- World Trade Organisation membership
- European Union Association Agreement with provisions for future full membership
- Free Trade Agreements with the current **CEFTA** member states

Current criteria since Zagreb meeting in 2005:

- WTO membership *or commitment to respect all WTO regulations*
- *any* European Union Association Agreement
- Free Trade Agreements with the current **CEFTA** member states

CURRENT MEMBERS

State	Accession	Population	Capital	GDP in millions (PPP)	GDP per capita (PPP)
Albania	1 January 2007	3,619,778	Tirana	21,828	6,859
Bosnia and Herzegovina	1 January 2007	4,590,310	Sarajevo	30,389	7,611
Croatia	1 January 2003	4,491,543	Zagreb	82,272	18,545
Macedonia	1 January 2006	2,061,315	Skopje	18,818	9,157
Moldova	1 January 2007	4,324,450	Chişinău	10,746	3,174
Montenegro	1 January 2007	678,177	Podgorica	6,944	11,111
Serbia	1 January 2007	7 400 000	Belgrade	79,662	10,792
UNMIK (Kosovo)	1 January 2007	2,126,708	Pristina	4,000	2,300

ORIGINAL AGREEMENT

Original CEFTA agreement was signed by Visegrád Group countries, that is by Poland, Hungary and Czech and Slovak republics (at the time parts of the Czech and Slovak Federative Republic) on 21 December 1992 in Kraków, Poland. It entered into force since July 1994. Through CEFTA, participating countries hoped to mobilize efforts to integrate Western European institutions and through this, to join European political, economic, security and legal systems, thereby consolidating democracy and free-market economics.

The agreement was amended by the agreements signed on 11 September 1995 in Brno and on 4 July 2003 in Bled.
Slovenia joined CEFTA in 1996, Romania in 1997, Bulgaria in 1999, Croatia in 2003 and Macedonia in 2006.

CEFTA 2006 AGREEMENT

All of the parties of the original agreement had now joined the EU and thus left CEFTA. Therefore it was decided to extend CEFTA to cover the rest of the Balkan states, which already had completed a matrix of bilateral free trade agreements in the framework of the Stability Pact for South Eastern Europe. On 6 April 2006, at the *South East Europe Prime Ministers Summit* in Bucharest, a joint declaration on expansion of CEFTA to Albania, Bosnia and Herzegovina, United Nations Interim Administration Mission on behalf of Kosovo, Moldova, Serbia and Montenegro was adopted. Accession of Ukraine has also been discussed. The new enlarged agreement was initialled on 9 November 2006 in Brussels and was signed on 19 December 2006 at the South East European Prime Ministers Summit in Bucharest. The agreement went into effect on 26 July 2007 for Albania, UNMIK, Macedonia, Moldova and Montenegro, and on 22 August for Croatia. Bosnia and Herzegovina ratified it on 6 September, while Serbia completed the final legal procedures on 24 September 2007. The agreement aims at establishing a free trade zone in the region by 31 December 2010.

RELATIONS WITH THE EU

All former participating countries had previously signed association agreements with the EU, so in fact CEFTA has served as a preparation for full European Union membership. Poland, the Czech Republic, Hungary, Slovakia, Slovenia joined the EU on 1 May 2004, with Bulgaria and Romania following suit on 1 January 2007. Croatia does not yet have a date specified, but is in the process of accession negotiations, and is expected to join EU in 2010 or 2011. Macedonia is also an official candidate country of the EU.

At the EU's recommendation, the future members prepared for membership by establishing free trade areas. A large proportion of CEFTA foreign trade is with EU countries.

EUROPEAN UNION FREE TRADE AGREEMENTS

The EU is firmly committed to the promotion of open and fair trade with all its trading partners. The EU has specific trade policies in place for all its partners and abides by the global rules on international trade set out by the World Trade Organisation.

The **European Union** has concluded **free trade agreements** (FTAs) with many countries world-wide and negotiating with many others.

FREE TRADE AGREEMENTS IN FORCE

State	Date	Notes	Relations
Albania	2009	SAA	Potential candidate for EU accession
Algeria	2005	AA	
Andorra	1991	Customs Union	Andorra–EU relations
Bosnia and	2008	Interim SAA	Potential candidate for

State	Date	Notes	Relations
Herzegovina			EU accession
Chile	2003		
Colombia	signed 2011 August 2013		
Egypt	2004	AA	
Faroe Islands	1997	autonomous entity of Denmark	Faroe Islands-EU relations
Honduras	August 2013		
Iceland	1973 (EEA since 1992)	EEA	Negotiating for EU accession
Israel	2000	AA	Israel–EU relations
Jordan	2002	AA	Jordan–EU relations
Lebanon	2003	AA (FTA provisions in force since 2003)	Lebanon–EU relations
Liechtenstein	1973	EEA	Liechtenstein–EU relations
Republic of Macedonia	2004	SAA	Candidate for EU accession
Mexico	2000	Details	Mexico–EU relations
Montenegro	2010	SAA	Negotiating for EU accession
Morocco	2000	AA	Morocco–EU relations
Nicaragua	August 2013		
Norway	1973 (EEA since 1992)	EEA	Norway–EU relations
Palestinian Authority	1997	AA	Palestine–EU relations
Panama	August 2013		
Peru	signed 2011 March 2013		
San Marino	1992	Customs Union	San Marino–EU relations
Serbia	2010	SAA	Candidate for EU accession
South Africa	2000		South Africa–EU relations
South Korea	2011 (PROVISIONAL)	Details, provisional application from 1 July 2011	South Korea–EU relations

State	Date	Notes	Relations
Switzerland	1973	EFTA	Switzerland–EU relations
Tunisia	1998	AA	
Turkey	1995	Customs Union: Details	Negotiating for EU accession

PENDING

A Deep and Comprehensive Free Trade Agreement with Ukraine was initialled on 19 July 2012. Ratification of the DCFTA, like an European Union Association Agreement, has been stalled by the EU due to concerns over the rule of law in Ukraine.

A European Union Central American Association Agreement was signed with the Central American Common Market in 2011 and is awaiting ratification.

ACP COUNTRIES

Economic Partnership Agreement (EPA) are being implemented for ACP countries.

State	Signed	Notes
Cameroon	2009	
CARIFORUM States	2008	Antigua and Barbuda, Bahamas, Barbados, Belize, Dominica, the Dominican Republic, Grenada, Guyana, Haiti, Jamaica, Saint Lucia, Saint Vincent and the Grenadines, Saint Christopher and Nevis, Suriname, Trinidad and Tobago
Ivory Coast	2009	
South Korea	2010	Provisionally applied from 2011 but not yet fully ratified

NEGOTIATING

- India (India–EU relations)
- ASEAN countries – now being pursued individually
- Comprehensive Economic and Trade Agreement with Canada (Canada–EU relations); agreement in principle reached.
- Gulf Cooperation Council (Bahrain, Kuwait, Oman, Qatar, Saudi Arabia, and United Arab Emirates)
- Russia (details)
- Mercosur (Argentina, Brazil, Paraguay, Uruguay, and Venezuela)
- Japan (Japan–EU relations)

CONCLUDED NEGOTIATIONS

Singapore and European Union concluded their Free Trade negotiations on 17 December 2012. They will sign the agreement after all translations and verifications are completed.

EU FREE TRADE POLICY WITH REGIONS AND COUNTRIES

EU TRADE POLICY AND ECONOMIC PARTNERSHIP AGREEMENTS

Economic Partnership Agreements:

date back to the signing of the Cotonou Agreement in 2000.

are "tailor-made" to suit specific regional circumstances.

go beyond conventional free-trade agreements, focusing on ACP development, taking account of their socio-economic circumstances and include co-operation and assistance to help ACP countries implement the Agreements.

opened up EU markets fully and immediately (unilaterally by the EU since 1st January 2008), but allowed ACP countries 15 (and up to 25) years to open up to EU imports while providing protection for the sensitive 20% of imports.

provide scope for wide-ranging trade co-operation on areas such as services and standards.

are also designed to be drivers of change that will kick-start reform and help strengthen rule of law in the economic field, thereby attracting foreign direct investment, so helping to create a "virtuous circle" of growth.

GENERALISED SCHEME OF PREFERENCES (GSP)

The EU's "Generalised Scheme of Preferences" (GSP) allows developing country exporters to pay lower duties on their exports to the EU. This gives them vital access to EU markets and contributes to their economic growth.

The reformed GSP, which will apply as from 2014, will further focus support on countries most in need.

Generalised Scheme of Preferences in a nutshell

There are three main variants (arrangements) of the scheme:

- the standard GSP scheme, which offers generous tariff reductions to developing countries. Practically, this means partial or entire removal of tariffs on two thirds of all product categories.

- the "GSP+" enhanced preferences means full removal of tariffs on essentially the same product categories as those covered by the general arrangement. These are granted to countries which ratify and implement international conventions relating to human and labour rights, environment and good governance;

- "Everything but Arms" (EBA) scheme for least developed countries (LDCs), which grants duty-free quota-free access to all products, except for arms and ammunitions.

The EU has adopted a reformed GSP law on 31 October 2012 - (Regulation No 978/2012). In order to allow ample time for economic operators to adapt to the new scheme, the new preferences will apply as of 1 January 2014.

Until the end of 2013, the preferences under the previous scheme will continue to apply on the basis of Regulation No 732/2008, extended by the GSP "Roll-over" Regulation.

In December 2012, the EU identified products exported by some of the beneficiaries of the new GSP that had become so competitive that they no longer need support to be successfully exported to the EU. These products will not receive GSP preferences as from 1 January 2014 to 31 December 2016, when the list will be reviewed.

In February 2013, the EU released procedural rules on how to treat the applications for the GSP+ arrangement under the new GSP.

Following South Sudan's independence in July 2011 and its recognition by the UN as a Least-Developed Country in December 2012, the EU included it among the beneficiaries of the EBA arrangement in May 2013, with retro-active application as from January 2013.

GSP preferences were withdrawn for Myanmar/Burma in 1997 due to serious and systematic violations of the principles of the International Labour Organisation (ILO) Convention on forced labour. Following the decision by the Conference of the ILO to lift its negative opinion on the country in June 2012, the EU reinstated GSP preferences for Myanmar/Burma in July 2013, with retro-active application as from June 2012.

EU trade and Generalised Scheme of Preferences

Main features of the reformed GSP:

■Concentrating GSP preferences on countries most in need. A number of countries, which do not require GSP preferences to be competitive, will no longer benefit from the scheme as from 1 January 2014, including:

■Countries that already have preferential access to the EU which is at least as good as under GSP – for example, under a Free Trade Agreement or a special autonomous trade regime.

■Countries which have achieved a high or upper middle income per capita, according to World Bank classification.

■A number of overseas countries and territories, which have an alternative market access arrangement for developed markets.

■Reinforcing the incentives for the respect of core human and labour rights, environmental and good governance standards through the GSP+ arrangement.

■Strengthen the effectiveness of the trade concessions for Least Developed Countries through the "Everything but Arms" scheme. Reducing GSP to fewer beneficiaries will reduce competitive pressure and make the preferences for LDCs more meaningful.

■Increasing predictability, transparency and stability. With the exception of EBA, which has no expiry date, the new scheme will last 10 years, instead of three previously. This will make it easier and more interesting for EU importers to purchase from GSP beneficiary countries. In addition, procedures will become even more transparent, with clearer, better defined legal principles and objective criteria.

WEST AFRICA

Benin, Burkina Faso, Cape Verde, Gambia, Ghana, Guinea, Guinea-Bissau, Ivory Coast, Liberia, Mali, Mauritania, Niger, Nigeria, Senegal, Sierra Leone, Togo

The focus of the ongoing negotiations for an Economic Partnership Agreement between the EU and Benin, Burkina Faso, Cape Verde, Ivory Coast, Gambia, Ghana, Guinea, Guinea-Bissau, Liberia, Mali, Niger, Nigeria, Senegal, Sierra Leone, Togo and Mauritania is strengthening regional integration. A key priority is developing the economies by enhancing competitiveness – mainly through capacity-building for West African companies and exporters. Another important part of the negotiations is promoting the agricultural sector in West Africa.

Economic Partnership Agreements set out to help African Caribbean and Pacific (ACP) countries to improve their trade.

The EU is currently in negotiations for an Economic Partnership Agreement with Benin, Burkina Faso, Cape Verde, Ivory Coast, Gambia, Ghana, Guinea, Guinea-Bissau, Liberia, Mali, Niger, Nigeria, Senegal, Sierra Leone, Togo and Mauritania. The EU signed an interim Economic Partnership Agreement with the Ivory Coast in November 2008. Ghana initialed an interim agreementin December 2007.

- The West African region is the EU's most important trade partner in the African, Caribbean and Pacific region. The West African countries account for 40% of all trade between the EU and the African, Caribbean and Pacific region.
- Of the West African countries the Ivory Coast, Ghana and Nigeria account for 80% of the exports to the EU.
- Despite advanced regional integration processes in the region, barriers to intra-regional trade remain a challenge for the economies in West Africa. Regional trade lags behind compared to trade with developed and emerging countries outside West Africa.
- All the countries in the West Africa region except for Liberia are members of the WTO. Liberia is currently going through the accession process with full support of the EU.
- EU exports to the Ivory Coast and Ghana are dominated by industrial goods, machinery, vehicles and transport equipment and chemicals.
- EU imports from the West African countries are dominated by a limited number of basic commodities. Nigeria is a major oil exporter, recently followed by Ghana. Ghana and Ivory Coast are the world's two largest cocoa exporters. They also export bananas and, together with Cape Verde and Senegal, processed fisheries products. Other exports from the region include a range of agricultural commodities (mango, pineapple, groundnuts, cotton etc.) and to a far lesser extent metals (copper, gold) and diamonds.

EASTERN AND SOUTHERN AFRICA (ESA)

Comoros, Djibouti, Eritrea, Ethiopia, Madagascar, Malawi, Mauritius, Seychelles, Somalia, Sudan, Zambia, Zimbabwe

The EU is currently negotiating an Economic Partnership Agreement withDjibouti, Eritrea, Ethiopia, Somalia and Sudan, Malawi, Zambia and Zimbabwe, Comoros, Mauritius, Madagascar and the Seychelles.

- Eastern and Southern Africa is a diverse Economic Partnership Agreement group, including Indian Ocean islands (Comoros, Madagascar, Mauritius and Seychelles), countries from the Horn of Africa (Djibouti, Ethiopia, Eritrea and Sudan) and some countries of Southern Africa (Malawi, Zambia and Zimbabwe). Regional integration remains a challenge for this region.

- All the countries in the Eastern and Southern Africa region, except Eritrea, are members of the WTO.
- Exports to the EU from the Eastern and Southern Africa region are dominated by sugar, coffee, fish, tobacco, copper and crude oil.
- Imports from the EU to the Eastern and Southern Africa region are dominated by machinery and mechanical appliances, equipment, vehicles and pharmaceutical products.

The interim Economic Partnership Agreement between the EU and Madagascar, Mauritius, Seychelles and Zimbabwe – signed in August 2009 – includes the elimination of duties and quotas for imports from these countries to the EU as well as a gradual liberalization of EU exports to these countries. The agreement also covers rules of origin, fisheries, trade defense, development cooperation provisions and mechanisms for settling disputes.

More information on the interim Economic Partnership Agreement between the EU and Madagascar, Mauritius, Seychelles and Zimbabwe fr

The ongoing negotiations for an Economic Partnership Agreement between the EU and Eastern and Southern Africa as a whole include areas such as rules and commitments on services and investment, sustainable development and competition, and trade facilitation. It also includes co-operation on technical barriers to trade. It also includes co-operation on technical barriers to trade and sanitary and phyto-sanitary standards.

Economic Partnership Agreements set out to help African Caribbean and Pacific (ACP) countries to improve their trade.

CARIBBEAN COUNTRIES[1]

Antigua and Barbuda, Bahamas, Barbados, Belize, Dominica, Dominican Republic, Grenada, Guyana, Haiti, Jamaica, St Lucia, St Vincent and the Grenadines, St Kitts and Nevis, Suriname, Trinidad and Tobago

In October 2008 Antigua and Barbuda, The Bahamas, Barbados, Belize, Dominica, Grenada, Guyana, Jamaica, Saint Lucia, Saint Vincent and the Grenadines, Saint Kitts and Nevis, Surinam, Trinidad, Tobago, and the Dominican Republic signed an Economic Partnership Agreement with the EU. Haiti signed the agreement in December 2009, but is not yet applying it pending ratification.

The Economic Partnership Agreement between the EU and the 15 Caribbean countries is in part a free trade agreement, or FTA. And like any FTA, it opens up trade in goods between the two regions.

But unlike other FTAs, the EU-Caribbean Economic Partnership Agreement goes further. In fact, it's a wide-ranging partnership putting trade at the service of development.

That is because the agreement:

[1] Please contact Global Investment and Business Center, USA at ibpusa3@gmail.com for a complete text of the EU-Caribbean Economic Partnership Agreement

also opens up trade in services and investment;

makes it easier to do business in the Caribbean - governments there have made commitments in many areas directly affecting trade, like rules to ensure fair competition;

comes with financial support from the EU to help Caribbean:

governments implement the accord; and

businesses to use the EPA to export more and attract more outside investment.

CARIFORUM stands for the Caribbean Forum of African, Caribbean and PacificStates. In recent years CARIFORUM countries have been integrating more closely with each other. This is part of their strategy to play a fuller role in global trade, and to offer the economies of scale and simpler rules which are vital to attract more foreign investment.

The EU-Caribbean Economic Partnership Agreement helps to consolidate this process, by making it easier to export goods and services between:

the fourteen countries of the Caribbean Community, or CARICOM, and the Dominican Republic, which together make up CARIFORUM;

these fifteen countries (CARICOM plus the Dominican Republic) and seventeen territories in the Caribbean with direct links to EU countries, and which make up two distinct groups:

four French 'outermost regions'; and

thirteen 'overseas territories' - six British, six Dutch and one French.

To strengthen the competitiveness of economic operators in Antigua and Barbuda, The Bahamas, Barbados, Belize, Dominica, Grenada, Guyana, Jamaica, Saint Lucia, Saint Vincent and the Grenadines, Saint Kitts and Nevis, Surinam, Trinidad, Tobago, and the Dominican Republic – as well as the integration process of these countries in the global economy – the EU provides development cooperation in the region.

The EU's trade and development partnership with the Caribbean stretches back over more than 30 years. At its heart today is the CARIFORUM-EU Economic Partnership Agreement, or EPA. This is a new partnership which CARIFORUM - a group of 15 Caribbean countries - and the EU signed in 2008. The agreement also comes with substantial EU aid for trade.

The purpose of the agreement is to make it easier for people and businesses from the two regions to invest in and trade with each other and thus to help Caribbean countries grow their economies and create jobs.

The EU is CARIFORUM's second largest trading partner, after the US. In 2011, trade between the two regions came to over €8 billion.

In 2011 CARIFORUM ran a trade deficit with the EU of some €2.2 billion. In other words, CARIFORUM countries exported €2.2 billion less in goods and services to the EU than they imported from the EU.

The main exports from the Caribbean to the EU are in:

- fuel and mining products, notably petroleum gas and oils;
- bananas, sugar and rum;
- minerals, notably gold, corundum, aluminium oxide and hydroxide, and iron ore products;
- fertilisers.

The main imports into the Caribbean from the EU are in:

- boats and ships, cars, constructions vehicles and engine parts;
- phone equipment;
- milk and cream;
- spirit drinks.

CENTRAL AFRICA

Cameroon, Central African Republic, Chad, Congo (Brazzaville), Congo - Democratic Republic of (Kinshasa), Equatorial Guinea, Gabon, São Tomé & Principe

The EU is currently in negotiations for an Economic Partnership Agreement with Cameroon, the Central African Republic, Chad, Congo, the Democratic Republic of Congo, Equatorial Guinea, Gabon, Sao Tome and Principe. Cameroon signed an interim Economic Partnership Agreement with the EU in 2009.

Regional integration remains a challenge for the economies in Central Africa. Regional trade lags behind compared to trade with developed countries outside Central Africa.

Oil dominates (70%) exports to the EU from the Central African countries. Only the Central African Republic do not export oil to the EU. Other main exports are cocoa, wood copper, bananas, and diamonds.

Imports from the EU into the Central African region are dominated by machinery and mechanical appliances, equipment, vehicles, foodstuffs and pharmaceutical products.

EU and Central Africa

The interim Economic Partnership Agreement between the EU and Cameroon - signed in 2009 - encompasses duty and quota-free EU access for all goods from Cameroon and a gradual removal of duties and quotas during the period 2010-2025 on up to 80% of EU exports to Cameroon. Besides trade in goods, the interim agreement also covers aid for trade, institutional issues, and dispute settlement. It also includes rendez-vous clauses on other Economic Partnership Agreement subjects. The beginning of the liberalization process started on 1 January 2010.

Gabon and Congo have not yet signed an Economic Partnership Agreement. They trade with the EU under the EU's Generalised Scheme of Preferences scheme. As an upper-middle income country (according to the World Bank classification), Gabon not be eligible for the new Generalized System of Preferences scheme as of 1 January 2014.

As Least Developed Countries Chad, the Central African Republic, the Democratic Republic of Congo, São Tomé and Equatorial Guinea all benefit from duty and quota-free EU access under the EU's "Everything but Arms" scheme.

The ongoing negotiations for a comprehensive Economic Partnership Agreement between the EU and Central Africa region include areas such as rules and commitments on goods and rules of origin, services and investment, sustainable development, competition and trade facilitation. Cooperation on technical barriers to trade and sanitary and phyto-sanitary standards are also foreseen.

Economic Partnership Agreements set out to help African Caribbean and Pacific (ACP) countries to improve their trade

SOUTHERN AFRICAN DEVELOPMENT COMMUNITY (SADC)

Angola, Botswana, Lesotho, Mozambique, Namibia, South Africa

The EU is currently in negotiations for an Economic Partnership Agreement with Angola, Botswana, Lesotho, Mozambique, Namibia, Swaziland and South Africa, as the Southern African Development Community Economic Partnership Agreement group.

The other six members of the Southern African Development Community region – the Democratic Republic of the Congo, Madagascar, Malawi, Mauritius, Zambia and Zimbabwe – are negotiating Economic Partnership Agreements with the EU as part of other regional groups, namely Central Africa or Eastern and Southern Africa.

An interim Economic Partnership Agreement was concluded with Botswana, Lesotho, Namibia, Swaziland and Mozambique in 2007. It was signed by Botswana, Lesotho, Swaziland and Mozambique in June 2009. The Namibia signature is still pending.

EU AND THE SOUTHERN AFRICAN DEVELOPMENT COMMUNITY

The Interim Partnership Agreement signed by Botswana, Lesotho, Namibia, Swaziland and Mozambique in 2007 (Namibia's signature still pending) includes a number of key areas that will boost trade from in the region.

The interim agreement includes the elimination of duties/quotas for imports to the EU from these countries as well as the elimination of duties/quotas on EU exports to Botswana, Lesotho, Namibia and Swaziland and Mozambique. The interim agreement makes it possible for all participating countries to re-introduce duties/quotas to help safeguard local economies.

The interim Economic Partnership Agreement includes EU commitments to foster trade within the region and help to exporters meet with EU import standards. It also includes a commitment of all interim partners – except Namibia – to conclude an Economic Partnership Agreement to cover services and investments.

Angola currently maintains market access through the EU's "Everything but Arms" scheme for least developed countries.

The interim agreement has not been ratified yet pending the negotiations on a comprehensive regional EPA agreement.

Negotiations for a comprehensive regional Economic Partnership Agreement are ongoing and the parties are discussing improved market access as requested by South Africa, but also how to deal with trade related issues, rules of origin and cumulation, as well as some textual provisions of the Interim EPA text (e.g. Most Favoured Nation clause, export taxes, sustainable development). Botswana, Mozambique, Lesotho and Swaziland have agreed to negotiate services.

The door will be open for others to join at a later stage. Several rounds took place in between 2010 and 2012 and the next round is scheduled to take place in November 2012.

Economic Partnership Agreements set out to help African Caribbean and Pacific (ACP) countries to improve their trade.

- The EU is the Southern African Development Community's largest trading partner, with South Africa accounting for the largest part of EU imports to and EU exports from the region.
- TheSouthern African Development Community countries are strong in the exports of diamonds and in South Africa, Botswana, Lesotho and Namibia these constitute a large to dominant share of their exports to the EU.
- Other products from the region include agricultural products (beef from Botswana, fish from Namibia or sugar from Swaziland), oil from Angola or aluminum from Mozambique. South Africa's exports to the EU are much diversified and range from fruit to platinum and from manufactured goods to wine.
- The EU exports a wide range of goods to the Southern African Development Community countries, including vehicles, machinery, electrical equipment, pharmaceuticals and processed food.
- The countries in the Southern African Development Community are members of the WTO.
- The Economic Partnership Agreement countries in the Southern African Development Community constitute a very diverse group. Lesotho, Mozambique and Swaziland are least developed countries (LDCs), but countries like Namibia and Botswana hold upper middle income status. Botswana, Lesotho, Namibia and South Africa form the Southern Africa Customs Union (SACU).
- Trade between the EU and South Africa is governed by the Trade, Development and Cooperation Agreement between the EU and South Africa. Most of the Southern African Customs Union members have aligned their import regime to this trade agreement. As the main point of entry into Southern African Customs Union, duties are mainly collected by South Africa, which then redistributes to the other members according to an agreed formula.

PACIFIC COUNTRIES[2]

The EU concluded an Interim Partnership Agreement with Papua New Guinea and Fiji in 2007. The agreement was ratified by the European Parliament in January 2011, and by Papua New Guinea in May 2011. Fiji is not yet implementing the agreement, and has access to the EU under the Market Access Regulation.

The EU is currently negotiating a comprehensive Economic Partnership Agreement with all fourteen countries of the region (Cook Islands, East Timor, Fiji, Kiribati, the Marshall Islands, Micronesia, Nauru, Niue, Palau, Papua New Guinea, Samoa, the Solomon Islands, Tonga,

[2] Please contact Global Investment and Business Center, USA at ibpusa3@gmail.com for a complete text of the Partnership Agreement with Papua New Guinea and Fiji

Tuvalu, and Vanuatu). The comprehensive agreement would cover trade in goods, trade in services, development co-operation and trade-related issues like food health and safety issues, technical barriers to trade, agriculture, sustainable development and competition.

- Regional trade is based on the Pacific Island Countries Agreement (PICTA), which is in the process of being implemented. The region is also negotiating a trade and cooperation agreement with Australia and New Zealand (PACER+).
- Only countries in the Pacific region are members of the WTO, namely: Fiji, Papua New Guinea, Samoa, Solomon Islands, Tonga and Vanuatu.
- Exports to the EU from the Pacific region are dominated by palm oil, coffee, coconut, and fish and caviar.
- Imports from the EU to the Pacific region are dominated by electrical machinery and equipment.
- Overall, trade between the EU and the Pacific countries is very small both in absolute and in relative terms.

EU AND THE PACIFIC REGION

The interim Economic Partnership Agreement concluded between the EU and Fiji and Papua New Guinea liberalizes trade with the EU in goods, but do not cover the trade in services. The agreement includes:

- duty and quota-free exports from Papua New Guinea and Fiji to the EU as of 1 January 2008
- assymetric and gradual opening of markets to EU goods, taking full account of differences in levels of development and sensitive sectors – for Papua New Guinea: liberalizing 88% of EU imports with the agreement, excluding the most sensitive economic sectors (e.g. meat, fish, vegetables, furniture and jewelry) and for Fiji: committed to liberalize 14% of EU imports to the country, rising to a maximum 87% over 15 years, excluding products from sensitive economic sectors and important for revenue, (e.g. meat, fish, fruits and vegetables, alcohol, tubes and iron)
- safeguard provisions: duties and quotas can be reintroduced if imports from the EU disturb or threaten to disturb the economy
- provisions on technical barriers to trade (TBT), and sanitary and phytosanitary (SPS) measures to help Pacific exporters meet EU import standards
- customs and trade facilitation – efficient customs procedures and better co-operation between administrations
- improved Rules of Origin for processed fisheries products from the Pacific which could boost development in the region

ANDEAN COMMUNITY COUNTRIES[3]

Bolivia, Colombia, Ecuador, Perú

The EU is the second largest trading partner of the Andean region after the US. Trade with the EU was worth 14.3% of the total trade of the Andean Community in 2010.

- The Andean countries export predominantly primary products (agricultural products (38%), fuels and mining products (54%) to the EU.

[3] Please contact Global Investment and Business Center, USA at ibpusa3@gmail.com for a complete text of the Peru and Colombia Trade Agreement

- EU exports consist mostly of manufactured goods, notably machinery and transport equipment (50%), and chemical products (19%).

In June 2012 the EU signed an ambitious and comprehensive Trade Agreement with Colombia and Peru. The agreement is provisionally applied with Peru since 1 March 2013 and with Colombia since 1 August 2013

Once fully implemented, it will open up markets on both sides as well as increase the stability and predictability of the trading environment.

Trade negotiations between the EU and with Colombia and Peru were successfully concluded in 2011. The text of the Trade Agreement (Peru and Colombia Trade Agreement - full text) - was signed on June 2012 and will now follow the process of translation, signature and adoption according to each Party's domestic procedures.

The Agreement provides for progressive and reciprocal liberalisation by means of an ambitious, comprehensive and balanced free trade area. This is important for enhancing trade between the two regions, attracting investment to the Andean countries and helping local businesses develop the strength in their regional market to compete internationally.

The EU grants the Andean countries preferential access to its market under the EU's Generalised Scheme of Preferences, including through the special incentive arrangement for sustainable development and good governance, known as the Generalised Scheme of Preferences Plus (GSP+).

BENEFITS OF THE AGREEMENT:

- opening markets for goods, services, government procurement and investment
- savings on import duties alone worth some half a billion Euros at the end of transition periods
- better conditions for trade through new disciplines on non-tariff barriers, competition, transparency and intellectual property rights
- a more stable and predictable environment for economic operators with a mediation mechanism for non-tariff barriers and a bilateral dispute settlement mechanism
- provisions for cooperation on competitiveness, innovation, production modernisiation, trade facilitation and technology transfer
- a comprehensive Trade and Sustainable Development title to promote and preserve a high level of labour and environmental protection, including a transparent arbitration system and an engagement of the civil society

SOUTH EAST ASIAN COUNTRIES

Brunei Darussalam, Myanmar/Burma, Cambodia, Indonesia, Laos, Malaysia, Philippines, Singapore, Thailand, Vietnam

The final negotiations for a Free Trade Agreement between Singapore and the EU were completed in December 2012, both parties initialed the text on 20 September 2013, whilst negotiations on investment protection are continuing.

The EU also finances regional projects relating to trade such as:

- Enhancing ASEAN FTA Negotiating Capacity Programme
- ASEAN Regional Integration Support Programme (ARISE)
- EU-ASEAN Statistical Capacity Building Programme (EASCAB)
- ASEAN Project on the Protection of Intellectual Property Rights (ECAP III)

The EU is negotiating Free Trade Agreements with Malaysia, Vietnam and Thailand.

The EU's door remains open to start negotiations with other partners in the region and hopes one day to complete these agreements with a region-to-regional trade agreement.

ASEAN as a whole represents the EU's 3rd largest trading partner outside Europe (after the US and China) with more than €206 billion of trade in goods and services in 2011.

The EU is ASEAN 2nd largest trading partner after China, accounting for around 11% of ASEAN trade.

The EU is by far the largest investor in ASEAN countries. EU companies have invested around €9.1 billion annually on average (2000-2009).

The EU's main exports to ASEAN are chemical products, machinery and transport equipment. The main imports from ASEAN to the EU are machinery and transport equipment, agricultural products as well as textiles and clothing.

CENTRAL AMERICAN COUNTRIES[4]

Panama, Guatemala, Costa Rica, El Salvador, Honduras, Nicaragua

The EU's central economic policy objective for Central America is to strengthen the process of regional integration between the region's countries. In practical terms this means the creation of a customs union and economic integration in Central America. The EU has supported this process through its trade agreement and its trade-related technical assistance in the region.

The EU and the Central American region concluded a new Association Agreement in 2011 and signed it in 2012. This new agreement aims at fostering sustainable development and deepening their process of regional integration and includes a major trade pillar. This closer economic integration between the countries of the Central American region is important for attracting investment to the region and helping local businesses develop the strength in their regional market to compete internationally.

The EU grants all Central American countries preferential access to its market under the EU's General Scheme of Preferences and particularly, the special incentive arrangement for sustainable development and good governance, known as GSP+).

[4] Please contact Global Investment and Business Centr, USA - ibpusa3@gmail.com - for the text of the EU-Central America association agreement

Trading with Central America

■Rules and requirements for trading with the countries of Central America

■The EU is present on the ground in Central America (+ Delegations in Costa Rica, El Salvador, Guatemala, Honduras, Nicaragua and Panama)

■Trade relations are part of the EU's overall political and economic relations with Central America

■Central America organisation

For the last decade the EU's share in Central American trade has remained largely stable at 8.1% in 2010. Historically the bulk of most Central America countries trade is with the USA and Latin America, and it is only recently that the region has actively sought to increase its trade with Europe.

- EU imports from Central America are dominated by office and telecommunication equipment (53.9%) and agricultural products (34.8% in 2010).
- The most important exports from the EU to Central America are machinery and transport equipment (48.2%) and chemicals (12.3%).

CENTRAL ASIAN COUNTRIES

Kazakhstan, Kyrgyzstan, Tajikistan, Turkmenistan, Uzbekistan

Central Asia is of geostrategic importance to the EU. The region represents a bridge to China as well as to Afghanistan and to the Middle East. The region is a source of significant energy imports for the EU.

All five Central Asian countries benefit from favourable access to the EU's market, through the Generalised Scheme of Preferences

EU trade with Central Asia has grown and the EU is now the main trading partner of the region, accounting for about a third of its overall external trade. Nevertheless, total turnover of the EU's trade with Central Asia remains low.

- Central Asian exports to the EU remain concentrated in a few commodities, especially crude oil, gas, metals and cotton fibre.
- EU exports are dominated by machinery and transport equipment, and other manufactured goods. Such products accounted for more than half of EU exports in the region in 2011.

Based on the EU Central Asia Strategy the EU aims to enhance relations with the region as a whole and each of its particular countries. In the area of trade and investment the Strategy focuses on

- the accession of the entire Central Asian region to the World Trade Organisation.
- It also aims to help Central Asian countries take greater advantage of the EU's Generalised Scheme of Preferences.

The overall institutional framework for the EU's cooperation with the region is as follows:

The EU's bilateral trade relations with Kazakhstan, Kyrgyzstan, Tajikistan and Uzbekistan are governed by a Partnership and Cooperation Agreement (PCA)

In terms of trade, these are non-preferential agreements – ensuring that there are no tariff reductions applied and that quantitative restrictions are prohibited in bilateral trade.

The Partnership and Cooperation Agreements envisage progressive regulatory approximation of the partner countries' legislation and practices to the most important EU trade-related standards including technical regulations, sanitary and phytosanitary requirements, intellectual property rights' protection and customs issues. This should lead to better access to the EU markets for goods originating in those countries.

The Partnership and Cooperation Agreement concluded with Turkmenistan in 1998 has not yet been ratified by all the Member States of the EU.

Pending ratification, an Interim Agreement on trade and trade related matters entered into force on 1 August 2010.

The other areas of cooperation remain based on the Trade and Cooperation Agreement signed with the Soviet Union in 1989 and subsequently endorsed by Turkmenistan.

WTO MEMBERSHIP

WTO membership of all the Central Asian countries is a pre-condition for closer trading and investment relations with the EU.

- Kyrgyzstan has been a WTO member since 1998.
- Tajikistan's accession package was adopted by the WTO General Council in December 2012 and Tajikistan becomes a WTO member on 2 March 2013.
- Kazakhstan's accession process is well advanced.
- There is limited progress in the accession of Uzbekistan
- Turkmenistan has not yet applied for WTO membership.

MEDITERRANEAN AND NORTH AFRICAN COUNTRIES

Algeria, Egypt, Israel, Jordan, Lebanon, Libya, Morocco, Occupied Palestinian Territory, Syria, Tunisia, Turkey

The Union for the Mediterranean aims to establish a common area of peace, stability, and shared prosperity in the Euro-Mediterranean region.

EU-Southern Mediterranean relations at bilateral level are managed mainly through the Euro-Mediterranean Association Agreements.

- Nearly all countries have concluded Association Agreements with the EU. Preparations are going to deepen these agreements through the establishment of deep and comprehensive free trade areas.
- Negotiations for a Framework Agreement between the European Union and Libya are currently suspended.

- Steps towards the signature of the initialled Association Agreement with Syria are currently suspended.

Country	Status	Date signed	Entry into Force
Algeria	Signed	April 2002	September 2005
Egypt	Signed	June 2001	June 2004
Israel	Signed	Nov 1995	June 2000
Jordan	Signed	Nov 1997	May 2002
Lebanon	Signed	June 2002	April 2006
Morocco	Signed	Feb 1996	March 2000
Occupied Palestinian Territory	Signed	Feb 1997	Interim Agreement July 1997
Syria	Initialled (December 2008)		
Tunisia	Signed	July 1995	March 1998
Turkey	Customs Union January 1996	Customs Union	December 1995

These agreements cover trade in goods and are complemented with a number of additional ongoing negotiations and preparations for future negotiations:

- to open up additional agricultural trade,
- liberalise trade in services and investment,
- to negotiate agreements on accreditation and acceptance of industrial products,
- to establish deep and comprehensive free trade areas.

Deepening South-South economic integration is a key goal of the Euro-Mediterranean trade partnership. It is an essential element towards the establishment of a fully-fledged Free Trade Area. However, regional economic integration between Southern Mediterranean countries is still limited: total intra-regional trade amounted to €15 billion in 2009, one of the lowest levels of regional economic integration in the World.
The EU supports the strengthening of trade relations amongst Southern Mediterranean countries:

- the Agadir Agreement between Tunisia, Morocco, Jordan, and Egypt, in force since 2007, remains open to other Arab Mediterranean countries;
- Israel and Jordan have signed a Free Trade Agreement;
- Egypt, Israel, Jordan, Lebanon, Morocco, the Palestinian Territories, Syria and Tunisia have signed bilateral agreements with Turkey.
- Negotiations are underway between other Mediterranean countries to establish similar agreements.

The EU works closely with each of its Southern Mediterranean partners to support economic and social transition and reform, taking into account each country's specific needs and characteristics. These programmes are funded under the European Neighbourhood Policy

The key objective of the trade partnership is the creation of a deep Euro-Mediterranean Free Trade Area, which aims at removing barriers to trade and investment between both the EU and Southern Mediterranean countries and between the Southern Mediterranean countries themselves. Euro-Mediterranean Association Agreements are in force with most of the partners (with the exception of Syria and Libya).

The scope of these agreements is essentially limited to trade in goods and a number of bilateral negotiations are on-going or being prepared in order to deepen the Association Agreements. These ongoing or future negotiations are related to further liberalisation of trade in agriculture, liberalisation of trade in services, accreditation and acceptance of industrial products and regulatory convergence.

GULF REGION COUNTRIES

Bahrain, Kuwait, Oman, Qatar, Saudi Arabia, United Arab Emirates

The EU is negotiating a free trade agreement with the Gulf Cooperation Council. Negotiations were suspended by the GCC in 2008. Informal contacts between negotiators continue to take place.

The Gulf Cooperation Council is currently the EU's fifth largest export market. Meanwhile, the EU is the first trading partner for the Gulf.

- EU exports to Gulf Cooperation Council are diverse but focused on machinery and transport materials (46.5%), for example power generation plants, railway locomotives and aircraft as well as electrical machinery and mechanical appliances.
- EU imports from Gulf Cooperation Council are mainly fuels and derivatives (81.9% of total EU imports from the region in 2011).

The EU-Gulf Cooperation Council negotiations for a Free Trade Agreement seek the progressive and reciprocal liberalisation of trade in goods and services. They aim to ensure a comparable level of market access opportunities, taking into account the countries' level of development.

A future EU-Gulf Cooperation Council agreement has been subject to a public sustainability impact assessment.

The current framework for economic and political cooperation is the 1989 EU-GCC cooperation agreement that seeks to improve trade relations and stability in a strategic part of Europe's neighbourhood.

- The agreement created a Joint Council and a Joint Co-operation Committee which meet annually.
- At the 2010 Joint Council, a EU-Gulf Cooperation Council Joint Action Programme for the years 2010-2013 has been agreed.

All six Gulf Cooperation Council countries currently benefit from preferential access to the EU market under the EU's Generalised Scheme of Preferences.

EU-GULF COOPERATION COUNCIL TRADE NEGOTIATIONS

Negotiations cover, *inter alia*:

- Market access for goods, services and public procurement
- Common rules and disciplines for intellectual property rights
- Competition
- Dispute settlement
- Rules of origin
- Human rights

- Illegal immigration
- Terrorism

SOUTH AMERICAN (MERCOSUR) COUNTRIES

Argentina, Brazil, Paraguay, Uruguay, Venezuela

Mercosur was established in 1991 and encompasses Argentina, Brazil, Paraguay, Uruguay and Venezuela which officially joined in July 2012. Paraguay is temporarily suspended from Mercosur since June 2012.

The EU has bilateral Partnership and Cooperation agreements with Argentina, Brazil, Paraguay and Uruguay

All Mercosur countries currently benefit from the GSP scheme, while Paraguay also benefits from GSP+[5]

- The EU is Mercosur's first trading partner, accounting for 20% of Mercosur's total trade.
- Mercosur is the EU's 8th most important trading partner, accounting for 3% of EU's total trade. EU's exports to the region have steadily increased over the last years, going up from € 28 billion in 2007 to € 45 billlion in 2011.
- Mercour's biggest exports to the EU are made of agricultural products (48% of total exports) while the EU mostly exports manufactured products to Mercosur and notably machinery and transport equipment (49% of total exports) and chemicals (21% of total exports).
- The EU is also a major exporter of commercial services to Mercosur (€13.4 bn in 2010) as well as the biggest foreign investor in the region with a stock of foreign direct investment that has steadily increased over the past years and which now amount to €236 billion in 2010 compared to € 130 billion in 2000.

The EU is currently negotiating a trade agreement with Mercosur as part of the overall negotiation for a bi-regional Association Agreement which also cover a political and a cooperation pillar.

These negotiations with Mercosur were officially relaunched at the EU-Mercosur summit in Madrid on 17 May 2010. The objective is to negotiate a comprehensive trade agreement, covering not only trade in industrial and agricultural goods but also services, improvement of rules on government procurement, intellectual property, customs and trade facilitation, technical barriers to trade.

Nine negotiation rounds (the last one from 22 to 26 October 2012) have taken place since then.

Until now, rounds have focused on the part of the agreement related to rules and the two regions are still working on the preparation of their market access offers. No date has been set yet for the exchange of market access offers.

[5] The EU's "Generalised Scheme of Preferences" (GSP) allows developing country exporters to pay lower duties on their exports to the EU. This gives them vital access to EU markets and contributes to their economic growth. The reformed GSP, which will apply as from 2014, will further focus support on countries most in need

SOUTH CAUCASUS COUNTRIES

Armenia, Azerbaijan, Georgia

The EU started negotiations with Armenia and Georgia for a Deep and Comprehensive Free Trade Area in early 2012. With Azerbaijan the EU is negotiating a non-preferential trade and investment agreement as Azerbaijan is not yet a member of the WTO.

The EU is the main trade partner of each country (in 2012 trade with the EU represented 27,3% of overall trade for Armenia, 45.6% for Azerbaijan and 26.6% for Georgia). Armenia's and Georgia's share of overall EU trade remains very low, at around 0.1% . Azerbaijan's share in total EU trade is higher due to imports of energy products, at 0.8%.

A deep and comprehensive free trade area is about closer economic integration, including:

- Complete elimination of customs duties - so that products can enter duty free and result in lower prices of goods to the benefit of consumers
- Improvement of customs procedures - bringing the partners' legislation closer to the EU one to unify procedures for imports
- Increased protection of intellectual property - to improve in particular enforcement of legislation and bring the level of IP protection on a par with that in the EU
- Application of EU sanitary and phytosanitary rules – to increase the level of food safety protection within the countries and so allow exports of products of animal origin to the EU
- Upgrade rules on public procurement and competition - thereby creating a transparent and predictable regime for economic operators both in private and public commercial transactions
- Removal of technical obstacles to trade - to facilitate trade in industrial products but also, by upgrading infrastructure and conformity assessment procedures, to gradually increase competitiveness of their industries

The South Caucasus region plays an important role both in supplying energy to the EU and as a transit route for it.

Azerbaijan is a major supplier of oil and gas to the EU, as recognised in the EU-Azerbaijan memorandum of understanding on energy concluded in 2006.

Oil and gas from the Caspian Sea is shipped to the EU through pipelines crossing Georgia and Turkey (Baku-Tbilisi-Ceyhan, Baku-Supsa and Baku-Tbilisi-Erzurum).

Caspian oil is also transported from Azerbaijan to the Georgian port of Poti and Batumi by rail.

In the future, energy supplies should be shipped via the 'southern corridor' that should include, *inter alia*, the Nabucco gas pipeline. All three countries participate in the Baku Energy Initiative

In December 2011 (Georgia) and in February 2012 (Armenia), the Commission concluded following a lengthy preparatory process that trade negotiations could start as an integral part of currently negotiated Association Agreements. Both countries embarked on talks for a Deep and Comprehensive Free Trade Area with the EU in early 2012.

Current relationship between the EU and South Caucasus countries is governed by the Partnership and Cooperation Agreements which entered into force with each of the three partners in 1999 and do not provide any trade preference for goods and a limited preference for trade in services.

Closer economic ties are dependent on the partner countries' membership in the World Trade Organisation. Georgia and Armenia have been WTO members since 2000 and 2003 respectively.

Azerbaijan applied for membership to the World Trade Organisation in 1997 and the process is ongoing. Azerbaijan first needs to accomplish its accession before a Deep and Comprehensive Free Trade Agreement can be considered.

With a view to supporting Azerbaijan's future WTO membership and subsequent eventual bilateral Deep and Comprehensive FTA, negotiations on upgrading the existing trade related provisions of the Partnership and Cooperation Agreement (non-preferential trade and investment agreement) were launched on 16 July 2010.

Azerbaijan is receiving technical assistance from the EU to help it to prepare for WTO membership.

All three South Caucasus countries benefit from the EU's Generalised Scheme of Preferences (GSP). Under the current GSP Regulation, applying from 1 January 2009, all qualify for the special incentive arrangement for sustainable development and good governance (GSP+), offering advantageous access to the EU market.

Under the reformed GSP scheme, as of 22 February 2014 preferences for Azerbaijan will be deferred and Azerbaijan will revert to the standard "Most Favoured Nation" treatment.
The new regime focuses preferences on poorer countries. Countries which are classified as “upper-middle income” economies by the World Bank for at least 3 years in a row, like Azerbaijan, have their preferences deferred.

The EU supports closer trade and economic integration with the EU through the European Neighbourhood Policy and its Easter Partnership dimension. Armenia, Azerbaijan and Georgia each have an Action Plan

- The Action Plans are a long-term reform agenda in various policy areas, including trade and trade-related matters. Both countries were required to speed up their efforts and demonstrate tangible results before negotiations on a trade area could be launched.
- The reform process, in line with the Action Plans, continues for Armenia and Georgia in parallel to ongoing trade negotiations.
- The Commission / EEAS prepare annual reports where the progress made is assessed. For more information

WESTERN BALKANS COUNTRIES

Albania, Bosnia and Herzegovina, the former Yugoslav Republic of Macedonia, Montenegro, Serbia, Kosovo. Croatia became member of the European Union on 1 July 2013

In 2000, the EU granted autonomous trade preferences to all the Western Balkans. These preferences, which were renewed in 2005 and subsequently in 2011 until 2015, allow nearly all exports to enter the EU without customs duties or limits on quantities. Only wine, baby beef and certain fisheries products enter the EU under preferential tariff quotas.

■This preferential regime has contributed to an increase in the Western Balkans' exports to the EU. In 2010, the EU was the region's largest trading partner for both imports (61,3%) and exports (64,5%).

- The EU is the Western Balkans' largest trading partner, accounting for about two thirds of the region's total trade. As a whole the region's share of overall EU trade was 1,4% in 2012, however individual countries' shares were very low - Croatia 0,5%, Serbia 0,4%, FYR Macedonia 0,2%, Bosnia and Herzegovina 0,2%, Albania 0,1%, Montenegro 0,0% and Kosovo 0,0%.

- In 2012, the EU's main imports from Western Balkans were manufactured goods classified chiefly by materials (21.7%), manufactured articles (20.9%), and machinery and transport equipment (20.7%). The EU's exports to the Western Balkans were mainly machinery and transport equipment (25.3%), manufactured goods classified mainly by material (21.2%), chemicals (15.1%), and mineral fuels (14.8%).

All the Western Balkans states have been offered Stabilisation and Association Agreements (SAAs) and have a clear EU perspective. The EU's strategy includes massive financial assistance, making it by far the largest donor to the region.

The EU strongly supports the membership of the Western Balkans states of the World Trade Organization (WTO).

■Albania (2000), the former Yugoslav Republic of Macedonia (2003) and Montenegro (2011) are already WTO members.

■The EU signed the bilateral agreement on Bosnia and Hercegovina's accession to the WTO (2012), which is a key step for the country to become a WTO member.

■The WTO accession negotiations with Serbia are on going.

The EU's relations with the Western Balkans are governed by the Stabilisation and Association process.

■There are three Stabilisation and Association Agreements (SAAs) in force: with the former Yugoslav Republic of Macedonia (2004), Albania (2009) and Montenegro (2010).

■The trade part of the SAAs came into force through an Interim Agreement with Bosnia and Herzegovina (2008) and Serbia (2010). The agreements aim to progressively establish a free trade area between the EU and the Western Balkans.

■Where trade is concerned, they focus on liberalizing trade in goods, aligning rules on EU practice and protecting intellectual property.

For more information, see also: Commission Communication on "Western Balkans : Enhancing the European perspective" (March 2008), Staff Working Paper 2009 (February 2009) and Commission Communication on "Enlargement Strategy and Main Challenges 2011-2012" (October 2011).

In order to further develop regional trade and to offer new opportunities for economic operators, a system of diagonal cumulation of origin has been set up between the European Union, the Western Balkans participating to the Stabilisation and Association Process and Turkey. This system allows a participating partner to use materials originating in other partner(s) of the zone under advantageous conditions in the manufacture of final goods which are exported to the European Union, the Western Balkans or Turkey.

Trading with Western Balkans

- The EU is present on the ground in the Western Balkans (EU Delegations in Albania, Bosnia and Herzegovina, the former Yugoslav Republic of Macedonia, Montenegro, Serbia and Kosovo)

- Trade relations are part of the EU's overall political and economic relations with the Western Balkans

- The Central European Free Trade Agreement (CEFTA) is a single Free Trade Agreement (FTA) linking all the Western Balkans and Moldova.

EU TRADE AND FINANCIAL INTEGRATION

EU FINANCIAL SERVICE POLICY

Today, the European Commission presented its new financial services strategy for the next five years. Although progress has been made through the successful completion of the Financial Services Action Plan (FSAP), the Commission concludes that the EU financial services industry (banking, insurance, securities, asset management) still has strong untapped economic and employment growth potential. The Commission's new strategy explores the best ways to effectively deliver further benefits of financial integration to industry and consumers alike. Priority N° 1 is to dynamically consolidate progress and ensure sound implementation and enforcement of existing rules. N° 2 is to drive through the better regulation principles into all policy making. N° 3 is to enhance supervisory convergence. N° 4 is to create more competition between service providers, especially those active in retail markets. N° 5 is to expand EU's external influence in globalizing capital markets.

Internal Market Commissioner Charlie McCreevy said: "*European financial integration has really moved forward in the last five years. The challenge now is to consolidate progress and work together on applying the better regulatory disciplines. Our aim should be to create the best financial framework in the world. It means creating real, tangible benefits for the citizens and businesses of Europe through lower capital costs, better pensions, and cheaper, safer retail financial products. Our new strategy is practical, economics driven and citizen focused. Only in a few, targeted areas are new initiatives foreseen.*"

Financial integration and the new initiatives

Studies show that the more integrated financial markets are, the more efficient the allocation of economic resources and long-run economic performance will be. Completing the single market in financial services is more and more recognised as one of the key areas for EU's future growth and jobs, essential for EU's global competitiveness and thus a crucial part of the Lisbon economic reform process.

Efforts need to continue in the next five years. Only when rules are implemented on time and enforced effectively, companies and citizens can benefit from access to pan-European markets. National regulators need to speed up on implementation. The current regulatory framework must be free of inconsistencies and legal ambiguities. Supervisory practices and standards need to converge across Europe. Cross-border investments need to be encouraged.

Unfinished business must be completed in a practical way. The new strategy has not identified and straitjacketed – ex ante – many new regulatory initiatives. However, if regulation is needed, each initiative will have to follow the better regulation principle, should be evidence based and comply with the subsidiarity principle.

Furthermore, while the FSAP focused mainly on the wholesale market, retail integration will become more important over the next period. Barriers associated with the use of bank accounts will be examined, with a view to enabling consumers to shop around all over Europe for the best savings plans, mortgages, insurance and pensions, with clear information so that products can be compared.

FREQUENTLY ASKED QUESTIONS (FAQS) ON EU FINANCIAL SERVICES POLICY FOR THE NEXT FIVE YEARS

What is the status of a White Paper and why is it important?

A White Paper sets out the Commission's final policy programme in a specific area. Before a White Paper is written, a Green Paper is published, which is a consultative document including suggestions and options for new policy. While Green Papers are open for public consultation, White Papers are not, as, in principle, a White Paper is the final say. However, each single proposal for legislation announced in a White Paper or deriving from a policy initiative announced in it will be subject to one or more rounds of open consultation and impact assessment.

What are the main differences between the content of this White Paper and the suggestions in the Green Paper published in May?

Not many. In the long and thorough consultation process that took place prior to the publication of the Green Paper (IP/05/527, MEMO/05/148), all stakeholders had been heard and all arguments expressed. From the public consultation on the Commission's Green Paper there was broad support from all concerned on the main issues. The analysis in the Green Paper and its Annex remain valid. However, in two areas the Commission has decided to use the White Paper to clarify and explain in more detail its envisaged policies: (1) the so-called "Single Financial Services Rulebook" and (2) Supervision (see below).

Why is financial integration beneficial?

Well-functioning financial markets influence the prosperity of all European citizens and businesses and are the motor for growth and jobs. The value of savings and pensions, the cost of mortgages and the cost of capital are ultimately determined in financial markets. Deep, liquid, dynamic financial markets will ensure the most efficient allocation and provision of capital and services throughout the European economy. The economic benefits of European financial integration are beyond doubt, as has been recognised in the Lisbon strategy. Integration of financial services is more and more recognised as one of the pioneer, flagship areas for strengthening Europe's future growth and jobs.

What has been done already to integrate financial markets?

One of the biggest achievements in Europe over the last six years has been the progress made towards an integrated, open, and more competitive and efficient European financial market. This year, the legislative phase for the Financial Services Action Plan (FSAP) drew to a close.

The FSAP has been a top EU policy priority since its launch in 1999. Major political and legislative agreements for example have been found on accounting, auditing, integrity, corporate governance, prospectuses, transparency, investment services, investment funds, marketing, intermediation, capital requirements, pensions and reinsurance.

The measures foreseen in the FSAP were agreed on time and are now being put in place. From a macro-perspective, the FSAP has laid the legislative foundations for an effectively integrated market for many segments of European finance. European capital markets are expanding (*e.g.* corporate bonds, Initial Public Offerings, Mergers & Acquisitions). Equity markets are strong, and financial services companies' profits are healthy. Integration of the European financial market is the best way to stimulate competition within the European industry and therewith the competitiveness of our industry in a global setting.

The new strategy does not introduce many new things in terms of legislation. Is this programme ambitious enough?

It is. The Commission's programme of dynamic consolidation is a major and very ambitious task which will require enormous effort and resources from all concerned: regulators, supervisors and industry alike. What could be more ambitious than to make all the FSAP measures actually work on the ground; creating real financial integration? What is needed now is practical implementation of the agreed measures – not a swathe of new legislation. Even though some actors (albeit limited in number) would like to see more rapid developments, especially in the area of supervision, there is full support for the Commission's approach on the way forward, *i.e.* practical steps to make the Lamfalussy approach work to the fullest extent possible. The Commission has identified concrete tasks and actions to assist in this consolidation process and to complete unfinished business in a practical way.

What are the main actions the Commission has announced in the White Paper for the next four years?

The new strategy has a strong focus on "delivering" the benefits of European integration and on getting things done right; the focus is *not* on proposing new legislative measures. Only when rules are implemented on time and enforced effectively, can companies and consumers benefit. To allow the financial market to function effectively, regulatory and supervisory mechanisms need to be strengthened and joined-up across the Member States and the conditions to facilitate cross-border consolidation in the EU need to improve.

While significant progress has been achieved to integrate the business-to-business markets, financial services offered to consumers remain deeply fragmented. Some areas have been identified that could bring clear economic benefits to industry, markets and consumers. Over the next five years there will probably only be a limited number of well-targeted new initiatives, focusing on retail financial services. Here, the Commission will look at the barriers related to cross-border use of bank accounts and the need for a regulatory framework in the area of credit intermediaries. Asset management is another area of interest, as is Clearing and Settlement, where an impact assessment is underway. In all areas no decisions have yet been taken on whether to bring forward new Commission proposals.

Aren't there too many implicit barriers to making retail integration possible?

The Commission agrees there are important implicit barriers to the integration of retail financial services markets. Integration of retail markets is complex and demanding. Product characteristics, distribution systems, consumer protection, contract law, differences in consumption culture or other economic or structural realities play a prominent role in the retail area – and create considerable complexity for cross-border supply. These barriers, however, have their origin in the fragmentation of the European market – for historic reasons. The Commission does not accept the argument that as European integration increases, this fragmentation is there to stay. Ten years from now, the retail market will look completely different compared to the market today. The role of the Commission is to anticipate and facilitate cross-border developments.

What can the Commission do to improve transposition and enforcement at Member State level?

Regrettably, the rate of transposition of Community law by Member States within agreed deadlines is weak. As a result, companies cannot benefit fully from pan-European access. Member States need to demonstrate real commitment and deliver proper implementation on time.

Enforcement mechanisms need to be strengthened and joined-up across the Member States. The Commission will work intensively with Member States to monitor progress, ensure accurate implementation and avoid regulatory additions, so-called 'goldplating'. Some practical processes (transposition matrices including hyperlinks to Member States' own implementing texts, transposition workshops) will facilitate effective monitoring. In the event of faulty implementation, the Commission will be swift in launching infringement proceedings.

How do the Commission's planned initiatives in the area of financial services fit in to the culture of "Better Regulation"?

Each possible new legislative initiative will have to follow the "better regulation principles", be evidence based and comply with the subsidiarity and proportionality principles of the Treaty. Consultation will be crucial and impact assessments will accompany all new proposals. These assessments will scope each issue and determine the most appropriate option. However, better regulation is a shared responsibility; impact assessments should take place at all levels involved in the policy-making process and be applied by all actors: (i) the Commission, (ii) the European Parliament and Council (when tabling substantive amendments to Commission proposals) and supervisors (when they give advice to the Commission).

The cycle of good policy making, in order, is:

- Open a consultation with interested parties;
- Ex-ante impact assessments;
- Examination of options based on evidence gathered;
- Where necessary, in line with the subsidiarity/ proportionality principles of the Treaty, a Commission proposal;
- Ex-post evaluation, normally around four years after the implementation deadline;
- If needed, evaluation could be followed up by simplification, codification and clarification;
- If specific legal texts have not worked, they will be modified or repealed.

Does the White Paper elaborate further on the ideas to develop a Single European Rulebook as suggested in the Green Paper?

In the Green Paper, the Commission suggested that work should be set in hand to simplify and consolidate all relevant financial services rules. This was elaborated further in Annex I to the Green Paper. The reference to the term "*Rulebook*" in the Green Paper without further clarification created confusion. It was not clear where the Commission stood on two main distinctions, namely between: (i) action at the level of Community law versus action at the level of national law; and (ii) a comprehensive consolidation of law into one single code of rules (thus, literally a single rulebook) versus pinpointed measures aimed at specific problems.

The White Paper clarifies this. The key idea is to get rid of regulatory overlaps, conflicts, duplication and ambiguities; in other words, to introduce an overall legal consistency check, "reading-across" Community directives and regulations. This will be carried out in areas where there are difficulties in implementing legislation because of successive amendments, overlapping or conflicting requirements, or where there is potential legal uncertainty resulting from inconsistent definitions or terminology. A first sectoral consistency check will be carried out in the securities area. Furthermore, a broad study will be carried out to review the appropriateness of information requirements and to signal possible inconsistencies. Also, clarification is needed on marketing rules in the area of collective investments.

Does the Commission envisage any further reinforcement of the interaction with other policy areas?

Yes. Exploiting policy synergies between financial services and other policy areas is key. Over the next 5 years, close cooperation with other policy areas, particularly competition (sectoral enquiries), consumer policy (consumer protection, contract law), trade, external policy and taxation will be further strengthened.

To what extent are consumer / user interests represented in the White Paper?
Representatives of consumers and shareholder organisations were invited to participate in the first step of the consultation exercise, the work of the expert groups. Despite a conscious effort to ensure effective representation of consumers/ shareholders in the expert groups, it remains difficult to get input from this perspective on the nuts and bolts of financial regulation. Unfortunately, only a few consumer organisations responded to the Green Paper's consultation, including the FIN-USE forum comprising twelve financial services experts conveying the user perspective about EU policy development.

How does the Commission intend to include the users and consumers of financial service more strongly in its future policy preparation?
The Commission will endeavour to ensure proportionate representation of users in all future advisory groups. Furthermore, to spread awareness of developments in financial services among consumers, the Commission intends to publish a periodic newsletter emphasising the most relevant user/consumer aspects of its ongoing work.
A permanent group of consumer representatives from the Member States is also planned, within which financial services issues of particular relevance to consumers will be discussed. The co-operation with UNI-Europa, grouping together trade unions of financial services employees, will also continue. FIN-NET plays an important role by providing users and consumers with easy access to out-of-court complaint procedures in cross-border cases.

Does the Commission have any plans in the area of consumer literacy and financial education?
Yes. We are aware of the need for increased awareness and direct involvement of citizens in financial issues, partly owing to the public sector's gradual disintermediation from financing some aspects of the social system. In order to promote good investment choices, *e.g.* for pensions, it is essential to increase transparency and comparability and to help consumers understand financial products. Although consumer education is the Member States' responsibility, the Commission wants to stimulate a pan-EU exchange of views on financial education, consumer literacy and best practice and plans to organise a conference on this subject in early 2007.

What is the Commission's view on Europe's future supervisory structure?
The Commission wants the Lamfalussy process to deepen and deliver its enormous potential. The supervisory committees in banking and insurance started their work at the beginning of 2004. For the moment, we therefore want to give the current supervisory structure the chance to demonstrate the strength of the new structure and prove that it can be used to its maximum potential.

However, supervisory and enforcement mechanisms need to be strengthened and joined-up across the Member States. Further convergence of supervisory practices is needed. The White Paper has set some clear goals on which the supervisors need to deliver: Existing and very costly duplicative supervisory reporting requirements should be eliminated by 2008. The level-3 committees should speed up their work in earnest to devise simplified common data and reporting templates, underpinned by real information sharing between national supervisors. A real European supervisory culture should develop, with mutual trust and confidence as a baseline condition for success. This will ensure more consistent supervisory practice. Supervisors should not only exchange information, they should also exchange personnel; and train staff together.

Is this a first step towards the introduction of a "Lead Supervisor"?
No. A major step forward has been made recently by the adoption of the Capital Requirements Directive in the banking area and the expansion of the consolidating supervisor concept. The

Commission is aware of the call for more centralised supervisory structures coming from large financial groups operating cross-border. The latter represent only a small proportion of total financial institutions in the EU, but a significant proportion of financial sector assets.
Before considering any further fundamental changes to the present supervisory arrangements (such as the "lead supervisor" concept) consideration must be given to a number of important issues such as:

- developments in Member States' financial sector and in particular the emergence of important branch operations and markets with high 'foreign' presence; and
- Implications of the division of responsibilities between supervisors for cross-border crisis management and other inter-related issues such as liquidity, lender of last resort and deposit guarantee arrangements or winding-up proceedings.

What are the Commission's plans on the external dimension?
The external dimension is another priority in the White Paper. Standards and best practices are increasingly set and defined at the global level. Here, the EU must have a leading role. Over the last years, good progress has been made in building open, *ex-ante* regulatory dialogues - exchanging information, identifying potential regulatory problems upstream and seeking mutually acceptable solutions. There is much support for the Commission's approach to these dialogues. Cooperation with our main trading partners – particularly the US – will therefore be further deepened.

The Commission is committed to an ambitious opening of global financial services markets, as modern and efficient financial markets are a prerequisite for further economic development in these countries. This commitment will therefore be reflected in the WTO negotiations on financial services. Financial relations with the emerging capital markets in Asia and other parts of the world become more important.

Furthermore, the EU needs to be represented more strongly in international bodies. And the European views need to be coordinated on the international scene. This makes Europe - and our case – much stronger.

For internationally mobile consumers, special 'pan-European' financial products may present an attractive option. Are you still sceptical on "26th regimes"?
Yes. The so-called 26th regime may sound attractive in its simplicity, but in practice it will require harmonisation across the board (legal, tax, language etc.). The benefits of the "26th regime" approach remain to be proven and reaching agreement on optional European standards designed only for certain products, might be very difficult. Furthermore, it is considered far too restrictive to focus exclusively on the expatriates / frontier workers business model. The benefits of financial integration are far broader. Access to a pan-EU market and increased competition leads to pressure on pricing, even in markets dominated by local players. The approach of creating pan-European passports for businesses and consumers seems to be still the most beneficial one. Also, consultation has shown widespread scepticism about the feasibility and usefulness of "26th regimes" in the area of financial services. The Commission, however, will listen to all arguments on the subject.

What about important initiatives on corporate governance, auditing, accounting, asset management and mortgages? Are they included in the White Paper?
Other horizontal and complementary policy areas (corporate governance, company law reform, accounting, statutory auditing) are also of immense importance in building confidence and transparency in European financial markets. Significant progress has been made. Although outside the scope of this Paper, work in these areas will progress in line with the agreed timetables and the *"better regulation"* principle-based and simplification approach.

The White Paper simply refers to asset management and mortgage credit. Initiatives in these areas have already advanced and do not require further reflection in this new strategy. The Commission published its Green Paper on enhancing the framework for investment funds in July 2005.
This Green Paper assesses the existing UCITS framework in the light of current developments in the funds industry. The Commission's views will be outlined in a White Paper, to be published by the second half of 2006. In addition, the Commission already spelled out its ideas on mortgage credit in a separate Green Paper, which was also published in July 2005. An exchange of views with all stakeholders on the way forward will take place on 7 December. The follow-up of these Green Papers will proceed in parallel with the White Paper's strategy, applying the same principles.

Will progress continue to be monitored, as the Commission used to do with the FSAP?
Yes. Detailed reports covering progress and developments in the areas outlined in this Paper will be published by the Commission on an annual basis.

Why is the White Paper only being made available in English, French and German – and the Annexes only in English?
The Commission regrets that it is unavailable to make translations available in other official languages due to the tremendous pressure on its translation services arising from the accession of ten new Member States. However, translations of the White Paper in the other EU languages will follow in the coming month.

LEGISLATION IN FORCE[6]

The key Directive in the banking sector is the Capital Requirements Directive, which is comprised of two directives:

- Directive 2006/48/EC of the European Parliament and of the Council of 14 June 2006 relating to the taking up and pursuit of the business of credit institutions (recast); and
- Directive 2006/49/EC of the European Parliament and of the Council of 14 June 2006 on the capital adequacy of investment firms and credit institutions (recast)

Other relevant directives are:

- Directive 2000/46/EC of the European Parliament and of the Council of 18.9.2000 on the taking up, pursuit of and prudential supervision of the business of electronic money institutions

- Directive 2002/87/EC of the European Parliament and of the Council of 16.12.2002 on the supplementary supervision of credit institutions, insurance undertakings and investment firms in a financial conglomerate

REGULATORY CAPITAL

CAPITAL REQUIREMENTS FOR CREDIT INSTITUTIONS AND INVESTMENT FIRMS

The objective of the capital requirements is to have in place a comprehensive and risk-sensitive framework and to foster enhanced risk management amongst financial institutions. This will maximise the effectiveness of the capital rules in ensuring continuing financial stability, maintaining confidence in financial institutions and protecting consumers.

[6] Please contact IBPUSA at ibpusa@comcats.net for texts of official documents and materials

ADOPTION OF THE CAPITAL REQUIREMENTS DIRECTIVE

The European Commission has welcomed the signing by the Council and the European Parliament of the Capital Requirements Directive for credit institutions and investment firms. The Directive introduces an updated supervisory framework in the EU which reflects the Basel II rules on capital standards agreed at G-10 level. Member States can now focus on transposing and implementing the Directive by the end of this year.

Internal Market and Services Commissioner Charlie McCreevy said: *"This is the last step in a long process – discussions in Basel to update the G-10 level rules began in 1998. The implementation of the CRD will be good for the EU economy and good for financial stability, bringing benefits to both firms and consumers. The next important step is to get this piece of legislation implemented in a coherent way across Europe".*

Excellent cooperation between Parliament, Council and Commission led to political agreement on this important measure in October 2005. The Directive, one of the measures required to complete the EU Financial Services Action Plan, modernises the existing capital framework to make it more comprehensive and risk-sensitive encouraging enhanced risk management by financial institutions. This will maximise the effectiveness of the framework in ensuring continuing financial stability, maintaining confidence in financial institutions and protecting consumers. Improved risk-sensitivity in the capital requirements will lead to more effective allocation of capital, contributing to boosting the competitiveness of the EU economy.

A key aspect of the new framework is its flexibility. This provides institutions with the opportunity to adopt the approaches most appropriate to their situation and to the sophistication of their risk management.

The new regime is also designed to ensure that the capital requirements for lending to small- and medium-sized enterprises (SMEs) are appropriate and proportionate, recognising the importance of SMEs in the EU economy.

Member States are to apply the Directive from the start of 2007, with the most sophisticated approaches being available from 2008. This is in line with the planned global introduction of the Basel II rules.

The Capital Requirements Directive, comprising Directive 2006/48/EC and Directive 2006/49/EC, was published in the Official Journal on Friday 30 June

- Directive 2006/48/EC of the European Parliament and of the Council of 14 June 2006 relating to the taking up and pursuit of the business of credit institutions (recast)
- Directive 2006/49/EC of the European Parliament and of the Council of 14 June 2006 on the capital adequacy of investment firms and credit institutions (recast)

EUROPEAN COMMISSION PROPOSAL FOR A NEW CAPITAL REQUIREMENTS FRAMEWORK FOR BANKS AND INVESTMENT FIRMS - FREQUENTLY ASKED QUESTIONS

What is the purpose of EU capital requirements rules?

Capital requirements rules stipulate the minimum amounts of own financial resources that credit institutions and investment firms must have in order to cover the risks to which they are exposed. The aim is to ensure the financial soundness of these institutions – in particular to ensure that they can weather difficult periods. This is aimed at protecting depositors and clients and the stability of the financial system. In the EU harmonised capital requirements are a key component in the single market in financial services: mutual recognition of requirements is the basis for banks' and investment firms' "single market passport", which basically means that they can operate throughout the EU on the basis of approval by the appropriate regulatory authority in their own Member State.

What is new about this proposal (as compared with the existing legislation)?

Capital requirements would become much more risk-sensitive. They would be far less crude than in the past and better cover the real risks run by the institution. This would enhance consumer protection and financial stability and lead to more efficient capital allocation.

Capital requirements would be more comprehensive than in the past. In particular they would be expanded to cover 'operational risk' (such as the risk of systems breaking down or people doing the wrong things). This is an increasingly important risk for financial institutions.

The new rules would comprise a new 'supervisory review process' (the so-called 'Pillar 2'). This part of the framework would require financial institutions to have their own internal processes to assess their capital needs and call for supervisors to evaluate institutions' overall risk profile to ensure that they hold adequate capital.

The new rules would also require credit institutions to disclose certain information publicly in order to increase the levels of 'market discipline' supporting the soundness and stability of financial institutions (the so-called 'Pillar 3').

Finally, the new framework would enhance the role of the 'consolidating supervisor' responsible for the top-level of supervision of an EU cross-border group – i.e. the national supervisory authority in the Member State where the group's parent institution is authorised.

This role would now include new responsibility and powers in coordinating the supervision of cross-border financial services groups. This would include coordinating the treatment of an application by such a group for approval to use the more sophisticated capital calculation rules made available by the proposed Directive.

All supervisors concerned in such an application should reach an agreed decision on the application within six months. In the case of failure to do so, the consolidating supervisor would be empowered to make a decision.

What is the 'Standardised Approach'?

This approach is similar to the existing rules, in that it is straightforward to use and does not require institutions to provide their own estimates of risks. It nonetheless incorporates enhanced risk-sensitivity by permitting the use of, for example, external ratings of rating agencies and export credit agencies. It also permits the recognition of a considerably expanded range of collateral, guarantees and other 'risk mitigants'. It includes reduced capital charges for retail lending (6% as compared with 8% previously) and residential mortgage lending (2.8% as compared with 4% previously).

What is the 'Internal Ratings Based (IRB) Approach'?

A significant step forward in prudential regulation, it allows institutions to provide their own 'risk inputs' – probability of default, loss estimates, etc – in the calculation of capital requirements. The calculation of these inputs is subject to a strict set of operational requirements to ensure that they are robust and reliable. They are incorporated into a 'capital requirement formula' which produces a capital charge for each loan or other exposure that the institution makes. The formula is designed to achieve a high level of soundness of the institution in the event of economic difficulties.

The IRB approach comes in two modes. The 'Advanced' mode allows institutions to use their own estimates of all relevant risk inputs. This approach is likely to be chosen by the biggest and most sophisticated institutions. The 'Foundation Approach' requires institutions only to provide the 'probability of default' risk input. This will enable a large number of less complex banks to reap the benefits of the risk-sensitivity provided by the IRB approach.

What is operational risk?

Operational risk is the risk that financial institutions suffer losses due to problems with their systems or processes or due to human error or as a result of external events. This is an important area of risk for financial institutions. The proposals introduce capital requirements to ensure that institutions are resilient to such risks.

In the proposal, three methods of calculating the capital requirements for such risks are made available ranging from the very simple based on a percentage of total gross income, through an intermediate approach which requires activities to be ascribed to eight different business lines, to an advanced approach which relies on institutions own calculations of operational risk.

Who will be covered by the new rules?

The new framework would – like the current rules – apply to all banks (or 'credit institutions') and investment firms in the EU.

How would investment firms be affected by the proposals?

The EU Single Market in financial services requires that the same activities giving rise to the same risks should be subject to the same capital charge.

However, the new framework recognises that the situation of certain investment firms is different to that of banks. Accordingly, investment firms which do not undertake the activities of dealing in securities on their own account, or underwriting the issue of securities, as a central activity, would be permitted to continue to use the existing 'expenditure-based capital requirement' instead of the specific operational risk requirement.

The treatment of 'trading book' exposures is an important aspect for investment firms. There is further work being undertaken on this area which is expected to come on stream relatively quickly.

How does the proposal benefit small-and-medium size enterprises (SMEs)?

Capital requirements are one of the factors that can affect the availability and cost of lending to (and other forms of financing of) SMEs.

The risk-sensitivity of the new framework means that it is possible to reflect the fact that it is less risky to have a large number of small loans than a small number of large loans. This results in lower capital requirements for lending to SMEs.

The proposal also recognises that for certain forms of equity financing (venture capital) carried out as part of a sufficiently diversified portfolio the risks are lower than in the case of individual equity exposures. Accordingly a preferential capital charge is provided for this kind of financing. A report prepared by PriceWaterhouseCoopers at the request of the European Council indicates an overall beneficial outcome for SMEs (see http://ec.europa.eu/internal_market/regcapital/index_en.htm)

What is the implementation date for the proposed Directive?

The implementation date is scheduled for the end of 2006. In order to allow reasonable transition arrangements, institutions would be able to continue to use the existing rules as an alternative until the end of 2007. Similarly, in order to allow sufficient time for the bringing on stream of the most sophisticated approaches while maintaining the Internal Market level playing field, the advanced approaches to credit risk and operational risk would be available at the end of 2007.

How will it be ensured that the implementation of the new framework does not give rise to differences between countries and to difficulties for cross-border groups?

The new framework incorporating harmonised state-of-the-art prudential rules means that the opportunities for regulatory arbitrage would be very significantly reduced. This would have significant beneficial effects in enhancing the level playing field within the Single Market.

The proposed Directive incorporates important requirements for supervisory authorities to work together so as to ensure an efficient and proportionate regulatory environment for cross-border groups. The Directive would also oblige supervisors themselves to publicly disclose how they implement and apply its rules in practice.

Another key example of this is that cross-border groups would only have to make one application for approval of their internal rating systems and/or models for all of the entities within the group.

This application should be channelled through the 'consolidating supervisor' – the supervisory authority responsible for the top-level of supervision of an EU cross-border group. The application should be determined jointly by the supervisory authorities concerned. But if they fail to reach a decision within six months, the consolidating supervisor would be empowered to make the decision.

The new Committee of European Banking Supervisors (CEBS) – recently established by a Commission decision – will have an important role to play in ensuring consistency and convergence in the application of the new framework. Such a role forms a key part of its mandate and of the reason for its establishment.

What is the Basel Committee?

The Basel Committee on Banking Supervision ('the Basel Committee') consists of central bank and supervisory authority representatives from the thirteen 'G10' countries. Nine EU Member States are represented – Belgium, France, Germany, Italy, Luxembourg, the Netherlands, Spain, Sweden, and the UK. The other countries represented are Canada, Japan, Switzerland and the US.

The European Commission, along with the European Central Bank, participates as an observer in the Committee itself and in its many working groups.

What is the Basel Accord?

The 'Basel Accord' is an agreement on capital requirements amongst the members of the Basel Committee. 'Basel 1' was agreed in 1988.

Although strictly speaking it only applies to internationally active banks in the G10, the Accord has been applied to most banks in 100 countries throughout the world.

While it has made a significant contribution to financial stability and consumer protection, Basel 1 is now viewed as outdated. Accordingly since 1998 an intensive exercise has been underway to revise the Accord ('Basel 2) and, in parallel, the EU capital requirements legislation.

What is the link between the Basel Accord and EU legislation?

The existing European legislation (originally the Solvency Ratio Directive of 1989 – now incorporated in the Codified Banking Directive of 2000) was based on the Basel 1 Accord. It applies to all banks and investment firms in the EU.

In order to maximise consistency between the EU legislation and the international framework, the European Commission and EU members of the Basel Committee have had as a primary objective ensuring the suitability of Basel 2 for application in the EU Single Market.

Accordingly, the new Basel agreement represents the appropriate basis for the proposed EU Directive on a new capital requirements framework. At the same time the EU legislative proposal has been designed to fully reflect the specific features of the European context – in particular its application to the full range of financial institutions including banks of all sizes and levels of complexity and investment firms.

Examples of such "EU adaptations" in the proposed Directive include:

- rules on partial use which would allow less complex institutions to make use of the more sophisticated methodologies for some of their portfolios while using the simpler methodologies for others
- tailoring of the new operational risk requirements in their application to low- and medium-risk investment firms. Such firms may be permitted to continue to use the existing 'expenditure-based requirement'
- specific rules on how the applications of cross-border groups for approval to use the more sophisticated methodologies should be handled. There would be only one application process which would be channelled through the 'consolidating supervisor'. A decision should be made within six months by the different supervisors acting together
- lower capital requirements for banks' 'venture capital' business, which is key for the financing of small start-up companies in some Member States and to achieving the Lisbon growth and competitiveness

EUROPEAN FREE TRADE ASSOCIATION

Secretariat	Geneva, Switzerland
Official languages	German, French, Norwegian, and Icelandic
Type	Trade bloc
Member states	Iceland Liechtenstein Norway Switzerland
Establishment	3 May 1960
- EFTA Convention	4 January 1960
	Area
- Total	529,600 km^2 204,518 sq mi
	Population
- 2007 estimate	12,660,623
- Density	100.6/km^2 59.82/sq mi
GDP (PPP)	2007 (IMF) estimate
- Total	$567.5 billion
- Per capita	$44,828
GDP (nominal)	(IMF) estimate
- Total	$743.3 billion
- Per capita	$58,714
Currency	Icelandic króna, Norwegian krone, Swiss franc (ISK, NOK, CHF)
Time zone	WET / CET (UTC+0 / +1)
- Summer (DST)	WEST / CEST (UTC+1 / +2)

The **European Free Trade Association** ((**EFTA**); French: ***Association européenne de libre-échange*** (***AELE***)) was established on 3 May 1960 as a trade bloc-alternative for European states who were either unable to, or chose not to, join the then-European Economic Community (EEC) (now the European Union (EU)).

The EFTA Convention was signed on 4 January 1960 in Stockholm by seven states. Today only Iceland, Norway, Switzerland, and Liechtenstein remain members of EFTA (of which only Norway and Switzerland are founding members). The Stockholm Convention was subsequently replaced by the Vaduz Convention.

This Convention provides for the liberalisation of trade among the member states. Three of the EFTA countries are part of the European Union Internal Market through the Agreement on a European Economic Area (EEA), which took effect in 1994; the fourth, Switzerland, opted to conclude bilateral agreements with the EU. In addition, the EFTA states have jointly concluded free trade agreements with a number of other countries.

In 1999 Switzerland concluded a set of bilateral agreements with the European Union covering a wide range of areas, including movement of persons, transport and technical barriers to trade. This development prompted the EFTA States to modernise their Convention to ensure that it will continue to provide a successful framework for the expansion and liberalization of trade among them and with the rest of the world.

POLITICAL HISTORY

British reaction to the creation of the EEC was mixed and complex. Consequently France vetoed British membership fearing that the Anglo-Saxons planned a federal super-state modeled on the USA. Britain was also preoccupied with the British Commonwealth, which was in a critical period. The UK brought together several countries (including some bordering the EEC) and decided to form the European Free Trade Association in about 1959, soon after the establishment of the 6-nation EEC. (France, Germany, Italy, Belgium, Luxembourg and the Netherlands. These last three are also known as the Benelux Union)

On January 4, 1960 the Treaty on European Free Trade Association was initialed in the Golden Hall of the Prince's Palace of Stockholm. This established the progressive elimination of customs duties on industrial products, but did not affect agricultural products or maritime trade.

The main difference between the early EEC and the EFTA was the absence of a common external customs tariff, and therefore each EFTA member was free to establish individual customs duties against trade with non EFTA countries.

Despite this modest initiative, the financial results were excellent, as it stimulated an increase of foreign trade volume among its members from 3 522 to 8 172 million US dollars between 1959 and 1967. This was however rather less than the increase enjoyed by countries inside the EEC. After the accession of Denmark and the UK to the EEC EFTA began to falter. For this reason most countries eased or eliminated their trade tariffs in preparation to join the EEC, but experienced declining revenue which reduced the importance of EFTA. Currently there are only 4 members remaining: Switzerland, Norway and Liechtenstein and Iceland which applied for EC membership in 2009 following the 2008–2009 Icelandic financial crisis.

MEMBERSHIP HISTORY

The founding members of EFTA were Austria, Denmark, Norway, Portugal, Sweden, Switzerland and the United Kingdom. During the 1960s these countries were often referred to as the **Outer Seven**, as opposed to the Inner Six of the then-European Economic Community.
Finland became an associate member in 1961 (becoming a full member in 1986) and Iceland joined in 1970. The United Kingdom and Denmark joined the European Communities in 1973 (together with Ireland), and hence ceased to be EFTA members. Portugal also left the EFTA for the European Community in 1986. Liechtenstein joined in 1991 (previously its interests in EFTA had been represented by Switzerland). Finally, Austria, Sweden and Finland joined the European Union in 1995 and thus ceased to be EFTA members.

CURRENT MEMBERS

State	Official name	Accession	Population	Capital	GDP in millions (PPP)	GDP per capita (PPP)
Iceland	Republic of Iceland	1 January 1970	320,000	Reykjavík	12,144	39,168
Liechtenstein	Principality of Liechtenstein	1 January 1991	34,247	Vaduz	4,160	118,000
Norway	Kingdom of Norway	3 May 1960	4,721,600	Oslo	247,416	53,152
Switzerland	Swiss Confederation (Confoederatio Helvetica)	3 May 1960	7,591,400	Berne	300,186	41,265

GENERAL SECRETARY

2006-present: Kåre Bryn

INSTITUTIONS

EFTA is governed by the EFTA Council and serviced by the EFTA Secretariat. In addition, in connection with the EEA Agreement of 1992, two other EFTA organisations were established, the EFTA Surveillance Authority and the EFTA Court.

EEA-RELATED INSTITUTIONS

The EFTA Surveillance Authority and the EFTA Court regulate the activities of the EFTA members in respect of their obligations in the European Economic Area (EEA). Since Switzerland is not an EEA member, it does not participate in these institutions.
The EFTA Surveillance Authority performs the European Commission's role as "guardian of the treaties" for the EFTA countries, while the EFTA Court performs the European Court of Justice's role for those countries.

The original plan for the EEA lacked the EFTA Court or the EFTA Surveillance Authority, and instead had the European Court of Justice and the European Commission were to exercise those roles. However, during the negotiations for the EEA agreement, the European Court of Justice informed the Council of the European Union by way of letter that they considered that giving the EU institutions powers with respect to non-EU member states would be a violation of the treaties, and therefore the current arrangement was developed instead.
The EEA and Norway Grants are administered by the Financial Mechanism Office, which is affiliated to the EFTA Secretariat in Brussels.

LOCATIONS

The EFTA Secretariat is headquartered in Geneva, Switzerland. The EFTA Surveillance Authority has its headquarters in Brussels, Belgium (the same location as the headquarters of the European Commission), while the EFTA Court has its headquarters in Luxembourg (the same location as the headquarters of the European Court of Justice).

PORTUGAL FUND

The Portugal Fund was established in 1975 when Portugal was still a member of EFTA, to provide funding for the development and reconstruction of Portugal after the Carnation Revolution. When Portugal left EFTA in 1985 to join the EEC, the remaining EFTA members decided to nonetheless continue the Portugal Fund, so Portugal would continue to benefit from it. The Fund originally took the form of a low-interest loan from the EFTA member states to Portugal, to the value of 100 million US dollars. Repayment was originally to commence in 1988, but EFTA then decided to postpone the start of repayments until 1998. The Portugal Fund has now been dissolved by the Member States.

EFTA IN ECONOMIC INDICATORS

	Iceland	Liechtenstein	Norway	Switzerland	EU27
GDP (in million € at market prices)	13,251	2,730.8	267,799	309,096	11,583,403
GDP per capita (PPS in €)	31,900	34,700	43,900	31,900	23,500
GDP growth (in %)	4.2%	3.9%	2.2%	3.2%	3.0%
Inflation	4.6	1.1	2.3	1.1	2.2
Unemployment (in %)	2.9	3.2	3.4	4.0	8.2
Exports: Goods (in million €)	2,774	n.a	97,356	118,054	1,157,900

Imports: Goods (in million €)	4,558	n.a	52,201	114,810	1,350,500
Exports: Services (in million €)	1,464	n.a	27,549	44,079	447,395
Imports: Services (in million €)	2,031	n.a	23,840	23,993	380,331
Exports of goods and services (in million €)	4,239	n.a	124,905	162,133	1,605,295
Imports of goods and services (in million €)	6,591	n.a	76,041	138,803	1,730,831
Total Trade (in million €)	10,830	n.a	200,946	300,936	3,336,125
Government Financial Balance (in % of GDP)	5.3	n.a	18.5	1.1	-1.6
Government debt (in % of GDP)	45.7	n.a	55.0	25.4	61.4

Sources: National Statistical Offices and EUROSTAT

Liechtenstein figures are from 2004

Liechtensteins inhabitants adjusted by cross-border commuter population

Liechtensteins trade figures are included in Switzerlands trade figures due to the existence of the Swiss-Liechtenstein Customs Union.

SOCIAL INDICATORS

	Iceland	Liechtenstein	Norway	Switzerland	EU27
Life expectancy at Birth - Women	83.0	82.1	82.7	84.0	81.2
Life expectancy at Birth - Men	79.4	78.7	78.1	79.1	75.1
Infant Mortality Rate (per 1 000 live births)	1.4	2.7	3.2	4.4	4.5
Population Growth Rate (in %)	2.2	0.8	0.9	0.7	0.5
Employment rate (in % of persons aged 15-64 in employment)	84.6	68.5	75.5	77.9	64.4
Women	80.8	58.6	72.3	71.1	57.2
Men	88.1	78.2	78.6	84.7	71.6
Unemployment rate	2.9	3.2	3.5	4.0	8.2

Sources: National Statistical Offices and EUROSTAT

Liechtenstein figures are from 2005

EU-27 figures are from 2004

INTERNATIONAL CONVENTIONS

EFTA also originated the Hallmarking Convention and the Pharmaceutical Inspection Convention, both of which are open to non-EFTA states.

EUROPEAN ECONOMIC AREA

The EFTA members, except for Switzerland, are also members of the European Economic Area (EEA).

Austria	Greece	Netherlands
Belgium	Hungary	Norway
Bulgaria	Iceland	Poland
Cyprus	Ireland	Portugal
Czech Republic	Italy	Romania
Denmark	Liechtenstein	Slovakia
Estonia	Latvia	Slovenia
Finland	Lithuania	Spain
France	Luxembourg	Sweden
Germany	Malta	United Kingdom

The **European Economic Area** (**EEA**) was established on 1 January 1994 following an agreement between member states of the European Free Trade Association (EFTA), the European Community (EC), and all member states of the European Union (EU). It allows these EFTA countries to participate in the European single market without joining the EU.

MEMBERSHIP

The contracting parties to the EEA Agreement are three of the four EFTA states—Iceland, Liechtenstein and Norway (except for Svalbard)—and the 27 EU Member States along with the European Community.

Switzerland is not part of the EEA. A referendum (mandated by the Swiss constitution) was held and rejected the proposal to join. Switzerland is linked to the European Union by the Swiss–EU bilateral agreements, with a different content from that of the EEA agreement.
Austria, Finland and Sweden joined the EEA in 1994, but the EEA agreement was superseded by EU membership in 1995.

FREEDOMS AND OBLIGATIONS

The EEA is based on the same "four freedoms" as the European Community: the free movement of goods, persons, services, and capital among the EEA countries. Thus, the EFTA countries that are part of the EEA enjoy free trade with the European Union. As a counterpart, these countries have to adopt part of the Law of the European Union. These states have little influence on decision-making processes in Brussels.

The EFTA countries that are part of the EEA do not bear the financial burdens associated with EU membership, although they contribute financially to the European single market. After the EU/EEA enlargement of 2004 there was a tenfold increase in the financial contribution of the EEA States, in particular Norway, to social and economic cohesion in the Internal Market (€1167 million over five years). EFTA countries do not receive any funding from EU policies and development funds

LEGISLATION

The non EU members of the EEA (Iceland, Liechtenstein and Norway) have agreed to enact legislation similar to that passed in the EU in the areas of social policy, consumer protection, environment, company law and statistics. These are some of the areas covered by the European Community (the "first pillar" of the European Union).

The non EU members of the EEA have no representation in Institutions of the European Union such as the European Parliament or European Commission. In February 2001, Norwegian Prime Minister Jens Stoltenberg described the situation as a "fax democracy", with Norway waiting for their latest legislation to be faxed from the Commission.

INSTITUTIONS

A Joint Committee consisting of the EEA-EFTA States plus the European Commission (representing the EU) has the function of extending relevant EU law to the non EU members. An EEA Council meets twice yearly to govern the overall relationship between the EEA members. Rather than setting up pan-EEA institutions, the activities of the EEA are regulated by the EFTA Surveillance Authority and the EFTA Court, which parallel the work of the EU's European Commission and European Court of Justice. See EEA institutions for further information.

EEA AND NORWAY GRANTS

The EEA and Norway Grants are the financial contributions of Iceland, Liechtenstein and Norway to reduce social and economic disparities in Europe. In the period 2004- 2009, €1.3 billion of project funding is made available for project funding in the 15 beneficiary states in Central and Southern Europe. The EEA and Norway Grants were established in conjunction with the 2004 enlargement of the European Economic Area (EEA), which brings together the EU, Iceland, Liechtenstein and Norway in the Internal Market.

INTERNATIONAL RELATIONSHIPS

EFTA has several free trade agreements with non-EU countries as well as declarations on cooperation and joint workgroups to improve trade. Currently, the EFTA States have established preferential trade relations with 20 States and Territories, in addition to the 27 Member States of the European Union.

FREE TRADE AGREEMENT

- Canada
- Chile
- Croatia
- Egypt
- Israel (Switzerland exempt)
- Jordan
- South Korea
- Lebanon
- Macedonia
- Mexico
- Morocco
- Palestinian National Authority
- Singapore
- Southern African Customs Union (Botswana, Lesotho, Namibia, Swaziland, South Africa)
- Tunisia
- Turkey

SIGNED AGREEMENT 2008, NOT YET RATIFIED

- Colombia

SIGNED AGREEMENT 2009, NOT YET RATIFIED

- Gulf Co-operation Council (Bahrain, Kuwait, Oman, Qatar, Saudi Arabia, United Arab Emirates)

FINALISED NEGOTIATIONS 2008

- Peru

CURRENTLY NEGOTIATING AGREEMENTS

- Thailand
- Algeria
- India

DECLARATIONS ON COOPERATION

- Albania
- Mercosur (Brazil, Argentina, Uruguay, Paraguay)
- Mongolia
- Serbia
- Ukraine

JOINT WORKGROUPS

- Indonesia
- Russia

FUTURE

The Norwegian electorate has rejected treaties of accession to the EU in two referenda. At the time of the first referendum (1972) their neighbour the Kingdom of Denmark joined. The second time (1994) two other Nordic neighbours, Sweden and Finland, joined the EU. The last two governments of Norway have been unable and unwilling to advance the question, as they have both been coalition governments consisting of proponents and opponents.
Since Switzerland rejected the EEA in 1992, referenda on EU membership have been initiated, the last time in 2001. These were rejected by clear majorities.

Iceland, on the other hand, may join the EU in the near future, following the global financial crisis of 2008, which has particularly affected the local economy. On 16 July 2009, the government formally applied for EU membership.

In mid-2005, representatives of the Faroe Islands hinted at the possibility of their territory joining EFTA. However, the chances of the Faroes' bid for membership are uncertain because, according to Article 56 of the EFTA Convention, only states may become members of the Association. The Faroes already have an extensive bilateral free trade agreement with Iceland, known as the Hoyvík Agreement.

ESTERNAL TRADE AND POLICIES

The European Union is the world's biggest trader, accounting for 20% of global imports and exports. Free trade among its members underpinned the launch of the EU 50 years ago. The Union is therefore keen to liberalise world trade for the benefit of rich and poor countries alike.

Trade boosts world growth to everybody's advantage. It brings consumers a wider range of products to choose from. Competition between imports and local products lowers prices and raises quality. Liberalised trade enables the most efficient EU firms to compete fairly with rivals in other countries. To help developing countries, the EU is ready to open its market to their exports even if they cannot reciprocate.

The disappearance of trade barriers within the EU made a significant contribution to its prosperity and has reinforced its commitment to global liberalisation. As EU countries removed tariffs on trade between them, they also unified their tariffs on goods imported from outside. This means that products pay the same tariff whether they enter the EU via the ports of Genoa or Hamburg. As a result, a car from Japan which pays import duty on arrival in Germany can be shipped to Belgium or Poland and sold there in the same way as a German car. No further duty is charged.

The EU has been a key player in international trade liberalisation negotiations. The latest of these is the so-called Doha Development Round which began in 2001. The aim of these negotiations, held in the framework of the World Trade Organisation (WTO), is to reduce tariffs and remove other barriers to world trade. Following earlier rounds, the EU's average tariff on industrial imports has now fallen to 4%, one of the lowest in the world.

Progress in the Doha Round has been slow. Wide and persistent differences have opened up between the rich and poor countries on issues concerning access to each other's markets and the long-running question of agricultural subsidies. Negotiations have lurched from crisis to crisis. The WTO hopes the Doha Round can be successfully concluded by the end of 2008.

THE RULES-BASED SYSTEM

The European Union has invested heavily in trying to make Doha a success. It is also a firm believer in the WTO's rules-based system which provides a degree of legal certainty and transparency in the conduct of international trade. The WTO sets rules whereby its members can defend themselves against unfair practices like dumping – selling at below cost – by which exporters compete against local rivals. It also provides a dispute settlements procedure.

A NETWORK OF AGREEMENTS

Trade rules are multilateral, but trade itself is bilateral – between buyers and sellers, exporters and importers. This is why the EU, in addition to its participation in Doha and previous WTO rounds, has also developed a network of bilateral trade agreements with individual countries and regions across the world.
It has partnership and cooperation agreements with its neighbours in the Mediterranean basin and with Russia and the other republics of the former Soviet Union.

TRADE AND DEVELOPMENT

The EU's trade policy is closely linked to its development policy. The Union has granted duty-free or cut-rate access to its market for most of the imports from developing countries under its generalised system of preferences (GSP). It goes even further for the world's 49 poorest countries, all of whose exports – with the sole exception of arms – enter the EU duty-free.

The EU has developed a new trade and development strategy with its 78 partners in the Africa-Pacific-Caribbean (ACP) group aimed at integrating them into the world economy. It also has a trade agreement with South Africa that will lead to free trade, and it is negotiating a free trade deal with the six members of the Gulf Cooperation Council (GCC) – Bahrain, Kuwait, Oman, Qatar, Saudi Arabia and the United Arab Emirates. The EU has agreements with Mexico and Chile and has been trying to negotiate a deal to liberalise trade with the Mercosur group – Argentina, Brazil, Paraguay and Uruguay.

TRADE WITH MAJOR PARTNERS

It does not, however, have specific trade agreements with its major trading partners among the developed countries like the United States and Japan. Trade is handled through the WTO mechanisms, although the EU has many agreements in individual sectors with both countries. The WTO framework also applies to trade between the EU and China which joined the world trade body in 2001. China is now the Union's second biggest trading partner after the United States.

TRADE LEGISLATION, REGULATIONS AND POLICY

TRADE POLICY FUNDAMENTALS

The common commercial policy is a pillar for the external relations of the European Union. It is based on a set of uniform rules under the Customs Union and the Common Customs Tariff and governs the commercial relations of the Member States with Non-EU Member Countries. The purpose of the instruments of trade defence and market access is mainly to protect European businesses from obstacles to trade. The EU has evolved during the process of globalisation by aiming for the harmonious development of world trade and fostering fairness and sustainability. It actively encourages the opening of the markets and the development of trade in the multilateral framework of the World Trade Organisation (WTO). At the same time, it supports developing countries and regions through bilateral relations with a view to involving them in world trade using preferential measures.

As part of the external aspect of the Lisbon Strategy promoting growth and employment, the Commission proposes an ambitious programme for the competitiveness of the European Union (EU) and its businesses that places the emphasis on open markets. Fundamental to the programme are the rejection of protectionism in Europe, the opening up of the principal markets outside Europe and the bringing together of the EU's internal and external policies.
In this context, the Commission presents an analysis of the foundations of the EU's common commercial policy and competitiveness. Furthermore, the Commission outlines the measures necessary to respond to both these priorities and the challenges of globalisation.
The global economy is characterised by an increasing integration facilitated, notably, by new information and communication technologies and the reduction in the costs of transport. This increasing integration leads to a strong interdependence between economies and industries at global level, bringing about as many opportunities as it does risks for both citizens and the planet.

THE FOUNDATIONS OF EUROPEAN COMPETITIVENESS

Faced with these challenges, the EU must reinforce its competitiveness through the use of transparent and effective rules.

Firstly, European competitiveness is based on **sound internal policies**, namely:

- **competitive markets** which encourage the competitiveness of European businesses. The Single Market benefits from high-quality, transparent rules that make it possible to benefit from economies of scale and use resources efficiently. Furthermore, competition encourages businesses to provide high-quality products. Despite the strong performance of European businesses compared with their global competitors in the sectors of manufacturing and services, high-technology sectors could still improve in terms of innovation, education, research and development.

- **economic opening up**: unlike protectionism, opening up to international trade and investment generates competitive pressures which benefit innovation, new technologies and investment, thereby facilitating the use of Single Market resources. In this context, trade defence instruments adapted to global trade remain indispensable to combat unfair commercial practices.
- **social justice**: the EU must be in a position to cope with the impact caused by an opening up of the markets, notably an acceleration in structural changes brought about by globalisation. This acceleration can have a negative impact on certain sectors, regions or workers. Therefore, not only must the effects of an opening up be predictable, but the values, particularly those concerning social and environmental issues, must also be promoted throughout the world.
- Secondly, European competitiveness is based on the **opening up of foreign markets** that are based on fair rules. The EU should in particular show a commitment to opening up markets in emerging countries, which account for a growing share of global trade. The opening up of the markets in China, India and Brazil has shown the benefits that this can bring in terms of development and the fight against poverty.
- Nevertheless, to draw the maximum benefit from an opening up of markets, new trade obstacles must be tackled head-on, going beyond customs duties. Against this background, the common commercial policy should place the emphasis on:
- **non-tariff barriers**: beyond customs tariffs, non-tariff barriers (trade-restricting regulations and procedures) are often less visible, more complex and more sensitive because they have a direct impact on domestic regulation. To promote trade that abides by transparent and non-discriminatory rules, the Commission, Member States and industry must define new ways of working in addition to the traditional methods at their disposal (mutual recognition, dialogues on standardisation and regulation, technical assistance to third countries).
- **access to resources**: European industry should have access to key resources such as energy, raw materials, metals and scrap. This access should not be restricted other than for environmental or security reasons. Accordingly, and in view of the essential nature of energy access for the EU, a coherent policy is needed to guarantee a diversified, competitive, secure and sustainable energy supply both within the Union (competitive market, promotion of a sustainable, efficient and diverse energy mix) as well as outside its borders (non-discriminatory access to export infrastructures for third and transit countries, assistance to third countries to strengthen their capacities and infrastructures). In this context, the link between trade and the environment should be strengthened because of the impact trade can have on the environment, in particular on biodiversity and the climate. Energy efficiency, renewable energy sources and the rational use of energy should be encouraged.
- **new growth sectors: intellectual property rights (IPRs), services, investment, internal markets and competition**. These sectors offer major opportunities for the European economy, provided that a gradual liberalisation of global trade and transparent, effective and respected rules (both national and international) facilitate exchanges between the EU and its trading partners. Bilateral and international cooperation should therefore be strengthened.

ACTION PLAN

The Commission proposes an action programme aimed at strengthening the EU's external competitiveness and meeting global challenges. To achieve this, the action plan identifies the necessary priorities and methods, comprising an internal and an external dimension.

Internal dimension

European businesses must benefit from the EU's competitiveness and its citizens should feel the advantages. The Lisbon Strategy constitutes the foundation of the EU's competitiveness. In this context, the communication from the Commission entitled "A Citizens' Agenda" of May 2006 offers an in-depth examination of the Single Market to guarantee businesses competitiveness through diversification, specialisation and innovation.

The process of framing EU policies should focus on the Union's capacity to respond to global challenges. Coherent regulation at European or international level is therefore essential, and international and bilateral cooperation is of equal importance. The EU encourages good practices to be imparted, but also an open and flexible approach towards drafting these rules.
Concerning the repercussions of an opening up of the markets, the Commission and the Member States will ensure that the European citizens reap the benefits, notably through the introduction of a systematic monitoring of both import and consumer prices.
Furthermore, adaptation to change is a key factor for growth and employment. Cohesion programmes and the Globalisation Adjustment Fund will make it possible to predict and respond to these changes. The European customs system will also be modernised (revision of customs code, introduction of e-customs).

EXTERNAL DIMENSION

Concerning external action, the EU maintains its commitment to **multilateralism**, which offers the means to eliminate trade barriers in a stable and sustainable manner. The World Trade Organisation (WTO) is the framework of choice to achieve these goals and the EU supports resuming the Doha round of trade negotiations.

As well as multilateralism, the EU must also endeavour to promote a faster and more comprehensive trade liberalisation within the framework of its bilateral relations. The **Free Trade Agreements(FTAs)** will be a driving force towards achieving this goal. These have the advantage of being able to cover domains not provided for either by an international regulation or the WTO. As well as serving the EU's neighbourhood and development policies, the FTAs should also bring increased benefits to the European Union's commercial interests. Nevertheless, the Commission notes that the FTAs should have a wider scope of content than the existing ones in the context of neighbourhood policy, the Economic Partnership Agreements (EPAs) currently being negotiated with the African, Caribbean and Pacific (ACP) countries, or the Association Agreements with Latin America and the Andean Community.

The EU must define economic criteria to negotiate and conclude FTAs and to identify its partners, such as the market potential measured in terms of size and economic growth, the level of protection vis-à-vis exports from the EU (customs tariffs, non-tariff barriers), etc. Other factors will also come into play, such as negotiations between the EU's potential partners and its competitors, the impact of these negotiations on the EU and the risk that they pose to the partners' preferential access to the Union's markets. Based on this, the partners to be privileged are the ASEAN countries, South Korea and Mercosur, which fulfil the criteria mentioned, and India, Russia, the Gulf Cooperation Council and China.

As regards content, these agreements must be more comprehensive, more ambitious and broader to encompass a wide range of areas covering services and investment as well as IPRs. The FTAs must provide for a regulatory convergence to effectively combat non-tariff barriers, stronger and stricter provisions (IPRs, competition), simple and modern rules of origin adapted to suit circumstances, and monitoring mechanisms to evaluate implementation and results. The FTAs will be adapted to the specific considerations of development (including impact studies) and sustainable development. They will also respond to the needs of each country in accordance with the EU's strategies towards these countries and the regions to which they belong.
Transatlantic trade is at the heart of the EU's bilateral relations, in particular with the aim of meeting global challenges. The EU will continue to encourage the elimination of non-tariff

barriers, given the economic advantages of a comFprehensive liberalisation of trade between the partners. To this end, negotiations under the transatlantic economic initiative are continuing.

China is both an essential partner and a challenge for the EU, offering growth and employment opportunities. China itself is faced with challenges while accounting for an increasing share of global trade. Therefore, as part of its strategy for China, the EU proposes focusing on these challenges, establishing priorities and pursuing closer cooperation in these areas.

The EU and its partners must agree to do more concerning respect for **intellectual property rights (IPRs).** This action will take the form of special provisions in the bilateral agreements, a strengthening of customs cooperation, dialogues, an increase in presence and resources in the field and awareness-raising among European businesses. The principal countries concerned will be China, Russia, the ASEAN countries, Korea, Mercosur, Chile, Ukraine and Turkey in connection with its accession negotiations.

The **Market Access Strategy** established in 1996 was renewed in 2007. The Commission proposes strengthening its work by refocusing action on certain countries and sectors as well as on the opening up of their markets to third countries. This effort must be made in cooperation with industry and the Member States.

The **internal markets** of third countries must be opened up to European suppliers. The Commission will launch an initiative aimed at reducing restrictive practices which are discriminatory. If necessary, targeted restrictions will be maintained for uncooperative countries with the aim of encouraging them towards a mutual opening up of markets.

Trade defence instruments will be a part of multilateralism. The EU will therefore ensure that its partners' instruments are justified, transparent and in compliance with international rules. Failing this, the EU could fall back on dispute settlement mechanisms such as that of the WTO. Furthermore, the EU will concentrate on improving its own instruments, which must respond to demands in terms of efficiency and adaptation to global changes in order to ensure that the diversity of European interests is taken into account.

COMMON TRADE POLICY REGIME AND BASIC REGULATIONS FOR EXPORT

EXPORTS

Council Regulation (EEC) No **2603/69** of 20 December 1969 establishing common rules for exports [Official Journal L 324, 27.12.1969].

This regulation lays down the principle that exports from the European Community to third countries are free, that is to say, they are not subject to any quantitative restrictions.

However, this principle of freedom of export does not preclude the Member States from maintaining or introducing quantitative restrictions or bans on exports on grounds of public morality, public policy, public security, etc.

In 1992, all derogations to the principle of freedom of export granted to the Member States in relation to exports of certain products were eliminated.

Scope

The regulation applies to all industrial and agricultural products covered by the EC Treaty. With regard to agricultural products, it is complementary to the regulations establishing common organisation of agricultural markets and the special regulations for processed agricultural products.

From a geographical point of view, it applies to all third countries. Council Regulation (EEC) No 2604/69 of 20 December 1969 extended the regulation to cover the French overseas departments.

Information and consultation procedures

The regulation establishes a Community procedure for information and consultation to be followed before implementing protective measures. If, as a result of unusual developments on the market, a Member State considers that protective measures might be necessary, it must inform the Commission accordingly, which will then advise the other Member States. Consultations may thus be held at any time within an advisory committee composed of representatives of each Member State and chaired by a representative of the Commission. These consultations relate, in particular, to the export conditions and trends for the product in question as well as the measures, if any, to be adopted.

The Commission may request Member States to supply statistical data on market trends in a given product for the purpose of assessing the economic and commercial situation. It may also ask them to exercise surveillance over given products in accordance with their national legislation and with the procedure specified by the Commission.

Protective measures

Protective measures may make it possible to prevent or remedy a critical situation brought about by a shortage of essential products, or allow international commitments entered into by the Community or all the Member States to be fulfilled, in particular those relating to trade in primary products. In addition, the Community's interests must require the adoption of appropriate measures, which generally means quantitative restrictions on exports.

These protective measures may be limited to exports to certain countries or exports from certain regions of the Community. They must not affect products already on their way to the Community frontier. However, the measures may not be adopted for agricultural products covered by common organisations of markets or processed agricultural products covered by special regulations adopted within the framework of Article 308 of the EC Treaty (ex-Article 235).

In principle, protective measures are adopted by the Council, acting by a qualified majority on a proposal from the Commission. The Commission may also implement such measures where immediate action is required. The Commission, acting at the request of a Member State or on its own initiative, may make the export of a product subject to the production of an export authorisation, the granting of which shall be governed by such provisions and subject to such limits as the Commission shall lay down pending subsequent action by the Council. The Council and the Member States shall be notified of the measures taken and they shall take effect immediately.

A Member State may also, as an interim protective measure, make the export of a product subject to production of an export authorisation, the granting of which shall be governed by such provisions and subject to such limits as that Member State shall lay down. The Commission shall be notified of these measures immediately and they shall apply only until the decision taken by the Commission or the Council takes effect.

During their application, protective measures are the subject of consultation on the advisory committee with a view to examining their effects and ascertaining whether the conditions for their application are still satisfied. As a result, they may be amended or revoked if they are longer necessary.

EXPORT CREDIT INSURANCE

The European Union wishes to reduce the distortions of competition between firms that are caused by differences between official medium and long-term export credit insurance systems and establish some transparency in this sector

Council Directive 98/29/EC of 7 May 1998 on the harmonisation of the main provisions concerning export credit insurance for transactions with medium and long-term cover

Each Member State has its own public export credit insurance system, with significant differences in guarantee arrangements, premium rates and cover policies that can create major distortions of competition between Community firms. This Directive is aimed at lessening those risks by harmonising the different rules of the Member States on export credit insurance.
The Directive applies to cover for transactions related to the export of goods and/or services originating in a Member State, provided directly or indirectly for the account of, or with the support of, one or more Member States, involving a total risk period of two years or more, that is to say, the repayment period including the manufacturing period.

Member States must ensure that any institution providing cover directly or indirectly in the form of export credit insurance, guarantees or refinancing on behalf of or with the support of the Member State, referred to as "the insurer", covers transactions related to export in accordance with the provisions set out in the Annex to the Directive, when destined for countries outside the Community.

The Annex to the Directive sets out the common principles for export credit insurance which insurers must comply with and which relate to the main constituents of cover (Chapter I), the premium (Chapter II) and country cover policy (Chapter III). It also lays down notification procedures that introduce greater transparency (Chapter IV).

The common principles relating to the constituents of cover concern the general principles and definitions, the scope of cover, causes of loss, exclusions of liability and the provisions applicable to indemnification of claims.

The common principles relating to the premiums applicable to export credit insurance transactions establish a framework intended to produce greater transparency in the setting of insurance premiums and, in particular, lay down a basic premise that is that premiums must converge. Last but most importantly, the framework also applies the guidelines negotiated within the OECD in June 1997 in this area.

The common principles concerning country cover policy establish a format necessary to the mutual information of credit insurers in this area. This information is supplemented by the data on the technical results produced annually by insurers (see notification procedure Chapter IV).
The common principles can be applied flexibly, since derogations from these rules are authorised provided that the changes to the quality of the guarantee granted are reflected in the premiums charged and are notified to other credit insurers and the Commission.
The Directive also provides for notification procedures that are aimed at creating greater transparency at Community level in this area; there are four such procedures:

- annual notification for information which details the activity of the insurer in the previous year and the cover policy it will apply in the forthcoming year;

- notification for decision, the scope of which is limited to disagreements on the status (public or private) of the debtor that will be the subject of a decision in accordance with the comitology rules;
- ex-ante notification for information, where an insurer notifies its intention to derogate from the provisions of the Annex to the Directive by giving more favourable conditions or covering transactions with debtors in countries for which it normally does not offer cover;
- ex-post notification for information, where an insurer decides to give less favourable conditions than those set out in the Annex or to adapt its cover policy or to give the more favourable conditions notified by another insurer.
- The notification procedures laid down by the Directive supplement those established by Decision 73/391/EEC. Directives 70/509/EEC and 70/510/EEC are repealed.

DUAL-USE ITEMS AND TECHNOLOGY

Council Regulation (EC) No 1334/2000 of 22 June 2000 setting up a Community regime for the control of exports of dual-use items and technology

This Regulation establishes Community rules for controlling exports of dual-use items and technologies *.

Scope

Any products, software or technology that can be used for both civil and military purposes are considered to be dual-use items.

The Regulation does not apply to the supply of services or the transmission of technology if this involves the cross-border movement of natural persons.

Exporting dual-use items

The export of dual-use items listed in the annex to the Regulation is subject to authorisation. The authorisation is valid throughout the European Community (EC). The list itself is divided into ten categories.

A general Community export authorisation has been set up for certain categories of products destined for the following countries: Australia, Canada, Japan, New Zealand, Norway, Switzerland and the United States of America.

Any other export authorisations required are to be granted by the competent authorities of the Member State in which the exporter is established.

In deciding whether or not to grant an export authorisation, the Member States must take into account their obligations as members of international non-proliferation regimes as well as any sanctions imposed by positions and decisions of the EU, OSCE or UN. Furthermore, they must give consideration to the European Union Code of Conduct on arms exports as well as the intended end-use and the risk of diversion.

An authorisation is also required for the export of dual-use items not listed in the annex if the exporter has been informed by the competent authorities that the items in question are or may be intended, in their entirety or in part, for use in connection with

- the development, production, handling, operation, maintenance, storage, detection, identification or dissemination of chemical, biological or nuclear weapons;
- the development, production, maintenance or storage of missiles capable of delivering such weapons.

Essential security interests

If an export might prejudice its essential security interests, a Member State may request another Member State not to grant an export authorisation or to annul, suspend, modify or revoke it. In such cases, the two Member States are to consult with each other immediately.
A Member State may provisionally suspend the process of export from its territory if it suspects that important information was not been taken into account when the authorisation was granted or that circumstances have materially changed.
Exporters must keep records of their exports. These records must contain information about the description and quantity of the items as well as the names and addresses of the exporter and consignee.

Background
Export controls at European level for dual-use items and technology will help ensure that the international commitments given by the EU and its Member States with regard to the non-proliferation of weapons of mass destruction and the dissemination of conventional weapons are honoured. These include, for example, participation in the Nuclear Suppliers Group (NSG), which seeks to prevent the proliferation of nuclear items and technology, and the Australia Group (AG), whose aim is to stop the proliferation of chemical and biological items and technology.

EXPORT OF CULTURAL GOODS

Council Regulation (EEC) No 3911/92 of 9 December 1992 on the export of cultural goods

The Regulation ensures uniform checks on exports of certain categories of cultural goods, listed in the Annex.

Export licence

An export licence must be presented for the export of cultural goods covered by the Regulation. Licences are valid throughout the Community.

The licence is issued by the competent authorities of the Member States at the request of the exporter.

The licence must be presented together with the export declaration during the completion of customs formalities at the competent customs office.

Member States may refuse to accept an export licence when the cultural goods in question are covered by legislation protecting national treasures of artistic, historical or archaeological value in the Member State concerned.

Administrative cooperation

The administrative authorities of the Member States provide mutual assistance and cooperate with the Commission in implementing the Regulation.

BAN ON TRADE IN INSTRUMENTS OF TORTURE

Council Reulation (EC) No 1236/2005 of 27 June 2005 concerning trade in certain goods which could be used for capital punishment, torture or other cruel, inhuman or degrading treatment or punishment

Under this Regulation, any export or import of goods which have no practical use other than for the purpose of capital punishment, torture and other cruel, inhuman or degrading treatment or punishment (see Annex II) is prohibited; moreover, an authorisation is required for the export of goods which could be used for purposes of torture or other cruel, inhuman or degrading treatment or punishment, listed in Annex III, irrespective of the origin of such equipment.

The national authorities of the Member States which are empowered to take decisions on requests for an import or export authorisation should distinguish between goods which have no practical use other than that of, on the one hand, carrying out capital punishment or inflicting torture * and other cruel, inhuman or degrading treatment or punishment *, and on the other, goods which could be used for such purposes, the import or export of which the authorities could authorise on the basis of criteria that are precisely defined in this Regulation. The goods covered by this Regulation are listed in Annexes II and III. The Commission may amend this list as soon as new equipment appears on the market.

This Regulation applies to the Community's customs territory, the Spanish territories of Ceuta and Melilla, and the German territory of Helgoland.

It prohibits any export or import of goods which have no practical use other than for the purpose of capital punishment, torture and other cruel, inhuman or degrading treatment or punishment (see Annex II), irrespective of the origin of such goods, and related technical assistance. The competent authorities may grant an exemption only if it is proved that the goods concerned will be used in the country of destination for purposes of public display in a museum, in view of their historical significance.

However, an export authorisation is required for goods which could be used for purposes of torture or other cruel, inhuman or degrading treatment or punishment, listed in Annex III irrespective of their origin. No authorisation is required for goods in transit through the Community's customs territory, on the other hand.

There is no obligation to issue an authorisation for exports of goods listed in Annex III to the territories of Member States that are listed in Annex IV but are not part of Community territory for customs purposes, provided that the goods in question are used by a law enforcement authority. Nor is there any obligation to issue an authorisation for exports of goods listed in Annex III which are to be used by the military or civilian personnel of an EU Member State in the context of a peacekeeping or EU or UN crisis management operation in the third country concerned or of an operation based on defence-related agreements between the Member States and third countries.

Decisions to grant export authorisations are taken on a case-by-case basis, taking all appropriate considerations into account, by the competent authority in the Member State where the applicant is based (listed in Annex I). The competent authority does not grant an authorisation if there is good reason to believe that the goods listed in Annex III could be used for purposes of torture or other cruel, inhuman or degrading treatment or punishment (including sentences involving corporal punishment handed down by the courts) carried out by a law-enforcement authority or any legal or natural person in a third country.

However, a Member State may exempt from these arrangements certain goods listed in Annex III by adopting or maintaining a total ban on the import and export of leg-irons, gang chains and portable electric shock devices.

In order to harmonise the authorisation procedures, export and import authorisations are issued using a form based on the model in Annex V and are valid throughout the Community. The competent authorities may refuse to grant an export authorisation and cancel, suspend, amend or withdraw an authorisation already granted. When completing customs formalities, the exporter or importer submits the form reproduced in Annex V, duly completed, as proof that the necessary authorisation has been obtained. If authorisation is not granted, the customs authorities keep the goods declared and draw attention to the option of applying for an authorisation. After six months, if a request for authorisation has not been submitted, the customs authorities may - if provision for this is made under national law - destroy the goods thus kept.

The authorities of the Member States notify all the other Member State authorities and the Commission of the decision rejecting a request for an authorisation and any decision rescinding an authorisation already granted. The Commission and the Member States inform each other about measures taken under this Regulation and provide one another with information concerning authorisations that have been granted or rejected.

A public annual activity report is drawn up by the Member States, in cooperation with the Commission if possible.

The Commission is assisted by the committee on the common rules applicable to exports of products set up by Regulation (EEC) No 2603/69. This committee examines all issues relating to the application of this Regulation.

The Member States themselves establish rules on the penalties applicable to violations of the Regulation's provisions. These rules must be notified to the Commission by 29 August 2006 at the latest.
Imports

COMMON TRADE POLICY REGIME AND BASIC REGULATIONS FOR EXPORT IMPORTS

COMMON RULES FOR IMPORTS

Council Regulation (EC) No 3285/94 of 22 December 1994 on the common rules for imports and repealing Regulation (EC) No 518/94

This Regulation applies to imports of products originating in third countries except for textile products covered by special rules for imports and products originating from third countries which are subject to that country's own import rules. It is also complementary to the regulations on agricultural products covered by organisations of the market. From a geographical point of view, it applies to imports from all third countries with the exception of Albania, the Commonwealth of Independent States (CIS) and certain Asian countries (North Korea, China, Mongolia and Vietnam) covered by Regulation (EC) No 519/94.

The regulation lays down the principle of freedom to import products originating in third countries, subject to possible safeguard measures.

Information and consultation procedure

The Member States must inform the Commission should trends in imports appear to call for safeguard measures. Consultations may be held either at the request of a Member State or on the initiative of the Commission. They take place within an advisory committee made up of representatives of each Member State with a representative of the Commission as chairman.

These consultations aim to examine the conditions of imports, the economic and commercial situation and the measures to be taken. Consultations may be conducted in writing if necessary and the Member States may express their opinion or request oral consultations within a period of five to eight working days.

Community investigation procedure

Where after consultations it is apparent that there is sufficient evidence to justify the initiation of an investigation, the Commission initiates an investigation within one month and publishes a notice in the Official Journal of the European Communities summarising the information justifying the initiation of the procedure.

The investigation seeks to determine whether imports of the product in question are causing or threatening to cause serious injury to the Community producers concerned. Once the investigation has been launched, the Commission seeks and verifies all information it considers necessary for the conduct of the investigation.

Within the framework of the investigation, the Commission seeks information on the following aspects: the volume of imports, the price of imports, the consequent impact on Community producers and factors other than trends in imports which are causing or may have caused injury to the Community producers concerned.

At the end of the investigation, the Commission submits a report to the advisory committee and, depending on the conclusion of its investigations, terminates the investigation or implements, or proposes to the Council that it implement, surveillance or safeguard measures.

This investigation procedure does not preclude the use, particularly in critical circumstances, of surveillance or safeguard measures. In this instance, the duration of such measures must not exceed 200 days.

Surveillance measures

Imports of products may have to undergo Community checks on the basis of a decision by the Council or the Commission should market trends in this product threaten to cause injury to the Community producers of like or competing products, and the Community's interests require such checks.

The decision to introduce surveillance measures is normally taken by the Commission. Such surveillance may involve retrospective checks of imports (statistical surveillance) or prior checks. In the case of the latter, products under prior Community surveillance may be put into free circulation only on production of an import document. This document is issued or endorsed by the Member States, free of charge, for any quantity requested and within a maximum of five days of receipt of a declaration by the importer. This document must be issued to all importers, regardless of their place of business in the Community.

Surveillance measures do not necessarily cover the entire Community. Where imports of a product have not been made subject to prior Community surveillance within eight working days of the end of consultations on the possibility of establishing Community surveillance, the Commission may introduce surveillance confined to imports into one or more regions of the Community.

Member States shall inform the Commission each month of the import documents that were issued (in cases of prior surveillance) and the imports received (in cases of prior and retrospective surveillance).

Safeguard measures

Safeguard measures may be applied where products are imported into the Community in such greatly increased quantities and/or on such terms or conditions as to cause, or threaten to cause, serious injury to Community producers. As regards members of the World Trade Organisation (WTO), these measures are cumulative.

Where these conditions are fulfilled, the Commission may change the period of validity of the import documents issued in respect of surveillance or establish an import authorisation procedure and, in particular, introduce a quota system for imports.

When establishing a quota, account is taken of the desirability of maintaining, as far as possible, traditional trade flows and the volume of contracts concluded before the entry into force of the measure. In principle, the quota should not be set lower than the average level of imports over the last three years. The quota may be allocated among the supplier countries.

Safeguard measures apply to every product which is put into free circulation after their entry into force. However, they do not prevent the release for free circulation of products already on their way to the Community. In exceptional cases, they may be confined to one or more regions of the Community.

These measures are taken by the Commission or by the Council. Where intervention by the Commission has been requested by a Member State, the Commission takes a decision within a maximum of five working days. The Commission's decision is communicated to the Council and to the Member States. Any Member State may, within one month, refer the decision to the Council. In this case, the Council, acting by a qualified majority, may confirm, amend or revoke that decision. If, within three months, the Council has not taken a decision, the decision taken by the Commission is deemed to be revoked.

In any event, where the interests of the Community so require, the Council, acting on a proposal from the Commission drawn up in accordance with the conditions set out above, may adopt safeguard measures.

No safeguard measure may be applied to a product originating in a developing country as long as that country's share of Community imports of the product concerned does not exceed 3%.

The duration of safeguard measures may not, in principle, exceed four years, unless they are extended under the same conditions as the initial measures were adopted. Under no circumstances may the duration of the measures exceed eight years.

In addition to safeguard measures as such, the regulation stipulates that the Commission may adopt appropriate measures to allow the rights and obligations of the Community or of all its Member States, in particular those relating to trade in commodities, to be exercised and fulfilled at international level.

This Regulation does not preclude the fulfilment of obligations arising from special agreements concluded between the Community and third countries. Nor does it preclude the adoption or application by the Member States of measures on grounds of public order, public morality, public security, the protection of health and life of humans, animals or plants, the protection of national treasures, the protection of industrial and commercial property, and special formalities concerning foreign exchange.

COMMON RULES FOR IMPORTS FROM CERTAIN NON-EU MEMBER COUNTRIES

Council Regulation (EC) No 519/94 of 7 March 1994 on common rules for imports from certain third countries and repealing Regulations (EEC) Nos 1765/82, 1766/82 and 3420/83 [Official Journal L 67 of 10.03.1994].

Amended by the following acts:

Council Regulation (EC) No 839/95 of 10 April 1995 [Official Journal L 85 of 19.04.1995];
Council Regulation (EC) No 139/96 of 22 January 1996 [Official Journal L 21 of 27.01.1996];
Council Regulation (EC) No 168/96 of 29 January 1996 [Official Journal L 25 of 01.02.1996];
Council Regulation (EC) No 1138/98 of 28 May 1998 [Official Journal L 159 of 03.06.1998];
Council Regulation (EC) No 427/2003 of 3 March 2003 [Official Journal L 65 of 08.03.2003].

SUMMARY

The existence of special import rules for former communist countries was justified by the State's monopoly in these countries in the area of foreign trade. Since the breakdown of the communist bloc, there has been a move towards liberalisation of the economy and foreign trade in these countries. This has led the Commission to remove most of these countries from the scope of the Regulation applicable to State-trading countries and to bring them under the standard procedure. However, the fact remains that certain countries are still subject to this specific legislation.
This regulation has many similarities with the regulation establishing common rules for imports (Regulation (EC) No 3285/94). As a result, only the aspects that differ from that regulation will be considered here.

Scope
This regulation applies to products originating in the Commonwealth of Independent States (CIS), Albania, China, Vietnam, North Korea and Mongolia.
In addition, its scope excludes textile products which are covered by special common rules for imports.

Rules for imports
Imports of products covered by this regulation are free and are not subject to any quantitative restrictions, without prejudice to the safeguard measures and quotas applied to China.
Community information and consultation procedure
This procedure is similar to that set out in Regulation (EC) No 3285/94 applicable to Non-EU Member Countries in general.

Community investigation procedure
This procedure is identical to that set out for the Non-EU Member Countries covered by Regulation (EC) No 3285/94. However, it is stipulated that the Commission must give consideration in its investigation to the specific economic system in the countries in question.

Surveillance measures
The conditions for implementing surveillance measures are the same as those applied to other Non-EU Member Countries. However, where surveillance measures are implemented, the conditions for the use or issue of import documents may be stricter than for other Non-EU Member Countries. In particular, where the Community's interests so require, the Commission may limit the period of validity of the import document, make issue of this document subject to certain conditions or even provide for the insertion of a revocation clause.

Safeguard measures

The conditions laid down for the introduction of safeguard measures with regard to the countries concerned are the same as those applied to other Non-EU Member Countries: increased imports or imports under conditions that cause injury to the Community industry. These two conditions are alternatives in the case of the countries in question, whilst they may be cumulative in the case of other Non-EU Member Countries.
Quotas
Quotas are applied to a number of products from China, including the following: certain footwear, tableware or kitchenware of porcelain, and tableware or kitchenware other than of porcelain. These quotas are administered by the Commission according to the procedure for administering quantitative quotas.

COMMUNITY PROCEDURE FOR ADMINISTERING QUANTITATIVE QUOTAS

Council Regulation (EC) No 520/94 of 7 March 1994 establishing a Community procedure for administering quantitative quotas [Official Journal L 66, 10.03.1994].

Amended by the following acts:

Council Regulation (EC) No 138/96 of 22 January 1996 [Official Journal L 21 of 27.01.1996];
Council Regulation (EC) No 806/2003 of 14 April 2003 [Official Journal L 122 of 16.05.2003].

SUMMARY

Scope
This regulation applies where the Community has established the quantities of goods likely to be imported or exported during a given period, whether autonomous or conventional.
The regulation does not apply to the agricultural products listed in Annex II to the Treaty of Rome, to textile products or to the products covered by special import rules laying down specific provisions for the administration of quotas.

Basic rules for administering Community quotas
The Commission shall publish a notice announcing the opening of quotas in the Official Journal of the European Communities, setting out the allocation method chosen, the conditions to be met by licence applications, time limits for submitting them and a list of the competent national authorities to which they must be sent.

Quotas shall be allocated among applicants as soon as possible after they have been opened. They may be allocated in several tranches.
Quantities that are not allocated, assigned or used shall be redistributed. Quantities for redistribution shall be determined by the Commission on the basis of the information provided by Member States.

The different methods for administering quantitative quotas
Quotas may be administered by one of the three methods set out in the regulation, by a combination of these methods or by any other appropriate method.
Method based on traditional trade flows: This method of allocation reserves as a priority one portion of the quota for traditional importers or exporters. The remainder is set aside for other importers or exporters. Importers or exporters deemed to be traditional are those able to demonstrate that in the course of a previous period, to be known as the reference period, they have imported into the Community or exported from it the product or products covered by the quota.

After examining the information provided by the Member States on the number and the aggregate amount of the import or export applications, the Commission establishes the criteria according to which traditional importers' or exporters' applications are to be met. Where aggregate applications are equal to or less than the amount set aside for traditional importers or exporters, applications will be met in full. Where aggregate applications exceed this amount, applications will be met on a pro rata basis, calculated in accordance with each applicant's share of the total reference imports or exports.

The portion of the quota set aside for non-traditional importers or exporters are allocated in accordance with the method based on the order in which applications are submitted.
Method based on the order in which applications are submitted: This method works on the basis of the "first come, first served" principle. The Commission determines the quantity to which operators are entitled until the quota is exhausted. In setting this quantity, the same for all operators, allowance is made for the need to assign economically significant quantities having

regard to the nature of the product concerned. When holders of import or export licences have used up their quota, they may submit a new licence application.

Method allocating quotas in proportion to the quantities requested: The competent authorities of the Member States inform the Commission of the licence applications they have received. This information should specify the number of applications and the aggregate quantities applied for. After examining this information, the Commission determines the quantity of the quota or of the tranches concerned for which the said authorities are to issue import or export licences. Where aggregate licence applications do not exceed the quantity of the quota concerned, applications are met in full. Where they exceed this quantity, they are met on a pro rata basis, in proportion to the quantities applied for.

Rules concerning import or export licences
Import or export licences authorise the import or export of products which are subject to quotas. Licences are issued immediately by the Member States when the "first come, first served" principle is used. In other cases, they are issued within ten days of notification of the Community decision indicating the quantities to be distributed.

They are valid throughout the Community, except in situations where a quota is limited to one or more regions of the Community, in which case these licences are only valid in the Member State(s) of the region(s) in question. These licences are valid for four months.

Decision-making procedures
This procedure provides for the intervention of an administration committee, composed of representatives of the Member States and chaired by a representative of the Commission. The committee delivers its opinions by a qualified majority as set out in Article 205(2) of the Treaty establishing the European Community. When the provisions envisaged are in accordance with the committee's opinion, the Commission adopts them itself. If not, they are communicated to the Council. The Commission may defer application of the measures by one month. The Council, acting by a qualified majority, may take a different decision within this period.

PRODUCTS DERIVED FROM SEALS

Proposal for a Regulation of the European Parliament and of the Council of 24 July 2008 concerning trade in seal products [COM(2008) 469 final – Not published in the Official Journal].

SUMMARY

This proposal for a Regulation establishes harmonised rules regarding the placing on the market of seal products *, as well as the import or transit of seal products within the Community and their export from the Community.
The placing on the market, import and transit in the Community, as well as the export of seal products from the Community is prohibited, except when it forms part of traditional hunting methods conducted by Inuit communities for subsistence purposes or when they are derived from seals killed and skinned under conditions which do not cause pain, distress or any other from of unnecessary suffering. Proof that these conditions have been complied with is provided in the form of a certificate, a label or marking.
Compliance with these regulations is assessed by the Commission, which grants derogations based on certain criteria as listed in Annex II of the Regulation. In particular, they concern:

- animal welfare principles;
- hunting tools and conditions;

- methods for killing seals and training hunters;
- hunt monitoring systems and the production of reports.

The certificates must include all relevant information necessary to attest that the seal products they refer to meet the conditions detailed in the paragraphs above. They will be validated by an independent body or public authority attesting the accuracy of the information displayed therein. Every five years Member States shall send a report outlining the actions taken to enforce this Regulation to the Commission.

Context

This Regulation aims to harmonise the legislative measures taken by certain Member States regarding the trade in seal products. The proposed ban also aims to respond to concerns expressed by citizens regarding seal hunting methods.

The Regulation supplements existing Community legislation regarding the protection of seals, in particular the Directive 83/129/EEC prohibiting the importation into Member States of skins of certain seal pups.

Animal welfare protection is an objective pursued by the Commission and is the focus of a Protocol annexed to the EC Treaty (Protocol No 33), which is at the heart of the Action Plan on the Protection and Welfare of Animals for the period 2006-2010.

COMMERCIAL DEFENCE STRATEGY

ANTI-DUMPING MEASURES

Regulation (EC) No 384/96 aims to transpose the provisions of the new agreement on the implementation of Article VI of the General Agreement on Tariffs and Trade 1994 (1994 Anti-dumping Agreement) into Community law with a view to ensuring appropriate and transparent application of the new anti-dumping rules.

ACT

Council Regulation (EC) No 384/96 of 22 December 1995 on protection against dumped imports from countries not members of the European Community

SUMMARY

Scope

From a geographical point of view, the Regulation applies to all countries that are not members of the European Community (EC). However, the Community may adopt specific provisions in relation to countries without a market economy or whose economy is in transition. The Regulation also stipulates that its provisions do not preclude the application of any special rules laid down in agreements concluded between the Community and third countries.

From a physical point of view, the Regulation applies to all products. However, with regard to agricultural products, particularly products where common market organisations protect Community production through the use of levies, the provisions of the anti-dumping regulation may be applied by way of complement to and in derogation from any provisions which preclude the application of anti-dumping duties.

The Regulation lays down two conditions for the application of anti-dumping duties: the existence of dumping and proof of injury to the Community industry as a result of this dumping.

Definition of dumping

Dumping must be distinguished from simple practices of low-price sales resulting from lower costs or greater productivity. The key criterion in this respect is not, in fact, the relationship between the price of the exported product and that on the market of the country of import, but the relationship between the price of the exported product and its normal value. Thus, a product is considered to be dumped if its export price to the Community is less than the comparable price for a like product established in the ordinary course of trade within the exporting country.
The normal value to be taken into account to determine if there is dumping is usually based on the prices paid or payable, in the ordinary course of trade, by independent customers in the exporting country.

However, where the exporter in the exporting country does not produce or does not sell a like product, the normal value may be established on the basis of prices of other sellers or producers. In addition, when there are no or insufficient sales of the like product in the ordinary course of trade (for example, sales by a company with a monopoly) or where because of the particular market situation such sales do not permit a proper comparison, the normal value may be calculated on the basis of the cost of production in the country of origin.

In the case of imports from non-market economy countries, the normal value is determined on the basis of the price or constructed value in a market economy third country, or the price from this country to other countries, or where those are not possible, on any other reasonable basis.
The second basis of comparison, the relationship with the normal value in the country of origin which determines the dumping margin, is the export price. This is the price actually paid or payable for the product when sold for export to the Community.

In cases where there is no export price or where the price is set under an association or a compensatory arrangement between the exporter and the importer or a third party, any reference to the export price becomes impossible. It may thus be constructed on the basis of the price at which the imported products are first resold to an independent buyer, or, if the products are not resold to an independent buyer, or are not resold in the condition in which they were imported, on any reasonable basis. In these cases, adjustments are made to take account of all costs incurred between importation and resale as well as for profits accruing.

Dumping margin
The dumping margin is the amount by which the normal value exceeds the export price. The comparison is made between sales at the same commercial stage and on dates which are as close to each other as possible. The necessary adjustments are made to take account of differences in sales conditions, taxation and other differences which affect price comparability.

Injury
The application of any anti-dumping duty presupposes the presence of a second key element: significant injury to a Community industry, be it injury caused to an industry established in the Community, the threat of injury or substantial retardation of the establishment of such an industry. The determination of injury must be based on positive evidence and involve an objective examination of the following elements:

- the volume of the dumped imports, particularly where there has been a significant increase, either in absolute terms or relative to production or consumption in the Community;
- the price of dumped imports, in particular to determine whether there has been significant price undercutting as compared with the price of a like product of the Community industry, or whether the effect has been to depress prices or prevent price increases;
- the consequent impact on the Community industry concerned, particularly in relation to production and utilisation of capacity, stocks, sales, market share, price changes, profits, return on investments, cash flow and employment.

The Regulation stipulates that there must be a causal link between dumping and injury. Known factors other than the dumped imports which at the same time are injuring the Community industry must also be examined.

Moreover, the effect of the dumping must be assessed in relation to the production of the like product by the Community industry, taking into account the narrowest production sector. The term "Community industry" means the Community producers as a whole or those of them whose collective output constitutes a major proportion of the total Community production. However, when producers are themselves importers of a dumped product, the term "Community industry" may be interpreted as referring to the other producers in this sector.

Initiation of proceedings
Proceedings are initiated upon a written complaint by any natural or legal person, or any association not having legal personality, acting on behalf of a Community industry. Where, in the absence of any complaint, a Member State is in possession of sufficient evidence of dumping and of resultant injury to the Community industry, it shall immediately communicate such evidence to the Commission.

The complaint must include evidence of dumping, injury and a causal link between these two elements. It shall contain such information on the following: identity of the complainant and a description of the volume and value of the Community production concerned, a complete description of the allegedly dumped product, the country of origin, the identity of each known producer/exporter and importer, information on prices at which the product in question is sold when destined for consumption in the domestic markets of the country of origin or export, export price of the product, volume of imports of the product concerned and effect of those imports on prices of the like product.

The complaint is considered to have been made by or on behalf of the Community industry if it is supported by those Community producers whose collective output constitutes more than 50% of the total Community production.

The complaint is examined by the Advisory Committee, which consists of representatives of each Member State, with a representative of the Commission as chairman. If this consultation reveals that the complaint does not contain sufficient evidence to justify initiating a proceeding, the complaint is rejected and the complainant duly informed.
Where, after consultation within the Committee, it is apparent that there is sufficient evidence to justify initiating a proceeding, the Commission must do so within 40 days. The Commission publishes in the Official Journal of the European Communities a notice of initiation of the investigation, indicating the product and countries concerned, giving a summary of the information received and stating the period within which interested parties may make themselves known and present their views.

The complaint may be withdrawn prior to initiation of the investigation.

Investigations
The investigation carried out by the Commission, in cooperation with the Member States, covers both dumping and injury simultaneously. An investigation period is selected which normally constitutes a period of not less than six months immediately prior to the initiation of the proceeding. The Commission sends questionnaires to the parties involved, who are given at least 30 days to reply.

The Commission may request Member States to supply information, carry out checks and inspections, particularly amongst importers, traders and Community producers, as well as carry out investigations in third countries (provided that the firms concerned give their consent and that

the government of the country in question raises no objection). Officials from the Commission may be authorised to assist the officials of Member States in carrying out their duties. More commonly, the Commission may carry out visits to examine the records of the parties concerned; it may also carry out investigations in third countries involved.
The Commission may meet with interested parties who request such a meeting. It may also organise meetings between these parties so that opposing views may be presented. The interested parties may examine all information provided to the Commission, with the exception of confidential documents.

An investigation is concluded with termination of the proceeding or with the adoption of a definitive measure. It should normally be concluded within 15 months of the initiation of the proceeding.

Termination of the proceeding without measures
The final outcome of the proceeding may be negative. Where, after consultation, protective measures are considered unnecessary and there is no objection raised within the Advisory Committee, the proceeding is terminated. If there are any objections, the Commission shall immediately submit to the Council a report on the results of the consultation, together with a proposal that the proceeding be terminated. The proceeding shall be deemed terminated if, within one month, the Council has not decided otherwise.

A proceeding is terminated where the dumping and injury are considered to be negligible. A proceeding may also be terminated without the imposition of provisional or definitive duties when commitments are undertaken and are considered acceptable by the Commission. These commitments may take the form of a price review or a freeze on exports such as is required to eliminate the injurious effects of the dumping.

Imposition of provisional anti-dumping duties
Provisional duties may be imposed if a provisional affirmative determination has been made of dumping and injury, and if the Community interest calls for immediate intervention to prevent such injury.

The amount of the duty must not exceed the margin of dumping, and it should be less than the margin if such lesser duty would be sufficient to remove the injury.
The duties must be imposed no more than nine months after the initiation of the proceeding. They are normally imposed for a period of six months.
These duties are imposed by the Commission, after consultation of the Committee or, in cases of extreme urgency, after informing the Member States. The Commission informs the Council and the Member States of these provisional measures. The Council may decide to take a different course of action.

Imposition of definitive anti-dumping duties
Where the facts as finally established show that there is dumping and injury caused thereby, and the Community interest calls for intervention, a definitive anti-dumping duty is imposed by the Council.

As with the provisional measures, the definitive duty may not exceed the dumping margin and should be less than the margin if it would be adequate to remove the injury.

The duty must be imposed on a non-discriminatory basis on imports of a product found to be dumped and causing injury. The regulation imposing the duty specifies the amount of duty applied to each supplier or, if that is impracticable, to the supplying country concerned.

Provisional and definitive duties may not be applied retroactively. However, a definitive duty may be levied on products which were entered for consumption not more than 90 days prior to the date of application of the provisional measures.

Community interest
Anti-dumping measures may not be applied if it is concluded that their imposition is not in the Community interest. To this end, all the various interests are taken into account as a whole, including the interests of the Community industry and of the users and consumers. All the parties concerned are given the opportunity to make their views known.

Duration and Review
The duties shall expire five years after their date of imposition or five years after the conclusion of the review of the measures concerned. This review is carried out on the initiative of the Commission or at the request of the Community producers. The duties shall remain in force during the period of the review.

Refund of duties
Duties collected may be refunded where the importer can show that the dumping margin has been eliminated or reduced to a level below the anti-dumping duty.
The importer must request a refund within six months of the date on which the amount of the definitive duties to be levied was duly determined or within six months of the date on which a decision was made definitively to collect the provisional duties. The application must be submitted via the Member State in which the product was released for free circulation. The Member State shall forward the application to the Commission, which comes to a decision after consultation of the Committee.

ANTI-SUBSIDY MEASURES

Regulation 2026/97 is designed to transpose the provisions of the Agreement on Subsidies concluded within the framework of the World Trade Organisation (WTO) with a view to ensuring appropriate and transparent application of the anti-subsidy rules.

ACT

Council Regulation (EC) No 2026/97 of 6 October 1997 on protection against subsidised imports from countries not members of the European Community [See amending acts].

SUMMARY

This Regulation provides for the imposition of countervailing duties for the purpose of offsetting any subsidy granted, directly or indirectly, for the manufacture, production, export or transport of any product from a third country whose release for free circulation in the Community causes injury.

Apart from the provisions on the definition of a subsidy, countervailable subsidies and the calculation of subsidies, this Regulation is identical to the anti-dumping Regulation particularly with regard to the determination of injury, the definition of Community industry, the initiation of the proceeding, the investigation, the provisional and definitive measures and the termination of the proceeding.

Definition of a subsidy
A subsidy is deemed to exist, firstly, if there is a financial contribution by a government or if there is any form of income or price support within the meaning of Article XVI of the 1994 GATT Agreement and, secondly, if a benefit is thereby conferred.

There is a financial contribution where:

- a government practice involves a direct transfer of funds (grants, loans, equity infusion) or potential direct transfers of funds or liabilities (loan guarantees);
- government revenue which is otherwise due is not collected (tax credits);
- a government provides goods or services other than general infrastructure, or purchases goods;
- a government makes payments to a funding organisation or entrusts a private body to carry out one or more of the functions which are normally its responsibility.

Countervailable subsidies
Subsidies are subject to countervailing measures only if they are specific to an enterprise or a group of enterprises or industries. They are specific in cases where the granting authority explicitly limits access to a subsidy to certain enterprises.
In addition, Annex I to the Regulation provides a list of examples of export subsidies considered to be specific.

The Regulation also defines non-countervailable subsidies. These include non-specific subsidies and subsidies which, although specific, relate to research activities, are granted to disadvantaged regions or promote protection of the environment.

Calculation of the amount of countervailable subsidies
This amount is calculated in terms of the benefit conferred on the recipient. As regards the calculation of this benefit, the following rules apply:

- government provision of equity capital is considered to confer a benefit if the investment can be regarded as inconsistent with the usual investment practice in the country of origin or export;
- a loan by a government is considered to confer a benefit if there is a difference between the amount that the firm receiving the loan pays on the government loan and the amount that the firm would pay for a comparable commercial loan;
- the provision of goods by a government is considered to confer a benefit if the provision is made for less than adequate remuneration in relation to prevailing market conditions or the purchase is made for more than adequate remuneration in relation to these conditions.

The amount of the subsidy is determined per unit of the subsidised product exported to the Community. Some elements may be deducted from the subsidy, such as any fees or costs incurred in order to qualify for the subsidy or export taxes intended to offset the subsidy. Where a subsidy is not granted by reference to the quantities, the amount of the subsidy is determined by spreading the value of the total subsidy over the level of production, sales or exports of the product.

PROTECTION AGAINST TRADE BARRIERS

This Regulation aims to establish a procedure enabling economic operators and the Member States to request the Community institutions to respond to any trade barriers put in place by third countries, with a view to eliminating the resulting injury or adverse trade effects in accordance with international trade rules.

ACT

Council Regulation (EC) No 3286/94 of 22 December 1994 laying down Community procedures in the field of the common commercial policy in order to ensure the exercise

of the Community's rights under international trade rules, in particular those established under the auspices of the World Trade Organisation [See amending acts].

SUMMARY

This regulation replaces the 1984 regulation on illicit practices. It covers trade barriers that may impede Community exports to third country markets.
The scope of the trade barriers regulation is broader than that relating to illicit practices. The regulation applies not only to goods but also to certain services, particularly cross-border services.

Definitions
The term "obstacle to trade" (i.e. trade barrier) refers to any trade practice adopted by a third country but prohibited by international trade rules which give a party affected by the practice a right to seek elimination of the effect of the practice in question. These international trade rules are essentially those of the WTO and those set out in bilateral agreements with third countries to which the Community is a party.

The regulation defines "injury" as any material injury which an obstacle to trade threatens to cause to a Community industry on the market of the Community.

"Adverse trade effects" are those which an obstacle to trade threatens to cause to Community enterprises on the market of any third country, and which have a material impact on the economy of the Community or of a region of the Community, or on a sector of economic activity therein.
The term "Community industry" means all Community producers or providers of products or services which are the subject of an obstacle to trade or all those producers or providers whose combined output constitutes a major proportion of total Community production of the products or services in question.

The term "Community enterprise" means a company formed in accordance with the law of a Member State and having its registered office, central administration or principal place of business within the Community, directly concerned by the production of goods or the provision of services which are the subject of the obstacle to trade.

Right of referral
Complaints under this regulation may be lodged in three ways:

- on behalf of a Community industry that has suffered material injury as a result of trade barriers that have an effect on the market of the Community;
- on behalf of one or more Community enterprises that have suffered adverse trade effects as a result of trade barriers that have an effect on the market of a third country;
- by a Member State denouncing an obstacle to trade.

The complaint must contain sufficient evidence of the existence of the trade barriersand of the injury or adverse trade effects resulting therefrom. In examining injury or adverse trade effects, the Commission will take account of certain factors such as the volume of Community imports or exports concerned, the prices of the Community industry's competitors, the rate of increase of exports to the market where the competition with Community products is taking place, the export capacity in the country of origin or export, and so on.

Examination procedures
Complaints must be submitted to the Commission in writing. The Commission will decide on the admissibility of a complaint within 45 days. This period may be suspended at the request of the complainant in order to allow the provision of complementary information.

The regulation has provided for a consultation procedure by establishing an advisory committee composed of representatives of each Member State and chaired by a representative of the Commission. This committee is used as the forum for providing the Member States with information and is where they can express their opinions either in writing or by requesting an oral consultation.

If a complaint is deemed admissible, an examination is initiated and announced through publication of an announcement in the Official Journal of the European Communities. This announcement will indicate the product or service and countries concerned. The Commission will then gather all the relevant information from the parties involved.

When it is found as a result of the examination procedure that the interests of the Community do not require any action to be taken, the procedure will be terminated. When, after an examination procedure, the third country or countries concerned take measures to eliminate the adverse trade effects or injury referred to by the complainant, the procedure may be suspended. It may also be suspended in order to try to find an amicable solution that may result in the conclusion of an agreement between the third country or countries concerned and the Community.

Adoption of commercial policy measures

Where it is found, as a result of the examination procedure, that action is necessary in the interests of the Community in order to ensure the exercise of the Community's rights, the appropriate measures will be determined on the basis of the regulation. These measures may include:

- suspension or withdrawal of any concession resulting from commercial policy negotiations;
- the raising of existing customs duties or the introduction of any other charge on imports;
- the introduction of quantitative restrictions or any other measures modifying import or export conditions or otherwise affecting trade with the third country concerned.

Where the Community's international obligations require it to follow prior international consultation or dispute settlement procedures, these measures may only be implemented at the end of these procedures and in accordance with their conclusions.
The Council must rule on the Commission proposal within 30 days of receiving the proposal.

PROTECTION AGAINST SUBSIDIES AND UNFAIR PRICING PRACTICES WHICH CAUSE INJURY IN THE AIR TRANSPORT SECTOR

This Regulation sets out the procedure for protecting against pricing practices of and subsidies to non-Member State air carriers which cause injury to the Community industry

ACT

Regulation (EC) No 868/2004 of the European Parliament and of the Council of 21 April 2004 concerning protection against subsidisation and unfair pricing practices causing injury to Community air carriers in the supply of air services from countries not members of the European Community.

SUMMARY

Background

This Regulation was approved following the air transport crisis at the end of 2001 that led some governments outside the EU to subsidise their national airlines, while the Community industry is subject to strict rules on government aid.

The Regulation
The Regulation allows **redressive measures** to be imposed when non-Community air carriers are subsidised directly or indirectly or when they carry out unfair pricing practices on one or more routes to or from the Community, thereby causing injury to the Community industry. These measures preferably take the form of **duties** and are imposed by regulation and enforced by the Member States themselves.

According to the Regulation, a **subsidy** exists when a government, regional body or other public organisation makes a financial contribution that confers a benefit. It may take the form of:

- grants, loans or equity infusion, potential direct transfer of funds or the assumption of liabilities;
- revenue that is otherwise due but which is foregone or not collected;
- the supply of goods or services other than general infrastructure, or their purchase by a public body;
- payments by a public body to a funding mechanism or the entrusting to a private body of one of the functions described above.

To be subject to redressive measures, the subsidies must be limited to an industry or group of enterprises or industries within the jurisdiction of the granting authority.

An **unfair pricing practice** exists where non-Community air carriers benefit from a non-commercial advantage and charge fares that are sufficiently low to cause injury to competing Community air carriers. The Regulation lays down elements to take into account when fares are compared.

Before proceedings are initiated, it must be shown, by the existing facts that **injury** is being caused. The determination of injury must be based on positive evidence and involves an examination of the level of fares charged, their effect on Community fares and the impact of the air services concerned on the Community industry.

An **investigation** is initiated when a written complaint is lodged by the Community industry or on the Commission's own initiative. Where sufficient evidence exists, the proceeding is initiated within 45 days of the lodging of the complaint, but this period may be extended by up to 30 days if there is a bilateral agreement. Notice of the initiation of the procedure must be published in the Official Journal and include the details specified in the Regulation. The Commission must notify interested parties. The Commission has 45 days within which to inform the complainant if insufficient evidence is presented.

This investigation should be **concluded** within nine months of proceedings being initiated. An extension may be allowed if a satisfactory resolution of the complaint appears imminent or if additional time is needed in order to achieve a resolution that is in the Community interest. Interested parties may be granted a hearing. However, if they refuse access to or fail to provide necessary information within the appropriate time limits, the final findings may be made on the basis of facts available.

Four possible scenarios may be the result of an investigation:

- **provisional measures**: these may be imposed for a maximum period of six months if it is determined that injury is being caused and that the Community interest calls for intervention to prevent further such injury;

- **termination of the proceedings without measures being imposed**: this happens when the complaint is withdrawn or a satisfactory remedy is obtained;
- **definitive measures**: these are imposed when it is established that unfair pricing practices or subsidies which cause injury exist. The level of measures imposed must not exceed the level of the subsidies or the difference between the fares charged by the two air carriers concerned (Community and non-Community);
- **undertakings**: an investigation may be terminated without measures being imposed if the public authorities or non-Community air carrier concerned undertake to eliminate the subsidies and revise its prices in order to prevent further injury. In the event of an undertaking being breached, a definitive measure will be imposed.

If the circumstances warrant, the Commission may review the imposition of the measures in their initial form with a view to repealing, modifying or maintaining them.

COMMUNITY STATISTICS

The Commission proposes a new legal framework for statistics relating to external trade in order to improve the quality and transparency of the statistical system of trade in goods with non-member countries (Extrastat) and respond to new user needs.

PROPOSAL

Proposal for a Regulation of the European Parliament and of the Council of 30 October 2007 on Community statistics relating to external trade with non-member countries and repealing Council Regulation (EC) No 1172/95.

SUMMARY

The Commission proposes revising the current statistical system of trade in goods with non-member countries (Extrastat). To this end, it has identified a new legal framework aiming to improve quality and transparency.
The revision of the Extrastat system aims to adjust the statistical system to the changes introduced through the simplified and centralised customs declaration procedures and respond to user needs by gathering more statistics on trade, concerning businesses, invoicing currency, imports and exports and the nature of the transaction.
The adoption of this proposal will lead to the repeal of the previous Regulation.

Role and objectives of external trade statistics

The Extrastat system records each month, through the data obtained from customs declarations, the imports and exports of goods between the Member States and non-member states. These data make it possible to determine, in particular, the balance of payments and commercial accounts, to set out Community economic and trade policies, and analyse market developments. This proposal for a Regulation aims to revise the statistical system in order to:

- make the **legislation clearer**, simpler and more transparent;
- **adjust the system of statistics to the changes** to be made to the procedures regarding customs declaration and centralised clearance;
- **reconsider the concept of 'importing' or 'exporting' Member State**, in order to identify the importing and exporting Member States with respect to trade that is declared according to the centralised clearance procedure and trade affected by quasi-transit (Rotterdam effect);
- **set up a system for quality assessment**, by increasing the relevance, accuracy, timeliness and comparability of statistics;
- **establish a link between trade statistics** and business statistics;

- **respond to user needs** by compiling more statistics relating to the trade in goods using information available in customs declarations.

Reforming the Extrastat system

In order to reform the system on external trade statistics, the Commission wishes to:

- **set up a new Extrastat system** for 2010, incorporating interim provisions that are valid until the customs provisions are adapted;
- **implement arrangements** between the customs and statistical authorities, in order to record the physical trade flow of goods and ensure the availability of data in the 'importing' or 'exporting' Member State;
- **compile information** on the 'Member State of final destination', for imports, and on the 'Member State of actual export', for exports.

The Commission has put forward the list of data to be collected by the Member States. It can also provide other specifications for cases of 'specific movements of goods'.

Each Member State is to record **exports** when goods leave the statistical territory of the EU and imports when they enter it. Once the data are collected, the Member States are required to compile:

- **monthly statistics** on the imports and exports of goods, expressed in value and quantity by: commodity, importing or exporting Member State, partner country, statistical procedure, nature of the transaction, tariff treatment on import, mode of transport;
- **annual statistics** on trade broken down by businesses' characteristics, linking the data on businesses with the data on imports and exports;
- trade **statistics on a two-year basis** broken down by invoicing currency, using a representative sample of records on imports and exports;
- **additional statistics** for national purposes, if they so wish, and if the data are mentioned on the customs declaration.

The Member States are not required to submit to Eurostat statistical data that are not mentioned on the customs declaration. This regards data on the Member States of final destination, those of actual export, and the nature of the transaction.

Quality assessment

The standards for quality assessment, which apply to the statistics to be transmitted, are the following: relevance, accuracy, timeliness, punctuality, accessibility, clarity, comparability and coherence.

The Member States must submit to Eurostat a report on the quality of the statistics sent every year. Eurostat assesses the quality of the statistics transmitted.

Exchange, transmission and dissemination

The Member States must ensure that the data kept by their national customs authorities are sent to the national statistical authorities of the Member State which is indicated on the record as the Member State of final destination or actual export. This provision will become applicable once a mechanism for the mutual exchange of relevant electronic data has been set up between the Member States.

The Member States must transmit to Eurostat the statistics in electronic form, no later than 40 days after the end of each monthly reference period. They must ensure to:

- provide up-to-date statistics;
- submit information on all the imports and exports carried out;
- make adjustments where records are not available;
- include in the data transmitted any information which is confidential.

The Commission may adopt provisions on the transmission deadlines, coverage, revisions and content of statistics, and implementing measures necessary for the dissemination of external trade statistics.
The dissemination of sensitive data may be subject to restrictions.

Procedures

The budget of the MEETS programme should cover the implementation costs of the new Extrastat system.

EXTERNAL TRADE AND GLOBALISATION

THE MULTILATERAL TRADE FRAMEWORK OF THE WORLD TRADE ORGANISATION (WTO)

ADOPTION OF THE WTO AGREEMENTS

By this Decision, the Council adopts the legal texts resulting from the Uruguay Round multilateral trade negotiations concluded through the signature of the Marrakesh Final Act and the creation of the World Trade Organisation.

ACT

Council Decision 94/800/EC of 22 December 1994 concerning the conclusion on behalf of the European Community, with regard to matters within its competence, of the agreements reached in the Uruguay Round multilateral negotiations (1986-1994) [Official Journal L 336 of 23.12.1994]

SUMMARY

Final Act embodying the results of the Uruguay Round multilateral trade negotiations

Through this Decision, the Council adopts, on behalf of the European Community and with regard to matters within its competence, the results of the Uruguay Round negotiations embodied in the Marrakesh Final Act signed on 15 April 1994 in Morocco by the representatives of the European Community and the Member States.

The Marrakesh Final Act includes a list of multilateral and plurilateral agreements and ministerial decisions and declarations that clarify provisions of certain agreements. The multilateral trade agreements are the agreements in question and the associated legal instruments are an integral part of the WTO agreements and binding on all WTO members. As far as the plurilateral agreements are concerned, although they form part of the WTO agreements, they do not create obligations or rights for WTO members that have not accepted them (e.g. the Agreement on Government Procurement).
The agreement establishing the World Trade Organisation incorporates several annexes containing the WTO agreements. Annex 1A encompasses the multilateral agreements on trade in goods. These are:

- the General Agreement on Tariffs and Trade 1994 (GATT 1994) (which included the GATT 1947);
- the Agreement on Agriculture;
- the Agreement on the Application of Sanitary and Phytosanitary Measures;
- the Agreement on Textiles and Clothing;
- the Agreement on Technical Barriers to Trade;
- the Agreement on Trade-Related Investment Measures;
- the Agreement on Anti-Dumping Measures;

- the Agreement on Customs Valuation;
- the Agreement on Preshipment Inspection;
- the Agreement on Rules of Origin;
- the Agreement on Import Licensing Procedures;
- the Agreement on Subsidies and Countervailing Measures;
- the Agreement on Safeguards.

Annex 1B of the WTO Agreement contains the General Agreement on Trade in Services (GATS) and Annex 1C consists of the Agreement on Trade-Related Aspects of Intellectual Property Rights (TRIPS), including trade in counterfeit goods.

Annex 2 incorporates the Understanding on Rules and Procedures Governing the Settlement of Disputes. Annex 3 relates to the mechanism for reviewing the trade policies of WTO members. Finally, Annex 4 deals with the plurilateral trade agreements. These are:

- the Agreement on Trade in Civil Aircraft;
- the Agreement on Government Procurement;
- the International Dairy Agreement;
- the International Bovine Meat Agreement.

The last two agreements were repealed at the end of 1997.

Agreement establishing the World Trade Organisation (WTO)
This agreement provided a common institutional framework for the conduct of international trade relations within the context of the rules resulting from the agreements and legal instruments mentioned above.

Contrary to its predecessor (the GATT), the WTO is a permanent organisation which benefits from a legal personality and its attributes. All members of the GATT by rights became original members of the WTO on 1 January 1995. Since that date, applicants wishing to join have had to follow the accession procedure set out in the Agreement establishing the WTO.
The WTO members have set themselves the following objectives:

- raising standards of living;
- ensuring full employment and a growing volume of real income and effective demand;
- expanding the production of and trade in goods and services;
- sustainable development and protection of the environment;
- taking account of the needs of developing countries.

The function of the WTO is to:

- facilitate the implementation, administration and operation of the various trade agreements;
- provide a forum for multilateral trade negotiations;
- resolve trade disputes, through the Dispute Settlement Body (DSB);
- review the national trade policies of its members;
- cooperate with other international organisations in order to ensure greater coherence in global economic policy-making.

From a structural point of view, the WTO has a Ministerial Conference, its highest body, composed of representatives of all the member countries, which meets at least once every two years. In the interval between these meetings, the General Council, made up of representatives of all the members, carries out the functions of the WTO and supervises the operation of the agreements and ministerial decisions. The General Council also meets to discharge the responsibilities of the Dispute Settlement Body and the Trade Policy Review Body provided for in the Trade Policy Review Mechanism (TPRM).

The General Council has under its guidance three subsidiary bodies, the Council for Trade in Goods, the Council for Trade in Services and the Council for Trade-Related Aspects of Intellectual Property Rights. Committees that are dependent on the General Council but not on these three councils are also established, such as the committees on 'trade and development', 'trade and the environment' and 'regional agreements'. Finally, two committees are responsible for administrating the two plurilateral agreements on trade in civil aircraft and government procurement.

The General Council appoints a Director-General, who is responsible for heading the Secretariat of the WTO.

In principle, the WTO takes its decisions by consensus. When a decision cannot be arrived at by consensus, decisions are taken by a majority of votes, each WTO member having one vote. The European Community, which is a full member of the WTO, has a number of votes equal to the number of its Member States, which are members of the WTO. The agreement stipulates that the number of votes of the EC and its Member States shall in no case exceed the number of the Member States of the EC.

Each member of the WTO may submit to the Ministerial Conference proposals to amend provisions of the WTO's various multilateral trade agreements.

Understanding on Rules and Procedures Governing the Settlement of Disputes
The WTO's dispute settlement system is an important element of the multilateral trading order. It is based on Articles XXII and XXIII of the GATT 1994 and on the rules and procedures subsequently drawn up and set out in the Understanding on Rules and Procedures Governing the Settlement of Disputes incorporated in the Agreement establishing the WTO.

The dispute settlement system covers all of the multilateral trade agreements. In fact, it applies to trade in goods, trade in services and intellectual property issues covered by the TRIPS Agreement. It also applies to disputes under the plurilateral Agreement on Government Procurement. Some of these agreements contain provisions concerning dispute settlement that only apply to disputes under the agreement in question and that may supplement or modify the rules of the Understanding.

The dispute settlement system is administered by a Dispute Settlement Body (DSB) set up by the Understanding. All WTO members may attend the DSB's meetings. However, where the DSB is administering provisions relating to the settlement of disputes concerning a plurilateral trade agreement, only the members that are parties to the agreement will be able to participate in decisions or actions taken by the DSB with respect to disputes under that agreement.
The dispute settlement process is launched when one member submits to another a request for consultations on a specific issue. These consultations must begin within 30 days of the request. If the consultations fail to settle a dispute, a member may call on the DSB to set up a panel, usually consisting of three independent experts, in order to deal with the issue. In addition, the parties may voluntarily agree to make use of other dispute settlement methods, including good offices, conciliation and mediation.

After listening to the parties, the panel submits a report to the DSB. The panel must complete its work within six months or, in cases of urgency, within three months. The report is considered for adoption by the DSB 20 days after it has been circulated to members. Within 60 days of the date of circulation it is adopted, unless the DSB decides by consensus not to adopt the report (opposite or negative consensus), or if one of the parties notifies its decision to appeal. Indeed, the WTO's dispute settlement procedure enables all parties to a panel case to appeal. The appeal is, however, limited to issues of law covered in the panel report and legal interpretations developed by the panel. The appeal is examined by a standing Appellate Body composed of seven members appointed by the DSB for a four-year term. Three of the members serve on any one case. The Appellate Body's report must be accepted unconditionally by the parties to the dispute and adopted by the DSB unless there is a negative consensus, in other words, a decision by consensus not to adopt the report.

The DSB keeps under surveillance the implementation of adopted recommendations or decisions, and all pending matters remain on the agenda of its meetings until they are resolved. Deadlines are also set for the implementation of recommendations set out in panel reports. When a party is unable to implement these recommendations within a reasonable period of time, it must enter into negotiations with the complaining party with a view to developing mutually acceptable compensation. If these negotiations are unsuccessful, the DSB may authorise the complaining party to suspend the application to the member concerned of concessions or obligations. Compensation and the suspension of concessions are, however, only temporary measures that may be applied until the DSB's recommendations are implemented by the member concerned. In all cases, WTO members agree that they will not determination themselves that there has been a violation of the obligations laid down within the framework of the WTO, nor suspend concessions. They must apply the rules and procedures for the settlement of disputes set out in the Understanding.

Furthermore, the Understanding on Rules and Procedures Governing the Settlement of Disputes recognises the special situation of the WTO's developing country members and least developed country members. Developing countries may opt for an accelerated procedure, request extended deadlines or request additional legal aid. WTO members are encouraged to give particular consideration to the situation of developing country members.

Trade Policy Review Mechanism (TPRM)

The Trade Policy Review Mechanism (TPRM) was set up as a temporary measure under the GATT in 1989 following the mid-term review of the Uruguay Round. This mechanism is now an integral part of the WTO system and encompasses all the fields covered by the WTO agreements (goods, services and intellectual property questions).

The TPRM aims, in particular, to achieve greater transparency in, and understanding of, the trade policies and practices of WTO members, to encourage members to adhere to the rules in force in the multilateral trading system and, thus, to promote the smooth functioning of the system. Within the framework of the TPRM, all WTO members are subject to review. This review is held every two years for the four members with the greatest share of world trade (currently the European Community, the United States, Japan and Canada), every four years for the next 16 members and every six years for the other members. A longer period may be set for least developed countries. In practice, a certain degree of flexibility has been introduced to the rate of reviews (up to a six-month interval). In 1996, it was agreed that every other review of each of the first four trading powers would be an interim review.

The review is carried out by the Trade Policy Review Body (TPRB) on the basis of a general policy declaration submitted by the member concerned and a report drawn up by the WTO Secretariat. In drawing up its report, the Secretariat seeks the support of the member concerned but retains full responsibility for the facts presented and views expressed. The Secretariat's report and the member's declaration are published following the review meeting, together with the minutes of the meeting and the text of the final comments made by the Chairman of the TPRB at the end of the meeting.

ASPECTS RELATING TO TRADE IN GOODS

The European Community undertakes to liberalise trade in industrial and agricultural goods under fair conditions of competition. To reduce tariff and non-tariff barriers to trade in goods.

ACT

Council Decision 94/800/EC of 22 December 1994 concerning the conclusion on behalf of the European Community, as regards matters within its competence, of the agreements reached in the Uruguay Round multilateral negotiations (1986-1994) [Official Journal L 336 of 23.12.1994]

SUMMARY

MARKET ACCESS

General Agreement on Tariffs and Trade (GATT 1994)

This is the basic text containing the general rules governing trade in goods, the specific rules being laid down in the sectoral agreements established in the Final Act. GATT 1994 encompassed GATT 1947 and all of the legal instruments adopted before the Agreement establishing the World Trade Organisation (WTO).

The General Agreement lays down a number of fundamental principles based on GATT 1947, in particular:

- The general principle of most favoured nation treatment: according to this principle, each WTO member accords to products of any other member treatment no less favourable than that it accords to like products of any other country (concept of non-discrimination).
- The principle of national treatment with regard to taxation and internal regulations: according to this principle, each WTO member accords products of another member regulatory and fiscal treatment no less favourable than that accorded to products of national origin.

The Agreement also provides for the reduction and binding of customs duties, the elimination of quantitative restrictions on imports and exports and the notification requirement for State trading enterprises. The Agreement covers anti-dumping duties and regulates subsidies and safeguard measures. The provisions concerning consultations and dispute settlement are dealt with in the WTO rules on dispute settlement.
In addition, it sets out a number of criteria concerning free trade areas and customs unions as well as requirements for the members of these areas and unions. Provisions added in 1965 lay down special rules and privileges for developing countries.

Marrakesh Protocol

The Marrakesh Protocol annexed to GATT 1994 is the legal instrument that incorporates into GATT 1994 the schedules of concessions and commitments for goods negotiated during the Uruguay Round, and establishes their authenticity and the arrangements for their implementation. Each WTO member draws up a schedule of goods concessions. This schedule forms an integral part of GATT 1994. Each schedule lists all of the concessions offered by the member concerned during the Uruguay Round or previous negotiations. In accordance with Article II of GATT 1994, each member must accord to the commerce of the other members treatment no less favourable than that provided for in the appropriate part of the corresponding schedule.

Industrial products

As far as industrial products were concerned, the aim of the Uruguay Round was to reduce tariff barriers by at least one third in five years and to increase the number of bound customs duties (where governments agree not to raise the level of duty). Thus, the tariff reductions agreed upon by each member are being implemented in five equal rate reductions, as of 1 January 1995, except as may be otherwise specified in the schedules of concessions.

As a result of these commitments, customs duties levied by developed countries on industrial products imported from all regions of the world have fallen by 40% on average, from 6.3% to 3.8%.

As regards the European Community, almost 40% of its industrial products will be free of duty. In fact, the customs duties levied by the EC on industrial products are amongst the lowest in the world and most of them will have disappeared by 2004, in line with the commitments made by the Community during the Uruguay Round.

Agricultural products
In accordance with the Agreement on Agriculture, access to agricultural markets is now covered by a regime based solely on customs duties. Non-tariff border measures are replaced by customs duties ensuring equivalent protection. The new customs duties resulting from the 'tariff fixing' process, together with the other duties levied on agricultural products, should be reduced by an average of 36% in six years for developed countries and 24% in ten years for developing countries. The least advanced countries are not obliged to reduce their duties.

WTO members are also required to reduce spending on export subsidies and the quantities of exports that are subsidised with regard to specific products. For products not subject to commitments regarding a reduction in export subsidies, the Agreement on Agriculture stipulates that no such subsidy may be used in the future. Developed countries are obliged to reduce the level of direct export subsidies by 36% in relation to the 1986-1990 base period levels over an implementing period of six years and to decrease the quantity of exports subsidised by 21% over the same period. Developing countries must ensure reductions equivalent to two thirds of the reductions carried out by developed countries, over a period of ten years (no reductions for the least advanced countries).

As regards domestic support measures for farmers (price support), these are regulated through a reduction in the total aggregate measurement of support (total AMS). Developed countries are committed to reducing their total AMS by 20% over six years (1986-1988 being the base period used to calculate the reductions). Developing countries must reduce their total AMS by 13% over ten years. These commitments do not apply to measures with a zero or minimal impact on trade (so-called 'green category' measures, such as agricultural research or training provided within the framework of public programmes).
This set of measures is designed to be a continuous process with the long-term aim of securing gradual substantial reductions in support and protection in the field of agriculture.

Textiles and clothing
The 1973 Multifibre Arrangement (MFA), which covers natural and synthetic fibres and related products, had left trade in textile products outside the common GATT system. In fact, this agreement had set up a derogatory system by legalising bilateral voluntary restraint agreements between states, in other words quantitative restrictions, prohibited by the GATT.
The Uruguay Round negotiations aimed to ensure the smooth integration of the textiles and clothing sector into GATT 1994. Thus, the Agreement on Textiles and Clothing (ATC) provides for the gradual dismantling of the Multifibre Arrangement by 1 January 2005. This involves the gradual elimination of quantitative restrictions, especially the bilateral quotas negotiated under the MFA. Integration means that once the product is integrated, trade in that product is governed by the general rules of GATT 1994. The integration programme has four stages and all products must be integrated no later than 1 January 2005. The Agreement also stipulates that all restrictions on imports of textiles and clothing not covered by the MFA must be notified and

brought into line with the GATT within one year of the entry into force of the ATC or gradually eliminated over a period not exceeding the duration of the agreement (by 2005).
Safeguard measures may be applied for countries whose local industries will have difficulties adjusting. These measures may last no longer than three years and will be strictly monitored by the Textiles Monitoring Body.

RULES CONCERNING NON-TARIFF MEASURES

Technical barriers to trade

The Agreement on Technical Barriers to Trade (TBT) aims to ensure that technical regulations and standards and conformity assessment procedures do not create unnecessary obstacles to international trade. The Agreement recognises the right of countries to adopt such measures in order to fulfil a legitimate objective, for example the protection of human health or safety or the protection of the environment. Technical regulations and standards must not discriminate between national products and like products that are imported. Indeed, the Agreement encourages the use of international standards and the harmonisation and mutual recognition of technical regulations, standards and conformity assessment procedures.

The Agreement contains a Code of Good Practice for the Preparation, Adoption and Application of Standards by central government bodies together with provisions concerning the preparation and application of technical regulations for local government bodies and non-governmental organisations. The Agreement stipulates that procedures for assessing conformity of products with national standards must not discriminate against imported products. The Agreement also provides for the establishment of national enquiry points to facilitate access to information on the technical regulations, standards and conformity assessment procedures in each member country.

Sanitary and phytosanitary measures

The Agreement on the Application of Sanitary and Phytosanitary Measures (SPS) relates to all SPS measures which may, directly or indirectly, affect international trade. SPS measures are defined as measures applied to protect human and animal life or to protect plant life from risks associated with additives, contaminants, toxins or diseases present in foodstuffs, or to protect a country in the event of the entry, establishment or spread of pests.

The Agreement affords members the right to take SPS measures based on scientific principles, but they must ensure that those measures do not discriminate against other countries. Moreover, the SPS measures must not be used for protectionist purposes. Members are encouraged to base their measures on international standards, guidelines or recommendations wherever possible. The application of standards may be contested and a dispute settlement procedure is established.

CUSTOMS AND TRADE ADMINISTRATION

Customs valuation

Where customs duties are levied on an ad valorem basis, it is important to establish a clear procedure to determine the customs value of the goods imported. Indeed, when carried out according to unfair rules, the customs valuation may have the effect of a non-tariff protective measure and be more restrictive than the customs duty itself.
The Agreement on customs valuation recognises that this value should, in principle, be based on the transaction value, in other words the real price of the goods. In very specific cases where the transaction value cannot be used as a basis for determining the customs value, the Agreement provides for five other methods of customs valuation, which must be applied in a particular hierarchical order.

Preshipment inspection

In order to prevent fraud and compensate for the shortcomings of their administrative structures, a number of developing countries have recourse to the services of private companies for the verification of the quality, quantity, price and/or customs classification of imported goods before they are exported from supplying countries. The Agreement on Preshipment Inspection sets out the requirements for user countries, mainly as regards non-discrimination, transparency, the protection of confidential business information and price verification.

Rules of origin
As necessary criteria for determining the country of origin of a product, rules of origin must not create unnecessary obstacles to international trade. The Agreement on Rules of Origin establishes disciplines for the application of these rules. It covers the rules used in non-preferential commercial policy instruments. The main objective of this Agreement is to harmonise non-preferential rules of origin so as to ensure that the same criteria are applied by all WTO members, irrespective of the purpose of their application.

Pending this harmonisation and during a transition period, WTO members must ensure that the conditions for determining origin are clearly defined and that the rules of origin do not create restrictive, distorting or disruptive effects on international trade. The rules should not pose unduly strict requirements or require the fulfilment of a certain condition not related to manufacturing or processing as a prerequisite for the determination of the country of origin.
After the transition period, and within three years, members must establish harmonised rules of origin. These rules must be applied equally and they must be objective, understandable and predictable. This harmonisation work is carried out within the WTO's Committee on Rules of Origin and a Technical Committee established under the auspices of the World Customs Organisation.

Annex 2 to the Agreement contains a Common Declaration with regard to Preferential Rules of Origin.

Import licensing procedures
Import licences may be defined as administrative procedures requiring the submission of an application or other documentation to the relevant administrative body as a prior condition for importation into the customs territory of an importing country. The main objectives of the Agreement on Import Licensing Procedures are to simplify these procedures and to ensure that they are transparent and predictable so that they can be applied and administered fairly and equitably.

TRADE PROTECTION MEASURES

Anti-dumping measures
Article VI of GATT 1994 authorises members to apply anti-dumping measures. However, these measures may only be applied if three conditions are fulfilled:

- the product is sold at an export price that is lower than its standard value, in other words at a price lower than the comparable price of the like product when destined for the exporting country;
- the dumped imports cause or threaten to cause significant injury to the domestic industry of the importing country;
- the existence of a causal relationship between the dumped imports and the significant injury to the domestic industry is clearly established.

The Agreement on the implementation of anti-dumping measures is based on the agreement negotiated during the Tokyo Round but it introduces more specific, clearer rules with regard to the method for determining dumping and the procedures to be followed when carrying out investigations. The Agreement provides greater transparency by stipulating that anti-dumping decisions must be notified immediately to the Committee on Anti-dumping Practices, established by the Agreement. It also provides for a dispute settlement procedure.

Subsidies and countervailing measures
The new Agreement on Subsidies and Countervailing Measures, contrary to that adopted at the Tokyo Round, defines the term 'subsidy' and stipulates that only those specific subsidies are subject to its provisions. It lays down the criteria for determining whether a subsidy is specific to an enterprise or industry or group of enterprises or industries. The Agreement divides the subsidies into the following three categories: prohibited, actionable and non-actionable. The Agreement provides for different remedies for each category of subsidies.
The Agreement also contains provisions concerning the use of countervailing measures, i.e. duties imposed by an importing country to compensate for the effect of a subsidy. These rules are similar to those that apply in the case of anti-dumping.

Safeguards
The Agreement on Safeguards lays down the rules for application of the safeguard measures provided for in Article XIX of GATT 1994. This article enables WTO members to apply safeguard measures on a non-discriminatory basis to limit imports where certain conditions are met in order to protect a domestic industry from serious injury or a threat of serious injury caused by an increase in imports.

The Agreement prohibits so-called 'grey zone' measures such as voluntary export restraint or other market sharing arrangements. The Agreement also provides for an extinction clause for all existing safeguard measures. In addition, it provides details on the procedures and rules to be followed when applying safeguard measures.

OTHER TRADE-RELATED RULES

Trade-related investment measures (TRIMs)
The Agreement on Trade-Related Investment Measures (TRIMs) recognises that certain investment measures may have a restrictive or distorting effect on trade. WTO members agree not to apply TRIMs that are inconsistent with the principle of national treatment established by the GATT or with the elimination of quantitative restrictions. The annex to the Agreement contains an illustrative list of TRIMs that are inconsistent with these provisions (requirement to purchase a specified quantity of products of national origin, etc.).

All TRIMs must be notified and eliminated within two years for developed countries, five years for developing countries and seven years for the least advanced countries. A Committee on Trade-Related Investment Measures is responsible for monitoring these commitments.
The members also decided to determine at a later date whether the Agreement should be complemented with provisions on investment policy and competition policy.

Balance-of-payments provisions
GATT 1994 authorises WTO members to impose restrictions on trade for balance-of-payments purposes. The Understanding on the Balance-of-Payments Provisions clarifies the GATT 1994 provisions and strengthens the procedures for consultations and notification of restrictive measures. It confirms the commitment made by the members at the Tokyo Round to give preference to price-based measures, such as import surcharges and import deposits, rather than quantitative restrictions applied for balance-of-payments purposes.

State trading enterprises
Article XVII of GATT 1994 governs the activities of State trading enterprises (government and non-government) with a view to ensuring that states do not use their enterprises as a mechanism to bypass the basic requirements they must fulfil under the GATT. The Understanding on the

Interpretation of Article XVII contains a precise definition of State trading enterprises and aims to increase supervision of their activities through enhanced notification and review procedures.

Government procurement
The Agreement on Government Procurement is one of the four plurilateral agreements included in Annex 4 to the Marrakesh Agreement (in December 1997, two of these, dealing with bovine meat and dairy products, were terminated; the other agreement relates to trade in civil aircraft). These agreements only apply to the WTO members that have expressly accepted them. The European Community is one of the twenty or so WTO members that have signed and adopted these agreements.

The Agreement on Government Procurement, replacing the previous agreement from the Tokyo Round, aims to liberalise government procurement as far as possible at international level within a framework guaranteeing transparency and non-discrimination in relation to foreign products and suppliers. It covers procurement involving non-central administrations (states in a federal grouping, provinces, cantons, major towns) and relates to goods, works and services. The legal framework established by this Agreement reflects to a large extent the Community rules on government procurement.

The Agreement governs government procurement where the value exceeds a specific amount: SDR 130 000 (Special Drawing Rights, an IMF accounting unit) for the acquisition of goods and services by central government bodies, SDR 200 000 for sub-central governments, SDR 400 000 for public utility companies and SDR 5 000 000 for construction contracts.
The Agreement covers five sectors of activity: ports, airports, water, electricity and urban transport. It is based on the principle of reciprocity: countries must only open government contracts in the sectors indicated to signatories to the Agreement involved in the same sector.

ASPECTS RELATING TO TRADE IN SERVICES

1) OBJECTIVE

To establish a multilateral framework of principles and rules for trade in services with a view to promoting the expansion of this trade and its gradual liberalisation through negotiations whilst ensuring transparent regulations and the increasing participation of developing countries.

2) ACT

Council Decision 94/800/EC of 22 December 1994 concerning the conclusion on behalf of the European Community, as regards matters within its competence, of the agreements reached in the Uruguay Round multilateral negotiations (1986-1994) [Official Journal L 336 of 23.12.1994].
General Agreement on Trade in Services

3) SUMMARY

The General Agreement on Trade in Services (GATS) is the first set of rules and disciplines agreed at multilateral level to govern international trade in services. It consists of three elements: a general framework containing fundamental requirements for all WTO members, national schedules of specific commitments concerning market access and, finally, annexes laying down special conditions to be applied to different sectors.

General framework
The agreement is distinguished by its universal scope. It applies to all services in all sectors with the exception of services provided by the public authorities. It also applies to all measures applicable to services taken at all levels of government (central, regional, local, etc.). The agreement defines four methods of supplying a service:

- Supplying a service from the territory of one member into the territory of any other member (e.g. international telephone calls);
- Supplying a service in the territory of one member to a consumer of any other member (e.g. tourism);
- Supplying a service through commercial presence of a member in the territory of any other member (e.g. banking services);
- Supplying a service through presence of natural persons of a member in the territory of any other member (e.g. construction projects, fashion models, consultants).

The agreement is based on the principle of most-favoured-nation treatment (MFN), according to which each member must accord unconditionally services and service suppliers of any other member treatment no less favourable than that it accords to services and service suppliers of any other country. However, certain exceptions are envisaged in the context of specific service activities within the framework of a list of exemptions from the MFN requirement. In fact, each government has included in its schedule the services for which it guarantees access to its market by setting out the limits it wishes to maintain for such access.

Moreover, members entering into an agreement involving economic integration are authorised to liberalise trade in services between the parties without having to extend the agreement to the other GATS members provided that it has substantial sectoral coverage and provides for the absence or elimination of practically all discrimination.

In order to ensure maximum transparency, the agreement requires governments to publish all relevant laws and regulations. These measures must be administered in a reasonable, objective and impartial manner.

The bilateral agreements concluded between governments on the recognition of qualifications must be open to other members who wish to negotiate their accession to these agreements. In addition, each member must ensure that monopolies and exclusive service suppliers do not abuse their position. Similarly, members must enter into consultations on business practices that may restrain competition with a view to eliminating them.

International transfers and payments for current transactions relating to specific commitments entered into under the GATS, must not be restricted except in cases of balance-of-payments difficulties and under certain circumstances.

Specific commitments

The provisions on market access and national treatment are not general requirements but specific commitments included in schedules annexed to the GATS and they form an integral part of the agreement. These schedules identify the services and service activities for which market access is guaranteed and set out the conditions governing this access. Once consolidated, these commitments can only be modified or withdrawn following negotiation of compensation with the country concerned.

Thus, each member must accord treatment to services and service suppliers of any other member, no less favourable than that provided for under the terms specified in its schedule.

The agreement is also based on the principle of national treatment. In fact, in the sectors inscribed in each member's schedule, and subject to any conditions set out therein, each government must accord to services and service suppliers of any other member, treatment no less favourable than that it accords to its own services and service suppliers.

Progressive liberalisation

The GATS provides for negotiations, beginning within five years, to achieve a higher level of liberalisation of trade in services. This liberalisation will be aimed at enhancing the commitments in the schedules and reducing the adverse effect of the measures taken by the governments.

Sectoral questions
A number of annexes relating to different service sectors form part of the GATS. These annexes were designed to take account of certain specific characteristics of the sectors in question.
The Annex on movement of natural persons authorises governments to negotiate specific commitments applying to the temporary stay of persons in their territory for the purpose of supplying services. The agreement does not apply to permanent employment nor to measures regarding citizenship or residence.

The Annex on air transport services excludes from the scope of the GATS traffic rights and services related to these rights (mainly bilateral agreements on air services that grant landing rights). The GATS does apply, however, to aircraft repair and maintenance services, the selling and marketing of air transport services and computer reservation system services.
The Annex on financial services (particularly banking services and insurance services) recognises a government's right to take measures to protect investors, depositors and insurance policy holders. The agreement excludes from its scope services supplied by central banks.
Finally, the Annex on telecommunications stipulates that governments must accord any service supplier of any other member access to public telecommunications networks on reasonable and non-discriminatory terms and conditions.

Institutional provisions
These provisions relate, in particular, to consultations and dispute settlement and to the establishment of a Council for Trade in Services. The responsibilities of this Council are defined in a ministerial decision.

Continuation of negotiations
At the end of the Uruguay Round, the governments agreed to continue negotiations in four areas: basic telecommunications, maritime transport, movement of natural persons and financial services. Other negotiations are due to be held on subsidies, government procurement and safeguard measures.

ASPECTS OF INTELLECTUAL PROPERTY RIGHTS

1) OBJECTIVE

To ensure effective and appropriate protection for trade-related intellectual property rights, taking into account differences in national legal systems. To draw up a multilateral framework of minimum rules to help combat counterfeiting.

2) ACT

Council Decision 94/800/EC of 22 December 1994 concerning the conclusion on behalf of the European Community, as regards matters within its competence, of the agreements reached in the Uruguay Round multilateral negotiations (1986-1994) [Official Journal L 336 of 23.12.1994].
Agreement on Trade-Related Aspects of Intellectual Property Rights (TRIPS)

3) SUMMARY

General provisions and basic principles
The principles are those of national treatment and most-favoured-nation treatment. Thus, members of the WTO must accord the nationals of other members treatment no less favourable than that they accord to their own nationals. Moreover, any advantage granted by a member to nationals of another member must be accorded immediately and unconditionally to the nationals of all other members even if this treatment is more favourable than that accorded to its own nationals.

Standards concerning the availability, scope and use of intellectual property rights
The Agreement aims to ensure that adequate rules on the protection of intellectual property are applied in all member countries, on the basis of the basic obligations laid down by the WIPO (World Intellectual Property Organisation) in the various conventions on intellectual property rights (the Paris Convention for the Protection of Industrial Property, the Berne Convention for the Protection of Literary and Artistic Works, the Rome Convention for the Protection of Performers, Producers of Phonograms and Broadcasting Organisations, and the Washington Treaty in Respect of Integrated Circuits). Numerous new rules or stricter rules are introduced in fields not covered by the existing conventions or where the existing conventions are inadequate.
With regard to copyright, the members of the WTO must comply with the basic provisions of the Berne Convention for the Protection of Literary and Artistic Works. Computer programs will from now on be protected as literary works. As regards rental rights, authors of computer programmes and producers of sound recordings may authorise or prohibit the commercial rental of their works to the public. A similar exclusive right applies to cinematographic works.

With regard to trademarks, the Agreement specifies the types of signs that may benefit from protection as trademarks as well as the minimum rights conferred on their owner. It also lays down the requirements relating to the use of trademarks, the duration of protection, licensing and the assignment of trademarks.

As far as geographical indications are concerned, members of the WTO must provide the means to prevent the use of any indications which mislead the public as to the origin of a product and any use which would constitute an act of unfair competition. The Agreement also made provision for additional protection for geographical indications for wines and spirits, even where there is no risk of consumers being misled.
Industrial designs are protected under the Agreement for ten years. Their owners have the right to prevent third parties from making, selling or importing articles embodying a design which is a copy of the protected design.

With regard to patents, members of the WTO have the general obligation to comply with the basic provisions of the 1967 Paris Convention. In addition, the TRIPS Agreement stipulates that it must be possible for all inventions to be protected by a patent for 20 years. Certain inventions may be excluded from patentability if their exploitation is prohibited for reasons of public order or morality. Other authorised exclusions relate to diagnostic, therapeutic and surgical methods for the treatment of humans or animals, as well as plants and animals (other than micro-organisms) and essentially biological processes for the production of plants or animals (other than non-biological and microbiological processes). However, members must provide for the protection of plant varieties either by patents or by a *sui generis* system.

As regards layout-designs of integrated circuits, WTO members must provide for their protection in accordance with the provisions of the Washington Treaty on Intellectual Property in Respect of Integrated Circuits. The TRIPS Agreement also sets out a number of other provisions, relating in particular to the term of protection.

According to the Agreement, trade secrets and technical knowledge that have commercial value must be protected against breaches of confidence and any act contrary to honest commercial practices. Furthermore, anti-competitive practices in contractual licences may be subject to measures on the part of members to prevent and/or control such practices.

Enforcement of intellectual property rights
The laws of the member countries of the WTO must include procedures to ensure that intellectual property rights are respected both by foreign right holders and by their own nationals. These procedures must permit effective action against any act of infringement of these rights. They must be fair and equitable, they must not be unnecessarily complicated or costly, and they must not

entail unreasonable time limits. Final administrative decisions may be reviewed by a judicial authority.

The Agreement provides details concerning evidence, injunctions, damages, provisional measures and other remedies.

Transition period
With regard to the application of the Agreement, developed countries have a period of one year to bring their legislation and practices into line with the Agreement. This period is extended to five years for developing countries and countries in the process of transformation from a centrally-planned economy to a market economy, and to eleven years for the least-developed countries.

Institutional framework
The Agreement created a Council for Trade-Related Aspects of Intellectual Property Rights. It is responsible for monitoring the operation of the Agreement, ensuring that members comply with their obligations and affording opportunities for consultations between members.
The settlement of disputes over intellectual property is governed by the dispute settlement procedures adopted following the Uruguay Round negotiations.

DEVELOPMENT

SCHEME OF PREFERENCES FROM 2006 TO 2015 - GUIDELINES

A SCHEME OF GENERALISED TARIFF PREFERENCES 2009-2011

The purpose of the generalised system of preferences (GSP) is to help developing countries to reduce poverty by using tariff preferences to help them obtain international trade revenue. In the Communication the Commission sets out the principles that should underpin regulations between 2006 and 2015 in order to achieve this objective. It proposes improving the current system (GSP for the period 2002-2005) in several areas by simplifying the GSP (reducing the five arrangements currently in place to three), targeting the system on the developing countries that need it most, encouraging regional cooperation and increasing the additional preferences granted for sustainable development, good governance etc.

ACT

Communication of 7 July 2004 from the Commission to the Council, the European Parliament and the European Economic and Social Committee on "Developing countries, international trade and sustainable development: the function of the Community's generalised system of preferences (GSP) for the ten-year period from 2006 to 2015" [COM(2004) 461 final - Official Journal C 242 of 29.9.2004]

SUMMARY

In this Communication the European Commission proposes guidelines for the generalised system of preferences for the period 2006-2015, based on experience of earlier systems. It advocates:
Maintaining generous tariff rates
There are a number of ways of maintaining and even improving the tariff preferences. Among other things the Commission proposes extending the GSP to some products not covered by the current system, under which almost one tenth of taxable products in the Customs Tariff are not covered.
Some products classed as sensitive could also be transferred to the category of non-sensitive products.
Preferential margins (currently 3.5% for sensitive products and 100% for non-sensitive products) will be maintained and, where possible, increased.

The enlargement of the European Union (EU) by ten new Member States on 1 May 2004 has helped to improve what the Community can offer since it has expanded the EU market to include a further 75 million potential consumers.

Targeting the GSP on the countries that most need it

The Commission proposes that the GSP should target the countries that need it most, such as the least developed countries (LDCs) and the most vulnerable among the other developing countries (small economies, land-locked countries and low-revenue countries) to help them to play a greater part in international trade.

The GSP should also have a mechanism for gradual withdrawal of a country from the special GSP, the everything-but-arms scheme, which gives duty-free and quota-free access to all products (except arms and munitions) from the fifty poorest countries.

A simpler GSP with easier access

The process of simplification, already started under the present GSP, should be enhanced. The Commission has proposed replacing the five GSP arrangements to three: the general arrangement, the special arrangement for the least developed countries and a new special arrangement (GSP+) to encourage sustainable development and good governance.

Making graduation more transparent and targeting it on the prime beneficiaries

The Commission proposes making graduation (withdrawal from the GSP) more transparent by withdrawing the most competitive product groups of certain beneficiary countries from the GSP. This means that the beneficiaries no longer need the GSP to increase their exports of those products to the EU. The smaller beneficiaries will not be graduated and so can enjoy a greater share of the benefits of the GSP.

The current criteria for graduation (share of preferential imports, development index and export-specialisation index) will be replaced with a single straightforward criterion: share of the Community market, expressed as a share of preferential imports.

Devising a new incentive to encourage sustainable development and governance

As already mentioned, the Commission proposes introducing a new incentive for sustainable development and good management of public affairs by replacing the separate "drugs", "social" and "environment" special arrangements with a single new category: GSP+.

GSP+ will provide special incentives for countries which have signed up to the main international agreements on social rights, environmental protection, governance and combating the production of and trafficking in illegal drugs.

The Commission will take account of the evaluations by the international organisations responsible for each international agreement concerned before deciding which of the applicant countries will be selected to benefit from the GSP+. This scheme will include a credible suspension clause that can be rapidly activated where a country fails to meet its commitments under the agreements.

Improving the rules of origin

The Commission proposes improving the rules of origin by changing their form (simplifying them), their substance (adjusting the origin criteria and cumulation rules) and their procedures (formalities and controls).

The new rules of origin should also be flexible in order to encourage development. One of the objectives must be to facilitate acquisition of origin to optimise the benefits of preferences.

The system could, for example, be improved by regional cumulation, promoting regional cooperation among beneficiary countries. The Commission attaches particular importance to regional integration for southern countries as a route to greater involvement of the southern countries in international trade.

Restoring the temporary withdrawal instruments, safeguard measures and anti-fraud measures

The Commission proposes redefining the GSP temporary withdrawal arrangements and the safeguard clause to take account of the new graduation focused on the most competitive beneficiary countries.

Even though they will still be for use in exceptional circumstances only, those arrangements must be made more credible, which will involve simplifying them and making the way they are used more flexible, particularly in cases of unfair trade practices. It is also essential that the Commission and Member States responsible for applying the GSP should apply these rules unwaveringly where fraud is detected.

As the beneficiary countries also have GSP management responsibilities, the Commission calls on them to establish effective and appropriate management structures to guarantee the validity of certificates or origin.

Background

The generalised system of preferences allows manufactured products and some agricultural products exported by developing countries access to the Community market with total or partial exemption from customs duties.

It is thus an instrument of both the European Community's trade policy and its development policy. As it is a cooperation instrument it is a provisional mechanism, the benefits of which are to be withdrawn from countries that no longer need it.

The EU absorbs one fifth of developing countries' exports. 40% of EU imports come from the developing countries. The EU is also the world's biggest importer of agricultural products from developing countries, importing more than the United States, Canada and Japan put together. Half the preferential imports under this system in 2002 were exempt from customs duties and reduced duties were applied to the other half.

RELATED ACTS

Communication from the Commission to the Council, the European Parliament and the European Economic and Social Committee - The rules of origin in preferential trade arrangements - Orientations for the future [COM(2005) 100 final - Not published in the Official Journal]

This communication follows the consultation launched by the Commission Green Paper on the future of rules of origin in preferential trade arrangements. It shows that the preferential rules of origin need to be reviewed. The review is also important because of the goal of integrating developing countries into the world economy. The review should also be accompanied by an adjustment of the procedures for their management and control.

The Commission is proposing actions in three areas:

- a revision of the conditions for a product to be considered as originating in a country;
- a change in the customs procedures necessary for the proper implementation and the control of the use of the preferences by the economic operators;
- the development of instruments ensuring that the beneficiary countries comply with their obligations.

Council Regulation (EC) No 980/2005 of 27 June 2005 applying a scheme of generalised tariff preferences [Official Journal L 169 of 30.06.2005]

This Regulation sets out the Community scheme of generalised tariff preferences which applicable from 1 January 2006 until 31 December 2008. It simplifies the preferential import arrangements for products originating in developing countries, thereby streamlining the preferential scheme and reconciling trade and development objectives.

TOWARDS AN EU AID FOR TRADE STRATEGY

This Communication aims to lay the bases for a joint European Union (EU) Aid for Trade strategy in favour of developing countries. The EU is the world's largest donor in the field of trade-related assistance, which is a key dimension of the Doha agenda for development and of Economic Partnership Agreements (EPAs) between the EU and the African, Caribbean and Pacific countries (ACP).

ACT

Communication from the Commission to the Council, the European Parliament, the European Economic and Social Committee and the Committee of the Regions entitled "Towards an EU Aid for Trade strategy – the Commission's contribution" [COM(2007) 163 final - Not published in the Official Journal].

SUMMARY

Trade is an important catalyst for growth and poverty reduction in developing countries. But successful integration of developing countries into world trade requires more than better market access and strengthened international trade rules. In order to fully exploit the benefits from trade, developing countries also need to remove supply-side constraints and address structural weaknesses. This includes domestic reforms in trade-related policies, trade facilitation, enhancement of customs capacities, upgrading of infrastructure, enhancement of productive capacities and building of domestic and regional markets. Complementary efforts are required in areas such as macroeconomic stability, fiscal reforms, promotion of investment, labour policy, capital and product market regulations and institutions, and human capital development.
Aid for Trade is a very important factor in this context. It is geared to generating growth, employment and income, thereby contributing to the first and eighth Millennium Development Goals, i.e. to reduce the proportion of people living on less than a dollar a day and to establish an open trading and financial system that is rule-based and non-discriminatory.
The objectives of Aid for Trade are:

- to enable developing countries, particularly the least-developed countries (LDCs), to use trade more effectively to promote growth, employment, development and poverty reduction and to achieve their development objectives;
- to facilitate the access of these countries to international markets by improving their supply-side capacity and trade-related infrastructure;
- to help these countries to implement and adjust to trade reform, including via labour market and social adjustments;
- to assist regional integration;
- to assist good integration into the world trading system.

An EU Aid for Trade strategy can contribute to these objectives through the following measures:

- increasing the volumes of EU Aid for Trade, in particular by taking trade-related assistance up to EUR 2 billion a year by 2010, but also by promoting an effective response to wider Aid for Trade needs;
- enhancing the quality of EU Aid for Trade;
- implementing effective monitoring and reporting.

Increasing the volumes of Aid for Trade
The Commission recalls that five categories of Aid for Trade were identified by the World Trade Organisation (WTO) Task Force on Aid for Trade, i.e.:

- trade policy and trade regulation;
- trade development;
- trade-related infrastructure;
- productive capacities;
- trade-related adjustment.

The first two categories are grouped under "trade-related assistance". They include:

- trade policy and trade regulation, which are aimed at ensuring effective participation of developing countries in multilateral trade negotiations and assisting these countries in the implementation of trade-related legislation;
- development of trade and the business climate, and improvement of business support services and institutions.

In 2005 the EU undertook to increase its trade-related assistance to EUR 2 billion per year by 2010, with half coming from the Commission and the other half from the Member States. The Commission currently provides EUR 840 million per year, whereas Member States contribute only EUR 300 million.
To increase the volume of aid, the Commission recommends that:

- the Member States reach a level of EUR 600 million per year by 2008, in order to attain the 1 billion target set for 2010;
- a significant share of the increased aid should be allocated to the African, Caribbean and Pacific (ACP) countries in support of regional integration and Economic Partnership Agreements (EPAs). In particular, the ACP countries must be given guidance on the actual amounts involved.

In addition, in all the developing countries, it is necessary to develop effective approaches to trade needs assessments at regional level and to ensure that these needs will be taken into account in the national development strategies of the partner countries. In particular, the EU should endeavour to apply effectively the instrument of the Integrated Framework * used with the LDCs and to extend the same type of approach to non-LDCs.
The EU must also continue to implement a wider Aid for Trade agenda in order to:

- support economic infrastructure, productive capacities and trade-related adjustment (fiscal reforms);
- develop coherent reporting practices for all categories of Aid for Trade.

Enhancing the quality of Aid for Trade
In order to improve the quality and effectiveness of Aid for Trade, the Commission recommends that the EU strategy focuses on the following aspects:

- lay down the means to ensure that the Aid for Trade actions produce results in this field, e.g. by **identifying the areas of Aid for Trade** which bring about the widest and most sustainable reduction in poverty;
- **ensure better ownership and participation** by integrating trade-related issues into poverty reduction strategies, with active participation by private-sector and civil-society stakeholders;
- **promote the institutional and financial sustainability of programmes** by stakeholder capacity-building and ownership in all operations. It is also necessary to guarantee **social and environmental sustainability** by means of sustainability impact assessment of trade policies and agreements. In the specific case of environmental sustainability, the EU must help partners develop sustainable production methods. Other important aspects are the promotion of decent work and the development of effective labour market and social adjustment mechanisms;
- **ensure joint analysis, programming and delivery** between EU partners. The joint analysis of trade-related needs must be undertaken by using the Integrated Framework instrument in the LDCs and by developing similar processes in other countries. The EU could then better coordinate its response strategies in countries and regions. The opportunities for joint delivery depend in particular on progress in working through sector-wide approaches (SWAPs) in the field of Aid for Trade. In particular, the SWAPs are to

permit the development of joint delivery methods, such as budget support and co-financing between EU partners;

- **aim for aid effectiveness in regional Aid for Trade**, and in particular supporting regional partners' capacity to own and lead Aid for Trade efforts, coordinating the programme in support of regional and trade integration, streamlining the methods of delivery and enhancing cooperation with non-EU donors. In particular, the EU strategy must give priority to regional interventions in the EPA context.

Implementing effective monitoring and reporting of aid

To make progress in all these areas, monitoring and reporting are essential, both at international and EU levels. In particular, global monitoring and reporting must include the quantitative dimension of Aid for Trade and the qualitative dimension (associated with the effectiveness of the aid). At EU level, the Commission recommends that progress in implementing the EU Aid for Trade strategy should be assessed yearly by the Council.

Finally, the three groups of measures mentioned above must be accompanied by building human capacity in donor organisations. On this subject, the Commission recommends taking stock of the EU's existing capacity and expertise and of joint European initiatives to develop and share expertise.

Background

This Communication is the Commission's contribution to further expanding EU support for Aid for Trade with a view to adoption of a joint EU strategy by the Council (see Related Acts). It belongs to a package of measures adopted by the Commission to monitor the honouring of the development policy commitments entered into by the EU (see Related Acts).

Key terms of the act

Integrated Framework: multi-donor programme introduced to support LDCs in increasing their participation in the global economy. Its objective is to support LDCs in mainstreaming trade into their national development plans and to assist in a coordinated delivery of trade-related assistance in response to needs identified by the LDCs.

SCHEME OF PREFERENCES FROM 2006 TO 2015 - GUIDELINES

The purpose of the generalised system of preferences (GSP) is to help developing countries to reduce poverty by using tariff preferences to help them obtain international trade revenue. In the Communication the Commission sets out the principles that should underpin regulations between 2006 and 2015 in order to achieve this objective. It proposes improving the current system (GSP for the period 2002-2005) in several areas by simplifying the GSP (reducing the five arrangements currently in place to three), targeting the system on the developing countries that need it most, encouraging regional cooperation and increasing the additional preferences granted for sustainable development, good governance etc.

ACT

Communication of 7 July 2004 from the Commission to the Council, the European Parliament and the European Economic and Social Committee on "Developing countries, international trade and sustainable development: the function of the Community's generalised system of preferences (GSP) for the ten-year period from 2006 to 2015" [COM(2004) 461 final - Official Journal C 242 of 29.9.2004]

SUMMARY

In this Communication the European Commission proposes guidelines for the generalised system of preferences for the period 2006-2015, based on experience of earlier systems. It advocates:

Maintaining generous tariff rates
There are a number of ways of maintaining and even improving the tariff preferences. Among other things the Commission proposes extending the GSP to some products not covered by the current system, under which almost one tenth of taxable products in the Customs Tariff are not covered.Some products classed as sensitive could also be transferred to the category of non-sensitive products.

Preferential margins (currently 3.5% for sensitive products and 100% for non-sensitive products) will be maintained and, where possible, increased.

The enlargement of the European Union (EU) by ten new Member States on 1 May 2004 has helped to improve what the Community can offer since it has expanded the EU market to include a further 75 million potential consumers.

Targeting the GSP on the countries that most need it
The Commission proposes that the GSP should target the countries that need it most, such as the least developed countries (LDCs) and the most vulnerable among the other developing countries (small economies, land-locked countries and low-revenue countries) to help them to play a greater part in international trade.
The GSP should also have a mechanism for gradual withdrawal of a country from the special GSP, the everything-but-arms scheme, which gives duty-free and quota-free access to all products (except arms and munitions) from the fifty poorest countries.

A simpler GSP with easier access
The process of simplification, already started under the present GSP, should be enhanced. The Commission has proposed replacing the five GSP arrangements to three: the general arrangement, the special arrangement for the least developed countries and a new special arrangement (GSP+) to encourage sustainable development and good governance.

Making graduation more transparent and targeting it on the prime beneficiaries
The Commission proposes making graduation (withdrawal from the GSP) more transparent by withdrawing the most competitive product groups of certain beneficiary countries from the GSP. This means that the beneficiaries no longer need the GSP to increase their exports of those products to the EU. The smaller beneficiaries will not be graduated and so can enjoy a greater share of the benefits of the GSP.
The current criteria for graduation (share of preferential imports, development index and export-specialisation index) will be replaced with a single straightforward criterion: share of the Community market, expressed as a share of preferential imports.

Devising a new incentive to encourage sustainable development and governance
As already mentioned, the Commission proposes introducing a new incentive for sustainable development and good management of public affairs by replacing the separate "drugs", "social" and "environment" special arrangements with a single new category: GSP+.
GSP+ will provide special incentives for countries which have signed up to the main international agreements on social rights, environmental protection, governance and combating the production of and trafficking in illegal drugs.

The Commission will take account of the evaluations by the international organisations responsible for each international agreement concerned before deciding which of the applicant countries will be selected to benefit from the GSP+. This scheme will include a credible suspension clause that can be rapidly activated where a country fails to meet its commitments under the agreements.

Improving the rules of origin
The Commission proposes improving the rules of origin by changing their form (simplifying them), their substance (adjusting the origin criteria and cumulation rules) and their procedures (formalities and controls).

The new rules of origin should also be flexible in order to encourage development. One of the objectives must be to facilitate acquisition of origin to optimise the benefits of preferences. The system could, for example, be improved by regional cumulation, promoting regional cooperation among beneficiary countries. The Commission attaches particular importance to regional integration for southern countries as a route to greater involvement of the southern countries in international trade.

Restoring the temporary withdrawal instruments, safeguard measures and anti-fraud measures

The Commission proposes redefining the GSP temporary withdrawal arrangements and the safeguard clause to take account of the new graduation focused on the most competitive beneficiary countries.

Even though they will still be for use in exceptional circumstances only, those arrangements must be made more credible, which will involve simplifying them and making the way they are used more flexible, particularly in cases of unfair trade practices. It is also essential that the Commission and Member States responsible for applying the GSP should apply these rules unwaveringly where fraud is detected.

As the beneficiary countries also have GSP management responsibilities, the Commission calls on them to establish effective and appropriate management structures to guarantee the validity of certificates or origin.

Background

The generalised system of preferences allows manufactured products and some agricultural products exported by developing countries access to the Community market with total or partial exemption from customs duties.
It is thus an instrument of both the European Community's trade policy and its development policy. As it is a cooperation instrument it is a provisional mechanism, the benefits of which are to be withdrawn from countries that no longer need it.

The EU absorbs one fifth of developing countries' exports. 40% of EU imports come from the developing countries. The EU is also the world's biggest importer of agricultural products from developing countries, importing more than the United States, Canada and Japan put together. Half the preferential imports under this system in 2002 were exempt from customs duties and reduced duties were applied to the other half.

RELATED ACTS

Communication from the Commission to the Council, the European Parliament and the European Economic and Social Committee - The rules of origin in preferential trade arrangements - Orientations for the future [COM(2005) 100 final - Not published in the Official Journal]
This communication follows the consultation launched by the Commission Green Paper on the future of rules of origin in preferential trade arrangements. It shows that the preferential rules of

origin need to be reviewed. The review is also important because of the goal of integrating developing countries into the world economy. The review should also be accompanied by an adjustment of the procedures for their management and control.
The Commission is proposing actions in three areas:

- a revision of the conditions for a product to be considered as originating in a country;
- a change in the customs procedures necessary for the proper implementation and the control of the use of the preferences by the economic operators;
- the development of instruments ensuring that the beneficiary countries comply with their obligations.

Council Regulation (EC) No 980/2005 of 27 June 2005 applying a scheme of generalised tariff preferences [Official Journal L 169 of 30.06.2005]
This Regulation sets out the Community scheme of generalised tariff preferences which applicable from 1 January 2006 until 31 December 2008. It simplifies the preferential import arrangements for products originating in developing countries, thereby streamlining the preferential scheme and reconciling trade and development objectives.

ASSISTING DEVELOPING COUNTRIES TO BENEFIT FROM TRADE

The European Union defines practical steps to improve the integration of trade into development strategies so that it contributes to the fundamental objectives of poverty reduction and sustainable development.

ACT

Communication from the Commission to the Council and the European Parliament, "Trade and development: assisting developing countries to benefit from trade" [COM(2002) 513 final - Not published in the Official Journal].

SUMMARY

STEPPING UP DIALOGUE WITH PARTNER COUNTRIES
Trade reform in poverty reduction strategies
The European Union is committed to placing greater emphasis on trade issues in its political dialogue with the developing countries to improve the integration of trade policies into poverty reduction strategies. Trade policy must be integrated in such a way that it contributes to the fundamental objectives of poverty reduction and sustainable development. It should foster equitable growth, promote human development, and ensure the proper management of natural resources and the protection of the environment.

Adapting trade-related assistance to each country's specific conditions
To that end, the Commission must ensure that the financing of trade-related assistance, which is one of the six priority areas for development policy laid down in 2000, is adapted to needs, particularly for least developed countries. Assistance should ideally be adapted in the light of a national dialogue involving government, the private sector and representatives from labour and civil society.

ENHANCED EFFECTIVENESS OF EU SUPPORT
Political dialogue is translated into practical assistance by country and regional strategy papers. Trade issues and their linkages with other policies important for sustainable development need to be addressed at each stage of the preparation of strategy papers.

The Commission also proposes reinforcing, where appropriate and in consultation with the partner country/region, the trade component when programming EU development assistance. This will be done by including:

- **Support for macroeconomic and fiscal reforms:** Support to enhance trade capacity should also aim for sound macro-economic and tax policies, to achieve a policy mix that is conducive to improved trading conditions and economic and financial stability.
- **Support for the restructuring and competitiveness of production:** In order to support the repositioning process and increase the competitiveness of the private sector in developing countries, a variety of private-sector facilities have been set up at both national and regional levels. Strengthening support services and improving infrastructure has been another core area of EU support.
- **Support for the restructuring and competitiveness of production:** Regional integration is supported in the framework of the development strategy. This is the South-South-North approach. Under this approach, the EU is negotiating agreements with regional groupings. It is doing so in South America, with the Mercosur countries, in the Mediterranean, and in South-East Asia. But this approach applies in particular to the economic partnership agreements between the African, Caribbean and Pacific states (ACP) and the EU, for which negotiations started in September 2002.
- **Support for genuine participation in the multilateral trading system:** EU assistance in this area is mainly oriented towards assistance for accession to the World Trade Organisation (WTO) and multilateral trade negotiations, support for the implementation of existing and future WTO agreements requiring major financial input, and support for the policy reforms and investment necessary to enhance economic efficiency and ensure greater participation in the world economy. This last area notably includes reform of customs administrations, standards and conformity assessment, services, investment, intellectual property rights, competition policy, the adoption of legislation for appropriate labour standards, and environmental standards.

The Commission is also examining the scope for funding trade-related assistance initiatives that benefit all developing countries, especially in collaboration with multilateral agencies. At present, practically all EU development assistance is provided on a country/region basis. Yet this is an area in which it is very important to support multilateral initiatives in collaboration with international organisations, without confining them to specific countries or regions.

CONTRIBUTION TO THE EFFECTIVENESS OF INTERNATIONAL ACTION

It is important to make the most of the linkages between trade and all other areas important for sustainable development, and to ensure the consistency between the various EU policies with an external dimension.

There is a need to review existing mechanisms to improve coordination with Member States and to promote a greater exchange of "best practices" between the Commission and Member States and between Member States themselves.

Closer cooperation with international organisations with specific expertise in trade and trade-related matters is also encouraged.

The EU should also encourage regional development banks (such as the African Development Bank, the Asian Development Bank and the Interamerican Development Bank) to devote additional resources to capacity-building programmes in the sphere of trade.
The communication encourages the EU to support the WTO Secretariat in matters of technical assistance, and to continue contributing to the Trust Fund for the Doha Development Agenda.

FAIR TRADE

This Communication aims to launch the process for the development of the Community's position on fair trade.

ACT

Communication from the Commission to the Council of 29 November 1999 on 'fair trade' [COM(1999) 619 final - Not published in the Official Journal].

SUMMARY

Background

The promotion of fair trade comes under the framework of the Community's broader objectives in relation to development cooperation, in other words the fight against poverty, economic and social development and, in particular, the gradual integration of developing countries into the world economy.

Trade has a fundamental role to play in the creation of wealth and thus development. This communication is a first stage in the development of the Community's position on this matter.

Definition of fair trade

The concept of fair trade applies in general to trade operations which strengthen the economic position of small-scale producers and landowners in order to ensure that they are not marginalised in the world economy. It mainly relates to developing countries and, under the present communication, covers two main aspects:

- ensuring that producers, including employees, receive a share of the total profit commensurate with their input;
- improving social conditions, particularly those of employees in the absence of developed structures for social services and worker representation (trade union representation for instance), etc.;

This concept has long-term development in mind. Participation in initiatives on fair trade is voluntary for both sellers and consumers.

It is important to note that the concept of 'fair trade' is not the same as that of 'ethical trade'. 'Ethical trade' usually relates to the operating methods of companies present in the country (codes of conduct, for example).

Fair trade in practice

Fair trade goods are always made available to consumers through private initiatives. The practical implementation of fair trade has changed considerably over the years.

The traditional fair trade movement

The concept was originally developed by non-governmental organisations (NGOs). The philosophy is based upon precise principles and was originally applied by alternative trading organisations often started by churches, charities, etc. The organisations are involved in every stage (sourcing, production, etc.) and the profits are often devoted to development causes. The products are not always labelled.

Labelling initiatives

Since the end of the 1980s, normal commercial companies (supermarkets, etc.) have been more likely to be involved in fair trade initiatives and the products are marketed according to the usual rules.

In this regard, systems for labelling products were introduced in order to ensure their authenticity. There are several fair trade labels ('Fairtrade Mark', etc.) and each has a certification agency which verifies all the stages in the production process to ensure that the product respects fair trade principles. The certification bodies also set the criteria that must be respected in order for a product to carry a fair trade label. These criteria are harmonised at international level. All the labels are members of the FLO (Fair Trade Labelling Organisations International) which is responsible for coordination at EU and international level.

Producers and importers who have been assessed as complying with the fair trade criteria are included in international fair trade registers. Fair trade labelling schemes are financed by licence fees paid by importers and traders. These fees are related to turnover and volume of sales.

European Union and fair trade

Fair trade accounts for a relatively substantial proportion of consumption in Europe. In 1997, the turnover in the EU of fair trade products was estimated to be in the region of EUR 200 to 250 million. Overall, 11% of the EU population buy fair trade products and surveys show that there is high demand for such products.

The EU has already implemented initiatives concerning fair trade, including European Parliament resolutions and financing of NGOs, labelling bodies and projects in developing countries. With regard to legislation, the Union implements these principles through various instruments, particularly measures concerning the EU's generalised system of preferences. Some of these regulations on fair trade benefit fair trade goods by facilitating their access to the Community market.

International community

The international community has recognised the important role played by fair trade in the development of poorer countries. The World Trade Organisation (WTO) has concluded that initiatives in this field do not represent an obstacle to the liberalisation of markets since they do not impose import restrictions or other forms of protectionism. They are thus in line with the general principles of the world economy.

Issues

The Commission identifies certain problems that should be addressed in order to ensure the continued success of fair trade initiatives. This involves ensuring greater consistency between the policies of the actors at various levels and establishing a legal definition of the concept as well as the criteria involved. Efforts should also be made to improve the substantiation, verification and control of fair trade products so as to allow consumers to make properly informed choices. In addition, consumers must be better informed about fair trade and dialogue should be continued with the movement, through the creation of a formal platform for example.

AGRICULTURAL COMMODITIES, DEPENDENCE AND POVERTY

The Commission has drawn up an action plan to help developing countries dependent on commodities such as coffee, sugar, cotton and cocoa, and the producers of those commodities. It sets two overall objectives: raising the earnings of producers of traditional and other commodities and reducing the vulnerability of earnings at both producer and macroeconomic levels.

ACT

Communication of 12 February 2004 from the Commission to the Council and the European Parliament: Agricultural commodity chains, dependence and poverty - a proposal for an EU Action Plan [COM(2004) 89 final - Not published in the Official Journal].

SUMMARY

The Communication establishes policy priorities for addressing the six main challenges facing commodity dependent developing countries (CDDCs):

- treating commodity chains and dependence as priority issues in combating poverty;
- remedying the long-term decline in prices;
- managing commodity risks and providing access to financing;
- diversifying production to include non-traditional commodities;
- promoting integration in the international trading system;
- encouraging the use of viable business and investment practices in the CDDCs.

The Communication focuses on agricultural (not mineral) commodities traded and marketed internationally, since these products are directly linked to poverty.
It does not cover timber as the Commission has already drawn up a strategy and provided a specific budget line for this product. The Commission has also implemented an action plan to combat illegal logging.

Treating commodity chains and dependence as priority issues in combating poverty
Commodity chains have a major impact on the poorest sections of the population and should be treated as a priority in development strategies and combating poverty.
To this end, the Commission proposes:

- helping the CDDCs develop national commodity strategies as part of the fight against poverty;
- enhancing the strategies developed in international commodity bodies for each commodity category.

Remedying the long-term decline in prices
As demand for commodities has been outstripped by the increase in supply on the world market, there has been a long-term decline in commodity prices.
To address this problem, the Commission proposes:

- encouraging implementation of commodity chain strategies in the CDDCs, particularly in terms of improving capacity and support services at producer level, establishing basic infrastructure in production regions and pursuing policy reforms at macroeconomic level;
- setting up support services at regional level to promote regional cooperation among farmers' networks, regulatory bodies, research institutions, the services responsible for infrastructure, etc.;
- supporting regional integration by concluding economic partnership agreements with the African, Caribbean and Pacific (ACP) countries.

Managing commodity risks and providing access to financing
There is high price volatility on the agricultural commodities markets, and this creates uncertainty and affects the willingness and capacity of farmers to invest.
To address this phenomenon the Commission proposes:

- improving producer access to commodity risk insurance and trade finance;
- encouraging the development of shock management tools for the macroeconomic level;
- improving the CDDCs' access to the Flex compensatory mechanism. Flex is an EU instrument that allows the countries concerned to compensate for sudden declines in export earnings.

Support for diversification
Expanding the markets for both inputs and output products would reduce investment risks. To achieve this the Commission proposes:

- offering CDDC governments technical assistance with policy choices concerning diversification;
- providing more support for implementation of diversification and growth strategies;
- supporting the preparation and implementation of a growth-focused strategy allowing products traded at national level to be developed; such a strategy would include abandoning unprofitable commodities;
- increasing aid to the private sector, drawing on the available instruments for private sector development in non-traditional sectors.

Promoting integration in the international trading system
International trade rules are important for the CDDCs and commodity producers. Rules on domestic support, export competition and market access all shape commodity producers' opportunities, as do measures and standards and other technical regulations.

The Commission therefore proposes:

- working to achieve a substantial and development-friendly outcome from the current negotiations under the Doha Development Agenda;
- pursuing reform of its agricultural polices so as to reduce trade distortions as much as possible and monitoring the impact of national aid policies;
- facilitating CDDC access to the EU market, in particular by revising the generalised preference system;
- supporting CDDC efforts to profit from their market access, in particular by enhancing helpdesk services.

Encouraging the use of viable business and investment practices in the CDDCs.
The international commodity companies and retailers play a central role in framing the future of the commodity sectors since local entrepreneurs are often unable to compete effectively with these large consolidated corporations whilst remaining independent. Their dependence on the corporate policies of multinational enterprises means that they need to improve their social and environmental practice.

The Commission therefore proposes:

- fostering social responsibility at international level by promoting the application of viable codes of conduct, supporting the pooling of experience and studying criteria for the establishment of voluntary fair and ethical trading schemes at Community level;
- supporting CDDCs' efforts to benefit from companies' social responsibility and setting up public-private partnerships in some countries to evaluate the experience gained;
- promoting competition by drawing up common guidelines within the WTO, in particular in the context of regional cooperation.

Background
The prices of some important agricultural commodities (for example, sugar, cotton, coffee and cocoa) fell by 30 to 60% between 1970 and 2000. This has led to macroeconomic imbalances in the developing countries concerned, reducing export earnings, debt repayment capacity, imports, credit availability, government revenue and the provision of basic services (health care and education).

There are about fifty highly commodity dependent developing countries (with export revenues based on a maximum of three commodities). They are located mainly in Sub-Saharan Africa, but also in the Caribbean and Central America. They are mainly least developed countries (LDCs), landlocked countries or islands.

Many of these countries are caught in a trap of declining income and investment, stagnating competitiveness, endemic poverty and dependence. A lack of resources means that their commodities sectors are finding it ever harder to take on international competition, handle change and deal with the situation facing them.

RELATED ACTS

Commission communication of 12 February 2004 to the Council and Parliament: Proposal for an EU-Africa partnership in support of cotton-sector development [COM(2004) 87 final - Not published in the Official Journal].

Concerned about the crisis in the cotton sector in African ACP countries - as highlighted at the WTO ministerial conference in Cancún - the Commission proposes, as part of its action plan for agricultural commodities, a partnership in the cotton sector centred on two series of measures. The first set of measures is designed to achieve more equitable commercial conditions on international cotton markets by giving priority to market access, the reduction of internal support, support for exports and trade-related technical assistance. The second concerns support for African regions and countries producing cotton, and comprise measures intended to consolidate the competitiveness of the African cotton sector, help the regions dependent on this product to diversify, and mitigate the effects of price volatility. The Commission stresses the importance of dialogue with the African countries concerned and identifies the financial instruments that can be used to support this partnership.

THE INTERNATIONAL COFFEE AGREEMENT 2007

The European Community is a member of the International Coffee Organization and a signatory to the International Coffee Agreement 2007 aiming to encourage the sustainable development of the coffee sector worldwide in economic, social and environmental terms.

ACTS

Council Decision 2008/579/EC of 16 June 2008 on the signing and conclusion on behalf of the European Community of the International Coffee Agreement 2007 [Official Journal L 186 of 15.7.2008].

SUMMARY

The European Community is a member of the International Coffee Organization (ICO) as an international institution along with 31 importing countries and 45 exporting countries. Signed by the 77 members of the ICO, the International Coffee Agreement 2007 aims to enhance and promote the sustainable development of the worldwide coffee sector through the following measures:

- promoting international cooperation on coffee matters;
- providing a forum for consultation among governments and with the private sector;
- encouraging signatories to develop a sustainable coffee sector in economic, social and environmental terms;
- seeking a balance between supply and demand and fair pricing for both consumers and producers;
- facilitating the expansion and transparency of international coffee trade and promoting the elimination of trade barriers;
- collecting, disseminating and publishing economic, technical and scientific information, statistics and studies on coffee-related issues;
- promoting the development of consumption and markets for all types of coffee, including in coffee-producing countries;
- developing and seeking finance for projects that benefit the world coffee economy;
- promoting coffee quality with a view to enhancing customer satisfaction and benefits to producers;
- supporting the development of food safety procedures in the sector;
- supporting the development of strategies to enhance the capacity of small-scale farmers to benefit from coffee production, which can contribute to poverty alleviation;
- facilitating the availability of information on financial tools and services that can assist producers.

In this context, the agreement stipulates that Members must try to limit tariff-related and regulatory barriers to coffee consumption such as preferential tariffs, quotas, government monopolies and subsidies. They must also give due consideration to the sustainable management of coffee resources, in accordance with the principles and objectives on sustainable development contained in Agenda 21, and the improvement of the standard of living and working conditions of populations engaged in the coffee sector.

The agreement also requires that each exporting Member implement the system of Certificates of Origin established by the ICC to facilitate the collection of statistics on the international coffee trade, and furnish to the ICC any information it judges necessary relating to production, imports, exports, consumption and prices.

Matters governed by the agreement fall within the exclusive competence of the European Community under the common commercial policy.

Context

The International Coffee Agreement 2007 is the seventh agreement of its kind to be signed since 1962 by members of the International Coffee Organization. A previous agreement was signed in 2001. The agreement remains in force for a period of 10 years unless it is extended or terminated before it expires.

GLOBAL PARTNERSHIP FOR SUSTAINABLE DEVELOPMENT

This communication highlights how the European Union contributes to global sustainable development and the action aimed at establishing a global deal for sustainable development.

ACT

Communication from the Commission to the European Parliament, the Council, the Economic and Social Committee and the Committee of the Regions, of 21 February 2002, entitled: "Towards a global partnership for sustainable development" [COM(2002) 82 final - Not published in Official Journal].

SUMMARY

The European Union (EU) established a strategy for sustainable development in May 2001. In endorsing this strategy, the Göteborg European Council recognised that the external dimension needed to be further developed. It also called on the Commission to consider the Union's contribution to global sustainable development. This communication responds to this request and contributes to developing the EU's position in relation to the World Summit on sustainable development, which was held in Johannesburg in 2002.

The communication takes as its starting point the idea that globalisation acts as a powerful force for sustaining global growth and providing ways of dealing with international problems such as health, education and the environment. However, left to develop unchecked, market forces cause and exacerbate inequality and exclusion and can cause irreparable damage to the environment. Globalisation must therefore go hand in hand with measures designed to prevent or mitigate these effects. In the crucial spheres of trade, development financing, environmental management and combating poverty and crime, it is essential that efforts be made to draw up joint rules which are implemented and monitored effectively. It is also necessary to improve global governance, i.e. to promote more efficient management of interdependence.

The communication presents a series of actions to contribute to global sustainable development. They complement the May 2001 strategy for sustainable development and cover economic, social, environmental and financial aspects, as well as coherence of Community policies and governance at all levels.

Harnessing globalisation: trade for sustainable development
To ensure that globalisation contributes to sustainable development, the specific economic activities set out by the Commission are as follows:

- within the framework of the World Trade Organisation (WTO), to improve the integration of developing countries into the world economy;
- to help developing countries benefit from the global trading system;
- to change the generalised system of preferences (GSP) to take account of sustainable development;
- to include sustainable development in the bilateral and regional agreements;
- to reduce the non-transparent use of the international financial system and to regulate it more efficiently;
- to encourage European businesses to be socially responsible;
- to promote cooperation between the WTO and international environmental organisations.

Fighting poverty and promoting social development
The aim is to reduce extreme poverty in the world by 2015 (people who live on $ 1 a day or less). Consequently, the quality, quantity, impact and sustainability of development cooperation must be increased. The activities to be carried out in this field are as follows:

- to focus EU development policy on poverty reduction;
- to ensure that EU policies contribute to combating hunger;
- to integrate water distribution and treatment policies with health and education policies;
- to mainstream the gender perspective in EU policies;
- to invest more in the fields of health, education, training and communicable diseases;
- to promote research relating to sustainable development.

Sustainable management of natural and environmental resources

The objective in this field is to reverse the trend of the loss of environmental resources by 2015 as well as to develop intermediate objectives in the sectors of water, land and soil, energy and biodiversity. The specific activities set out are as follows:

- at the Johannesburg World Summit, to launch an initiative to promote sustainable water resource management;
- to launch an initiative on cooperation in the field of energy and development;
- to promote the application of international environmental agreements;
- to partially replenish the Global Environment Facility;
- to draw up an action plan to combat illegal logging;
- to invest in sustainable modes of transport;
- to promote sustainable fishing;
- to deal with the prevention of natural disasters;
- to extend the Global Monitoring for Environment and Security (GMES) system to developing countries.

Improving the coherence of European Union policies
The aim is to integrate sustainable development into all EU policies. The activities to be implemented are as follows:

- to establish a system to assess the economic, social and environmental impact of all major policy proposals of the Union;
- to continue the process of adapting policies to the objectives of sustainable development;
- to sign the United Nations Protocol on the Illicit Manufacturing and Trafficking of Firearms;
- to combat the negative effects of emigration.

Better governance at all levels
This area deals with strengthening the participation of civil society, and the legitimacy, coherence and effectiveness of global economic, social and environmental governance. The communication proposes the following specific action:

- strengthening public institutions and civil society in developing countries;
- stepping up the fight against corruption;
- ensuring that core labour standards are respected;
- at the Johannesburg Summit, encouraging the adoption of decisions which improve global governance;
- stepping up the fight against discrimination against women.

Financing sustainable development
The objectives are those of the Millennium Declaration, namely: to eradicate poverty and hunger; to achieve universal primary education; to promote gender equality; to reduce child mortality; to improve women's health; to combat communicable diseases; to promote sustainable development; and to develop a global partnership. The suggested actions are:

- to make progress towards achieving the target of allocating official development assistance of 0.7% of GNI (gross national income) and achieving the intermediate target of at least 0.33% of GNI for all countries of the European Union from 2006;
- to reduce the debt of the heavily indebted poor countries;
- to take part in the debate on the possibility of States offering global public goods.

RELATED ACTS

Joint declaration by the Council and the representatives of the governments of the Member States meeting within the Council, the European Parliament and the Commission on the development policy of the European Union, entitled The European Consensus**[Official Journal C 46/01 of 24 February 2006].**
In this declaration, the European Union reaffirms that the objective of its development policy is to reduce poverty worldwide in the context of sustainable development.

INTEGRATION OF THE ENVIRONMENTAL DIMENSION IN DEVELOPING COUNTRIES

The European Union lays down the procedure for allocating Community economic and technical aid to promote the full integration of the environmental dimension in cooperation projects between the Community and developing countries (DCs). As of 1 January 2007 those rules have been replaced by the Regulation establishing a financing instrument for development cooperation.

ACT

Regulation (EC) No 2493/2000 of the European Parliament and of the Council of 7 November 2000 on measures to promote the full integration of the environmental dimension in the development process of developing countries.

SUMMARY

1. Because of the direct impact they have on economic development, the depletion of natural resources and the impairment of the environment may thwart efforts to alleviate poverty in developing countries.

2. This has been recognised in several agreements concluded, with the Community's participation, in the framework of the United Nations (Framework Convention on climate change, Convention on biological diversity, etc.) and the OECD (Shaping the 21st century strategy).

3. The Regulation lays down the rules under which cooperation projects initiated by various players (governments, public bodies, regional authorities, traditional or local communities, cooperatives, international organisations, non-governmental organisations and private stakeholders) in developing countries and intended to promote sustainable development may receive financial aid and technical assistance from the Community.

4. Activities eligible for aid and assistance address, in particular:

- global environmental issues (climate change, desertification, biological diversity, etc.);
- transboundary issues (air, water and soil pollution);
- the environmental impact of the integration of developing countries into the world economy and of their macroeconomic and sectoral policies;
- the inclusion in development cooperation projects of environmental considerations for evaluating the sustainable management of such activities;
- conservation of biological diversity, sustainable management and use of natural resources, and fair and equitable sharing of the benefits drawn from these resources;
- issues relating to fishing and the management of coastal zones, estuaries and wetlands;
- desertification;
- urban environment problems (waste, noise and air pollution, water quality, etc.);
- sustainable production and use of energy;
- sustainable production and use of chemical products;

- environmental problems related to industrial activities;
- sustainable patterns of production and consumption.

5. They may take the following forms:

- pilot projects in the field;
- schemes to build up the institutional and operational capacities of actors in the development process (governments, civil society, NGOs, etc.);
- drawing up of policies, plans, strategies and programmes for sustainable development;
- formulation of guidelines, operating manuals and instruments aimed at promoting sustainable development (databases on the Internet);
- support for the development and application of environment assessment tools;
- inventory, accounting and statistical work to improve the quality of environmental data;
- making local populations and key actors in the development process aware of sustainable development issues;
- promotion of trade in environment-friendly products;
- support for multilateral processes.

6. In selecting activities eligible for support, particular attention is given to the following criteria:

- linkage with the overall objective of eradicating poverty;
- local initiatives involving innovative measures;
- active involvement of indigenous communities;
- the specific role and contribution of women in the sustainable management and use of natural resources;
- consistency with other development cooperation programmes;
- strengthening of regional cooperation on sustainable development;
- internalisation of environmental costs.

7. For each cooperation activity, the Community requires a contribution from the actors concerned according to their means. Community financial support is provided in the form of non-refundable aid. Such funding may cover technical assistance, studies, training, supplies, minor works, missions and small grant funds.

8. The Regulation emphasises that participation in invitations to tender and the award of contracts is open to all persons and all companies of the Member States and of the recipient country on equal terms. It may also be extended to other developing countries and, in exceptional cases, to other third countries. A guide setting out the criteria applicable in the selection of projects will be published and provided to interested parties.

9. The Commission is responsible for decisions and management relating to projects undertaken pursuant to the Regulation and will take all necessary coordination measures. It reports to the European Parliament every two years on strategic guidelines and priorities for the years ahead. It must also submit an annual report to Parliament and the Council summarising the activities financed during that year and evaluating the implementation of the Regulation. The Commission must regularly inform the Member States of the activities that have been approved, stating their cost and nature, the country concerned and the cooperation partners.

10. In the case of projects involving financing of EUR 2.5 million or more, the Commission is assisted in its management tasks and its decision-making by the geographically determined committee responsible for development.

11. The budget for applying the Regulation over the period 2000-2006 is EUR 93 million.

12. As of 1 January 2007 the Regulation has been repealed and replaced by the Regulation establishing a financing instrument for development cooperation (see "Related acts" below).

BACKGROUND

13. In Council Regulation (EC) No 722/97 on environmental measures in developing countries in the context of sustainable development [Official Journal L 108, 25.4.1997], the Council lays down a framework for Community aid to help developing countries integrate the environmental dimension into their development process. As Regulation (EC) No 722/1997 ceased to apply on 31 December 1999, the purpose of Regulation (EC) No 1905/2006 is to continue the Community action on the basis of experience acquired during the implementation of the former Regulation.

REFERENCES

Act	Entry into force - Date of expiry	Deadline for transposition in the Member States	Official Journal
Regulation (EC) No 2493/2000	18.11.2000	-	OJ L 288, 15.11.2000

RELATED ACTS

Regulation (EC) No 1905/2006 of the European Parliament and of the Council of 18 December 2006 establishing a financing instrument for development cooperation [Official Journal L 378, 27.12.2006].

In the context of the 2007-2013 financial perspective, this Regulation establishes a financing instrument for development cooperation providing direct support for the Community's policy in this field. The policy is aimed at achieving the objectives of poverty reduction, sustainable economic and social development and the smooth and gradual integration of developing countries into the world economy. The Regulation repeals and replaces Regulation (EC) No 2493/2000 as of 1 January 2007.

Council Conclusions of 31 May 2001: Strategy for the integration of environmental considerations into development policy to promote sustainable development.
In this strategy, the Council underlines the importance of integrating environmental considerations into all Community initiatives in the field of development cooperation. Priority should be given to:

- enhanced policy dialogue with partner countries on environmental issues;
- systematically incorporating environmental considerations into the preparation of all strategic plans and programmes for EC development cooperation;
- mainstreaming environmental considerations into the six priority themes for EC development cooperation, namely trade and development, regional cooperation, poverty reduction, transport, food security and institutional capacity building;
- monitoring the progress made.

PROMOTING CORPORATE SOCIAL RESPONSIBILITY

The Communication proposes to promote corporate social responsibility (CSR) in the European Union and globally. As part of the mid-term review of the Lisbon Strategy and the Sustainable Development Strategy, it traces the development of CSR in the European Union (EU) and sends a message to businesses to play a part in the partnership for growth and jobs. It gives its political support to the creation of a European Alliance on CSR. It also sets priorities with regard to CSR and announces a series of measures to achieve them, including cooperation with Member States, support for multi-stakeholder initiatives, research, SMEs and global action.

ACT

Communication from the Commission of 22 March 2006 to the European Parliament, the Council and the European Economic and Social Committee - Implementing the partnership for growth and jobs: making Europe a pole of excellence on corporate social responsibility [COM(2006) 136 final - Not published in the Official Journal].

SUMMARY

Corporate social responsibility * is part of the debate on globalisation and sustainable development. The Commission regards CSR as an aspect of the European social model and a means of defending solidarity, cohesion and equal opportunities against a backdrop of increasing global competition. CSR is also a way of addressing population ageing and can help to achieve a high quality of life in a healthy environment. The importance attached to CSR is reflected in the many related instruments and meetings:

- in March 2000, the Lisbon European Council appealed to companies' sense of social responsibility;
- in 2001, the Commission published a Green Paper promoting a European framework for CSR;
- in 2002, a Communication proposed a Community strategy promoting CSR;
- the European Parliament made valuable contributions to the debate in its resolutions of 2002 and 2003
- an opinion of the European Parliament is in the process of being adopted;
- the European Economic and Social Committee (EESC) has adopted several opinions on CSR. An opinion was adopted in December 2006;
- the European Multistakeholder Forum on CSR was set up in 2002 and submitted its final report in 2004. Businesses and stakeholders reached consensus on the need for further awareness-raising and competency-building activities in relation to CSR. There was no consensus, however, on topics such as company reporting requirements or the need for European standards on CSR. The Commission continued to attach great importance to dialogue with and among stakeholders and undertook to hold regular review meetings of the Multistakeholder Forum;
- the Commission convened the Forum two years later, on 7 December 2006, including the Member States and academic institutions;
- the Lisbon Strategy's new partnership for growth and jobs invited businesses to step up their commitment to CSR, including cooperation with other stakeholders;
- in the Social Agenda, the Commission announced that it would improve the transparency of CSR;
- in its contribution to the Spring European Council of March 2005, the Commission recognised that CSR could contribute to sustainable development while enhancing Europe's innovative potential and competitiveness. In return for the efforts made by the business community, the European Council stressed the importance for the EU of completing its internal market and making its legislation more business-friendly;
- in the Integrated Guidelines for Growth and Jobs (2005-2008), the Council recommended that Member States should encourage enterprises to develop their corporate social responsibility;
- the informal Hampton Court meeting in October 2005 proposed innovative solutions to the challenges posed by globalisation;

- the revised Sustainable Development Strategy called on businesses, which it regarded as key partners, to reflect on the medium- and long-term policies needed for sustainability;
- the Commission's 2006 Annual Progress Report on Growth and Jobs identified the promotion of entrepreneurial culture as a priority for Europe.

Uptake of CSR has improved in recent years thanks to social dialogue and European Works Councils. However, trade unions and other external stakeholders, such as investors, consumers and non-governmental organisations (NGOs), could further increase the uptake of CSR by playing a more active role and rewarding responsible business conduct.

Objectives
CSR practices cannot replace public policy, but they can contribute to a number of public policy objectives, such as:

-
- the inclusion of disadvantaged groups in the labour market;
- lifelong learning, which increases employability in the global knowledge economy and helps cope with the ageing of the working population;
- improvements in public health, for example by means of voluntary labelling;
- innovations that address societal and environmental problems, as a result of interaction with external stakeholders;
- reduced levels of pollution and a more rational use of natural resources (adoption of environmental management systems, the Ecolabel scheme and investments in eco-innovation);
- cultivating more favourable attitudes towards entrepreneurship;
- respect for human rights, environmental protection and core labour standards, in developing countries and throughout the world;
- poverty reduction and progress towards the Millennium Development Goals.

Alliance
In order to further encourage the adoption of socially responsible practices in the business community, the Commission is supporting an alliance which will act as an umbrella for CSR initiatives. The new instrument is open to European enterprises of all sizes, on a voluntary basis. There are no formal requirements for enterprises wishing to take part, and it does not imply any new financial obligations for the Commission. The Alliance will involve businesses and stakeholders in achieving the objectives of the renewed Lisbon Strategy and will provide increased support for their efforts through Community policies and instruments. The Commission will encourage participating enterprises to publicise their efforts in the area of CSR (strategies, initiatives, results, best practice) and will support stakeholders in developing their capacity to evaluate this information from businesses.

Dialogue with stakeholders
Recognising that CSR cannot flourish unless all stakeholders are involved, the Commission plans to hold a wide, inclusive debate on the subject. It proposes to hold regular meetings of the Multistakeholder Forum in order to review progress.

Proposed actions
The Commission will also focus on the following aspects:

-
- raising awareness of CSR and promoting the exchange of best practice in a strengthened partnership that is broader than the alliance, including not only businesses but also all

relevant stakeholders and national and regional authorities (particularly in Member States where CSR is a less well-known concept, as well as in acceding and candidate countries);

- support for multi-stakeholder initiatives, involving social partners and NGOs at sectoral level;
- cooperation with Member States within the Group of High-Level National Representatives on CSR in order to mobilise the range of national and regional instruments available to promote CSR;
- raising consumer awareness of the impact of their choices and providing clearer information (on the supply chain, public health issues, etc.) to help them exercise critical choice;
- interdisciplinary research under the 6th and 7th Research Framework Programmes to gain a greater understanding of CSR's contribution and the factors preventing or encouraging it;
- incorporation of CSR, as a cross-cutting issue, into the curricula of business schools and other education institutions;
- a specific approach to promote CSR among small and medium-sized enterprises (SMEs) through representative bodies, which is essential in order to harness the potential contribution of SMEs. Further research is needed to identify what SMEs already do in this area;
- promoting instruments which propose international benchmarks for CSR, such as the UN Millennium Development Goals, the ILO Tripartite Declaration of Principles the Organisation for Economic Cooperation and Development's Guidelines for multinational enterprises (MNEs), and the UN Global Compact. In bilateral trade negotiations the Commission will address the issues of sustainable development, CSR and respect for the main international principles. In addition, since 1 January 2006 it has had the new Generalised System of Preferences, "GSP Plus", to encourage trade partners to have greater respect and sensitivity in this area. It will discuss how to promote CSR in the framework of the Cotonou Agreement, the New Strategy for Africa and the EU-Africa Business Forum to be held in autumn 2006. It will also follow other relevant international processes, such as the work of the UN Special Representative on Human Rights and Transnational Corporations and Other Business Enterprises, the development of an International Standardisation Organisation (ISO) guidance standard on social responsibility, as well as sectoral initiatives.

Report
One year after the publication of this Communication, following the discussion within the Multistakeholder Forum, the Commission will assess the development of CSR in Europe.

Background
The Communication is a response to the call to promote CSR within the new partnership for growth and jobs and the revised Sustainable Development Strategy. CSR can contribute to innovation and employability, which influence competitiveness and job creation and are key components of sustainable development.

STRATEGY FOR THE CUSTOMS UNION

The Commission defines a new strategy to be adopted for customs activities in the European Union in order to adapt to the present and future changes and to propose concrete actions to be taken.

ACT

Communication from the Commission to the Council, the European Parliament and the Economic and Social Committee of 8 February 2001 concerning a strategy for the Customs Union [COM (2001) 51 final – Not published in the Official Journal]

SUMMARY

This Communication reviews the challenges confronting customs activities at present and in the short term: enlargement of the European Union, the fight against fraud, organised crime, the role of Customs in revenue collection, developments in international trade, the safety of citizens, new trading techniques, influence on the competitiveness of EU businesses and the increasing importance of indirect taxes.

The Communication refers to best practices, cooperation between the structures involved, training of officials and operators, simplification of legislation and investments in infrastructure and equipment as instruments to meet the above-mentioned challenges.
The European Union's strategic objectives in the field of customs for the coming years are:

- to provide a framework based on transparent, stable and appropriate rules for the development of international trade;
- to provide the Community and Member States with the necessary resources;
- to protect society from unfair trading and to safeguard its financial, commercial, health and environmental interests.

The Commission has indicated five areas of action for introducing the new strategy for the Customs Union: simplifying and rationalising legislation, improving customs controls, providing a good service to the business community, improving training and improving international cooperation in the customs field.

Simplifying and rationalising legislation
Amendments to the customs legislation are necessary to confront issues of fraud and to take account of changes in the business world. The Communication proposes the following practical actions:

- to involve economic operators in the preparation of legislation and to assist them with complex legislation;
- to continue the harmonisation of sanctions;
- to ensure that all regulations allow data to be transmitted electronically;
- to improve the implementation of legislation.

Improving customs controls
Several actions are proposed in this field:

- to improve the standards and application of controls;
- to improve cooperation between the customs administrations and between them and the tax authorities, police authorities, etc.
- to use risk analysis more effectively;
- to reinforce the fight against counterfeiting, piracy and false origin marking;
- to introduce a new computerised transit system (NCTS);
- to apply the new information technologies to the customs;
- to develop joint audit modules between the Commission and the Member States.

Providing a good service to the business community
The Communication lists the following actions to improve the service to the business community:

- to simplify and improve procedures;
- to facilitate electronic access to customs information;
- to continue the work on facilitating trade;
- to use memoranda of understanding to strengthen cooperation.

Improving training
Training is obviously necessary for customs officials and economic operators. The Commission is proposing:

- to set up common training modules;
- to complete the feasibility study on the European Customs Academy;
- to direct training towards problem areas and business compliance with the legislation.

Improving international cooperation
In order to improve cooperation between the customs administrations, the Communication emphasises the need:

- to represent the Community appropriately in the international forums dealing with customs issues;
- to promote international cooperation in view of the challenges of enlargement and combating fraud, among other things.

RELATED ACTS

Communication from the Commission to the Council, the European Parliament and the European Economic and Social Committee of 1 April 2008 entitled: "Strategy for the evolution of the Customs Union" [COM(2008) 169 final – Not published in the Official Journal]
The present strategy aims to complete the customs reform. After the modernisation of the customs legal and technological environment, this process is to be applied in the customs administrations, bringing out the human dimension.
Resolution – Official Journal C 171 of 15.6.2001
Council Resolution of 30 May 2001 concerning a strategy for the Customs Union.
Full version of the Council Resolution

Resolution – Official Journal C 247 of 15.10.2003
Council Resolution of 2 October 2003 concerning a strategy for customs cooperation.

CUSTOMS 2013 (2008-2013)

The customs administrations of European Union (EU) Member States play an important role in protecting the interests of the European Community (EC). They also ensure an equal level of protection throughout EC territory for citizens and economic operators within the Community. This Decision establishes the Community action programme Customs 2013 (2008-2013). The programme aims to support the development of a pan-European electronic customs environment which ensures that customs activities match the needs of the internal market, guarantees the protection of the financial interests of the EC and increases safety and security.

ACT

Decision No 624/2007/EC of the European Parliament and of the Council of 23 May 2007 establishing an action programme for customs in the Community (Customs 2013).

SUMMARY

The aim of the Customs 2013 programme is to help customs administrations in participating countries to facilitate legitimate trade and to simplify and speed up customs procedures. The programme will start on 1 January 2008 and end on 31 December 2013.

Objectives

The main objectives of the Customs 2013 programme are:

- supporting the development of a pan-European electronic customs environment which ensures that customs activities match the needs of the internal market, guarantees the protection of the EC's financial interests and increases safety and security;
- contributing to the creation of a modernised customs code;
- increasing cooperation between customs administrations so that they carry out their tasks as effectively as if they were a single administration;
- increasing international customs cooperation between EU customs administrations and third countries customs authorities in the field of supply chain security;
- preparing for enlargement, including the sharing of experience and knowledge with the customs administrations of the countries concerned;
- developing cooperation and exchange of information and best practices with the customs administrations of third countries, in particular candidate countries, potential candidate countries and partner countries of the European Neighbourhood Policy;
- standardising and simplifying customs systems and controls to reduce the administrative burden and the cost of compliance for economic operators;
- identifying, developing and applying best working practices.

Action

Customs 2013 will include activities in the field of communications systems and exchange of information, comparative analyses, seminars and workshops, project groups and steering groups, working visits, training activities and monitoring activities.

Participation in the Programme

The countries participating in the Customs 2013 programme are the EU Member States. The programme is also open to candidate countries benefiting from a pre-accession strategy, potential candidate countries (after the conclusion of framework agreements concerning their participation in Community programmes) and certain partner countries of the European Neighbourhood Policy (provided that a sufficient level of proximity has been attained and in compliance with relevant framework agreements).

Budgetary implications

The Customs 2013 programme will run for a period of six years, in accordance with the Financial Perspectives 2007-13. The amount to be borne by the Community budget is EUR 328.8 million.

BACKGROUND

Customs 2013 continues the activities carried out in the framework of the previous customs programmes, in particular Customs 2007, and supports the increasingly important development of e-customs.

REFERENCES

Act	Entry into force - Date of expiry	Deadline for transposition in the Member States	Official Journal
Decision No 624/2007/EC	4.7.2007	-	OJ L 154 of 14.6.2007

RELATED ACTS

Communication from the Commission to the Council and the European Parliament of 20 July 2005, 'Common actions for growth and employment: The Community Lisbon Programme' [COM(2005) 330 final - Not published in the Official Journal].
The Customs 2013 programme also aims to contribute to the revival of the Lisbon Strategy.
Communication from the Commission to the Council and the European Parliament of 6 April 2005, 'Community programmes "Customs 2013" and "Fiscalis 2013"' [COM(2005) 111 final - Not published in the Official Journal].

Pending its proposal for the future Customs 2013 (2007-2013) programme, the Commission proposes extending the Customs 2007 programme. The Commission believes that the Customs programme contributes to the aim of sustainable economic growth. One of the objectives of the 2013 programme is to ensure the smooth flow of external trade, while applying effective controls on goods. As in previous programmes, activities are intended to contribute to the smooth functioning of the internal market and preparing and ensuring the common implementation of Community customs legislation. In addition, the new programme must respond to new challenges and changes currently taking place, for example with respect to safety (management of external borders and control of the whole international supply chain), the creation of an electronic customs environment and the fight against counterfeiting and piracy.

Decision No 253/2003/EC of the European Parliament and of the Council of 11 February 2003 adopting an action programme for customs in the Community (Customs 2007).
The Customs 2007 programme (2003-2007) is intended to support and complement operations undertaken by the Member States to safeguard the functioning of the internal market in the customs field. This Decision will be repealed with effect from 1 January 2008.

THE CONTRIBUTION OF TAXATION AND CUSTOMS POLICIES TO THE LISBON STRATEGY

The Commission has launched a plan for EU-wide taxation and customs measures that would help the EU to achieve its Lisbon objectives. The co-existence of 25 national taxation systems makes it impossible to take full advantage of the single market. The proposed measures are aimed at reducing the negative effects these co-existing national tax systems can have on market integration

ACT

Communication from the Commission of 25 October 2005 to the Council and the European Parliament - The Contribution of Taxation and Customs Policies to the Lisbon Strategy [COM(2005) 532 final - Not published in the Official Journal].

SUMMARY

In 2005 the Commission proposed to reinvigorate the Lisbon Strategy. This communication describes the measures and initiatives taken by the European Community to reach the Lisbon Strategy's taxation and customs objectives.

These measures are aimed at:

- making the European Union a more attractive place to invest and work;
- boosting growth by increasing and improving knowledge and innovation.

INVESTMENT AND MARKET INTEGRATION
The taxation and customs measures proposed in the communication are aimed at making the EU a more attractive place to invest and work by:

- extending and deepening the internal market;
- ensuring open and competitive markets inside and outside the EU;
- improving European and national legislation.

Extending and deepening the Internal Market
National tax systems have a negative effect on EU market integration. Remaining obstacles should be lifted to take full advantage of the single market. The Commission proposes five categories of measures.
Because different **company taxation systems** co-exist, cross-border activities are treated differently to similar domestic activities. The first measure is to introduce a Common Consolidated Corporate Tax Base for EU businesses (CCCTB), a strategy the Commission has been working towards since 2001.
A second series of measures is aimed at simplifying the **tax environment**. In order to create a level playing field, corporate taxation obstacles have to be removed concerning:
VAT compliance obligations;

- experimental application of the Home State Taxation approach;
- VAT rules concerning international services;
- the VAT rules on financial services;
- the rules governing the exemptions of services in the public interest.

A third series of measures is aimed at removing **cross-border tax barriers** faced by EU businesses. Pending the introduction of the CCCTB, the Commission plans to put in place:

- a system of cross-border loss relief;
- a system to manage transfer pricing;
- measures to abolish a number of indirect taxes, such as capital duty.

The fourth measure is aimed at creating a new **car taxation** strategy to replace Member State registration taxes.
The fifth measure concerns a new policy to combat distortions due to **fraud** and tax evasion.
Open and competitive markets
Pirated and counterfeit products violate the industrial and intellectual property rights of EU businesses. That is why it action to protect intellectual property rights is necessary. In October 2005, the Commission adopted a communication on a customs response to latest trends in counterfeiting and piracy.
To improve customs legislation and promote **eCustoms** the Commission has adopted communications on:

- creating a simpler and paperless environment for customs and trade (eCustoms). This communication is part of the modernisation of the Community Customs Code and the eGovernment programme;

- the role of customs in the integrated management of external borders to simplify administrative formalities.

Improving European and national legislation

The modernisation of VAT rules contained in the 6th VAT Directive is necessary to provide clear rules to traders. A more uniform application of these rules in combination with binding provisions would help to eliminate the current divergences at the Community level. Thus, a more uniform application of the VAT system will help European businesses.

KNOWLEDGE AND INNOVATION

With a view to boosting growth by increasing and improving knowledge and innovation, this communication presents tax and customs measures aimed at:

- favouring investment in research and development (R&D);
- facilitating the sustainable use of resources.

Research and development (R&D)

The Commission proposes to adopt guidelines on R&D tax incentives to increase and improve R&D investment. These guidelines should:

- set out the key EU legal conditions for such tax incentives;
- highlight best practices as regards R&D tax treatment and incentives in some Member States;
- set out the political message and contents of possible future initiatives directed to Member States.

Sustainable use of resources

Indirect taxation can play a significant role in the sustainable use of resources, especially in the fields of energy, transport and the environment. The Directive on the taxation of energy products and taxation of commercial diesel, energy and cars are examples of this.

RELATED ACTS

COMPANY TAXATION

Communication from the Commission to the European Parliament, the Council and the European Economic and Social Committee - Implementing the Community Programme for improved growth and employment and the enhanced competitiveness of EU business: Further Progress during 2006 and next steps towards a proposal on the Common Consolidated Corporate Tax Base (CCCTB) [**COM(2007) 223** final - Not published in the Official Journal].

Communication from the Commission to the Council, the European Parliament and the European Economic and Social Committee - Implementing the Community Lisbon Programme - Progress to date and next steps towards a Common Consolidated Corporate Tax Base (CCCTB) [COM(2006) 157 final - Not published in the Official Journal]]

Communication from the Commission to the Council, the European Parliament and the Economic and Social Committee - Tackling the corporation tax obstacles of small and medium-sized enterprises in the Internal Market - outline of a possible Home State Taxation pilot scheme [...] [COM(2005) 702 final - Not published in the Official Journal]

Communication from the Commission to the Council, the European Parliament and the European Economic and Social Committee of 24 November 2003 - An Internal Market without company tax obstacles: achievements, ongoing initiatives and remaining challenges [COM(2003) 726 final - Not published in the Official Journal]

Communication from the Commission to the Council, the European Parliament and the Economic and Social Committee of 23 October 2001 - Towards an Internal Market without tax obstacles - A strategy for providing companies with a consolidated corporate tax base for their EU-wide activities [COM(2001) 582 final - Not published in the Official Journal]

CAR TAXATION

Proposal for a Council directive of 5 July 2005 on passenger car related taxes [**COM(2005) 261** final - Not published in the Official Journal] [Procedure **CNS/2005/0130**]

ENHANCING POLICE AND CUSTOMS COOPERATION IN THE EUROPEAN UNION

Cooperation between Member States' police forces and customs administrations is crucial to the maintenance of an area of security. In this Communication, the Commission is reviewing the measures and actions taken in this field since the adoption of the Treaty of Amsterdam, which entered into force on 1 May 1999. It proposes improvements that are necessary to enhance police and customs cooperation between Member States.

ACT

Communication from the Commission to the European Parliament and the Council: enhancing police and customs cooperation in the European Union [COM (2004) 376 final - Not published in the Official Journal].

SUMMARY

Area of security: On 18 May 2004 the European Commission adopted a communication to enhance police and customs cooperation. It recommends increasing information exchange and strengthening cross-border cooperation. It was considered necessary to create a common culture and common instruments and methods. The need to make progress in this policy area is highlighted by the challenges of today's world, in particular combating terrorism. The Commission focuses on the following factors that adversely affect police and customs cooperation:

- the nature of police work;
- the lack of a strategic approach;
- the proliferation of non-binding instruments;
- the decision-making procedures in the Third Pillar;
- insufficient implementation of legal instruments adopted by the Council;
- the lack of empirical research on police and customs cooperation;
- databases and communication systems.

The Commission analyses police and customs cooperation in the European Union since the entry into force of the Treaty of Amsterdam in 1999. It focuses exclusively on cooperation between Member States' police and customs authorities in combating crime. The Communication does not address matters relating to judicial cooperation, administrative assistance in customs matters under the First Pillar and preventive measures, or does so only to a limited degree, Police cooperation within the Union supplements existing bilateral cooperation between Member States. The AGIS programme provides financial support for police and customs cooperation within the European Union.

POLICE COOPERATION

The Commission covers and assesses the achievements of the police and other competent services in the context of Schengen cooperation, Europol, police cooperation at operational level, the European Police College (CEPOL) and other areas mentioned in Article 30 of the Treaty on European Union (TEU), such as investigative techniques and combating terrorism.

The Schengen Convention

The Treaty of Amsterdam incorporated the Convention implementing the Schengen Agreement of 1990 into the framework of the European Union. The aim of Schengen is to abolish checks at the common border on the movement of persons. Police cooperation appears as one of the complementary measures to safeguard internal security. Member States are subject to a number of obligations regarding police cooperation at the external borders of the Schengen territory (land, international airports and sea) to counteract any security deficit caused by the abolition of checks at the internal borders. The Vienna Action Plan of 1998 and the Conclusions of the 1999 Tampere European Council further underpin this area of freedom, security and justice.
The Commission takes stock of the articles in the Schengen Convention that it considers most relevant to police cooperation:

- **Article 39** stipulates that Member States' police authorities are to assist each other to prevent and detect criminal offences. It finds that disputes occur because the competences of police in the different Member States differ widely. Nevertheless, it considers that bilateral and trilateral cooperation between Member States on the establishment of cooperation and information exchange structures in the form of Joint Police Stations and Police and Customs Cooperation Centres (PCCC) at internal frontiers has made good progress. Such cooperation centres have proved effective in addressing the "security deficits" in border regions caused by the abolition of border controls and the fact that law-enforcement services' intervention has to stop at the internal borders. The Vienna Action Plan calls for the extension of such cross-border cooperation;
- **Article 44** seeks to improve communication links such as telephone, fax, computers in border areas. Since no data are available for cross-border operations, the Commission cannot assess whether real communication needs remain unattended but considers that the main obstacle to radio communications is a lack of interoperable communication systems;
- **Article 45** stipulates that Member States must undertake to adopt the necessary measures to ensure that non-nationals complete and sign registration forms and confirm their identity by providing a valid identity document. This information can be crucial for the police. It is unclear to the Commission precisely how Member States implement this obligation and how the information is used in law-enforcement practice. It therefore considers that the matter needs to be discussed in the Council;
- **Article 46** gives police authorities the right to exchange information with another Member State on their own initiative to prevent crime and threats to public order. In practice, it is not known whether the right is exercised. The Commission therefore proposes that the Council examine this question;
- **Articles 93***et seq.* are intended to maintain public order and security, including security of the State, through information exchange via the Schengen Information System (SIS).

En 1999, ten Member States were using the SIS and their number has now grown to 17. The current SIS was conceived for only 18 users and the ten Member States that acceded on 1 May 2004 must be connected in the future. The Commission has therefore been entrusted with the development of a second-generation SIS (SIS II). It considers that the SIS is crucial to police cooperation in Europe;

- The other articles of the Schengen Convention establish cooperation instruments concerning discreet surveillance of a suspect (Article 40) and where a person is caught in the act and avoids arrest by crossing international borders (Articles 41-43). The Commission finds that these instruments are rarely used.

Cooperation within Europol
Various measures concerning Europol that are listed in the TEU and the Vienna Action Plan have been implemented, producing mixed results, however. For example, a protocol extending

Europol's competence to money laundering was adopted by the Council in 2000, but nine Member States had yet to ratify it on the date of the Communication. Moreover, the reluctance of Member States to transmit information and intelligence to Europol is hampering its operational development. The Communication reviews progress achieved through signing cooperation agreements with third countries, such as the United States, following the events of 11 September. The Commission notes that a key prerequisite for Europol's effective functioning will be the existence of the Europol Information System (EIS), which Europol has been working on for the past few years. The EIS will allow decentralised storage and retrieval of information on organised crime held by Member States. The Commission has made recommendations to improve democratic control of Europol. It takes the view that an awareness programme is essential to improve mutual understanding and cooperation between Europol and the Member States' law-enforcement services.

The Task Force of EU Police Chiefs

The Tampere European Council called for the establishment of a "European Police Chiefs Operational Task Force" (TFPC) to exchange experience, best practices and information on current trends in cross-border crime, in cooperation with Europol. It meets twice a year. It has taken a large number of initiatives, particularly regarding the protection of the euro, which have, however, failed to lead to an operational added value at EU level. The Commission explains this lack of effectiveness by the fact that leading police officials of the Member States usually have to deal with a great number of issues, so that European issues are only one of many priorities. In addition, there are considerable differences in the competences of police representatives. In some Member States there is one national head of police, whereas in countries with federal systems the representation is quite complex. In addition, organisational weaknesses have added to the problems of the TFPC's work: since only one meeting of the Task Force is held per Council Presidency, agendas are overloaded, which does not make for effective work. Nevertheless, TFPC meetings are considerably improving bilateral contacts. A meeting in March 2004 discussed a reflection document dealing with the future of the TFPC in the light of the proposals set out in the Treaty on a Constitution for Europe.

The European Police College

By decision of 22 December 2000 [Official Journal L 336 of 30 December 2000] the Council established the European Police College (CEPOL). CEPOL assists the national police in increasing their knowledge of the operational structures of police in other Member States. In addition it aims to improve mutual understanding of Europol and police cooperation in the EU and at international level.

CEPOL has had a difficult beginning: it lacked a budget, did not have legal personality and faced administrative difficulties. By decision of 24 July 2004 the Council gave CEPOL legal personality [Decision 2004/556/JAI, Official Journal L 251 of 27 July 2004]. Despite the institution's difficult beginning considerable progress has been achieved in the following areas:

- its range of specialised training is constantly increasing, extending from cooperation in counter-terrorism to public order and border control at the Union's internal frontiers, etc.;
- it has set up its own CEPOL website;
- it has established the European Police Learning Network (EPLN), an Internet site offering virtual police training. The Commission has supported the development of the EPLN through the OISIN and AGIS programmes.

The Commission notes that insufficient knowledge of foreign languages among members of European police forces may hinder effective cooperation. CEPOL should draw up joint programmes and courses for priority areas of policy cooperation.

Other subjects of police cooperation

The Communication deals with other significant subject areas of police cooperation:

- investigative techniques;
- forensic science;

- terrorism;
- public order and security of high-level meetings;
- Article 32 of the TEU requiring the Council to fix the conditions and limitations under which the authorities of a State may operate in the territory of another Member State.

CUSTOMS COOPERATION

Customs cooperation plays a vital role in combating serious international crime such as elicit traffic in drugs, weapons, munitions, explosive materials, the theft of cultural goods, materials or equipment intended for the manufacture of atomic, biological and/or chemical weapons, etc. The Vienna Action Plan sets out more specific aims for customs cooperation, in particular the ratification of the following:

- **Convention on mutual assistance and co-operation between Member States** (Naples II). The Commission considers that the Member States do not make sufficient use of the special forms of cooperation such as hot pursuit, cross-border surveillance, etc. provided for in the Convention;
- **Convention on the use of information technology for customs purposes (**CIS**)**. The Commission, with the support of the Member States, has made good progress with the technical development of the database. It calls on the Member States to supplement the CIS database.

Customs cooperation was introduced into the intergovernmental part of the Maastricht Treaty on European Union in 1992. However, an important element in customs cooperation comes under the First Pillar: Article 135 of the Treaty establishing the European Community authorises the Council, acting on the Commission's proposal, to take measures to strengthen customs cooperation between Member States.

PROGRESSING TOWARDS EFFECTIVE COOPERATION

The Commission is focusing on the following improvements:

- **the nature of police work**: police work goes to the heart of what constitutes a sovereign State. It is therefore understandable that States are reluctant to participate in international arrangements which encroach on national sovereignty. The Commission hopes to build up a culture of trust and cooperation with the competent authorities for sharing information that is essential for international cooperation. It considers it essential to designate central national contact points for the international exchange of information. Member States must have an electronic system for the safe and rapid exchange of information. Technical investigative tools facilitating cooperation must be used effectively by the judicial authorities;
- **strategic approach**: the Commission regrets the lack of a strategic approach. Thus every Council Presidency defines a set of priorities according to its own priorities. The requirement of unanimity in decision-making in this area slows progress even more. The Convention on the future of Europe proposes improved decision-making mechanisms;
- **proliferation of non-binding instruments**: a problem with intergovernmental cooperation under the Third Pillar remains the non-binding nature of the instruments approved, such as recommendations. If Member States consider a given subject important enough to be discussed at Council level, then such discussions should result in measures which are effectively implemented by all;
- **decision-making procedures in the Third Pillar**: the Commission considers that the slow progress in police and customs cooperation can be linked to the decision-making rules. The Council, in relation to third-pillar subjects, must decide by unanimity. The right of initiative is shared between the Commission and the Member States. The Commission believes that the balance achieved in the Constitutional Treaty well reflects the respective competences of the Member States and the Union. The Constitution offers a

considerable improvement in the decision-making procedure. It provides that decisions relating to the framework and mechanisms for cooperation (e.g. Europol) are to be taken by qualified majority and co-decision. Decisions on operational cooperation (e.g. operation by one Member State in the territory of another) remain subject to unanimity;

- **implementation of legal instruments**: the Commission is critical of the slow implementation of legal instruments adopted by the Council. It points out that the Laeken European Council of December 2001 reaffirmed the need for decisions taken by the Union to be transposed quickly into national law;
- **research on police and customs cooperation**: the Commission finds that scientific research into police and customs cooperation has a number of shortcomings. Adequate funding needs to be made available for research, as a shared responsibility of the Member States and the Union;
- **cooperation between police and customs**: the Commission hopes to secure more effective coordination and communication between police forces and customs authorities;
- **databases and communication systems**: a number of databases and communication systems exist at European level. The main examples are: the EIS, the SIS, the CIS and the Customs Files Identification Database. There is a risk of duplication between some of them. The Commission also questions their interoperability. Three possible options should be considered:

  - to merge the existing systems into a single "Union Information System";
  - to keep the systems independent and allow the creation of new systems as required;
  - to investigate and implement the harmonisation of the data formats and the respective access rules between the various systems.

The Commission recalls the legal obligations and political commitments for police and customs cooperation under the Treaty and European Council decisions. In addition, it analyses the main factors preventing police and customs cooperation.

Legal obligations and political commitments for police and customs cooperation arise under the following measures:

- the Treaty on European Union;
- the Schengen Convention;
- the 1998 Vienna Action Plan;
- the Conclusions of the Tampere European Council of October 1999.

The Commission points out that certain events have given a political impulse to move forward in this area. The public order disturbances during the European Councils at Nice and Gothenburg in 2001 led to an intensification in cooperation in the maintenance of public order. Similarly, the events of 11 September 2001 in the United States have given rise to increased cooperation in the fight against terrorism.

RELATED ACTS

Council Recommendation of 27 April 2006 on the drawing up of agreements between police, customs and other specialised law enforcement services in relation to the prevention and combating of crime [Official Journal C 124 of 25.5.2006]

CUSTOMS RESPONSE TO LATEST TRENDS IN COUNTERFEITING AND PIRACY

The Commission proposes a series of customs measures aimed at protecting the EU more effectively against counterfeiting and piracy. These measures include improving legislation, strengthening partnership between customs and businesses and increasing international cooperation.

ACT

Communication of 11 October 2005 from the Commission to the Council, the European Parliament and the European Economic and Social Committee on a customs response to latest trends in counterfeiting and piracy [COM(2005) 479 final - not published in the Official Journal].

SUMMARY

This Communication sets out a range of initiatives aimed at cracking down on counterfeiting and piracy. The measures in question will be implemented by customs.

Problems and threats

The industrial production of counterfeit goods poses a threat to:

- the health, safety and jobs of EU citizens (e.g. fake medicines or foodstuffs);
- the competitiveness and trade of the European Community (EC);
- investment in research and innovation in the EC.

There was a 1000% increase in counterfeiting and piracy between 1998 and 2004. In 2004 alone, 103 million fake or pirated articles were seized by customs officials in the EC; 4.4 million of these were fake foodstuffs and alcoholic drinks. Much of this traffic is sold on the black market, which means losses of tax revenue for Member States.

Most of the products seized are household items, with growing numbers of sophisticated hi-tech products being faked. The quality of these counterfeits is now so good that it is becoming difficult to distinguish the real article from the fake. What is more, high profits and relatively low risks make counterfeiting and piracy lucrative for those involved in organised crime.

Recommendations and Action Plan

The Commission proposes a range of recommendations aimed at tightening customs controls to help combat counterfeiting and piracy in the Community.
In its action plan, the Commission considers measures to be necessary in the following areas:

- increasing protection at the level of Community legislation and operational performance;
- strengthening the partnership between customs and businesses;
- improving international cooperation.

Legislation

Customs controls on inbound traffic need to be improved and the suitability of the existing legal and operational measures has to be examined. Two concerns in particular must be addressed. The first involves the simplified destruction procedures that will reduce costs to businesses and public administrations alike. The second relates to the fact that travellers are currently permitted to import small quantities of personal-use items that may be counterfeit.

Operational performance

New techniques and instruments are needed to ensure that operational capacity is consistently high. Actions have to be developed and brought together in a new operational control plan based on risk management. The EU's Customs Information System (CIS) enables the national customs services of Member States to exchange and search for customs information.

Partnership

Effective customs enforcement can be guaranteed only if businesses are also fully involved. Improving the early exchange of information between businesses and customs is also important. A possible solution could take the form of an EU electronic information system for intellectual property rights.

International cooperation

The main region producing counterfeit goods is Asia, and China in particular. International cooperation is crucial in halting the production and export of counterfeit goods. The Commission intends to:

- introduce export and transhipment controls;
- exploit and extend Customs Cooperation Agreements to cover regions where there is a significant level of counterfeit production;
- enhance the World Trade Organization (WTO) agreement on trade-related aspects of intellectual property rights (TRIPS);
- strengthen cooperation with the World Customs Organization (WCO), Europol and Interpol;
- enter into bilateral arrangements, especially with China.

RELATED ACTS

Council Resolution of 13 March 2006 on a customs response to latest trends in counterfeiting and piracy [Official Journal C 67 of 18.3.2006]
Commission Regulation (EC) No 1891/2004 of 21 October 2004 laying down provisions for the implementation of Council Regulation (EC) No 1383/2003 concerning customs action against goods suspected of infringing certain intellectual property rights and the measures to be taken against goods found to have infringed such rights [Official Journal L 328 of 30.10.2004].

Directive 2004/48/EC of the European Parliament and of the Council of 29 April 2004 on the enforcement of intellectual property rights [Official Journal L 157 of 30.4.2004].
Council Regulation (EC) No 1383/2003 of 22 July 2003 concerning customs action against goods suspected of infringing certain intellectual property rights and the measures to be taken against goods found to have infringed such rights [Official Journal L 196 of 2.8.2003].

This Regulation sets out measures and conditions for the customs authorities to take action against goods found to have infringed IPR.
Council Regulation (EC) No 515/97 of 13 March 1997 on mutual assistance between the administrative authorities of the Member States and cooperation between the latter and the Commission to ensure the correct application of the law on customs and agricultural matters [Official Journal L 82 of 22.3.1997].

EUROPEAN ANTI-COUNTERFEITING AND ANTI-PIRACY PLAN

The Council is hereby calling upon the Commission and the Member States to take action to fight against counterfeiting and piracy more effectively.

ACTS

Council Resolution of 25 September 2008 on a comprehensive European anti-counterfeiting and anti-piracy plan [Official Journal C 253 of 4.10.2008].

SUMMARY

With this Resolution, the Council is calling on the Commission to put into effect the actions to combat counterfeiting and piracy set out in its Communication on an industrial property rights strategy for Europe [COM(2008) 465]. This Communication provides a set of measures aimed at enforcing industrial property, copy- and related rights such as customs initiatives, completing legislation, concluding inter-industry agreements, enforcing cross-border judgements, enforcing intellectual property rights in third countries and working towards a plurilateral anti-counterfeiting trade agreement (ACTA).

In this regard, the Commission is invited to establish a European counterfeiting and piracy observatory based on its existing structures. It should define in detail the arrangements and financing for the establishment and future operations of the observatory. The aim of the observatory should be to allow for regular evaluations and more accurate analysis of the counterfeiting and piracy situation in Europe. The data for this should be provided on a voluntary basis by both the private and public sectors.

The Commission should also communicate with actors taking part in the fight against counterfeiting and piracy. This should involve the diffusion of related information, in particular by using the Internet.
Finally, the Commission is also invited to develop awareness-raising activities in order to inform consumers of the dangers of counterfeiting. These should include operational guides and events to mark the European awareness day related to counterfeiting and piracy.
At the same time, the Council is also inviting the Commission and the Member States to take action to fight against counterfeiting and piracy. This should, among others, consist of drawing up an anti-counterfeiting customs plan for the period 2009-12. This plan should prioritise information sharing via electronic means, along with collaboration between border authorities, namely customs authorities, and rights holders. The Commission and the Member States should also review the customs law with a view to enhancing the legal framework so that the fight against counterfeiting is made more effective.

In addition, the Commission and the Member States should:

- establish a rapid information exchange network for counterfeit products and services by stepping-up cross-border administrative collaboration with the help of national contact points and modern information and communication tools;
- ensure that the institutions fighting against counterfeiting and piracy may coordinate properly by promoting the sharing of best practice between national administrations;
- review the legal framework relating to intellectual property rights in order to evaluate its effectiveness;
- encourage partnerships between the public and private sector for fighting counterfeiting and piracy, propose good practice and promote collaboration between professionals.

Furthermore, the Commission and the Member States should promote the protection of intellectual property rights within the international context, including in cooperation activities with third countries. This should consist of endorsing the inclusion and enforcement of intellectual property rights in bi- and multilateral agreements and actively working towards the conclusion of a plurilateral anti-counterfeiting trade agreement.

Background
In March 2008, the Council launched the new cycle of the renewed Lisbon strategy for growth and jobs (2008-10). In this context, the European Union was invited to fight against counterfeiting more effectively by working towards a more efficient system of protection of intellectual property rights.

MONEY LAUNDERING: PREVENTION THROUGH CUSTOMS COOPERATION

The Regulation places an obligation on any natural person entering or leaving the Community and carrying cash * of a value of EUR 10 000 or more to declare that sum to the competent authorities * of the Member States. The aim of the Regulation is to introduce preventive action to combat money laundering and terrorist financing through more effective customs cooperation.

ACT

Regulation (EC) No 1889/2005 of the European Parliament and of the Council of 26 October 2005 on controls of cash entering or leaving the Community.

SUMMARY

This Regulation complements the provisions of Directive 91/308/EEC on prevention of the use of the financial system for the purpose of money laundering. Directive 91/308/EEC was replaced by Directive 2005/60/EC, which in particular extends the scope of the preventive measures to terrorist financing. The competent authorities of the Member States now have harmonised rules for the control of cash entering or leaving the Community.

Obligation to declare

The Regulation places an obligation on any natural person entering or leaving the Community and carrying cash of a value of EUR 10 000 or more to declare that sum to the competent authorities. The information provided must be correct and complete, otherwise the declaration is invalid.

The declaration is provided in writing, orally or electronically, to be determined by the Member State, and must contain information on:

- the declarant, including full name, date and place of birth and nationality;
- the owner and the amount and nature of the cash;
- the intended recipient of the cash;
- the provenance and intended use of the cash.

The information obtained either from the declaration or as a result of controls must be recorded and processed. It is made available to the authorities responsible for combating money laundering or terrorist financing in the Member State of entry or of exit. The information provided may be communicated to third countries by Member States or by the Commission, subject to the consent of the competent authorities. The national and Community provisions on the transfer of personal data must be complied with.

Professional secrecy covers all information which is by nature confidential or which is provided on a confidential basis. It must not be disclosed without the express permission of the person or authority providing it. However, the competent authorities may be obliged by law to disclose this information, for instance in connection with legal proceedings. In such a case, any disclosure or communication of information must fully comply with prevailing data protection legislation.

Checking compliance with the obligation to declare

Officials of the competent authorities may check compliance with the obligation to declare by carrying out controls on natural persons. This includes controls on the natural persons themselves, their baggage and their means of transport. Such controls must comply with national legislation in this area.

In the event of failure to comply with the obligation to declare, cash may be detained by administrative decision in accordance with national legislation.

The information obtained may be made available to other Member States, in particular where there is evidence of illegal activities. In such cases, Regulation (EC) No 515/97 on mutual assistance between the administrative authorities of the Member States and cooperation between the latter and the Commission to ensure the correct application of the law on customs and agricultural matters applies mutatis mutandis. Where there are indications that the financial interests of the Community are adversely affected, the information will also be transmitted to the Commission.

Where it appears from the controls that a natural person is entering or leaving the Community with sums of cash lower than EUR 10 000 and where there is evidence of illegal activities associated with the movement of cash, that information may also be recorded and processed.

Penalties
By 15 June 2007 at the latest, Member States must lay down the penalties applicable in the event of failure to comply with the obligation to declare. Such penalties must be effective, proportionate and dissuasive.

Key terms used in the act

- Cash: the term "cash" covers currency (banknotes and coins), but also other monetary instruments such as cheques, promissory notes, money orders, etc.;
- Competent authorities: "competent authorities" means the customs authorities of the Member States or any other authorities empowered by Member States to apply this Regulation

EU TRADE AND COMMERCIAL POLICY REGULATIONS

11.60.10 General (number of acts: 28)

11.60.20 Extension or renewal of agreements with State-trading countries (number of acts: 1)

11.60.30 Trade arrangements (number of acts: 265)

11.60.40 Trade protection (number of acts: 303)

11.60.50 Other commercial policy measures (number of acts: 40)

11.60.60 Statistics on external trade (Nimexe) (number of acts: 0)

- **31999R1488**
  Commission Regulation (EC) No 1488/1999 of 7 July 1999 concerning the classification of certain goods in the Combined Nomenclature
  (OJ L 172, 8.7.1999, p. 25–26)
- **31999R1836**
  Commission Regulation (EC) No 1836/1999 of 24 August 1999 concerning the classification of certain goods in the Combined Nomenclature
  (OJ L 224, 25.8.1999, p. 6–7)
- **31999R2113**
  Commission Regulation (EC) No 2113/1999 of 5 October 1999 concerning the classification of certain goods in the combined nomenclature
  (OJ L 259, 6.10.1999, p. 3–4)
- **31999R2376**
  Commission Regulation (EC) No 2376/1999 of 9 November 1999 concerning the classification of certain goods in the Combined Nomenclature
  (OJ L 287, 10.11.1999, p. 4–5)

- **31999R2795**
  Commission Regulation (EC) No 2795/1999 of 29 December 1999 concerning the classification of certain goods in the Combined Nomenclature
  (OJ L 337, 30.12.1999, p. 36–37)
- **31999Y0707(01)**
  Resolution of the Council of 24 June 1999 on the management of Agreements on mutual recognition
  (OJ C 190, 7.7.1999, p. 2–2)
- **32000R0184**
  Commission Regulation (EC) No 184/2000 of 26 January 2000 concerning the classification of certain goods in the Combined Nomenclature
  (OJ L 22, 27.1.2000, p. 48–49)
- **32000R0289**
  Commission Regulation (EC) No 289/2000 of 3 February 2000 concerning the classification of certain goods in the Combined Nomenclature
  (OJ L 33, 8.2.2000, p. 3–5)
- **32000R0323**
  Commission Regulation (EC) No 323/2000 of 11 February 2000 concerning the classification of certain goods in the Combined Nomenclature
  (OJ L 37, 12.2.2000, p. 12–13)
- **32000R0442**
  Commission Regulation (EC) No 442/2000 of 25 February 2000 concerning the classification of certain goods in the Combined Nomenclature
  (OJ L 54, 26.2.2000, p. 33–35)
- **32000R0709**
  Commission Regulation (EC) No 709/2000 of 4 April 2000 concerning the classification of certain goods in the Combined Nomenclature
  (OJ L 84, 5.4.2000, p. 3–7)
- **32000R0710**
  Commission Regulation (EC) No 710/2000 of 3 April 2000 concerning the classification of certain goods in the Combined Nomenclature
  (OJ L 84, 5.4.2000, p. 8–9)

  Amended by 32005R0705

- **32000R0738**
  Commission Regulation (EC) No 738/2000 of 7 April 2000 concerning the classification of certain goods in the Combined Nomenclature
  (OJ L 87, 8.4.2000, p. 10–13)
- **32000R0961**
  Commission Regulation (EC) No 961/2000 of 5 May 2000 concerning the classification of certain goods in the Combined Nomenclature
  (OJ L 109, 6.5.2000, p. 16–22)
- **32000R1508**
  Commission Regulation (EC) No 1508/2000 of 11 July 2000 concerning the classification of certain goods in the Combined Nomenclature
  (OJ L 174, 13.7.2000, p. 3–6)
- **32000R1564**
  Commission Regulation (EC) No 1564/2000 of 18 July 2000 concerning the classification of certain goods in the combined nomenclature
  (OJ L 180, 19.7.2000, p. 5–7)
- **32000R2354**
  Commission Regulation (EC) No 2354/2000 of 24 October 2000 concerning the

classification of certain goods in the Combined Nomenclature
(OJ L 272, 25.10.2000, p. 10–11)

Amended by 32005R0705

- **32001R0305**
  Commission Regulation (EC) No 305/2001 of 12 February 2001 concerning the classification of certain goods in the Combined Nomenclature
  (OJ L 44, 15.2.2001, p. 22–24)
- **32001R0306**
  Commission Regulation (EC) No 306/2001 of 12 February 2001 concerning the classification of certain goods in the Combined Nomenclature
  (OJ L 44, 15.2.2001, p. 25–26)
- **32001R0646**
  Commission Regulation (EC) No 646/2001 of 30 March 2001 concerning the classification of certain goods in the Combined Nomenclature
  (OJ L 91, 31.3.2001, p. 42–43)
- **32001R1694**
  Commission Regulation (EC) No 1694/2001 of 24 August 2001 concerning the classification of certain goods in the Combined Nomenclature
  (OJ L 229, 25.8.2001, p. 3–4)

  Amended by 32005R0705

- **32001R2064**
  Commission Regulation (EC) No 2064/2001 of 22 October 2001 concerning the classification of certain goods in the combined nomenclature
  (OJ L 278, 23.10.2001, p. 3–5)
- **32001R2147**
  Commission Regulation (EC) No 2147/2001 of 31 October 2001 concerning the classification of certain goods in the Combined Nomenclature
  (OJ L 288, 1.11.2001, p. 23–24)
- **32001R2180**
  Commission Regulation (EC) No 2180/2001 of 9 November 2001 concerning the classification of certain goods in the Combined Nomenclature
  (OJ L 293, 10.11.2001, p. 5–7)
- **32001Y0111(02)**
  Council conclusions of 14 December 2000 — Implementation of the Council Resolution of 24 June 1999 on the management of agreements on mutual recognition
  (OJ C 8, 11.1.2001, p. 4–4)
- **32002R0141**
  Commission Regulation (EC) No 141/2002 of 25 January 2002 concerning the classification of certain goods in the Combined Nomenclature
  (OJ L 24, 26.1.2002, p. 11–13)
- **32002R0142**
  Commission Regulation (EC) No 142/2002 of 25 January 2002 concerning the classification of certain goods in the Combined Nomenclature
  (OJ L 24, 26.1.2002, p. 14–15)
- **32002R0471**
  Commission Regulation (EC) No 471/2002 of 15 March 2002 concerning the classification of certain goods in the Combined Nomenclature
  (OJ L 75, 16.3.2002, p. 13–17)

- **32002R0687**
Commission Regulation (EC) No 687/2002 of 22 April 2002 concerning the classification of certain goods in the Combined Nomenclature
(OJ L 106, 23.4.2002, p. 3–6)
- **32002R0763**
Commission Regulation (EC) No 763/2002 of 3 May 2002 concerning the classification of certain goods in the Combined Nomenclature
(OJ L 117, 4.5.2002, p. 3–4)
- **32002R0849**
Commission Regulation (EC) No 849/2002 of 22 May 2002 concerning the classification of certain goods in the Combined Nomenclature
(OJ L 135, 23.5.2002, p. 10–11)
- **32002R1017**
Commission Regulation (EC) No 1017/2002 of 13 June 2002 concerning the classification of certain goods in the Combined Nomenclature
(OJ L 155, 14.6.2002, p. 23–24)
- **32002R1380**
Commission Regulation (EC) No 1380/2002 of 29 July 2002 concerning the classification of certain goods in the Combined Nomenclature
(OJ L 200, 30.7.2002, p. 12–13)
- **32002R2014**
Commission Regulation (EC) No 2014/2002 of 7 November 2002 concerning the classification of certain goods in the Combined Nomenclature
(OJ L 311, 14.11.2002, p. 11–12)
- **32002R2049**
Commission Regulation (EC) No 2049/2002 of 19 November 2002 concerning the classification of certain goods in the Combined Nomenclature
(OJ L 316, 20.11.2002, p. 15–16)

  Amended by 32005R0705

- **32003R0055**
Commission Regulation (EC) No 55/2003 of 13 January 2003 concerning the classification of certain goods in the Combined Nomenclature
(OJ L 8, 14.1.2003, p. 3–4)
- **32003R0218**
Commission Regulation (EC) No 218/2003 of 4 February 2003 concerning the classification of certain goods in the Combined Nomenclature
(OJ L 29, 5.2.2003, p. 5–6)
- **32003R0627**
Commission Regulation (EC) No 627/2003 of 4 April 2003 concerning the classification of certain goods in the Combined Nomenclature
(OJ L 90, 8.4.2003, p. 34–36)

  Amended by 32005R0705

- **32003R1020**
Commission Regulation (EC) No 1020/2003 of 13 June 2003 concerning the classification of certain goods in the Combined Nomenclature
(OJ L 147, 14.6.2003, p. 10–11)
- **32003R1021**
Commission Regulation (EC) No 1021/2003 of 13 June 2003 concerning the

classification of certain goods in the Combined Nomenclature
(OJ L 147, 14.6.2003, p. 12–13)

- **32003R1224**
  Commission Regulation (EC) No 1224/2003 of 9 July 2003 concerning the classification of certain goods in the Combined Nomenclature
  (OJ L 172, 10.7.2003, p. 4–5)
- **32003R1386**
  Commission Regulation (EC) No 1386/2003 of 1 August 2003 concerning the classification of certain goods in the Combined Nomenclature
  (OJ L 196, 2.8.2003, p. 19–21)
- **32003R1887**
  Commission Regulation (EC) No 1887/2003 of 27 October 2003 concerning the classification of certain goods in the Combined Nomenclature
  (OJ L 277, 28.10.2003, p. 11–12)
- **32004R1849**
  Commission Regulation (EC) No 1849/2004 of 21 October 2004 concerning the classification of certain goods in the Combined Nomenclature
  (OJ L 323, 26.10.2004, p. 3–4)

IMPORTANT OFFICIAL MATERIALS AND REGULATIONS

MAKING GLOBALISATION WORK FOR EVERYONE: THE EUROPEAN UNION AND WORLD TRADE[7]

Globalisation means that the flows of goods, services, capital, technologies and people are spreading worldwide, as countries everywhere open up to wider contact with each other. Globalisation can create more wealth for everybody, but it can also be disruptive and needs to be harnessed by international rules. When business goes global, the rules for fair play must also be set globally.

The European Union (EU) represents all its Member States on questions of trade policy and within the World Trade Organisation. This booklet describes how the EU works for transparent and fair trade rules worldwide, and tries to mitigate the negative sides of globalisation by making sure that the developing countries benefit from free trade. The European Union involves citizens in trade policy and includes environmental and social rules in trade agreements.

TRADE FOR A BETTER WORLD

Trade is everybody's business. Trade policy may seem a complex, technical subject that only experts can understand, but it actually involves us all, every day, whatever we do and wherever we live. Think global. Think of morning tea or coffee, the cars we drive, the computers on which we increasingly depend. Think of a favourite oriental rug or a holiday on another continent.

Globalisation means that more and more countries, both rich and poor, are taking part in the world economy. This process is changing the pattern of world trade and increasingly permeating our everyday lives.

The wealth that trade can generate helps European Union (EU) countries to give their citizens a better quality of life — now, and for future generations too. Taking part in world trade — if properly managed — also gives developing countries a much-needed opportunity for economic growth.

As the world's leading trade power, the EU has a strong interest in creating conditions in which trade can prosper. The EU's position also gives it responsibilities towards the rest of the world. That is why it plays a leading role in international trade negotiations, **working towards fair trade and seeking to harness globalisation** through the World Trade Organisation (WTO).

The EU works to ensure that its trading partners in the developing world can join in the system, giving them a hand where needed. This applies particularly to the poorest countries, for which the benefits of globalisation remain elusive.

This booklet describes how EU trade policy works. It outlines the EU's trade relationships with the rest of the world and the role the EU plays in the World Trade Organisation. And it explains how the EU intends to make sure that the whole world can benefit from the international trade negotiations that were launched in Doha in November 2001. Known as the 'Doha development agenda', the new round of negotiations will be a decisive force in shaping trade in the 21st century.

ROLE AND RESPONSIBILITIES OF THE EUROPEAN UNION

[7] *European Commission*

The European Union, with its 15 member countries, represents just 6 % of the world's population. But it accounts for more than a fifth of global imports and exports. This makes the Union the world's biggest trader.

Trade was one of the first areas in which EU countries agreed to pool their sovereignty, transferring to the European Commission the responsibility for handling trade matters, including negotiating international trade agreements on their behalf.

This means that the EU's 15 Member States negotiate as one, both with their trading partners and at the WTO, thus maximising their influence on the international scene.

But a wide range of players are involved in drawing up the EU's trade policy. Representatives of the governments of the EU countries are regularly and closely consulted, and ministers themselves take the key decisions. The European Parliament is closely involved in all developments. The Commission is continually organising a wide consultation of civil society, such as non-governmental organisations (NGOs), trade unions, and business.

This enables the EU to be sensitive to all interests as it works to expand trade and to create a win–win situation for all players.

Europeans trade a lot

The European Union is:

- the world's leading exporter of goods: over 973 billion euro in 2001, almost a fifth of the world total;
- the world's leading exporter of services: 291 billion in euro 2000, 23.9 % of the world total;
- the world's leading source of foreign direct investment (362 billion euro in 2000) and the second largest home for foreign investment (176.2 billion euro in 2000) after the United States (304.9 billion euro)
- the main export market for some 130 countries around the globe;
- a relatively open economy: international trade accounted for over 14 % of its gross domestic product in 2000, compared with 12 % for the United States and 11 % for Japan.

What do we buy and sell?

There are four main categories of things that are traded internationally or flow across borders. Trade rules vary by category, and different countries are strong in different categories.

- **Goods:** This covers all types of physical goods, such as food, clothing, raw materials and machinery.
- **Services:** This covers things like tourism, banking and telecommunications.
- **Intellectual property:** This covers trade and investment in ideas and creativity: copyright, industrial design, artists' rights, etc.
- **Foreign direct investment (FDI):** This is when a company from one country buys or establishes a company in another country. This is an alternative to trade and an important part of 'globalisation'. The concept does not include financial investments, where the owner of the money has no direct influence on the running of a company in which he or she owns shares.

FREE AND FAIR

The European Union's aim is free but fair world trade. In other words, a system where all countries trade freely with one another on equal terms and without protectionist barriers. The EU wants a 'level playing field' for all countries and clear 'rules of the game' for everyone to follow. The system should be transparent — fully open to public scrutiny.

To achieve this, the EU's strategy is to open up its own market while others do likewise. It seeks to remove obstacles to trade gradually, at a pace the EU and others can sustain, to settle disputes peacefully and to build up a body of internationally agreed rules.

To 'open up' or to 'liberalise' trade must be seen in comparison with the situation created in years gone by when almost all governments in the world restricted imports into their country, with the intention of helping the economy in their country.

Opening up markets means removing trade barriers between countries. This was a basic goal of the Union from the earliest days. In the 1960s, it created a 'customs union' between its member countries. In other words, any EU country could trade any quantity of goods with any other EU country without having to pay customs duties and tariffs.

A 'single external tariff' was also introduced. In other words, non-EU countries exporting products to the EU were charged the same tariff regardless of which EU country was importing the goods. This made life simpler for traders and cut down their paperwork.

But although the tariff barriers were removed, many 'non-tariff' barriers to trade still remained. For example, different EU countries had different administrative requirements and different rules on things like packaging and labelling — all of which hindered trade between them.

That is why, in 1992, the EU launched its 'single market', removing non-tariff barriers to trade in goods, and also opening up trade in services within the Union.

Trade in the EU treaty

EU trade policy is enshrined in Article 131 of the EC Treaty. This article sets the objectives of the common commercial policy as being to 'contribute, in the common interest, to the harmonious development of world trade, the progressive abolition of restrictions on international trade and the lowering of customs barriers'.

This blends seamlessly with the aims of the Treaty in general (Article 2): 'to promote [...] harmonious, balanced and sustainable development of economic activities, a high level of employment and social protection, [...] a high degree of competitiveness and improvement of the quality of the environment, the raising of the standard of living and quality of life ...'.

(Treaty establishing the European Community)

DOING WHAT YOU ARE GOOD AT

Opening up trade stimulates the economy as a whole. It boosts the revenues of exporting countries and offers consumers in the importing countries a wider choice of goods and services at lower prices because of increased competition. Ultimately it allows all countries to produce and export the goods and services with which they are best placed to compete.

So globalisation can boost economic growth. But it can also be disruptive. Larger and more open markets mean increased competition between businesses and also between countries. By pitting unequally developed economies against one another, globalisation may, if unharnessed, widen the gap between rich and poor countries and further sideline the poorest economies.

Individual nation States cannot deal with this problem. When business goes global, the rules of fair play must also be set globally. Only through international agreement can we harness globalisation and make it work for the good of all.

So EU trade policy now covers a broader canvas, beyond trade liberalisation. It is about updating and improving international rules, and giving them a wider coverage to ensure fair trade and harnessed globalisation. It is about promoting an international agenda that benefits the developing world, and addressing issues of general public concern. One of the key challenges today is to ensure that world trade rules take account of non-market concerns, particularly the environment, public services, food safety, agriculture and culture.

Multilateral and bilateral

EU trade policy works on two complementary levels:

- **the 'multilateral' level** refers to the system of trading rules agreed by all WTO member countries worldwide;
- **the 'bilateral and regional' level** means trade between the EU and individual trading partners or with groups of countries that form a single trading bloc in a particular region of the world.

THE EU AND THE WORLD TRADE ORGANISATION

The European Union has always backed the multilateral trading system. The EU is indeed convinced that the best way to encourage and foster world trade — and thus to promote economic development and prosperity — is to have multilateral trading rules agreed by consensus.

That is why the EU played a major role in setting up the World Trade Organisation, and it is a very active participant in the WTO.

FORUM FOR THE WHOLE WORLD

The World Trade Organisation is the core of the international rules-based system for world trade. Based in Geneva, it provides a forum for multilateral negotiations on trade, together with a rule book and mechanisms for ensuring that its members play by the rules. These mechanisms include a procedure for settling disputes.

As the world economy globalises, the WTO is the most legitimate forum for removing obstacles to trade, creating and enforcing global rules and making them compatible with rules drawn up by other multilateral bodies. The aims of the EU's work in the WTO effort are:

- to open up markets in goods, services and investment in accordance with clear rules and following a timetable that enables all countries to implement them;
- to make the WTO more open, accountable and effective by engaging in discussion with other groups and organisations;
- to bring developing countries fully into the WTO's decision-taking processes, helping them to integrate with the world economy.

World Trade Organisation

Established: 1 January 1995 (but with its predecessor GATT dating back to the 1940s).
Membership: 144 countries at the start of 2002, accounting for over 90 % of all trade in the world.
Rounds: Countries tend to negotiate over several years on new agreements for a group of subjects. These series of negotiations are called 'rounds'. Examples are the 'Uruguay Round' 1986–94 and the round that started in 2001 called 'The Doha development agenda'.
Functions:

- Administering WTO trade agreements
- Forum for trade policy discussions and negotiations
- Handling and resolving trade disputes
- Monitoring national trade policies
- Technical assistance and training for developing countries
- Cooperation with other international organisations

The WTO was set up in 1995, but the multilateral trading system on which it is based is far older. Eight separate rounds of international negotiations under the General Agreement on Tariffs and Trade (GATT) have progressively abolished tariffs and other trade barriers over the past 50 years.

The WTO now has 144 members, including China and Taiwan which joined in 2001. It is the only international body policing trade in goods, services and intellectual property rights among its members.

Agreements are negotiated by governments whose aim is to ensure there is a comprehensible, reliable framework of rules for importers and exporters worldwide, enabling them to operate in the certainty there will be no sudden, unpredictable changes in policy.

The more members there are, the more effective the WTO's rules are likely to be. That is why the EU actively encouraged China to join, and is now working hand in hand with Russia and a number of other countries to help them prepare for WTO entry.

ENSURING COUNTRIES PLAY BY THE RULES

The **dispute settlement system** is one of the cornerstones of the WTO. It gives all WTO members confidence that the commitments and obligations they have negotiated are honoured.

The dispute settlement mechanism, which was introduced in 1995, is a forum that parties may use to assert their rights under multilateral trade agreements. WTO member countries are not allowed to take revenge on one another in response to alleged violations of the agreed rules. Instead, all 144 members have exactly the same right to seek redress via the WTO if they believe one of their trading partners is breaking the rules. Thus, the mechanism protects weaker members against arbitrary or unilateral action by the strongest.

The procedures for dispute settlement encourage the parties to settle their differences through consultation. Otherwise, panels of experts make rulings, which have to be endorsed or rejected by the WTO's full membership.

All WTO members, developing countries as well as the big players, are making more use of the mechanism, and it has helped to ensure real market opening. However, the EU believes there is still room for improvement, notably in respect of speed and the types of sanctions possible.

The EU has put forward proposals for making the procedures more transparent to the outside world, and for helping developing countries handle the process.

Share of world trade

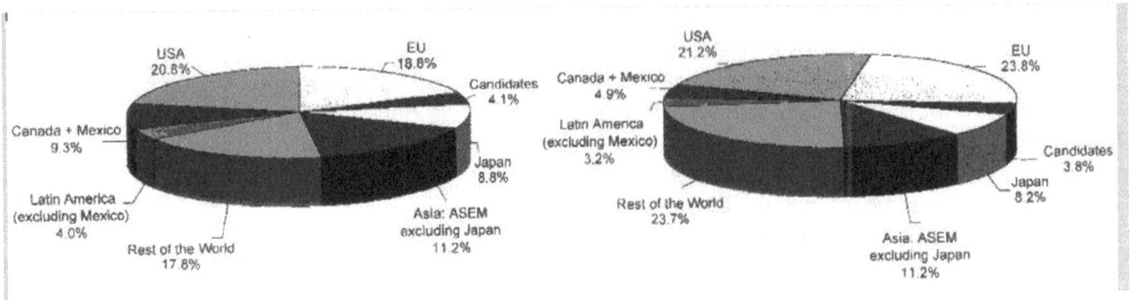

Goods	**Services**
United States 20.8 %	United States 21.2 %
EU 18.8 %	EU 23.8 %
Candidate countries 4.1 %	Candidate countries 3.8 %
Japan 8.8 %	Japan 8.2 %
Asia: ASEM excluding Japan ([1]) 11.2´ %	Asia: ASEM excluding Japan ([1]) 11.2´ %
Rest of the world 17.8 %	Rest of the world 23.7 %
Latin America excluding Mexico: 4.0 %	Latin America excluding Mexico: 3.2 %
Canada and Mexico: 9.3 %	Canada and Mexico: 4.9 %

([1]) ASEM: The nine Asian partners of the 'Asia–Europe meeting' (ASEM) other than Japan: Brunei, China, Indonesia, Malaysia, Philippines, Thailand, Singapore, South Korea, Vietnam.
Figures for 2000, imports and exports together.
Source: Eurostat.

THE EU'S BILATERAL TRADE AGREEMENTS

The European Union is the world's biggest trading power. Though it operates according to trade rules that are set multilaterally, the actual exchange of goods and services takes place bilaterally — between the EU and individual trading partners. However, what takes place bilaterally and what happens at the multilateral level often reinforce each other. The EU's bilateral agreements with individual trading partners, or with regional groupings of countries, are often designed to pursue goals that are subsequently achieved through multilateral negotiations.

EU tariffs on industrial products are among the lowest in the world and most of them will disappear in 2004 in line with the Union's commitments from 1994 under the Uruguay Round of international trade negotiations.

As it is, most of the EU's imports are already duty free or enter the EU at preferential rates under the terms of bilateral trade agreements or the EU's generalised system of preferences regime. For example, more than 50 % of finished steel imports enter the EU duty free from countries in central and eastern Europe with which the EU has bilateral association agreements.

DOING BUSINESS WITH NEIGHBOURS

Trade has helped the EU establish closer links with its immediate neighbours. In the first place, the Union has stepped up its trade with the **candidate countries** of central and eastern Europe that are due to join the EU. The agreements with these countries, known as 'Europe agreements', are intended to create a free trade area between them and the EU before they actually join.

Thanks to these agreements, a much greater proportion of the exports from these countries now goes to the EU. The agreements also relate to the free movement of services, payments and capital for trade and investment.

In addition, these countries will have to bring their national trade legislation into line with EU law before they become EU members. Association agreements with the other candidate countries — Cyprus, Malta and Turkey — contain similar provisions.

For the **Balkan countries**, which could eventually join the EU, trade is an instrument of reconstruction. The EU has removed customs duties on 95 % of exports from these countries in order to boost their economic recovery and strengthen their trade links with western Europe.

At the same time, the EU intends to conclude 'stabilisation and association agreements' with these countries, similar to those signed with the candidate countries. Agreements have already been signed with Croatia and with the Former Yugoslav Republic of Macedonia.

The EU also has a regional strategy for relations with its neighbours in the **Mediterranean region**. In 1995, it began what is called the 'Barcelona process'. This seeks, by means of a network of bilateral agreements and regional arrangements, to establish a Euro-Mediterranean free trade area by 2010.

To move this process forward, association agreements have been signed with Algeria, Egypt, Israel, Jordan, Lebanon, Morocco, the Palestinian Authority and Tunisia. Negotiations are ongoing with Syria.

EU TRADE: THE BIG PLAYERS

Trade partner	*Imports into the EU (billion euro)*	*Exports from the EU (billion euro)*	*Percentage of total trade (imports + exports)*
EU global trade	*985*	*990*	*100*
1. United States	*174*	*239*	*20.9*
2. The 10 countries due to join the EU in 2004	*107*	*125*	*11.7*
3. Switzerland	*59*	*71*	*6.5*
4. China	*81*	*34*	*5.8*
5. Japan	*68*	*42*	*5.6*
6 African, Caribbean and Pacific countries (ACP)	*46*	*40*	*4.4*
7. Russia	*48*	*30*	*3.9*
8. Norway	*45*	*26*	*3.6*

Figures for 2002, trade in goods.
Source: Eurostat.

OPENING UP TRADE AROUND THE WORLD

The EU is encouraging countries in Africa, Asia and Latin America and other regions of the word to forge closer ties with one another, just as the countries of Europe have done. Europe's own experience of 'regional integration' has brought many advantages, and the EU believes that integration in other regions of the world will put its trading partners in a better collective position to benefit from globalisation.

The EU is committed to ensuring that its agreements are compatible with WTO obligations. The EU expects the same of other WTO members and hopes the current international negotiations under the auspices of the WTO will be a useful opportunity to clarify and strengthen rules in this field for the benefit of all members.

The **United States** is by far the EU's biggest trading partner, accounting for nearly 22 % of the EU's total trade (exports plus imports).

Given the volume of their bilateral trade, it is not surprising that the EU and the United States have trade disputes from time to time. While a number of these are handled bilaterally, some end up before the WTO dispute settlement body. Although these disputes make the headlines, the amounts of trade involved are very small in comparison with total US–EU trade flows (less than 2 % of trade).

The EU's relationship with **Japan** is also of high importance. The EU's focus here is on the need for Japan to open up its market more to European goods and investments and to get the government to take effective action to reflate the economy.

The EU is also negotiating the establishment of a free trade area with the six members of the **Gulf Cooperation Council** (GCC), which is the regional organisation grouping Bahrain, Kuwait, Qatar, Oman, Saudi Arabia and the United Arab Emirates.

The EU is examining ways of promoting bilateral economic relations with **Iran** through a trade and cooperation agreement which is under negotiation. In addition, the EU has concluded partnership and cooperation agreements with Russia and a number of other countries of the **former Soviet Union** — Azerbaijan, Kazakhstan, Kyrgyzstan, Moldova and Ukraine. The agreements with Moldova, Russia and Ukraine are part of a process that could lead to the establishment of a free trade area between them and the EU.

The EU has recently been very active in its trade relations with **Latin America**.

A free trade agreement with **Mexico** came into force in July 2000. This agreement will give EU exports the same access to the Mexican market as those coming from the United States and Canada, its partners in the North American Free Trade Agreement (NAFTA). The EU is scheduled to remove all duties on imports from Mexico by 2003, while Mexico will lift all duties on EU goods by 2007.

The EU and **Chile** have recently concluded the negotiations for an association agreement, delivering the most ambitious and innovative results ever for a bilateral agreement by the EU.

Negotiations are currently under way to liberalise trade with **Mercosur**, the South American Common Market consisting of Argentina, Brazil, Paraguay and Uruguay. The EU is already the most important trading partner of the Mercosur countries and the biggest foreign investor in the region. The negotiations will cover not only the liberalisation of trade in goods and services, but also public procurement, intellectual property rights, competition policy and foreign investments.

South Africa concluded a bilateral agreement with the EU on trade, cooperation and development in 2000. According to this agreement, within 12 years, South Africa and the EU will grant free trade status to each other's exports.

FOCUS ON DEVELOPMENT

The globalisation of trade must not sideline poorer countries. The EU wants to find ways of helping these countries catch up with the rest of the world, instead of facing marginalisation. Improving their access to global markets for agricultural and industrial goods and services is crucial.

The EU demonstrated its support for the 49 **'least developed countries'** by launching the 'Everything but arms' initiative in March 2001. This means the EU is opening its markets to unlimited quantities of all products (except weapons) from those countries and without charging any duties whatsoever.

As Trade Commissioner Pascal Lamy said: 'This sends a signal to the rest of the world that we are serious about getting the most disadvantaged to share in the fruits of trade liberalisation.'

Everything but arms

This initiative is a world first. On 5 March 2001, the EU became the first major trading power to open its market completely to exports from the world's least developed countries (LDCs). On that date, remaining tariffs and quotas were removed from all products (barring arms), though the import duties on bananas, sugar and rice are being removed in stages between 2002 and 2009. In taking this initiative, the EU was mindful of the interests of its own producers, the interests of developing countries as a whole and of traditional suppliers of these products to the European market. The EU hopes other industrialised countries will follow its example by adopting similar initiatives.

EU OPENNESS TO EXPORTS FROM DEVELOPING COUNTRIES

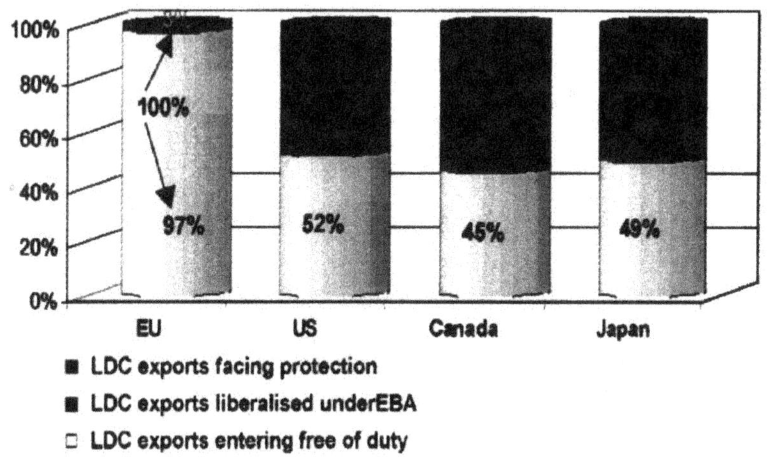

EU 3 % 97 % 100 %
United States 52 %
Canada 45 %
Japan 49 %

LDC exports facing protection
LDC exports liberalised under 'Everything but arms'
LDC exports entering free of duty

In 1999, 97 % of the exports from the world's least developed countries entered the EU free of duties. Since then, the access has been further liberalised under the 'Everything but arms' initiative. *Source:* United Nations Conference on Trade and Development/European Commission.

AID AND TRADE TOGETHER

The EU has a tradition of close relationship with the countries in **Africa, the Caribbean and the Pacific**. Under the Cotonou Agreement concluded with 77 African, Caribbean and Pacific (ACP) countries in February 2000, the European Union adopted an integrated trade and development strategy aimed at bringing the ACP countries smoothly into the world economy.

The Cotonou Agreement will run until 2007. It will then be replaced by agreements of a new type, called **economic partnership agreements** (EPAs). Negotiations between the EU and ACP countries on these new agreements started in September 2002. The EPAs will deal with political questions, economic and trade cooperation and development aid. They are likely to take the form of agreements between the EU and groups of neighbouring ACP countries.

This new approach is a response to the debate on globalisation, from which it is clear that neither European-funded development projects nor trade rules with increasingly open markets have led to acceptable living conditions in the poorest countries of the world.

A key strategy in the new approach is to strengthen the regional economic integration within different ACP subregions. Poor countries should not only try to sell more to EU countries, they should also trade more with each other. Free trade agreements between neighbouring countries can create larger, more effective markets which are attractive to local and foreign investors. The EPAs should deal with all factors that constrain business activities in ACP countries. The EU will continue to give wide-ranging economic support to these countries.

LEAST DEVELOPED COUNTRIES EXPORTS TO THE EU

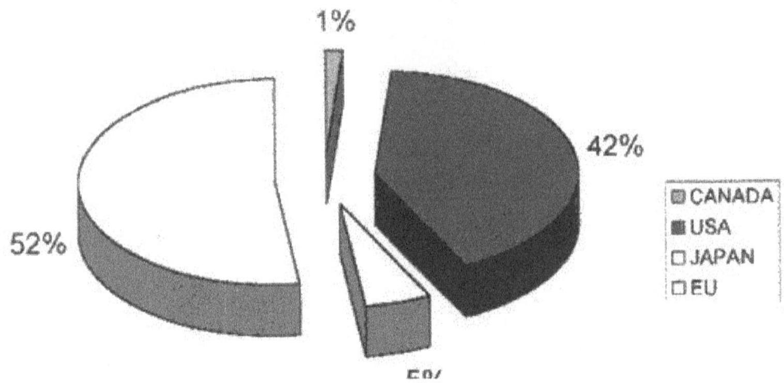

EU 52 %
United States 42 %
Japan 5 %
Canada 1 %

The value of exports from developing countries to the EU has been rising steadily, and in 2000 amounted to EUR 432 billion, double the total in 1990. The EU is the world's biggest importer of goods from the 49 least developed countries (LDCs). The chart shows the distribution of LDC exports to the four richest trading blocs. Figures for 2000. *Source:* European Commission.

THE DOHA DEVELOPMENT AGENDA: A NEW ERA FOR WORLD TRADE

On 14 November 2001, the 142 members of the WTO concluded the fourth ministerial conference with a decision to launch a new round of world trade talks. Called the 'Doha development agenda', this round will include both further trade liberalisation and a review of trade rules.

It is underpinned by the commitment of WTO members to help developing countries benefit fully from future WTO decisions. The negotiations will last three years — until January 2005.

The EU believes that the new WTO round, which it helped to launch, is the best way to ensure that trade expansion strikes a balance between economic growth, environmental protection and the promotion of social equity — in other words, sustainable development.

The EU finds the new round timely because:

- globalisation is accelerating. Its positive effects need to be harnessed in the interests of both developing and industrialised countries. This should be done by boosting opportunities for trade while creating a regulatory framework that offers predictability, stability and transparency;

- people are becoming increasingly aware of global issues such as the environment, investment, competition, consumer protection, and public health and safety. The world trade community needs to take all of these public concerns into account.

PRIORITIES FOR THE FUTURE

The new agenda sets WTO members on the path towards the following.

Further opening up their markets for goods and services: This is the traditional task of the WTO. Members need to do more to open their markets on the basis of predictable and non-discriminatory rules. Trade should be liberalised as comprehensively as possible, so that countries can negotiate concessions in one sector against gains in another.

Helping developing countries get better access to the markets of advanced countries: As developed countries open up their markets, businesses and citizens in those countries will have better access to imported products. This should happen at a pace that allows developing countries to adjust successfully to increased competitive pressures.

Focusing on development: This was a crucial aspect of the position which the EU took in Doha, and the outcome of the conference reflects it faithfully. The EU is committed to helping developing countries integrate into the world trading system and reap the benefits of liberalisation. WTO members must not only give developing countries better market access and a say in the rule-making, but must also provide them with the skills and tools to become effective players in the world trade arena.

TRADE-RELATED ASSISTANCE

The EU is a clear proponent of trade-related technical assistance (TRTA). From 1996 to 2000, it devoted more than 700 million euro to TRTA, and is providing an additional 300 million euro for ongoing bilateral or regional TRTA initiatives.

Examples of trade-related technical assistance for African, Caribbean and Pacific (ACP) countries include:
- a major 42 million euro programme to improve the health conditions of ACP fishery exports;
- a 29 million euro pesticide initiative programme for horticultural products;
- support for the installation and maintenance of an ACP office in Geneva.

The EU is committed to providing trade-related technical assistance and capacity-building for developing countries. It will make a special effort to help developing countries define and defend their interests in the new negotiations. It will also provide assistance for the medium- to long-term efforts needed to implement the results and take advantage of the trading opportunities which will flow from it.

The EU particularly welcomed a separate declaration in Doha on access to essential medicines at affordable prices. This confirms that the WTO agreements (here the Trade-Related Aspects of Intellectual Property Rights Agreement) can be interpreted in a way that allows members to take action to protect public health if need be.

Updating the world trade rule book: A fair and transparent rules-based system to govern world trade is just as important for developing countries as it is for industrialised ones. But as globalisation advances, the WTO will inevitably have to update its rules. The EU pressed successfully for the new round to include issues such as investment, competition, government procurement and measures to simplify trade procedures (known as 'trade facilitation'). The EU also supports plans to improve WTO rules on anti-subsidy measures and anti-dumping procedures, so as to reduce the scope for abusing the system.

Protecting the environment within sustainable development: Ministers at Doha agreed with the EU that trade and environmental issues can and should be dealt with in a multilateral context. In an increasingly interdependent world, challenges such as climate change, the protection of the ozone layer and the disposal of toxic waste cannot be solved by one country or even by a group of countries acting alone.

The EU has long argued that multilateral environmental agreements have to mesh smoothly with agreements in the international trading system, so they become mutually supportive.

Promoting trade and social development: There will be more cooperation between the WTO and the International Labour Organisation (ILO) so as to ensure progress on the social aspects of globalisation, including labour standards.

The EU will encourage the world community to pursue this issue via the ILO, and it will work to make sure that the WTO contributes constructively to this process.

The EU already includes social and environmental incentives in its trade relations with developing countries (the generalised system of preferences). It grants extra tariff reductions to countries that implement ILO conventions.

TAKING ON BOARD ISSUES OF GENERAL PUBLIC CONCERN

The EU has been keen to promote a debate within the WTO on issues of general public concern. Among these, **consumer protection**, and in particular food safety, is a top EU priority.

Quality and safety standards must be maintained at a high level. The WTO rules already allow countries to take trade measures to protect the health and well-being of their citizens, provided the measures taken are scientifically justified. When scientific proof is not available, countries may take action provisionally on the basis of the precautionary principle, pending the availability of scientific evidence that is being sought.

Dialogue with civil society

Demonstrations against globalisation have focused public attention as never before on the way trade policy is made. Concerned that globalisation was pushing trade policy in directions hostile to the interests of many, representatives of civil society around the world sought to make their views known.

The European Commission started its dialogue with civil society in 1998, recognising that trade policy must reflect the competing interests and values of the broadest cross-section of society and that their views need to be heard before difficult trade-offs are made. Since then, the Commission has held regular meetings with representatives of trade unions, academic institutions, employers' organisations (including small businesses) and non-governmental organisations (Internet: trade-info.cec.eu.int/civil_soc).

Further market access negotiations on **services** are expected to bring considerable market opportunities for business as well as benefits to consumers worldwide. In this respect, the EU does not seek general deregulation or privatisation of markets in sectors where principles of public interest are at stake, such as healthcare and education, or where the public authorities have a historic involvement, like energy or postal services.

The EU is also committed to maintaining its right to **cultural diversity** in negotiations. Audiovisual services are essential purveyors of culture and are therefore unlike other commercial services. Trade negotiations cannot be allowed to create standardised cultural products; rather, they should help them to be traded in a way that respects their diversity.

Overall, the Doha development agenda takes the World Trade Organisation into a new era. Not only will it continue improving conditions for worldwide trade and investment, but it will now be able to play a much fuller role in promoting economic growth, job creation and the fight against poverty.

Better world governance and the promotion of sustainable development are the ambitious backdrop to the agenda. The EU will actively pursue its work on this agenda by tabling proposals on all aspects of the negotiations and acting as a broker among different players, particularly between developed and developing countries. It will maintain close contacts with a wide range of ministers and seek to reshape trade policy so that it serves the interests of the majority of WTO members, namely the developing countries.

COMMON RULES FOR IMPORTS REGULATIONS

COUNCIL REGULATION (EC) No 3285/94 of 22 December 1994 on the common rules for imports and repealing Regulation (EC) No 518/94

Having regard to the Treaty establishing the European Community, and in particular Article 113 thereof,

Having regard to the instruments establishing the common organization of agricultural markets and the instruments concerning processed agricultural products, in particular in so far as they provide for derogation from the general principle that quantitative restrictions or measures having equivalent effect may be replaced solely by the measures provided for in the said instruments,

Having regard to the proposal from the Commission,

Having regard to the opinion of the European Parliament, (1)

Whereas the common commercial policy should be based on uniform principles; whereas Council Regulation (EC) No 518/94 of 7 March 1994 on common rules for imports and repealing Regulation (EEC) No 288/82 (2) is an important part of the policy;

Whereas due account was taken when Regulation (EC) No 518/94 was adopted from the Community's international obligations, particularly those deriving from Article XIX of the General Agreement on Tariffs and Trade (GATT);

Whereas the completion of the Uruguay Round has led to the foundation of the World Trade Organization (WTO); whereas Annex 1A to the Agreement establishing the WTO contains inter alia the General Agreement on Tariffs and Trade 1994 (GATT 1994) and an Agreement on Safeguards;

Whereas the Agreement on Safeguard meets the need to clarify and reinforce the disciplines of GATT 1994, and specifically those of Article XIX; whereas that Agreement requires the

elimination of safeguard measures which escape those rules, such as voluntary export restraints, orderly marketing arrangements and any other similar import or export arrangements;
Whereas the Agreement on Safeguards also covers ECSC products; whereas the common rules for imports, especially as regards safeguard measures, therefore also applies to those products without prejudice to any possible measures to apply an agreement specifically concerning ECSC products;

Whereas in the light of these new multilateral rules the common rules for imports should be made clearer and if necessary amended, particularly where the application of safeguard measures is concerned;

Whereas the starting point for the common rules for imports is liberalization of imports, namely the absence of any quantitative restrictions;
Whereas the Commission should be informed by the Member States of any danger created by trends in imports which might call for Community surveillance or the application of safeguard measures;

Whereas in such instances the Commission should examine the terms and conditions under which imports occur, the trend in imports, the various aspects of the economic and trade situations and, where appropriate, the measures to be applied;
Whereas if Community surveillance is applied, release for free circulation of the products concerned should be made subject to presentation of an import document meeting uniform criteria; whereas that document should, on simple application by the importer, be endorsed by the authorities of the Member States within a certain period but without the importer thereby acquiring any right to import; whereas the document should therefore be valid only during such period as the import rules remain unchanged;

Whereas the Member States and the Commission should exchange the information resulting from Community surveillance as fully as possible;

Whereas it falls to the Commission and the Council to adopt the safeguard measures required by the interests of the Community; whereas those interests should be considered as a whole and should in particular encompass the interest of Community producers, users and consumers;
Whereas safeguard measures against a Member of the WTO may be considered only if the product in question is imported into the Community in such greatly increased quantities and on such terms or conditions as to cause, or threaten to cause, serious injury to Community producers of like or directly competing products, unless international obligations permit derogation from this rule;
Whereas the terms 'serious injury', 'threat of serious injury' and 'Community producers' should be defined and more precise criteria for determining injury be established;

Whereas an investigation must precede the application of any safeguard measure, subject to the reservation that the Commission be allowed in urgent cases to apply provisional measures;
Whereas there should be more detailed provisions on the opening of investigations, the checks and inspections required, access by exporter countries and interested parties to the information gathered, hearings for the parties involved and the opportunities for those parties to submit their views;
Whereas the provisions on investigations introduced by this Regulation are without prejudice to Community or national rules concerning professional secrecy;
Whereas it is also necessary to set time limits for the initiation of investigations and for determinations as to whether or not measures are appropriate, with a view to ensuring that such determinations are made quickly, in order to increase legal certainty for the economic operators concerned;

Whereas in cases in which safeguard measures take the form of a quota the level of the latter should be set in principle no lower than the average level of imports over a representative period of at least three years;

Whereas in cases in which a quota is allocated among supplier countries each country's quota may be determined by agreement with the countries themselves or by taking as a reference the level of imports over a representative period; whereas derogations from these rules should nevertheless be possible where there is serious injury and a disproportionate increase in imports, provided that due consultation under the auspices of the WTO Committee on Safeguards takes place;

Whereas the maximum duration of safeguard measures should be determined and specific provisions regarding extension, progressive liberalization and reviews of such measures be laid down;

Whereas the circumstances in which products originating in a developing country Member of the WTO should be exempt from safeguard measures should be established;
Whereas surveillance or safeguard measures confined to one or more regions of the Community may prove more suitable than measures applying to the whole Community; whereas, however, such measures should be authorized only exceptionally and where no alternative exists; whereas it is necessary to ensure that such measures are temporary and cause the minimum of disruption to the operation of the internal market;

Whereas in the interests of uniformity in rules for imports, the formalities to be carried out by importers should be simplified and made identical regardless of the place where the goods clear customs; whereas it is therefore desirable to provide that any formalities should be carried out using forms corresponding to the specimen annexed to the Regulation;
Whereas import documents issued in connection with Community surveillance measures should be valid throughout the Community irrespective of the Member State of issue;
Whereas the textile products covered by Council Regulation (EC) No 517/94 of 7 March 1994 on common rules for imports of textile products from certain third countries not covered by bilateral agreements, protocols or other arrangements, or by other specific Community import rules (3) are subject to special treatment at Community and international level, except for the products listed in Annex II which are integrated into GATT 1994; whereas they should therefore be excluded from the scope of this Regulation;

Whereas the provisions of this Regulation are applicable without prejudice to Articles 77, 81, 244, 249 and 280 of the Act of Accession of Spain and Portugal;
Whereas national restrictions with respect to products falling under the ECSC Treaty will be progressively dismantled in accordance with the provisions of the WTO;
Whereas Regulation (EC) No 518/94 should consequently be repealed,
HAS ADOPTED THIS REGULATION

TITLE I GENERAL PRINCIPLES

Article 1
1. This Regulation applies to imports of products originating in third countries, except for:
- textile products covered by Regulation (EC) No 517/94, other than the products listed in Annex II in so far as those products originate in a country which is a member of the WTO,
- the products originating in certain third countries listed in Council Regulation (EC) No 519/94 on common rules for imports from certain third countries (4).
2. The products referred to in paragraph 1 shall be freely imported into the Community and accordingly, without prejudice to the safeguard measures which may be taken under Title V, shall not be subject to any quantitative restrictions.

TITLE II COMMUNITY INFORMATION AND CONSULTATION PROCEDURE

Article 2
The Commission shall be informed by the Member States should trends in imports appear to call for surveillance or safeguard measures. This information shall contain the evidence available, as determined on the basis of the criteria laid down in Article 10. The Commission shall immediately pass this information on to all the Member States.

Article 3
Consultations may be held either at the request of a Member State or on the initiative of the Commission. They shall take place within eight working days of the Commission receiving the information provided for in Article 2 and, in any event, before the introduction of any Community surveillance or safeguard measure.

Article 4

1. Consultation shall take place within an Advisory Committee, hereinafter called 'the Committee', made up of representatives of each Member State with a representative of the Commission as chairman.

2. The Committee shall meet when convened by its chairman. He shall provide the Member States with all relevant information as promptly as possible.
3. Consultations shall cover in particular:
- terms and conditions of import, import trends and the various aspects of the economic and commercial situation with regard to the product in question,
- the measures, if any, to be taken.
4. Consultations may be conducted in writing if necessary. The Commission shall in this event inform the Member States, which may express their opinion or request oral consultations within a period of five to eight working days, to be decided by the Commission.

TITLE III COMMUNITY INVESTIGATION PROCEDURE

Article 5
1. Without prejudice to Article 8, the Community investigation procedure shall be implemented before any safeguard measure is applied.
2. Using as a basis the factors described in Article 10, the investigation shall seek to determine whether imports of the product in question are causing or threatening to cause serious injury to the Community producers concerned.
3. The following definitions shall apply:
(a) 'serious injury' means a significant overall impairment in the position of Community producers,
(b) 'threat of serious injury' means serious injury that is clearly imminent;
(c) 'Community producers' means the producers as a whole of the like or directly competing products operating within the territory of the Community, or those whose collective output of the like or directly competing products constitutes a major proportion of the total Community production of those products.

Article 6
1. Where after consultations referred to in Article 3, it is apparent to the Commission that there is sufficient evidence to justify the initiation of an investigation, the Commission shall:
(a) initiate an investigation within one month of receipt of information from a Member State and publish a notice in the Official Journal of the European Communities; such notice shall give a summary of the information received, and stipulate that all relevant information is to be communicated to the Commission; it shall state the period within which interested parties may make known their views in writing and submit information, if such views and information are to be taken into account during the investigation; it shall also state the period within which interested

parties may apply to be heard orally by the Commission in accordance with paragraph 4;
(b) commence the investigation, acting in cooperation with the Member States.

2. The Commission shall seek all information it deems to be necessary and, where it considers it appropriate, after consulting the Committee, endeavour to check this information with importers, traders, agents, producers, trade associations and organizations.
The Commission shall be assisted in this task by staff of the Member State on whose territory these checks are being carried out, provided that Member State so wishes.
Interested parties which have come forward pursuant to paragraph 1 (a) and representatives of the exporting country may, upon written request, inspect all information made available to the Commission in connection with the investigation other than internal documents prepared by the authorities of the Community or its Member States, provided that that information is relevant to the presentation of their case and not confidential within the meaning of Article 9 and that it is used by the Commission in the investigation.

Interested parties which have come forward may communicate their views on the information in question to the Commission; those views may be taken into consideration where they are backed by sufficient evidence.

3. The Member States shall supply the Commission, at its request and following procedures laid down by it, with the information at their disposal on developments in the market of the product being investigated.

4. The Commission may hear the interested parties. Such parties must be heard where they have made a written application within the period laid down in the notice published in the Official Journal of the European Communities, showing that they are actually likely to be affected by the outcome of the investigation and that there are special reasons for them to be heard orally.

5. When information is not supplied within the time limits set by this Regulation or by the Commission pursuant to this Regulation, or the investigation is significantly impeded, findings may be made on the basis of the facts available. Where the Commission finds that any interested party or third party has supplied it with false or misleading information, it shall disregard the information and may make use of facts available.
6. Where it appears to the Commission, after the consultation referred to in Article 3, that there is insufficient evidence to justify an investigation, it shall inform the Member States of its decision within one month of receipt of the information from the Member States.

Article 7
1. At the end of the investigation, the Commission shall submit a report on the results to the Committee.

2. Where the Commission considers, within nine months of the initiation of the investigation, that no Community surveillance or safeguard measures are necessary, the investigation shall be terminated within a month, the Committee having first been consulted. The decision to terminate the investigation, stating the main conclusions of the investigation and a summary of the reasons therefor, shall be published in the Official Journal of the European Communities.

3. If the Commission considers that Community surveillance or safeguard measures are necessary, it shall take the necessary decisions in accordance with Titles IV and V, no later than nine months from the initiation of the investigation. In exceptional circumstances, this time limit may be extended by a further maximum period of two months; the Commission shall then publish a notice in the Official Journal of the European Communities setting forth the duration of the extension and a summary of the reasons therefor.

Article 8
1. The provisions of this Title shall not preclude the use, at any time, of surveillance measures in accordance with Articles 11 to 15 or provisional safeguard measures in accordance with Articles 16, 17 and 18.
Provisional safeguard measures shall be applied:
- in critical circumstances where delay would cause damage which it would be difficult to repair, making immediate action necessary, and
- where a preliminary determination provides clear evidence that increased imports have caused or are threatening to cause serious injury.

2. The duration of such measures shall not exceed 200 days.

3. Provisional safeguard measures should take the form of an increase in the existing level of customs duty (whether the latter is zero or higher) if such action is likely to prevent or repair the serious injury.

4. The Commission shall immediately conduct whatever investigation measures are still necessary.

5. Should the provisional safeguard measures be repealed because no serious injury or threat of serious injury exists, the customs duties collected as a result of the provisional measures shall be automatically refunded as soon as possible. The procedure laid down in Article 235 et seq of Council Regulation (EEC) No 2913/92 of 12 October 1992 establishing the Community Customs Code (5) shall apply.

Article 9
1. Information received pursuant to this Regulation shall be used only for the purpose for which it was requested.

2. (a) Neither the Council, nor the Commission, nor the Member States, nor the officials of any of these shall reveal any information of a confidential nature received pursuant to this Regulation, or any information provided on a confidential basis without specific permission from the supplier of such information.
(b) Each request for confidentiality shall state the reasons why the information is confidential. However, if it appears that a request for confidentiality is unjustified and if the supplier of the information wishes neither to make it public nor to authorize its disclosure in general terms or in the form of a summary, the information concerned may be disregarded.

3. Information shall in any case by considered to be confidential if its disclosure is likely to have a significantly adverse effect upon the supplier or the source of such information.

4. The preceding paragraphs shall not preclude reference by the Community authorities to general information and in particular to reasons on which decisions taken pursuant to this Regulation are based. The said authorities shall, however, take into account the legitimate interest of legal and natural persons concerned that their business secrets should not be divulged.

Article 10
1. Examination of the trend of imports, of the conditions in which they take place and of serious injury or threat of serious injury to Community producers resulting from such imports shall cover in particular the following factors:
(a) the volume of imports, in particular where there has been a significant increase, either in absolute terms or relative to production or consumption in the Community;
(b) the price of imports, in particular where there has been a significant price undercutting as

compared with the price of a like product in the Community;
(c) the consequent impact on Community producers as indicated by trends in certain economic factors such as:

- production,
- capacity utilization,
- stocks,
- sales,
- market share,
- prices (i. e. depression of prices or prevention of price increases which would normally have occurred),
- profits,
- return on capital employed,
- cash flow,
- employment;

(d) factors other than trends in imports which are causing or may have caused injury to the Community producers concerned.

2. Where a threat of serious injury is alleged, the Commission shall also examine whether it is clearly foreseeable that a particular situation is likely to develop into actual injury. In this regard account may be taken of factors such as:
(a) the rate of increase of the exports to the Community;
(b) export capacity in the country of origin or export, as it stands or is likely to be in the foreseeable future, and the likelihood that that capacity will be used to export to the Community.

TITLE IV SURVEILLANCE

Article 11
1. Where the trend in imports of a product originating in a third country covered by this Regulation threatens to cause injury to Community producers, and where the interests of the Community so require, import of that product may be subject, as appropriate, to:
(a) retrospective Community surveillance carried out in accordance with the provisions laid down in the decision referred to in paragraph 2,
(b) prior Community surveillance carried out in accordance with Article 12.

2. The decision to impose surveillance shall be taken by the Commission according to the procedure laid down in Article 16 (7) and (8).

3. The surveillance measures shall have a limited period of validity. Unless otherwise provided, they shall cease to be valid at the end of the second six-month period following the six months in which the measures were introduced.

Article 12
1. Products under prior Community surveillance may be put into free circulation only on production of an import document. Such document shall be endorsed by the competent authority designated by Member States, free of charge, for any quantity requested and within a maximum of five working days of receipt by the national competent authority of a declaration by any Community importer, regardless of his place of business in the Community. This declaration shall be deemed to have been received by the national competent authority no later than three working days after submission, unless it is proven otherwise.

2. The import document and the declaration by the importer shall be made out on a form corresponding to the model in Annex I.
Additional information to that provided for in the aforementioned form may be required. Such

information shall be specified in the decision to impose surveillance.

3. The import document shall be valid throughout the Community, regardless of the Member State of issue.

4. A finding that the unit price at which the transaction is effected exceeds that indicated in the import document by less than 5 % or that the total value or quantity of the products presented for import exceeds the value or quantity given in the import document by less than 5 % shall not preclude the release for free circulation of the product in question. The Commission, having heard the opinions expressed in the Committee and taking account of the nature of the products and other special features of the transactions concerned, may fix a different percentage, which, however, should not normally exceed 10 %.

5. Import documents may be used only for such time as arrangements for liberalization of imports remain in force in respect of the transactions concerned. Such import documents may not in any event be used beyond the expiry of a period which shall be laid down at the same time and by means of the same procedure as the imposition of surveillance, and shall take account of the nature of the products and other special features of the transactions.

6. Where the decision taken pursuant to Article 11 so requires, the origin of products under Community surveillance must be proved by a certificate of origin. This paragraph shall not affect other provisions concerning the production of any such certificate.

7. Where the product under prior Community surveillance is subject to regional safeguard measures in a Member State, the import authorization granted by that Member State may replace the import document.

Article 13
Where import of a product has not been made subject to prior Community surveillance within eight working days of the end of consultations, the Commission, in accordance with Article 18, may introduce surveillance confined to imports into one or more regions of the Community.

Article 14
1. Products under regional surveillance may be put into free circulation in the region concerned only on production of an import document. Such document shall be endorsed by the competent authority designated by the Member State(s) concerned, free of charge, for any quantity requested and within a maximum of five working days of receipt by the national competent authority of a declaration by any Community importer, regardless of his place of business in the Community. This declaration shall be deemed to have been received by the national competent authority no later than three working days after submission, unless it is proven otherwise. Import documents may be used only for such time as arrangements for imports remain liberalized in respect of the transactions concerned.
2. The import document and the declaration by the importer shall be made out on a form corresponding to the model in Annex I.
Additional information to that provided in the aforementioned form may be required. Such particulars shall be specified in the decision to impose surveillance.

Article 15
1. Member States shall communicate to the Commission within the first 10 days of each month in the case of Community or regional surveillance:
(a) in the case of prior surveillance, details of the sums of money (calculated on the basis of cif prices) and quantities of goods in respect of which import documents were issued or endorsed during the preceding period;
(b) in every case, details of imports during the period preceding the period referred to in

subparagraph (a).
The information supplied by Member States shall be broken down by product and by country. Different provisions may be laid down at the same time and by the same procedure as the surveillance arrangements.

2. Where the nature of the products or special circumstances so require, the Commission may, at the request of a Member State or on its own initiative, amend the timetables for submitting this information.

3. The Commmission shall inform the Member States accordingly.

TITLE V SAFEGUARD MEASURES

Article 16
1. Where a product is imported into the Community in such greatly increased quantities and/or on such terms or conditions as to cause, or threaten to cause, serious injury to Community producers, the Commission, in order to safeguard the interests of the Community, may, acting at the request of a Member State or on its own initiative:
(a) limit the period of validity of import documents within the meaning of Article 12 to be endorsed after the entry into force of this measure;
(b) alter the import rules for the product in question by making its release for free circulation conditional on production of an import authorization, the granting of which shall be governed by such provisions and subject to such limits as the Commission shall lay down.
The measures referred to in (a) and (b) shall take effect immediately.

2. As regards Members of the WTO, the measures referred to in paragraph 1 shall be taken only when the two conditions indicated in the first subparagraph of that paragraph are met.

3. (a) If establishing a quota, account shall be taken in particular of:
- the desirability of maintaining, as far as possible, traditional trade flows,
- the volume of goods exported under contracts concluded on normal terms and conditions before the entry into force of a safeguard measure within the meaning of this Title, where such contracts have been notified to the Commission by the Member State concerned,
- the need to avoid jeopardizing achievement of the aim pursued in establishing the quota.
(b) Any quota shall not be set lower than the average level of imports over the last three representative years for which statistics are available unless a different level is necessary to prevent or remedy serious injury.

4. (a) In cases in which a quota is allocated among supplier countries, allocation may be agreed with those of them having a substantial interest in supplying the product concerned for import into the Community.
Failing this, the quota shall be allocated among the supplier countries in proportion to their share of imports into the Community of the product concerned during a previous representative period, due account being taken of any specific factors which may have affected or may be affecting the trade in the product.
(b) Provided that its obligation to see that consultations are conducted under the auspices of the WTO Committee on Safeguards is not disregarded, the Community may nevertheless depart from this method of allocation in case of serious injury if imports originating in one or more supplier countries have increased in disproportionate percentage in relation to the total increase of imports of the product concerned over a previous representative period.

5. (a) The measures referred to in this Article shall apply to every product which is put into free circulation after their entry into force. In accordance with Article 18 they may be confined to one or more regions of the Community.
(b) However, such measures shall not prevent the release for free circulation of products already

on their way to the Community provided that the destination of such products cannot be changed and that those products which, pursuant to Articles 11 and 12, may be put into free circulation only in production of an import document are in fact accompanied by such a document.

6. Where intervention by the Commission has been requested by a Member State, the Commission shall take a decision within a maximum of five working days of receipt of such a request.

7. Any decision taken by the Commission pursuant to this Article shall be communicated to the Council and to the Member States. Any Member State may, within one month following the day of such communication, refer the decision to the Council.

8. If a Member State refers the Commission's decision to the Council, the Council, acting by a qualified majority, may confirm, amend or revoke that decision.
If, within three months of the referral of the matter to the Council, the Council has not taken a decision, the decision taken by the Commission shall be deemed revoked.

Article 17
Where the interests of the Community so require, the Council, acting by a qualified majority on a proposal from the Commission drawn up in accordance with the terms of Title III, may adopt appropriate measures to prevent a product being imported into the Community in such greatly increased quantities and/or on such terms or conditions as to cause, or threaten to cause, serious injury to Community producers of like or directly competing products.

Article 16
(2), (3), (4) and (5) shall apply.

Article 18
Where it emerges, primarily on the basis of the factors referred to in Article 10, that the conditions laid down for the adoption of measures pursuant to Articles 11 and 16 are met in one or more regions of the Community, the Commission, after having examined alternative solutions, may exceptionally authorize the application of surveillance or safeguard measures limited to the region(s) concerned if it considers that such measures applied at that level are more appropriate than measures applied throughout the Community.
These measures must be temporary and must disrupt the operation of the internal market as little as possible.
The measures shall be adopted in accordance with the provisions laid down in Articles 11 and 16 respectively.

Article 19
No safeguard measure may be applied to a product originating in a developing country Member of the WTO as long as that country's share of Community imports of the product concerned does not exceed 3 %, provided that developing country Members with less than a 3 % import share collectively account for not more than 9 % of total Community imports of the product concerned.

Article 20
1. The duration of safeguard measures must be limited to the period of time necessary to prevent or remedy serious injury and to facilitate adjustment on the part of Community producers. The period should not exceed four years, including the duration of any provisional measure.
2. Such initial period may be extended, except in the case of the measures referred to in Article 16 (4) (b), provided it is determined that:
- the safeguard measure continues to be necessary to prevent or remedy serious injury,
- and there is evidence that Community producers are adjusting.
3. Extensions shall be adopted in accordance with the terms of Title III and using the same

producers as the initial measures. A measure so extended shall not be more restrictive than it was at the end of the initial period.
4. If the duration of the measure exceeds one year, the measure must be progressively liberalized at regular intervals during the period of application, including the period of extension.
5. The total period of application of a safeguard measure, including the period of application of any provisional measures, the initial period of application and any prorogation thereof, may not exceed eight years.

Article 21
1. While any surveillance or safeguard measure applied in accordance with Titles IV and V is in operation, consultations shall be held within the Committee, either at the request of a Member State or on the initiative of the Commission. If the duration of a safeguard measure exceeds three years, the Commission shall seek such consultations no later than the mid-point of the period of application of that measure. The purpose of such consultations shall be:
(a) to examine the effects of the measure;
(b) to determine whether and in what manner it is appropriate to accelerate the pace of liberalization;
(c) to ascertain whether its application is still necessary.

2. Where, as a result of the consultations referred to in paragraph 1, the Commission considers that any surveillance or safeguard measure referred to in Articles 11, 13, 16, 17 and 18 should be revoked or amended, it shall proceed as follows:
(a) where the measure was enacted by the Council, the Commission shall propose to the Council that it be revoked or amended. The Council shall act by a qualified majority;
(b) in all other cases, the Commission shall amend or revoke Community safeguard and surveillance measures.
Where the decision relates to regional surveillance measures, it shall apply from the sixth day following that of its publication in the Official Journal of the European Communities.

Article 22
1. Where imports of a product have already been subject to a safeguard measure no further such measure shall be applied to that product until a period equal to the duration of the previous measure has elapsed. Such period shall not be less than two years.

2. Notwithstanding paragraph 1, a safeguard measure of 180 days or less may be reimposed for a product if:
(a) at least one year has elapsed since the date of introduction of a safeguard measure on the import of that product; and
(b) such a safeguard measure has not been applied to the same product more than twice in the five-year period immediately preceding the date of introduction of the measure.

TITLE VI FINAL PROVISIONS

Article 23
Where the interests of the Community so require, the Council, acting by a qualified majority on a proposal from the Commission, may adopt appropriate measures to allow the rights and obligations of the Community or of all its Member States, in particular those relating to trade in commodities, to be exercised and fulfilled at international level.

Article 24
1. This Regulation shall not preclude the fulfilment of obligations arising from special rules contained in agreements concluded between the Community and third countries.
2. (a) Without prejudice to other Community provisions, this Regulation shall not preclude the adoption or application by Member States:
(i) of prohibitions, quantitative restrictions or surveillance measures on grounds of public morality,

public policy or public security; the protection of health and life of humans, animals or plants, the protection of national treasures possessing artistic, historic or archaeological value, or the protection of industrial and commercial property;
(ii) of special formalities concerning foreign exchange;
(iii) of formalities introduced pursuant to international agreements in accordance with the Treaty.
(b) The Member States shall inform the Commission of the measures or formalities they intend to introduce or amend in accordance with this paragraph. In the event of extreme urgency, the national measures or formalities in question shall be communicated to the Commission immediately upon their adoption.

Article 25
1. This Regulation shall be without prejudice to the operation of the instruments establishing the common organization of agricultural markets or of Community or national administrative provisions derived therefrom or of the specific instruments applicable to goods resulting from the processing of agricultural products; it shall operate by way of complement to those instruments.

2. However, in the case of products covered by the instruments referred to in paragraph 1, Articles 11 to 15 and 22 shall not apply to those in respect of which the Community rules on trade with third countries require the production of a licence or other import document.

Articles 16, 18 and 21 to 24 shall not apply to those products in respect of which such rules provide for the application of quantitative import restrictions.

Article 26
1. Residual national restrictions relating to products covered by the ECSC Treaty shall be progressively dismantled in accordance with the provisions of the WTO.

2. Until 31 December 1995, Spain and Portugal may maintain the quantitative restrictions on agricultural products referred to in Articles 77, 81, 244, 249 and 280 of the Act of Accession.

Article 27
Regulation (EC) No 518/94 is hereby repealed. References to the repealed Regulation shall be understood as referring to this Regulation.

Article 28
This Regulation shall enter into force on 1 January 1995.
This Regulation shall be binding in its entirety and directly applicable in all Member States.
Done at Brussels, 22 December 1994.
For the Council
The President
H. SEEHOFER

(1) Opinion delivered on 14 December 1994 (not yet published in the Official Journal).(2) OJ No L 67, 10. 3. 1994, p. 77.(3) OJ No L 67, 10. 3. 1994, p. 1.(4) OJ No L 67, 10. 3. 1994, p. 89.(5) OJ No L 302, 19. 10. 1992, p. 1.

ANNEX I LIST OF PARTICULARS TO BE GIVEN IN THE BOXES OF THE SURVEILLANCE DOCUMENT

SURVEILLANCE DOCUMENT
1. Applicant
(name, full address, country)
2. Registration No
3. Consignor (name, address, country)

4. Competent authorities of issue
(name and address)
5. Declarant (name and address)
6. Last day of validity
7. Country of origin
8. Country of consignment
9. Proposed place and date of importation
10. Reference to Regulation (EC) which imposed surveillance
11. Description of goods, marks and numbers, number and kind of packages
12. Goods code (CN)
13. Gross mass (kg)
14. Net mass (kg)
15. Additional units
16. Cif value EC frontier in ecu
17. Further particulars
18. Certification by the applicant:
I, the undersigned, certify that the information provided in this application is true and given in good faith.
Date and place
(signature)(stamp)
19. Stamp of the competent authorities

COMMON RULES FOR EXPORTS REGULATIONS

REGULATION (EEC) No 2603/69 OF THE COUNCIL of 20 December 1969 establishing common rules for exports

Whereas common rules should therefore be established for exports from the EEC;

Whereas exports are almost completely liberalised in all the Member States ; whereas it is therefore possible to accept as a Community principle that exports to third countries are not subject to any quantitative restriction, subject to the exceptions provided for in this Regulation and without prejudice to such measures as Member States may take in conformity with the Treaty;

Whereas the Commission must be informed if, as a result of unusual developments on the market, a Member State considers that protective measures might be necessary;

Whereas it is essential that examination should take place at Community level, in particular on the basis of any such information and within an advisory committee, of export terms and conditions, of export trends, of the various aspects of the economic and commercial situation, and of the measures, if any, to be taken;

Whereas it may become apparent from this examination that the Community should exercise surveillance over certain exports, or that interim protective measures should be introduced as a safeguard against unforeseen practices ; whereas the need for rapid and effective action makes it justifiable for the Commission to be empowered to decide upon such measures, but without prejudice to the subsequent position of the Council, whose responsibility it is to adopt a policy consistent with the interests of the Community;

Whereas any protective measures necessitated by the interests of the Community should be adopted with due regard for existing international obligations;

Whereas it is desirable that Member States be impowered, in certain circumstances and provided that their actions are on an interim basis only, to take protective measures individually;

Whereas it is desirable that while such protective measures are in operation there should be an opportunity for consultation for the purpose of examining the effects of the measures and of ascertaining whether the conditions for their application are still satisfied;

Whereas certain products should be provisionally excluded from Community liberalisation until the Council shall have acted to establish common rules in respect of those products;

Whereas this Regulation is to apply to all products, whether industrial or agricultural ; whereas its operation should be complementary to that of the instruments establishing common organisation of agricultural markets, and to that of the special instruments adopted under Article 235 of the Treaty for processed agricultural products ; whereas any overlap between the provisions of this Regulation and the provisions of those instruments, particularly the protective clauses thereof, must however be avoided;

HAS ADOPTED THIS REGULATION:

TITLE I

Basic principle

Article 1

The exportation of products from the European Economic Community to third countries shall be free, that is to say, they shall, not be subject to any quantitative restriction, with the exception of those restrictions which are applied in conformity with the provisions of this Regulation.

TITLE II

Community information and consultation procedure

Article 2

If, as a result of any unusual developments on the market, a Member State considers that protective measures within the meaning of Title III might be necessary, it shall so notify the Commission, which shall advise the other Member States.

Article 3

1. Consultations may be held at any time, either at the request of a Member State or on the initiative of the Commission.

2. Consultations shall take place within four working days following receipt by the Commission of the notification provided for in Article 2, and in all cases before the introduction of any measure pursuant to Articles 5 to 7.

Article 4

1. Consultation shall take place within an advisory committee (hereinafter called "the Committee"), which shall consist of representatives of each Member State with a representative of the Commission as Chairman.

2. The Committee shall meet when convened by its Chairman. He shall provide all the Member States, as promptly as possible, with all relevant information.

3. Consultation shall in particular cover: (a) terms and conditions of export, export trends, and the various aspects of the economic and commercial situation as regards the product in question;

(b) the measures, if any, to be adopted.

Article 5

For the purpose of assessing the economic and commercial situation as regards a particular product, the Commission may request Member States to supply statistical data on market trends in that product and, to this end, acting in accordance with their national legislation and with a procedure to be specified by the Commission, to exercise surveillance over exports of such product. Member States shall take whatever steps are necessary in order to give effect to requests from the Commission and shall forward to the Commission the data requested. The Commission shall inform the other Member States.

TITLE III

Protective measures

Article 6

1. In order to prevent a critical situation from arising on account of a shortage of essential products, or to remedy such a situation, and where Community interests call for immediate intervention, the Commission, acting at the request of a Member State or on its own initiative, and taking account of the nature of the products and of the other particular features of the transactions in question, may make the export of a product subject to the production of an export authorisation, the granting of which shall be governed by such provisions and subject to such limits as the Commission shall lay down pending subsequent action by the Council under Article 7.

2. The Council and the Member States shall be notified of the measures taken. Such measures shall take effect immediately.

3. The measures may be limited to exports to certain countries or to exports from certain regions of the Community. They shall not affect products already on their way to the Community frontier.

4. Where intervention by the Commission has been requested by a Member State, the Commission shall take a decision within a maximum of five working days of receipt of such request. Should the Commission refuse to give effect to the request, it shall forthwith communicate its decision to the Council, which may, acting by a qualified majority, decide differently.

5. Any Member State may, within twelve working days of the day of their communication to the Member States, refer the measures taken to the Council. The Council may, acting by a qualified majority, decide that different action be taken.

6. Where the Commission has acted pursuant to paragraph 1, it shall, not later than twelve working days following the entry into force of the measure which it has taken, make a proposal to the Council on appropriate measures as provided for in Article 7. If, at the end of six weeks following the entry into force of the measure, taken by the Commission, the Council has taken no decision on this proposal, the measure in question shall be deemed revoked.

Article 7

1. Where the interests of the Community so require, the Council may, acting by a qualified majority on a proposal from the Commission, adopt appropriate measures: - to prevent a critical situation from arising owing to a shortage of essential products, or to remedy such a situation;

- to allow international undertakings entered into by the Community or all the Member States to be fulfilled, in particular those relating to trade in primary products.

2. Such measures may be limited to exports to certain countries or to exports from certain regions of the Community. They shall not affect products already on their way to the Community frontier.

3. When quantitative restrictions on exports are introduced, account shall be taken in particular of: - the volume of goods exported under contracts concluded on normal terms and conditions before the entry into force of a protective measure within the meaning of this Title and notified by the Member State concerned to the Commission in conformity with its national laws ; and

- the need to avoid jeopardising achievement of the aim pursued in introducing quantitative restrictions.

Article 8

1. Where a Member State considers that there exists in its territory a situation such as that defined as regards the Community in Article 6 (1), it may, as an interim protective measure, make the export of a product subject to the production of an export authorisation, the granting of which shall be governed by such provisions and subject to such limits as that Member State shall lay down.

2. The Member State shall take such a measure after hearing the opinions expressed in the Committee or, where urgency precludes such a procedure, after notifying the Commission. The latter shall advise the other Member States.

3. The Commission shall be notified by telex of the measure immediately following its adoption ; such notification shall be equivalent to a request within the meaning of Article 6 (4). The measure shall operate only until the coming into operation of the decision taken by the Commission.

4. The provisions of this Article shall apply until 31 December 1972. Before that date the Council shall, by a qualified majority on a proposal from the Commission, decide on the adjustments to be made thereto.

Article 9

1. While any measure referred to in Articles 6 to 8 is in operation, consultations within the Committee shall be held, either at the request of a Member State or on the initiative of the Commission. The purpose of such consultations shall be: (a) to examine the effects of the measures;

(b) to ascertain whether the conditions for its application are still satisfied.

2. Where the Commission considers that any measure provided for in Article 6 or in Article 7 should be revoked or amended, it shall proceed as follows: (a) where the Council has taken no decision on a measure taken by the Commission, the latter shall amend or revoke such measure forthwith and shall immediately deliver a report to the Council;

(b) in all other cases, the Commission shall propose to the Council that the measures adopted by the Council be revoked or amended. The Council shall act by a qualified majority.

TITLE IV

Transitional and final provisions

Article 10

Until such time as the Council, acting by a qualified majority on a proposal from the Commission, shall have introduced common rules in respect of the products listed in the Annex to this Regulation, the principle of freedom of export from the Community as laid down in Article 1 shall not apply to those products.

Article 11

Without prejudice to other Community provisions, this Regulation shall not preclude the adoption or application by a Member State of quantitative restrictions on exports on grounds of public morality, public policy or public security ; the protection of health and life of humans, animals or plants ; the protection of national treasures possessing artistic, historic or archaeological value, or the protection of industrial and commercial property.

Article 12

1. This Regulation shall be without prejudice to the operation of the instruments establishing common organisation of agricultural markets, or of the special instruments adopted under Article 235 of the Treaty for processed agricultural products ; it shall operate by way of complement to those instruments.

2. However, in the case of products covered by such instruments, the provisions of Articles 6 and 8 shall not apply to those in respect of which the Community rules on trade with third countries make provision for the application of quantitative export restrictions. The provisions of Article 5 shall not apply to those products in respect of which such rules require the production of a licence or other export document.

Article 13

This Regulation shall enter into force on 31 December 1969.

This Regulation shall be binding in its entirety and directly applicable in all Member States.

GLOBAL EUROPE EUROPE'S TRADE DEFENCE INSTRUMENTS IN A CHANGING GLOBAL ECONOMY

A Green Paper for public consultation

Introduction

The European Union, like most other importing economies, operates a system of trade defence instruments. These instruments – Anti-Dumping, Anti-Subsidy and Safeguard measures – allow the European Union to defend its producers against unfairly traded or subsidised imports and against dramatic shifts in trade flows in so far as these are harmful to the EU economy. It is important that we use these instruments effectively and rigorously to ensure respect of international trade rules and protect European interests against unfair trade.

The EU's use of these instruments is based on rules derived from the WTO agreements that establish trade defence instruments and the principles on which they operate as a legitimate part of the multilateral system of free trade. Like the urgent work to suppress counterfeiting and intellectual property theft, including through the abuse of electronic communications, defending against unfair trade is a politically and economically crucial part of defending free trade. It allows us to support the interests of European workers and European competitiveness, and is therefore an important part of helping Europe manage the consequences of globalisation.

The economic rationale for Anti-Dumping and Anti-Subsidy trade defence measures essentially follows from the fact that the international economy has no mechanism for correcting anti-competitive practice similar to the competition authorities that operate in almost all national economies. Furthermore, very few jurisdictions have formal rules or institutions for subsidy control similar to the European Union's state aid rules. Trade defence instruments have developed in international law as a means of correcting the trade distorting effects of uncompetitive practice at the international level.

European trade defence action over the last decade has eliminated the trade distorting effects of dumping in important sectors such as steel, chemicals and microprocessors that threatened the continued viability of these industries and their thousands of workers in Europe.

The EU has gone further than any other WTO member in unilaterally building on WTO rules to tighten conditions for use and focus the impact of trade defence action in its own market. The EU has produced a system of trade defence instruments that is arguably more open and more balanced than any other WTO member. The EU has also led the debate on reforming WTO rules on trade defence, which has been an integral part of the Doha Round. The faithful application of those internationally agreed rules by all members of the WTO is crucial for the functioning of the international trading system. This insistence that all must adhere to the agreed rules in this field must remain a guiding objective for our policy in future.

Nevertheless, in the decade since the 1994 Agreement on Anti-Dumping and the last major reform of EU trade defence instruments, there have been far-reaching changes in the global economy and in the structure of the EU economy. These have been an important factor in the overall priorities of this Commission in promoting a new growth and competitiveness agenda. These priorities are set out in the Commission's contribution to the Hampton Court European Council: European values in a globalised world .

Many more EU companies now produce goods outside the EU for import into the EU, or operate supply chains that stretch beyond the EU market. These changes challenge familiar understandings of what constitutes EU production and the EU's economic interests. Because it is precisely these things that trade defence instruments are intended to defend, a periodic review can help us to ensure that the EU's trade defence instruments remain an effective response to unfair trading practices. This may also help to maintain strong political support behind the use of these necessary instruments across the EU.

The Commission has recently highlighted a new policy agenda designed to reinforce the EU's capacity to compete in a global economy marked by the growing fragmentation and complexity of the process of production and supply chains and the growth of major new economic actors, particularly in Asia (Global Europe: Competing in the World). This reflection on the EU's trade defence instruments is an integral part of that agenda. The Green Paper does not question the fundamental value of trade defence instruments, but invites a public reflection on how the EU can continue to use them to best effect in the European interest.

The Green Paper draws on the European Commission's experience of managing the use of trade defence instruments as well as on the results of a recent evaluation study of them. It also reflects informal contacts with EU Member States and the European Parliament and a series of papers submitted to EU Trade Commissioner Peter Mandelson by experts in the field of trade defence instruments in July 2006.

The paper groups the issues into six themes;

1. the role of trade defence instruments in a changing global economy;

2. the weighting of different EU interests in trade defence investigations;

3. the launch and conduct of trade defence investigations;

4. the form, timing and duration of trade defence measures;

5. the transparency of trade defence investigations and;

6. the institutional structure of trade defence investigations.

For each group of issues it raises a series of questions to which participants to the consultation are invited to respond.

Box 1: Europe's trade defence instruments

Anti-Dumping. Anti-Dumping rules are the European Union's most used form of trade defence instrument. Anti-Dumping measures address the import of goods to the European Union at less than their normal value in their home market – usually as a result of the lack of competition and/or state interference in the production process that allows an exporter to artificially lower the cost of an export. Dumping harms both EU producers but also other producers in third countries that compete for access to the EU market. Typical examples of distortions leading to dumping include: significant tariff and non-tariff barriers, insufficient enforcement of competition rules, export tax breaks; artificially low raw material and/or energy prices. Where an EU investigation shows that these imports are harming EU producers Anti-Dumping rules allow for remedial measures to correct the injury. Normally this is the imposition of a duty on the dumped import.

Anti-Subsidy. Anti-subsidy measures are similar to Anti-Dumping measures except they specifically correct the trade-distorting effect of WTO-actionable subsidies to foreign producers, where these subsidies can be shown to be harming EU producers.

Safeguards. Safeguard measures are different in that they do not focus on whether trade is fair or not, but on shifts in the volume of trade that are so swift and on such a scale that EU producers cannot reasonably be expected to adapt to changed trade flows. In these circumstances, WTO and EU rules allow for short-term restrictions on imports to give industry temporary relief in order to adapt to this sudden surge. This temporary breathing space goes hand in hand with the clear obligation to restructure.

Between January 1996 and December 2005, the EU imposed 194 definitive Anti-Dumping measures. The countries most frequently found to be involved in dumping were China (38 measures) and India (16 measures) during this period. As of 31 October 2006, the EU has 12 Anti-Subsidy measures in force. The EU has only ever imposed eight definitive safeguard measures under WTO rules: only one of these is still in force. In the EU, Anti-Dumping and Anti-Subsidy measures against unfair trade represent less than 0.45% of the value of total imports.

In comparison, the US imposed 201 definitive measures and India imposed 309 definitive measures between 1996 and 2005. In the same period the EU initiated 294 investigations, the US 352 and India 419 investigations.

The European Commission is responsible for the conduct of Anti-Dumping, Anti-Subsidy and Safeguard investigations, including decisions on whether to open investigations in response to industry complaints, and reviews during the life of current measures. It may also impose provisional measures and proposes definitive measures to the Council, where these are warranted. The Council imposes definitive Anti-Dumping/Anti-Subsidy measures by simple majority while Safeguard measures require the support of a qualified majority of Member States.

PART 1. WHAT IS THE ROLE OF TRADE DEFENCE MEASURES IN A GLOBAL ECONOMY?

The economic justification for Anti-Dumping measures derives chiefly from the fact that international markets are imperfectly competitive – there is no international competition authority to regulate anti-competitive behaviour between countries. In contrast to an internal market like the EU, there are few rules that regulate business behaviour on international markets.

Anti-Dumping measures are the only tool provided for in international law to address the effects of unfairly traded imports from such markets on EU industry. Similarly Anti-Subsidy measures counter unfair subsidisation of producers in third countries in the absence of fully developed international means of limiting such intervention. Safeguard measures are targeted against imports that increase in such quantities as to cause or threaten to cause serious injury to the EU industry.

The EU currently initiates significantly more Anti-Dumping investigations than Anti-Subsidy investigations. One reason why companies are reluctant to request Anti-Subsidy cases is that they fear retaliation by the governments concerned. One solution to this might be for the Commission itself to initiate more Anti-Subsidy cases.

The economic justification for trade defence instruments remains controversial amongst economists. Some argue that trade defence instruments are needed in the absence of internationally agreed competition rules. Others believe trade defence measures cannot be economically justified from the perspective of the overall welfare of a country. Others argue that they could potentially be misused by sectoral interests as a means of obtaining protection from competitive imports. Yet others argue that Anti-Dumping action is only justified if an exporter in a third country benefits from a lack of, or insufficient enforcement of, domestic competition rules.

Question 1: What is the role of trade defence instruments in the modern global economy? Do trade defence instruments remain essential in order to ensure respect for international trade rules and to protect European interests? Should the EU consider how they might be improved?

Question 2: Should the EU make greater use of Anti-Subsidy and Safeguard instruments alongside its Anti-Dumping actions? Should the Commission, in particular circumstances, be ready to initiate more trade defence investigations on its own initiative provided it is in possession of the required evidence?

Question 3: Are there alternatives to the use of trade defence instruments in the absence of internationally agreed competition rules?

PART 2. WEIGHING DIFFERENT EU INTERESTS IN TRADE DEFENCE INVESTIGATIONS

Trade defence measures must serve the overall economic interest of the EU, including that of producers and workers. EU rules need to continue to address situations in which lower import prices are not driven solely by true comparative advantages in labour and production costs in third countries, but reflect the fact that those advantages are topped up by unfair competitive conditions such as subsidies or other state induced distortions.

Changes in the structure of both the global and EU economies have made determining the EU's economic interests more complex. Globalisation increases the international division of labour as transportation and communication costs have substantially decreased. Increasingly, European companies are using production bases outside the European Union whilst maintaining significant operations and employment in Europe. From the perspective of trade defence instruments, the challenge is to consider whether EU rules take sufficient account of the reality of outsourced production by European businesses, which are then in competition with EU-based production and might be negatively affected by trade defence measures.

It is not in the EU's long-term economic interest to tolerate dumping, even where it benefits European companies that have outsourced production to third countries. But we do need to reflect on the fact that action to limit the injury caused by dumping can impact on the employment and viability of EU companies that are operating legitimately through outsourced production. Striking the right balance between free trade and fair trade is crucial. We need clear rules that help us address this situation.

This part of the paper relates to four key issues related to the Community interest test.

Box 2: Case study - Anti-dumping measures on leather shoes, August 2006

In October 2006 the European Union imposed duties of 16.5% and 10% on certain leather shoes imported to the European Union. These duties were the result of an investigation that found both dumping of these exports from certain third countries and consequent injury to EU producers. The application of EU and WTO rules in this highly complex case provoked divisions among EU economic operators and EU Member States. The case illustrated two of the important issues that this Green Paper considers.

Outsourcing by EU producers. Although many EU companies still produce leather footwear in the European Union, a significant number of EU companies have outsourced the production of footwear to third countries while keeping other parts of their operations in the EU. Those EU companies that produce leather shoes in the third countries concerned are subject to the Anti-Dumping duty. Moreover, under the existing rules for Anti-Dumping investigations, only producers that keep their production within the EU were considered in determining whether the required proportion of Community industry for the case to be initiated was met. Yet the number of EU companies that are moving elements of their production is growing and these companies account for thousands of jobs in the EU.

Consumer interest. The footwear case also illustrated another problem in the context of determining what is in the wider economic interest of the EU. In the majority of cases, especially those which do not concern consumer products, the impact of Anti-Dumping measures on the prices paid by the consumer have typically not been significant. Nonetheless, it is important to reflect on the question of whether and how consumer interests can be better reflected in Anti-Dumping investigations, and any measures taken.

2.1. The Community interest test. The EU is one of the few trade defence users that applies a public interest test in the form of the Community interest rule before applying Anti-Dumping measures. The Community interest rule states that measures can only be imposed where the Commission determines that imposing them is not against the wider interest of the EU economy. Such a test is not required by the WTO Anti-Dumping Agreement but it has proved a useful factor in weighing the balance of interests in Anti-Dumping cases.

However, some argue that the Community interest test is too strongly weighted towards EU producers and does not take sufficient account of the impact of measures on importing businesses that have moved some of their production outside the EU. There is also concern that consumer interests are not adequately weighted, especially when trade defence instruments are applied to finished consumer products. While the principal concern of the EU's instruments is responding to the effect of unfair competition, recent cases have also raised the question of using the Community interest test to weigh the impact of measures on the overall coherence of EU policy. For example, the EU might consider whether in some cases Anti-Dumping measures reduce the effectiveness of EU development assistance to a given country.

Question 4: Should the EU review the current balance of interests between various economic operators in the Community interest test in trade defence investigations? Alongside the interests of producers and their employees in Europe, how should we take into account the interests of companies which have retained significant operations and employment in Europe, even though they have moved some part of their production out of the EU? How should we take into account the interests of importers or producers who process affected imports?

Question 5: Do we need to review the way that consumer interests are taken into account in trade defence investigations? Should the Commission be more proactive in soliciting input from consumer associations? How could such input be weighted? How could the impact of trade defence measures on consumers be assessed and monitored?

Question 6: Should the EU include wider considerations in the Community interest assessments in trade defence investigations, such as coherence with other EU policies? With regard to development policy, should the EU make a formal distinction between least developed countries and developing countries in the application of trade defence measures?

Question 7: What kinds of economic analysis might help in making these assessments?

2.2. Using the Community interest test to fine-tune trade defence measures. Currently the findings of the Community interest test can only conclude that measures should either go ahead or not be imposed. In principle, this "either/or" test does not allow for Community interest analysis to be used as a rationale for adapting or modifying measures. However, it may be appropriate to introduce more flexibility in this respect provided that any adjustment of measures fully reflects the objective findings of the case. Such flexibility would be limited to downward adjustments by the EU's lesser duty rule which requires that duties be set at the injury margin or the dumping margin, whichever is lower. It could also in theory extend to the ability to exempt certain products from duties for Community interest reasons.

Question 8: Should it be explicitly foreseen that the level of proposed measures might be adjusted downwards following the results of the Community interest test in trade defence investigations? Should the EU explicitly allow for exclusion of certain product types under Community interest considerations? If so, what criteria should be applied?

2.3. Deciding when to apply the Community interest test. Currently, a Community interest test is foreseen only following the initiation of an investigation at the time of determining measures. WTO rules prohibiting the publicizing of anti-dumping complaints prior to launching an investigation currently preclude the use of the Community interest test in assessing the strength of an initial complaint. However some stakeholders have suggested that the EU should press to see these rules changed.

Question 9: Should the EU seek to have WTO rules changed to allow Community interest tests to be used at the complaints stage in Anti-Dumping and Anti-Subsidy investigations? Are there other situations where the community interest test would be appropriate – for example before the initiation of expiry reviews?

2.4. Viability assessments. The overall viability of the industry in the EU is an element investigated in the Community interest test. Where there are good prospects for the viability of a particular sector this is an important factor in assessing whether to impose trade defence measures.

Question 10: Are viability assessments relevant in reaching decisions on using trade defence instruments? If so, what criteria should be used in assessing the viability of EU industries in trade defence investigations, e.g. level of production, employment, market share?

PART 3. THE LAUNCHING AND CONDUCT OF TRADE DEFENCE INVESTIGATIONS

Stakeholders have identified a number of technical areas related to the launching and conduct of trade defence investigations where changes could further improve the proportionality, efficacy and fairness of EU trade defence investigations. Eight of these issues are addressed below:

3.1. Early consultations with the exporting third countries. While WTO rules prohibit contact with companies that may be investigated prior to the launch of a case, some stakeholders proposed contacts with exporting third countries' governments prior to launching investigations to help to avoid political frictions and discuss the products and practices likely to be implicated in an investigation.

Question 11: Should the EU consider consultations with exporting third countries after receiving complaints and prior to launching Anti-Dumping investigations?

3.2. The use of the Anti-Subsidy instrument in transition economies. Current practice does not foresee the initiation of Anti-Subsidy investigations in cases involving economies in transition because of the widespread nature of distortions of costs and prices in such economies. However, the use of the Anti-Subsidy instrument could be considered in cases in which individual companies in economies in transition are awarded market economy treatment.

Question 12: Should the EU more specifically foresee the use of the Anti-Subsidy instrument in cases involving companies in transition economies that receive market economy treatment?

3.3. Standing requirements . The EU imposes certain requirements that must be met for a trade defence investigation to be launched. WTO rules require that an investigation normally be initiated only when producers expressly supporting the complaint account for more than 25% of total production of the product implicated in the market concerned.

Under current rules businesses that both produce and import the allegedly dumped product may be excluded from the standing assessment. This has the effect of lowering the number of companies required to establish standing in a given case, and excluding companies that may object to a complaint. Some stakeholders consider these so-called ‘standing requirements’ too low.

Question 13: Should the EU review the ‘standing requirements’ for the definition of Community industry in Anti-Dumping and Anti-Subsidy cases? Is the level of support needed to endorse a complaint and thus launch an investigation appropriate? Should we review the possibility of excluding companies which themselves import or are related to exporters from standing assessments?

3.4. De-minimis rules for dumping, subsidy and injury. Under current rules, thresholds exist below which cases under investigation are not considered of sufficient importance to merit EU intervention. EU Anti-Dumping law stipulates that an investigation shall be terminated if the margin of dumping is less than 2% expressed as a percentage of the export price – this is called the ‘ de-minimis threshold’.

A de-minimis threshold is also applicable in the determination of injury from dumped goods. Proceedings are not initiated against countries whose imports represent less than 1% of the EU market. The current de-minimis thresholds could be higher or lower, depending on the perceived economic impact of low dumping/subsidy margins and injury thresholds.

Besides these percentage thresholds, a second " de-minimis test" could be considered by making the opening of a case dependent on the value of imports in Euro.

Question 14: Should the EU change the de-minimis thresholds (in percentage and absolute terms) that currently apply to dumping and injury in trade defence investigations?

3.5. Dumping margin calculations. An important part of an Anti-Dumping investigation is the determination of the production costs and normal value of a product in the home market. Some stakeholders have suggested that the EU does not take sufficient account of the extent to which low volumes produced and sold at the start-up phase of a product can distort per-unit costs and might make them appear unrealistically high. This in turn could possibly inflate dumping margins.

Question 15: Should the Commission refine the approach on "start-up costs" for dumping calculations in Anti-Dumping investigations in order to give a longer "grace period" to exporters in start-up situations?

Question 16: Are there other changes to the dumping margin calculation methodology in Anti-Dumping investigations – for example existing rules on the "ordinary course of trade-test" – that need to be considered?

3.6. Treatment of new exporters. Stakeholders have proposed refining the provisions on the treatment of new exporters who begin exporting goods while an investigation is underway. New exporters raise the problem of basing findings on a very small number of transactions. The Commission can also currently only address new exporters that start to operate during the investigation through a separate newcomer review.

Question 17: Should the EU refine the provisions on the treatment of new exporters in Anti-Dumping and Anti-Subsidy investigations? Should the EU introduce the possibility of dealing with newcomers that start to operate during the investigation of the main case more expeditiously?

3.7. Restructuring plans. Some stakeholders think that EU producers should be required to present a restructuring plan before they benefit from Anti-Dumping measures. Others take the view that where the problems of an industry are the direct consequence of unfair trade practices, restructuring is irrelevant.

Question 18: Is evidence of restructuring by an EU industry in any way relevant in Anti-Dumping and Anti-Subsidy investigations? If yes, in what way, and at what stage?

3.8. Involvement of SMEs. Many stakeholders think that SMEs have difficulties in launching and participating in trade defence investigations because of the complexity and high costs involved.

Question 19: What are the particular obstacles for SMEs to participate in trade defence investigations and how could they be addressed?

PART 4. THE FORM, TIMING AND DURATION OF TRADE DEFENCE MEASURES

Stakeholders have identified a number of areas related to the imposition, form, duration and expiry of trade defence measures that could be reviewed. We address four issues in this section.

4.1. Timing of provisional measures. Some stakeholders have raised the issue of faster adoption of provisional Anti-Dumping measures. At present they are adopted by the Commission between two and nine months after the launch of an investigation, if preliminary evidence points to a finding of injurious dumping.

Question 20: Bearing in mind that any shortening of deadlines could impose limitations on the conduct and transparency of investigations, should the EU consider shortening the deadlines in Anti-Dumping and Anti-Subsidy investigations within which it must decide whether or not to impose provisional measures? Should these deadlines be made more flexible?

4.2. Form, timing and duration of measures. Many stakeholders have said that the EU should have a greater choice of possible measures at its disposal than the standard ad valorem duties, fixed duties, minimum prices and price undertakings. This would give greater flexibility in dealing with complex cases which involve important consumer products. For example, should the Commission, to the extent that the Community's international obligations allow, generally have the possibility to apply a duty that phases in over time or with import volume, so as to give the market time to adapt?

Some stakeholders have also said that measures should take account of the impact on products that may have been ordered long before measures have been adopted or that are being shipped at the time of adoption.

Currently measures are normally in force for five years – the WTO maximum. It has been suggested that the duration of measures could be shorter, depending, for example, on the type of product, the market situation or the characteristics of an industry. The duration of measures imposed following expiry reviews could also be shorter.

Question 21: Should the EU make greater use of more flexible measures in Anti-Dumping and Anti-Subsidy investigations?

Question 22: Do EU measures in Anti-Dumping and Anti-Subsidy investigations need to be adapted so as to take better account of products with a long order or shipment time? If yes, how?

Question 23: Should it be made explicitly possible for the duration of definitive measures in Anti-Dumping and Anti-Subsidy investigations to be shorter than 5 years? If yes, in what type of situations would a shorter duration of measures be justified?

4.3. Reimbursement of duties after expiry reviews. Measures currently expire after five years unless an expiry review is initiated before that date. During the ensuing investigation (which can run for up to 15 months beyond the five-year period), measures remain in force. If the expiry review concludes that measures should not be maintained, consideration could be given to paying back any duties collected beyond the 'normal' five year period. An alternative could be to carry out and conclude expiry reviews before the maximum lifetime of measures ends. With this approach reimbursement would not be an issue.

Question 24: Should duties collected beyond the 5-year duration of the measures in Anti-Dumping and Anti-Subsidy investigations be reimbursed if the expiry review concludes that measures are not to be continued?

Question 25: Should expiry reviews in Anti-Dumping and Anti-Subsidy investigations be timed to end on the fifth anniversary of measures rather than to start on that date?

4.4. Higher thresholds for expiry reviews. Some stakeholders think that it is too easy for Anti-Dumping measures to be renewed. Under WTO and EU rules, industry needs to show that there is "likelihood of recurrence of injurious dumping". A higher threshold for industry might be a "clearly foreseeable and imminent threat of injury".

Question 26: Should the EU increase thresholds for expiry reviews in Anti-Dumping and Anti-Subsidy investigations? For example should the EU consider introducing the "threat of injury"- standard instead of the "likelihood of recurrence"?

PART 5. TRANSPARENCY IN TRADE DEFENCE INVESTIGATIONS

Effective transparency is vital to the credibility of trade defence instruments. EU rules represent a balance between openness in managing investigations and the need to respect the confidentiality of commercial information. The quality of analysis and resulting proposals depends strongly on the quality of the confidential information provided during an investigation. Stakeholders have raised a number of possible ways that the European Commission could nevertheless improve the transparency of trade defence investigations. Four of the aspects related to transparency are addressed below:

5.1. Hearing officer. Current EU rules foresee the possibility for interested parties to request hearings. Some parties have argued that a hearing officer would be helpful to ensure that parties in trade defence investigations can better exercise their right to be heard and to ensure that the rights of the parties are respected.

Question 27: The Commission is going to create the position of a hearing officer for trade defence investigations - what precise functions should such a person carry out?

5.2. Public hearings for country-wide Market Economy Status decisions. Certain countries are not considered market economies for the purpose of trade defence investigations – China and Vietnam for example. These countries can be awarded the status of market economy if they fulfil certain technical criteria. In view of the importance, complexity and political sensitivity of decisions to award country-wide Market Economy Status (MES), many stakeholders recommend holding public hearings prior to the Commission proposing to grant MES to a country.

Question 28: Should the Commission conduct public hearings in Anti-Dumping investigations for decisions to award country-wide Market Economy Status to a country?

5.3. A level playing field for information. Stakeholders have expressed concern about the uncertainty caused by rumours of possible complaints or investigations. The question has been raised whether the work of the advisory Anti-Dumping Committee could be rendered more transparent.

Question 29: Should there be greater openness regarding the working of the Anti-Dumping Committee, e.g. publication of its agenda and/or the minutes of its meetings?

5.4. Better access to non-confidential files. If parties want to consult the non-confidential file of an Anti-Dumping investigation, they currently have to do this in person at the premises of the European Commission. It would be possible to provide access to these materials on-line. However, some stakeholders might consider this an undesirably wide dissemination of non-confidential business facts.

Question 30: Would it be desirable for the non-confidential files in trade defence investigations to be accessible via the internet? Would intermediary solutions be more appropriate – for example the publication of a file index?

PART 6. INSTITUTIONAL PROCESS

While the use of trade defence instruments can be politically sensitive, the credibility of those instruments depends on their use being transparent, predictable and subject to stringent review. The decisions which are taken must be based on the results shown by investigations. The current institutional structure, as set out by the EU's Basic Regulations on trade defence instruments, divides responsibilities between the Commission and the Council. Decisions are subject to review by the European Court of Justice, and must also be compliant with the EU's WTO obligations. This institutional framework has worked well, but some stakeholders are concerned that it sometimes allows decisions to be influenced by factors not directly linked to the facts of the investigation itself.

Question 31: Should current institutional arrangements for adopting Anti-Dumping, Anti-Subsidy and Safeguard measures be maintained? Are there ways to improve the way those decisions are taken?

Contributing to this Green Paper consultation

Comments are invited from all interested parties, including the European Parliament and Member States, on the questions raised in this Green Paper. A structured questionnaire is available on-line to assist those responding and the Commission would welcome the views of all interested actors, including the views of public authorities in third countries.

The Commission invites respondents to raise issues related to the EU's trade defence instruments that are not directly addressed in the preceding questions.

Question 32: Is there any other aspect of the EU's trade defence instruments that you would like to see addressed?

The consultation response forms can be found at:

http://ec.europa.eu/trade/issues/respectrules/anti_dumping/comu061206_en.htm

Replies to the questionnaire should reach the Commission by 31 March 2007. Comments received will be made available on-line unless a specific request for confidentiality is made, in which case only an indication of the contributor will be given. Towards the end of the consultation period the Commission's services intend to organise a seminar with stakeholders. Following this public debate, the Commission will communicate the results of this consultation and consider if further action is appropriate.

GLOBAL EUROPE: A STRONGER PARTNERSHIP TO DELIVER MARKET ACCESS FOR EUROPEAN EXPORTERS[8]

1. INTRODUCTION

In today's global economy European companies have never been more dependent on effective access to the markets of our trading partners. European companies are making capital-intensive investments in third countries and creating supply chains that are both complex and global. European exporters are increasingly looking to succeed not just in the large economies of the developed world, but in emerging economies such as China, India, Brazil and Russia.

[8] SEC(2007) 452}{SEC(2007) 453

The Global Europe framework of 2006 argued that trade policy can make a key contribution to growth and jobs in Europe by ensuring that European companies remain competitive and that they have genuine access to the export markets they need. Europe is right to open its own markets in a way that stimulates competitiveness and innovation, provides access to raw materials and attracts inward foreign investment: this is the right response to globalisation. In parallel, we can and should expect open markets and fair trading conditions abroad. In particular, the emerging economies that have benefited from the global trading system to achieve high growth rates should now bring down their own barriers and further open their markets. This is in their own interests, as well as those of the global trading system more widely. In a highly competitive global economy, market access will significantly influence our economic export strength.

Europe's first and clearest priority in maintaining open global markets is through its commitment to the WTO, the multilateral trading system and the Doha Round. Progressive global liberalisation is not only the most effective way of creating an open trading system, but it is the only way that genuinely delivers for all, developing and developed countries alike. However, a renewed policy on market access that focuses on particular problems or markets is an essential part of the EU's wider strategy.

This Communication proposes a stronger Partnership to deliver market access between the Commission, Member States, and business, based on extensive public consultation. It sets out a clearer, more results-oriented approach that focuses on concrete problems that EU businesses face in third country markets. It identifies both the weaknesses of the current system, and the extent to which EU policy has to change to reflect a changing global economy.

It foresees a greater decentralisation of the current system and better use of local knowledge and initiative through the development of locally based EU Market Access Teams drawn from Commission Delegations, Member State Embassies and business organisations. It also asks if we could better prioritise the use of our capacities to ensure that, while all market access complaints are properly considered, the EU targets the most pressing problems. It sets out how we can make the current system more efficient, and more transparent for EU businesses.

A strong market access policy is a key function of the common commercial policy, and a key area in which the EU can deliver real economic benefits for its Member States. When it comes to taking action against trade barriers, we need to identify ways to improve the use of the existing tools and – where possible - to develop new ones. This paper sets out how we can strengthen that policy for the future.

2. MARKET ACCESS IN A CHANGING GLOBAL ECONOMY

Progress since 1996

The EU Market Access Strategy was launched in 1996 with the aim of enforcing multilateral and bilateral trade agreements and ensuring that third country markets were open to EU exports. This strategy aimed to provide exporters with information on market access conditions and a framework within which to tackle the barriers to trade in goods, services, intellectual property and investment.

The Market Access Database was created as the main operational tool of this strategy. It is a free, on-line service for EU exporters, incorporating information on market access conditions in around 100 countries and an evolving public record of currently around 500 market access barriers reported, primarily by business, to the Commission. The information sections of the database are well utilised and generally very popular with users.

As a result of the priority the EU has given to multilateral efforts to reduce trade barriers, the Commission's focus has to some extent shifted away from specific barrier removal. There is a strong need to correct this, both because of the growing importance and complexity of non-tariff barriers and because of the demands of stakeholders. This can be achieved through improved consultation with business and Member States and a more focused approach to tackling barriers and optimum deployment of resources. Failure to improve coordination will make it much more difficult to detect, analyse and assess priority cases, and to achieve systematic success in eliminating barriers.

The changing nature of barriers in the global economy

The nature of barriers to trade in the global economy has changed. Where market access once focused on border tariffs, non-tariff and other "behind the border" barriers in the markets of our trading partners are increasingly important (see box below). A clear distinction should be drawn between unnecessary barriers to trade and justified and legally defensible measures to fulfil legitimate policy objectives, such as security, protection of human, animal and plant health and of the environment. While it is necessary to regulate trade, this must be done in a transparent and non-discriminatory manner, which is not more trade-restrictive than necessary in pursuing other legitimate policy objectives.

These new types of barriers are more complicated, technically challenging and time consuming to detect, analyse and remove. Many market access problems now arise because existing rules are not correctly implemented or enforced. Furthermore, the expansion of WTO rules has not fully kept pace with the expanding range of barriers in the global economy. While the GATT and the WTO has been remarkably effective in removing tariff barriers to trade, and has moved into areas such as the policing of sanitary restrictions on trade, there are still many areas where WTO rules need to be developed and evolve in order to address non-tariff barriers. In addition, the more we can share best practice and approximation of environmental and social standards with trading partners, the better for EU business.

Trade barriers in the modern global economy

1. Tariff barriers . Although these have been eroded by successive multilateral trade rounds, high tariffs still pose problems for EU exporters.

2. Burdensome customs procedures for import, export and transit as well as unfair or discriminatory tax rules and practices .

3. Technical regulations, standards and conformity assessment procedures that are not in line with WTO rules on Technical Barriers to Trade (TBT Agreement).

4. Misuse of s anitary and phytosanitary measures i.e. those that are not justified on health and safety grounds within existing WTO rules.

5. Restrictions on access to raw materials , particularly restrictive export practices, including export taxes, which drive up prices for products such as hides and skins, and key mineral and metal goods, as well as dual pricing practices.

6. Poor protection of intellectual property rights including geographical indications and the lack of proper implementation and enforcement.

7. Barriers to trade in services and foreign direct investment such as unjustified foreign ownership caps, joint venture obligations and discriminatory treatment.

8. Restrictive government procurement rules and practices that prevent EU companies from bidding effectively for public contracts in third countries.

9. Abusive and/or WTO-incompatible use of trade defence instruments by third countries.

10. Unfair use of state aids and other subsidies by third countries in a way that constitutes market access barriers.

Stakeholders' support for change

In 2006 the Commission commissioned an evaluation study and undertook an internet consultation on the European Union's approach to market access. The consultation attracted more than 150 responses from

Member States, EU business, and other stakeholders. The evaluation and consultation process established the following key conclusions:

- The EU needs to improve the mix of policy instruments it brings to securing and preserving market access – combining a commitment to multilateral and bilateral trade negotiations with committed action to ensuring those agreements are enforced.

- While export promotion rightly remains the essential role of EU Member States, many European companies work on a European, and increasingly a global, scale. The Commission, Member States and business need to work more closely together in partnership to maximise our leverage in tackling and preventing barriers, both in Brussels and third countries.

- The EU needs to be better at prioritising action against barriers in order to achieve the greatest economic impact for the EU.

- The EU needs a more efficient and transparent service for businesses. Small and medium sized enterprises (SMEs) are increasingly active in export markets and often face the greatest challenges in addressing trade barriers. SME problems with market access need to be taken carefully into account in the practical implementation of the strategy. The Commission adopted a Communication in November 2005, which includes specific reference to addressing the needs of SMEs in this area. The Commission can further improve its Market Access Database to make it more user friendly.

The results of our evaluation and consultations make clear that market access is felt to be an area that deserves stronger action at the EU level. EU business wants a more result-oriented approach to help overcome the concrete problems they face in accessing third country markets with a speed and effectiveness that reflect modern commercial reality. Member States have consistently expressed their view that a more effective and assertive EU policy is needed.

3. PROPOSALS FOR A STRONGER PARTNERSHIP TO DELIVER MARKET ACCESS

The reasons for focusing on market access are as valid today as they were in 1996, if not more so. Our task is to strengthen and adapt the existing framework for market access policy and improve the concrete tools that are part of that framework.

3.1. The right mix of policy instruments

The WTO system and multilateral cooperation remain the single most important mechanism for securing and guaranteeing market access in the global trading system, although others such as the World Customs Organisation also play an important role. But we cannot rely on a single avenue or mechanism to tackle trade barriers. We must use multilateral and bilateral, as well as both formal and informal, instruments.

In the WTO, successful completion of an ambitious Doha Round of trade negotiations is the priority for the EU. The scope for using accession negotiations to secure greater market access is diminishing, as some of the most important trading countries such as China have now joined the WTO, and others such as Russia are entering the closing stretch of negotiations. Multilateral activity will be complemented by the launch of negotiations on a new generation of bilateral Free Trade Agreements, going beyond current WTO rules, with regions and countries such as ASEAN, Korea, India, Andean countries and Central America, as well as the pursuit of ongoing negotiations with Mercosur and the Gulf Cooperation Council, and by the conclusion of sectoral agreements.

We should also seek to reinforce our position in international normative bodies such as the International Standards Organisation (ISO). This will help us better influence international regulatory cooperation, for example by promoting the use of voluntary international standards drawn up by the international standardisation bodies. In addition new generation FTAs should include a regulatory approximation component. The EU should also facilitate the active participation of developing countries in such regulatory dialogues.

However, agreeing rules is only the start of the process. A clear focus must be maintained on enforcement and in ensuring that third countries comply with their obligations under bilateral and multilateral agreements. To facilitate this, rights under the WTO Dispute Settlement Understanding should be pursued actively. Multilateral and bilateral negotiations should be used to establish flexible dispute avoidance and resolution mechanisms, based on mediation, in order to address problems with partner countries. We should also encourage others to make greater use, as the EU has, of the notification procedures under the Agreements on Technical Barriers to Trade to head off trade restrictions. In addition, we should amend the Trade Barriers Regulation to include complaints against violation of bilateral treaties to which we are a party. The EU may also further develop co-operation with third countries to address barriers of common concern. For example, the EU should integrate such discussions into existing strategic partnerships with key emerging and developed country markets: we are already working closely with the United States on market access issues.

The absence of efficient competition laws can also limit market access. We need to continue our efforts to promote the introduction of appropriate competition rules in third countries.

Enforcement of market access rules also depends on an effective technical and administrative system. Many developing countries in particular do not have sufficient administrative capacities, training or technical equipment. Trade related assistance can assist in reducing these constraints. The Commission, and the EU as a whole, is committed to increasing trade-related assistance as part of its overall strategy on Aid for Trade.

Finally, political contacts and trade diplomacy will play an increasingly important role in the joint efforts of the Commission, Member States and business effectively to tackle barriers, and will complement other, more medium to long-term, policy instruments.

3.2. A new relationship with Member States and business

The Commission's role at the centre of the common commercial policy is vital. But it is clear that to be more effective the Commission needs to establish a new partnership with both Member States, who have their own competences in this area, and European business.

The Commission, Member States and business need to establish improved ways of working. This implies much more systematic contact and cooperation at all levels, both within the EU and in third countries. The Commission, Member States and business should work better together to establish priorities for action in barrier removal, as well as linking up databases and developing a network of market access specialists.

This is particularly important on the ground in key third country markets, where local knowledge is strongest. Commission Delegations, Member State embassies and European businesses operating in foreign markets are familiar with the local administrative structures and processes and usually best placed to offer initial reviews of market access problems, identify cases requiring coordinated action with specialists in Brussels in areas such as intellectual property, technical barriers to trade (TBT) and sanitary / phytosanitary (SPS) protection, and conduct local follow-up. In practical terms, there is much already going on in third countries to pool resources and contacts. However more systematic contacts and coordination would improve intelligence gathering, make it possible to identify and react to relevant legislative proposals before they are adopted and use local knowledge and leverage to apply diplomatic pressure to tackle market access barriers quickly and effectively.

The Commission proposes the creation of Market Access Teams in third country markets involving the Commission, Member States, the private sector (for example EU Chambers of Commerce), and where appropriate other EU stakeholders. In the short term, a list of pilot countries will be established to set up stronger networks and Market Access Teams.

The Commission also believes that the Market Access Advisory Committee, composed of representatives of Member States and chaired by the Commission, should become more technically focused on market access issues, including consideration of particular cases and exchange of best practices. It should also have a renewed emphasis on co-ordination, based on feedback from local Market Access Teams, and work closely with the Trade Barriers Regulation Committee. The 133 Committee, the overall advisory committee on trade policy, should continue to be the forum for discussion of the most important market access cases. However, owing to the complexity and variety of market access issues, other specialist committees will also continue to take the lead where appropriate. The Commission will also continue to discuss these issues on a regular basis with the European Parliament.

It is clear that there is a strong desire from business for more active participation in barrier removal. The Commission sees merit in more regular trilateral discussions between the Commission, EU business and Member States and proposes to create a specific forum for a regular Member State / Commission services / EU business meeting, possibly linked to the Market Access Advisory Committee meeting.

As a general principle for working together, we should use existing mechanisms better and create a framework for regular contacts, rather than creating additional institutions for intra-EU cooperation.

3.3. Prioritising to make the best use of resources

The anticipated increase in the already substantial number of trade barriers reported, coupled with the increasing complexity and difficulty of tackling them, means that it is important to ensure that we focus and act on the highest priority barriers.

All complaints received should continue to be examined, but in the light of objective prioritisation indicators discussed with EU Member States and EU business, including small and medium sized enterprises. These could include:

- the potential economic benefits for EU business as a whole in the short and the medium term,

- whether or not the barrier in question represents a serious infringement of bilateral or multilateral agreements, and

- the likelihood of resolution of the problem within a reasonable timeframe.

In terms of the outcomes of the prioritisation process, priorities could be defined in terms of:

- countries (both industrialised economies and emerging economies, but excluding least developed countries);

- sectors (a number of sectors have been identified, for example, in the consultation and in the framework of the industrial policy); and/or

- categories of problem - IPR infringements for example.

However, prioritisation must not be a straitjacket, but must help provide guidance to using resources better.

3.4. A more effective, efficient and transparent service

...preventing new barriers coming into effect...

A prevention based, "early warning" approach to monitoring regulations in third countries has the advantage of identifying possible barriers at an early stage, and tackling them at source, and letting our trade partners know of our concerns before draft legislation or regulations are set in stone. The Commission will encourage others to notify under the Technical Barriers to Trade Agreement and increase intelligence gathering efforts on upcoming legislation in third countries directly on the ground by the Market Access Teams.

...improving the process leading to barrier removal...

The biggest gap between the expectations created in 1996 and the results achieved is in the time taken for the successful removal of trade restrictions even in the most clear-cut cases of breaches of multilateral or bilateral agreements. Feedback from business makes clear that they need quicker, more responsive action. The Commission will improve and streamline the way it registers, analyses and tackles market access complaints, and the way in which it provides feedback to business.

We will rely on EU business to provide much of the information on the barriers which affect their trade or investment with third counties, and ensure Commission-wide sharing of such incoming information. The objective would be to register in the Market Access Database all market access complaints received. We will establish web-links with other databases elsewhere in the EU (including with Member States and business, where possible) to ensure that all recorded barriers are accessible via the Market Access Database. Cases would be given a unique case number to facilitate their tracking through the system in a transparent manner.

Analysis of barriers needs to involve all actors, including the locally established Market Access Teams. And EU business should be kept regularly informed on ongoing work.

The identification and analysis of barriers is the area where closer partnership with business and Member States could be expected to have its greatest impact in efficiency and transparency.

...and improving the Market Access Database

The European Commission's Market Access Database provides rapidly accessible and reliable information with regard to applied tariffs, import formalities and documentary requirements for imports into third countries and also incorporates information on trade barriers restricting access to those markets. While users are generally satisfied with the existing system, improvements should be made.

There will be a greater focus on user-friendliness and simplification of the Market Access Database that will make it easier to identify and report problems. The Commission will establish improved reaction times to on-line enquiries and commit to regular updates of the information available in the Database. The current 'Comments' section of the Database will be upgraded to encourage more issues and problems to be brought to the attention of the Commission via e-mail. A promotional campaign will be launched in and with Member States, to publicise widely the services of the Market Access Partnership, especially among SMEs via the forthcoming EU-wide network supporting business and innovation, and to encourage EU companies to register their complaints about barriers.

In response to requests from users and in order better to match the current challenges and needs of EU exporters, new sections of the Market Access Database will be developed over time to improve its coverage in areas such as services, IPR enforcement, and investment.

Locally based Market Access Teams should produce regular reports on trade barriers in their host countries which will update and strengthen the picture offered by the Market Access Database .

The Commission will also look at ways to link the Market Access Database and the Export Helpdesk for Developing Country exporters. Providing access to this information for developing countries' exporters would raise their capacity for export to other countries – a helpful boost to south-south trade in particular.

4. CONCLUSION

A stronger Partnership to deliver market access is an essential component of the Global Europe Strategy and a significant contribution to the Lisbon agenda for growth and jobs. European companies – from strong global companies to up and coming SMEs – are fighting to succeed in global markets. A strong market access policy is a key function of the common commercial policy, and a key area in which the EU can deliver real economic benefits for its Member States and European citizens and businesses. The EU's policy of 1996 needs to be strengthened and adapted to a changing global economy in which both the markets to which we seek access and the barriers that prevent it are changing.

The Commission therefore proposes:

- A reinforced commitment to using multilateral institutions, such as the WTO, and bilateral channels, like the new generation FTAs to encourage progressive – and enforceable – liberalisation, market opening, and approximation of standards and norms between the EU and its trading partners.

- Establishing a stronger relationship between the Commission, Member States, and EU business, to support directly economic operators in overcoming the concrete difficulties they encounter in accessing third country markets and in a manner and timeframe that is compatible with business reality.

- Decentralising the current system and encouraging local initiative in third countries through the development of locally based EU Market Access Teams involving Commission Delegations, Member State embassies and business organisations.

- Closer technical cooperation in Brussels between Member State officials and the Commission on market access issues, and intensified consultation with a wide range of industry representatives.

- Stronger prioritisation in choosing which barriers to focus on to make best use of our resources in certain target markets, (but excluding the least developed countries), key sectors, and/or key areas such as intellectual property rights.

- An overhaul of the European Commission's Market Access Database.

- Improved efficiency and transparency in the Commission's analysis of trade barrier complaints, including a new streamlined system for registering complaints.

The success of this initiative will depend on the strength of the new partnership that we are able to establish, dedicating sufficient resources to it, and making best use of these resources that we bring, collectively, to the project. The Commission is committed to taking up this challenge and invites all involved parties to contribute to implementing this new partnership.

Communication from the Commission to the Council, the European Parliament, the European Economic and Social Committee and the Committee of the Regions – Global Europe – Competing in the world – A contribution to the EU's Growth and Jobs Strategy - COM(2006) 567, 4.10.2006.

Communication from the Commission to the Council, the European Parliament, the Economic and Social Committee and the Committee of the Regions: The Global Challenge of International Trade: A Market Access Strategy for the European Union - COM(96) 53, 14.2.1996.

This report can be downloaded at:http://trade.ec.europa.eu/doclib/docs/2006/november/tradoc_130518.2.pdf.

This report can be downloaded at http://ec.europa.eu/trade/issues/sectoral/mk_access/cs101106_en.htm

Commission Communication "Implementing the Community Lisbon Programme – Modern SME Policy for Growth and Employment" - COM(2005) 551, 10.11.2005.

Communication from the Commission to the Council and the European Parliament: "Towards an EU Aid for Trade Strategy - the Commission's contribution" - COM(2007) 163, 4.4.2007.

Within the existing remit provided for by Council Decision 98/552/EC of 24 September 1998.

Commission Communication: "Implementing the Community Lisbon Programme: A policy framework to strengthen EU manufacturing - towards a more integrated approach for industrial policy" - COM(2005) 474, 5.10.2005. Its technical update of 4.9.2006

EU AID FOR TRADE STRATEGY

1. ORIGIN OF THE EU AID FOR TRADE STRATEGY

Trade is an important catalyst for growth and poverty reduction in developing countries. But successful integration of developing countries into world trade requires more than better market access and strengthened international trade rules. In order to fully exploit the benefits from trade, developing countries also need to remove supply side constraints and address structural weaknesses. This includes domestic reforms in trade-related policies, trade facilitation, enhancement of customs capacities, upgrading of infrastructure, enhancement of productive capacities and building of domestic and regional markets. Complementary efforts are required in areas such as macroeconomic stability, fiscal reforms, promotion of investment, labour policy, capital and product market regulations and institutions, and human capital development.

This is what Aid for Trade is for. Aid for Trade should have a global scope and support all developing countries, in particular the least developed, in their efforts to reform and to adjust to the world trading system, in the wider context of sustainable development. Aid for Trade is geared to generating growth, employment and income. It is therefore a contribution to the first of the Millennium Development Goals namely to reduce the proportion of people living on less than a dollar a day (MDG 1). It also supports MDG 8, which is to establish a global partnership for development, in particular to develop further an open trading and financial system that is rule-based, predictable and non-discriminatory. Aid for Trade is a key complement to trade negotiations. It is not a substitute for a pro-development outcome of these negotiations but should be delivered independently of progress in the negotiations.

The concepts behind Aid for Trade are well known to the EU. The EU is collectively the biggest donor in the field of Trade Related Assistance (TRA). The European Consensus for Development identifies trade and regional integration as an important area for Community action. One case in point are the ongoing negotiations of Economic Partnership Agreements (EPAs) with the African Caribbean and Pacific (ACP) countries. TRA commitments are also significant for other EU partner countries such as those in Asia or in Latin America.

This Communication is the Commission's contribution to further expanding EU support for Aid for Trade, with a view to adoption of a joint EU strategy by the Council in the second half of 2007, as agreed by the Council in October 2006. Anchored in well-established policy commitments, and building on the recommendations of a WTO Task Force, the value added of an EU Aid for Trade strategy lies in agreeing on the specific action to deliver. Such EU cooperation will reinforce the impact of EU Aid for Trade and contribute to the global debate on this topic.

2. OBJECTIVES

Aid for Trade has multiple objectives: to enable developing countries, particularly the least developed countries (LDCs), to use trade more effectively to promote growth, employment, development and poverty reduction and to achieve their development objectives; to help them build and modernise supply-side capacity and trade-related infrastructure in order to facilitate their access to markets and to export more; to help them implement and adjust to trade reform and liberalisation, including via labour market and social adjustments; to assist regional integration; to assist smooth integration into the world trading system and to assist with implementing trade agreements, all in the context of sustainable development, preservation of natural resources and the environment, and promotion of decent work.

Following the Council's guidelines, an EU Aid for Trade strategy can contribute to these objectives by addressing the following issues:

1. Increasing the volumes of EU Aid for Trade, in particular by taking Trade Related Assistance up to € 2 billion a year by 2010; but also by promoting an effective response to wider Aid for Trade needs.

2. Enhancing the quality of EU Aid for Trade, in particular by applying commitments to making development cooperation more effective.

3. Supporting effective monitoring and reporting.

4. Ensuring that Commission and Member States have sufficient capacity to implement the above mentioned objectives.

As the Council drew specific attention to the Aid for Trade needs related to the ongoing negotiations of Economic Partnership Agreements (EPAs) with ACP countries, the EU strategy should pay similar specific attention to these developments, in order to help realise the full development potential of EPAs. Aid for Trade is also an important element of EC assistance in Asia and in Latin America.

3. INCREASING THE VOLUME OF EU AID FOR TRADE

3.1. A Roadmap for meeting the EU's financial commitments on trade related assistance

TRA comprises two categories: "trade policy and regulation"; and "trade development". The first refers to support for the effective participation of developing countries in multilateral trade negotiations, analysis and implementation of multilateral trade agreements, trade-related legislation and regulatory reforms (including Technical Barriers to Trade and Sanitary and Phytosanitary measures), tariff structures, support to regional trade arrangements, trade facilitation, including customs regimes and equipment, and issues such as security of the supply chain. The second category covers business development and activities aimed at improving the business climate, business support services and institutions, access to trade finance, trade promotion and market development in the productive and services sectors, including at the institutional and enterprise level.

During the baseline period 2001-2004, the TRA commitments of Community and Member States were, on average € 840 million and € 300 million per year respectively. The Council requested a roadmap for delivering in 2010 on the Community's and Member States' commitment to take this volume to € 1+1 billion a year. After analysing the available figures, the Commission concludes that it is on track to meet its commitment. Due to lack of forecasting data, the Commission is however not in a position to assess whether Member States are collectively on track to attain their 2010 target.

The Council decided that a substantial share of the increased EU TRA should go to ACP countries, in support of regional integration and EPAs. Guidance on the actual amounts involved is important for ACP partners at this point in time. On the basis of current plans the share of Community TRA which will go to ACP is expected to remain relatively stable. Whilst this reflects an increase in absolute terms, it means that the bulk of additional TRA resources for the ACP will have to come from the Member States.

EU Member States and the Community (as well as other donors) provide aid on the basis of priorities expressed by partner countries in their national development strategies. To deliver on their commitments the EU depends largely on the extent to which trade-related needs are articulated in these national strategies. Assisting developing countries with identifying and prioritising trade related assistance needs is therefore an integral part of meeting the EU's financial commitments. One key instrument for doing so is the Integrated Framework (IF) to which both the Commission and several MS are already contributing. Key challenges are to enhance the IF agenda and impact and expand the approach to other developing countries. At regional level, effective approaches to trade needs assessments must be developed.

Commission recommendations A linear trend from the present situation to their 1 billion target would imply that the collective commitments to TRA by EU Member States should rise to at least € 600 million by 2008. The strategy should, however, consider which measures to take should TRA from the Member States fail to reach this level by 2008. The strategy should provide guidance on the amounts involved in the Council commitment to allocate a "substantial share" of the additional TRA to ACP countries, in support of regional integration and EPAs with a view to increasing the share of overall TRA allocated to the ACP. The EU strategy should underline the importance of integrating trade-related concerns into national development strategies and identify criteria for when it is acceptable to finance trade-related priorities in anticipation of national development strategies being updated. The strategy should demonstrate the EU's commitment to engage actively in the enhanced IF, in particular by active in-country participation; and to extend the IF methods to non-LDCs, including via a plan for joint EU engagement in the creation of an IDA-only mechanism. The strategy should outline how to support regional trade needs assessments in support of regional integration. |

- 3.2. EU support to the wider Aid for Trade agenda

The Commission fully supports the wider Aid for Trade agenda identified by the WTO Task Force, i.e. inclusion of trade-related infrastructure, productive capacities and trade-related adjustment. This broad approach is reflected for example in the 2004 EU Commodity Action Plan. Although the EU Council did not set specific numerical targets on the new Aid for Trade categories, the EU is already providing substantial support to such areas. For instance, support for trade related infrastructure averaged € 1.480 billion a year from the Member States and € 1.290 billion a year from the Community during the period 2001-2004.

There is some lack of clarity in the new Aid for Trade categories, and some overlaps with the already existing categories of TRA. This has to be tackled if monitoring and reporting are to be developed usefully for Aid for Trade. This is recognised by the Aid for Trade community, including within the EU, and work is in progress, in particular within the OECD/DAC, to clarify and simplify the scope and use proxies from longstanding ODA categories. The EU, as a key partner in the Aid for Trade initiative, should participate in the unfolding discussions.

In this regard, the Commission considers that economic infrastructure is a helpful proxy for trade related infrastructure. For productive capacities, existing reporting categories can be used. In the context of trade-related adjustment, the Commission considers that this should include support to fiscal reforms aiming at introducing more sustainable forms of tax systems. Linked to this, budget support can be an appropriate means to tackle falls in customs revenue following trade liberalisation, or to support trade-related social safety nets to facilitate adjustment to trade opening and globalisation .

Commission recommendations In addition to TRA, the EU strategy should include a political commitment to strengthen EU support for trade-related infrastructure, productive capacity and trade-related adjustment, starting by supporting good coverage of such issues in trade needs assessments. This is particularly relevant for small, vulnerable and land-locked economies, many of which are ACP. The EU strategy should state the intent to develop coherent EU reporting practices for all categories of Aid for Trade and to continue to participate actively and jointly in relevant discussions at international level. The strategy should make it clear that the intent of the EU financial commitment to TRA is solid and will be maintained regardless of the evolving international debate. |

4. ENHANCING THE QUALITY OF EU AID FOR TRADE

Increasing levels of Aid for Trade raise the questions of quality and effectiveness. Without due attention to these matters, additional financial resources will not bring about the improvements desired by partner countries.

The EU strategy will not be starting from scratch. Based on the conclusions of the EU Ad Hoc Working Party on Harmonisation, the EU made a substantial contribution to the Paris Declaration on Aid Effectiveness. It is already fully committed to the Paris principles and has gone further to act on several of these. In particular, in April 2006, the Council agreed on principles and a format for joint programming and issued a mandate for further work on complementarity and co- financing.

The EU Aid for Trade strategy should offer a practical application of the agreed principles, focusing on five quality aspects: poverty and Aid for Trade; ownership and participation; sustainability; joint analysis, programming and delivery; and effectiveness of regional Aid for Trade.

4.1. Poverty and Aid for Trade

Within each category of Aid for Trade, choices made will have an impact on poverty levels. Sometimes, there are trade-offs between indirect and direct poverty reduction effects. The Commission has noted that the poverty linkages are not always well articulated in trade development strategies and Aid for Trade operations, in particular for traditional TRA.

Deeper reflection on how to ensure poverty reduction through Aid for Trade is necessary, for each category of Aid for Trade. More could be done to identify the areas of Aid for Trade which bring about the widest and most sustainable reduction in poverty. In individual operations, the EU should support analysis of implications on poverty and incorporate conclusions in a transparent way. Efforts should specifically include the gender dimension.

The decent work agenda is of relevance here, to address trade related issues of labour market and social adjustment. Similarly, the strategy should confirm support for the world-wide implementation of ILO's core labour standards. Voluntary initiatives giving consumers assurances relevant to sustainable development, such as Fair Trade, eco-labels, and comparable corporate schemes, are also important instruments with potential for reducing poverty and promoting socio-economic development, which a joint EU strategy should address.

Commission recommendation The strategy should stress the importance that the EU attaches to the impacts of Aid for Trade on poverty, and lay down steps to ensure that the activities undertaken under the strategy deliver in this regard. |

- 4.2. Ownership and participation

Ownership and participation are two aid effectiveness principles of special importance to Aid for Trade. Better ownership, manifested by integration of trade-related issues into poverty reduction and equivalent strategies, is necessary for increasing Aid for Trade. Identifying pertinent trade priorities, building consensus for reform policies and developing effective remedies to address bottlenecks to trade require active participation by the private sector, social partners and civil society. Often, partner governments need assistance to manage such consultation processes. Effective participation of a wide range of stakeholders can inter alia be facilitated by strengthening intermediate organisations such as chambers of commerce.

Commission recommendation The EU strategy should emphasise the key role that the private sector and civil society can play in Aid for Trade. It should outline ways of supporting the capacity of governments to manage consultation processes, and of weaker interest groups to engage in these processes. |

- 4.3. Sustainability

Sustainability is the underpinning principle of the EU Aid for Trade strategy and should be dealt with in all its dimensions - institutional, financial/economic, social and environmental.

The key to institutional and financial sustainability of programmes lies in ensuring stakeholder capacity-building and ownership in all operations, as discussed elsewhere in this Communication.

To fully integrate both social and environmental considerations into Aid for Trade programmes, existing impact assessment regulations and procedures , both of partners and donors, need to be applied. Sustainability impact assessments of trade policies and agreements should be further developed and the results better used both by the EU and partners.

As regards environmental issues specifically, EU Aid for Trade should help partners develop more sustainable production methods and assist producers in complying with (public and private) health, safety and environment standards in export markets and improve the capacity of customs to help implement trade-related aspects of Multilateral Environmental Agreements.

Other important related issues are the promotion of decent work and the development of effective labour market and social adjustment mechanisms. For example, the EU will continue to assist producers in complying with recognised labour standards, practices and regulations and in promoting occupational health and safety.

Commission recommendation The EU strategy should promote the sustainability of Aid for Trade, including by foreseeing support to stakeholder ownership, capacity building and participation; pursuing social and environmental goals; applying EU and partner countries' tools and procedures for environment, social, gender and sustainability impact assessments; integrating results from such work into in-country trade needs assessments; promoting sustainable production methods; and helping comply with relevant product standards in exports markets. |

- 4.4. Joint analysis, programming and delivery

Recent trends in EU development aid all point in the same direction: greater complementarity and cooperation is needed between EU partners, across all stages of the programme cycle and for all types of instruments. This must also apply to Aid for Trade.

As regards joint analysis of trade related needs, IF processes should be the preferred framework for EU coordination in LDCs. Similar processes should be developed for joint analysis in other countries. In ACP regions, Regional Preparatory Task Forces are important complements, in the context of EPAs.

As a further step, there is scope for the EU to coordinate better its response strategies in countries and regions. The Joint Trade and Development Expert Group could develop into an informal coordination forum for multilateral initiatives.

Opportunities for joint delivery will depend largely on progress in working through s ector wide approaches (SWAPs), as these are one of the preconditions for embarking on sector budget support . Good trade needs assessment processes and in-country coordination will help prepare the ground for successful SWAPs.

The possibilities for use of general budget support in Aid for Trade should be examined, including the issue of developing appropriate indicators. Finally, EU co-financing of Aid for Trade could allow increasing Aid for Trade without stretching partners' absorption capacity, by opening up existing EC programmes to Member States or by allowing some Member States to take the lead based on their comparative advantage and expertise.

Commission recommendations The strategy should lay down actions to facilitate the EU leading the way on coordinated response strategies in Aid for Trade. This could include preparing an overview of partner countries with a strong EU Aid for Trade presence, and assigning EU Aid for Trade contact points to facilitate in-country EU coordination and joint identification. Looking ahead to future opportunities to engage in Joint Programming (such as those related to the mid term review of the Commission's country strategies, including for the 10th EDF), the strategy should prepare the ground for good coverage of trade-related issues in the countries concerned. The strategy should lay down actions to further develop use of SWAPs in Aid for Trade. It should propose measures to build the confidence which is needed to facilitate application of joint delivery methods such as budget support and co-financing. The strategy should highlight the role that the Joint Trade and Development Expert Group could play in coordination for multilateral initiatives. |

- 4.5. Aid effectiveness in regional Aid for Trade

Support for regional integration is a distinctive feature of EU development cooperation and relations with non-EU countries, in particular through trade and customs policy. The regional level is therefore important for the delivery of Aid for Trade, in particular for regions deeply engaged in regional integration efforts. This corresponds to the growing number of regional trade and cooperation agreements, the growing interest on the part of developing country partners in regional integration and the priority given to regional integration in the European Consensus for Development, the Cotonou Agreement and the EC Development Cooperation Instrument.

Programming and delivery at regional level are not different in nature from that at national level . The same aid effectiveness principles should be applied, although this could be more challenging at regional level. Key actions for aid effectiveness at regional level include:

- supporting regional partners' capacity to own and lead Aid for Trade efforts , in particular by building regional organisations' capacity to assess the implications of trade or regional integration and/or trade agreements with third countries and strengthening their capacity to monitor and implement commitments, including for issues such as fiscal reforms;

- coordinating programming in support of regional and trade integration . Joint EU efforts could be developed to assess needs and identify areas where the EU could support the integration agenda of the region concerned, including on issues of economic and social integration. Much can be done at regional level by building on existing efforts on private sector development, productive capacity and infrastructure;

- pursuing more streamlined methods of delivery . The strategy should define enhanced coordination modalities with a view to stepping up collective mobilisation of AfT finance. Regional methods of delivery equivalent to budget support and co-financing should be developed. For example, the Commission is developing contribution agreements to facilitate financial management of its regional cooperation. Some ACP regions have begun to create regional funding mechanisms to facilitate management of regional programmes, including contributions from the Commission and, possibly, other donors in support of EPAs;

- enhancing cooperation with other donors . The Commission and the Member States should jointly encourage non EU donors to consider increasing their support to regional trade integration. Regional development banks and international financial institutions are particularly important.

Commission recommendations The EU strategy should underline the EU's commitment to applying aid effectiveness principles at regional level by supporting regional partners' capacity to own and lead Aid for Trade, coordinating programming, pursuing more streamlined delivery modes and enhancing cooperation with other donors. Having regard to the ongoing EPA negotiations, the EU strategy should indicate a priority for regional interventions in the EPA context, particularly as regards coordinating programming and supporting regionally owned initiatives, such as regional EPA funds. |

5. SPECIFIC ACP ANGLES OF THE PROPOSALS

The October Council paid specific attention to the EPA-related Aid for Trade agenda in ACP countries. The measures outlined above are all essential for supporting ACP regions and countries in the context of the EPAs. Some recommendations are particularly important; they are repeated below:

Commission recommendations The EU strategy should provide guidance on the amounts involved in the Council's commitment to allocate a "substantial share" of the additional TRA to ACP countries with a view to increasing the share of overall TRA allocated to the ACP. The strategy should include a political commitment on the part of the EU to strengthen its support for trade-related infrastructure, productive capacity and trade-related adjustment, starting by supporting good coverage of such wider issues in trade needs assessments. The strategy should support, as a priority, integration of trade-related concerns into ACP national development strategies. The strategy should outline how to strengthen support to regional trade needs assessments, in support of regional integration. In the EPA context, this includes a particular emphasis on the EPA Regional Preparatory Task Forces. The strategy should underline the commitment of the EU to applying aid effectiveness principles at the regional level by supporting regional partners' capacity to own and lead Aid for Trade, coordinating programming, pursuing more streamlined delivery modes and enhancing cooperation with other donors. The strategy should indicate a priority to EPA regions as regards coordinating delivery modes and supporting regionally owned initiatives, such as regional EPA funds. |

- 6. MONITORING AND REPORTING

Monitoring and reporting are the key to making progress in the areas discussed above. Both process monitoring and outcome monitoring is necessary, according to criteria to be agreed. The global monitoring and reporting foreseen within the WTO/OECD framework and the EU level monitoring of implementation of the EU Aid for Trade strategy are closely interlinked.

Monitoring and reporting at the global level

The global review mechanism proposed by the WTO Task Force on Aid for Trade should assess Aid for Trade delivery both quantitatively and qualitatively:

- Quantitatively: Monitoring should include global Aid for Trade flows as reported to the WTO/OECD by donors plus reports by beneficiaries on the implementation of their trade capacity building strategies. The Commission does not intend to duplicate the WTO/OECD work in compiling quantitative data on Aid for Trade but could, with the Member States, use the existing data for analysis at EU level to deepen understanding of efforts already made and planned.

- Qualitatively: The global review should also provide a platform for discussing all issues relevant to the effectiveness of Aid for Trade, building international consensus on these issues, and exchanging experience between donor and partner countries. It should monitor adherence to agreed processes recognised important to aid effectiveness, and outcomes. Monitoring should support results-based management of Aid for Trade, in particular by promoting development of clear and measurable objectives and indicators. Impacts on poverty deserve special attention. The review mechanism should also help increase understanding of the most efficient ways of spending funds on Aid for Trade, including the nexus between domestic markets, demand and institutional capacities, and the ability of developing countries to participate in international trade, the importance of the policy framework, the sequencing of trade liberalisation and Aid for Trade, the best way of integrating Trade issues into poverty reduction strategies etc.

Support for beneficiary countries' own monitoring and evaluation frameworks for Aid for Trade will be crucial.

Monitoring and reporting at EU level

The EU will need to report on implementation of the EU Aid for Trade strategy, for example to the European Parliament. Progress on implementing the EU strategy should be assessed yearly by the Council, on the basis of a progress report by the Commission and Member States. Joint programme evaluations should be promoted. If necessary, the strategy should be adjusted.

Commission recommendations The EU strategy should actively contribute to monitoring and reporting at global level, including by supporting developing countries in their reporting and monitoring. The strategy should assist in streamlining Commission and Member States reporting of quantitative Aid for Trade flows to the Doha database so that the data can be used for deeper analysis at EU level. The EU strategy should lay down action to support results-based management and commit the EU to carry out annual joint programme evaluations in the area of Aid for Trade in order to assess progress in the priority areas of the EU strategy and in those agreed internationally. |

- 7. EU CAPACITY FOR AID FOR TRADE

Building human capacity in donor organisations, both at headquarters and in the field is a precondition for scaling up Aid for Trade. Without this capacity, trade will figure less prominently in the policy dialogue and donor organisations will find it more difficult to respond to the needs of partner countries. Capacity means both numbers of staff and skills.

The specific needs to scale up capacity will differ between Member States and depend on the manner in which Member States have chosen to expand their Aid for Trade. Implementing the aid effectiveness agenda will be staff-intensive. However, sharing expertise could also help to reduce the need for an increase in human resources in the field.

Commission recommendations The Commission recommends taking stock of the EU's existing Aid for Trade capacity and expertise. The EU strategy should explore joint EU initiatives to develop and share expertise, such as trainings on Aid for Trade. |

- See background in Annex.

See details in Annex.
The strategy will have a much wider coverage than the recently created EC budget line on Aid for Trade.
See definitions in Annex.
In line with the World Customs Organisation Framework of Standards.
Includes funds both from the European Development Fund and the EC general budget.
See details on Member States in the Commission Staff Working paper accompanying the Monterrey report - SEC(2007) 415 - and details on EC commitments in Annex.
The IF is a multi-donor program whose objectives are to support LDCs mainstream trade into their national development plans; and to assist in the co-ordinated delivery of TRA in response to needs identified by the LDC. In August 2006, 42 LDCs were participating in the programme.
The IDA-only countries are: Mongolia, Tonga, Vietnam, Albania, Armenia, Georgia, Kyrgyz Republic, Moldova, Tajikistan, Guyana, Honduras, Nicaragua, Sri Lanka, Cameroon, Republic of the Congo, Cote d'Ivoire, Ghana and Kenya.
See discussion in Annex.
In line with the principles of good governance in the tax area.
See Annex for details.
Cf. Council Conclusions on Decent Work for All of 1 December 2006, and the Commission Staff Working Paper on Promoting Employment through EU development cooperation.
See Annex.

COMMUNITY PROGRAMMES CUSTOMS 2013 AND FISCALIS 2013

1. BACKGROUND

When the Internal Market was created in 1993 the most visible change was the abolition of border controls between the EU Member States making the free movement of goods and services possible. Intra-Community trade in goods is now worth around EUR 1 500 billion per year and has almost doubled since the internal borders were removed.

Customs and tax administrations play a crucial role in the Community in maintaining and developing the internal market, applying controls at the external frontier and protecting the Community's financial and other interests. The customs and tax programmes are essential in this work and, without them, Europe's commerce would be severely disrupted, its competitiveness weakened and the safety and security of its citizens threatened. In the face of new challenges and ongoing change, enhancements and developments, especially in the field of IT, are unavoidable. This communication sets out a coherent strategy to provide a response to these challenges through the future EU customs and tax programmes.

This Communication on the Customs 2013 and Fiscalis 2013 Community programmes that are expected to run during the 2007–2013 period, pre-empts the Commission proposal for the successor programmes Customs 2013 and Fiscalis 2013 pending the outcome of the intermediate evaluations.

1.1. Customs

Today's customs must ensure the smooth flow of external trade on the one hand while applying effective controls on the international supply chain in order to:

- ensure the safety and security of the citizens of the EU;

- facilitate legitimate trade while protecting the Community from unfair and illegal trade;

- increase the competitiveness of European business via modern working methods supported by an easily accessible electronic customs environment;

- protect the financial interests of the EU and its Member States;

- manage the external border as a project of mutual interest for the European Union and its neighbours;

- cooperate nationally and internationally to combat fraud and promote legitimate trade.

1.2. Indirect taxation

1.2.1. VAT

As a direct consequence of the abolition of controls at the internal frontiers of the Community, tax administrations are required to exchange information to ensure that taxable persons are properly accounting for VAT. The principles of the internal market, particularly that of the free movement of goods have created greater interdependence between tax administrations. This interdependence arises in two ways. Firstly, tax administrations are dependent on one another for the electronic information which flows through the VAT Information Exchange System (VIES), and which provides the information necessary for the tax administrations to ensure that the VAT arising from the trade in goods between Member States is correctly accounted for. Secondly, tax administrations must cooperate closely to ensure that they identify fraudulent traders quickly and deal with them to prevent any distortion of competition in the single market.

1.2.2. Excise duties

The destination principle enshrined in EU excise law has complicated the administration of the excise system and has required administrative systems to physically monitor the movement of excise products between Member States.

1.3. Direct taxation

Direct taxes also have an impact on the functioning of the common market. Taxation policies must therefore clearly take into account important Union objectives, such as further deepening and supporting the functioning of the single market and promoting growth and employment while at the same time protecting tax bases against harmful tax competition and tax fraud as well as making life easier for legitimate business.

1.4. Financial perspectives

By ensuring the smooth functioning of the Internal Market, the Fiscalis and Customs programmes will contribute to the broader objective of sustainable economic growth set out in the Commission Communication on the financial perspectives 2007-2013. The second Commission Communication on these perspectives explicitly refers to the Fiscalis and Customs programmes as one of the practical measures required. The programmes fall into subheading 1a – Competitiveness for growth and employment.

2. THE PRESENT PROGRAMMES

The Customs 2007 programme aims to guarantee the effective functioning of the internal market in the field of customs while the Fiscalis 2003–2007 programme aims to improve the operation of taxation systems in the internal market.

The interim evaluation for both programmes which started at the beginning of 2005, and the impact assessment will provide further material for supporting the successor programmes. Their recommendations will be incorporated in the proposals for the successor programmes, which are planned to be submitted for adoption in early 2006.

2.1. The backbone of the Trans-European computerised networks

The backbone for the electronic exchange of information is the secure network CCN/CSI (Common Communication Network/Common System Interface) used by customs and tax administrations and financed under both programmes. Via CCN/CSI, national and Community records are made available in a highly secure way at a European wide level. Some 180 million messages were handled by CCN/CSI in 2004.

Most of the Community databases (EBTI, TQS, ECICS) and some of the national information records are available for consultation via Internet through a portal setup on the EUROPA web site and called DDS (Data Dissemination System). More than 34 million queries were made in 2004.

2.2. Trans-European computerised networks for customs

In the field of customs, the New Computerised Transit System (NCTS) assures the transmission of the customs transit declaration of goods simultaneously with and prior to the physical transport of the goods. It increases the capacity of customs both to ensure correct customs control of these movements and to reduce operators' costs. In 2004, more than 5,5 million international transit movements were recorded. The Common Community Tariff system (TARIC) provides information vital for the correct and uniform application of tariff legislation to external trade by all Member States. Some 27 million queries were made in 2004.

With the launching of the electronic customs initiative the first steps have been taken on the road to a paperless customs environment.

2.3. Trans-European computerised networks for taxation

The VAT Information Exchange System (VIES) brings together national VAT databases. Its primary purpose is to allow the exchange of information between Member States regarding exempt intra-Community supplies of goods, thereby allowing the tax administrations to correctly control the taxation of supplies of goods in the single market. In 2004, 80 million messages were exchanged through VIES.

The Commission is also developing the Excise Movement Control System (EMCS) project establishing an IT system to monitor the movement of excise products under suspension of excise duty. Meanwhile, a number of intermediate systems allowing for the exchange of data on excisable goods, warehouses and traders in excise goods have been put in place and are constantly updated and improved.

2.4. Joint actions

Experience with the organisation of activities for officials is longstanding and has its roots in the predecessors of Customs and Fiscalis programmes, launched in 1991.

These joint actions have proved to be extremely useful for developing and disseminating best administrative practice, confidence building and for stimulating and developing cooperation between national administrations.

3. POLICY CHALLENGES TO BE ADDRESSED BY THE SUCCESSOR PROGRAMMES

3.1. Customs

Common implementation of Community customs law is essential in order to avoid distortions of the market. In terms of the globalisation of trade, customs activities must be consistent with the aim of ensuring that the European Union remains competitive. Customs must therefore ensure the smooth flow of trade whilst applying the necessary checks for risks that external trade might present to security, health, safety and the economic interests of the Union.

Customs has a unique position in relation to the new challenge of securing the supply chain. Having control over all aspects of international movements, customs has an overview of all the players, within the EU, at the physical external frontier and in third countries. With the burden of controlling the Community's external land frontier falling disproportionately on the newer Member States, it is also important to consider the possibility of financial support for joint operations in order to improve the consistency of controls.

Effective control can only be achieved through the use of common risk management. Risk management must be incorporated into all aspects of customs work, including IT systems and must also be constantly monitored and developed. For risk management and profiling to be effective, there is a need to ensure rapid exchange of information between customs control points as well as with other agencies.

In order to avoid serious distortions of trade and threats to the Community's security, continued efforts will be needed to ensure that controls are implemented effectively at every point of the Community's customs territory. This will require operational actions specifically targeted at setting and monitoring control standards and ensuring that national customs administrations have adequate means to achieve these objectives. The development and implementation of new working practices, strengthened cooperation, and systematic sharing of common practice, supported by measurement, monitoring and reporting will be a prerequisite to meet new threats to security and safety and to guarantee a high standard of effective customs controls. Actions in this area will also contribute to meeting the expectations of the different stakeholders, particularly in the reduction of compliance costs for economic operators. It is also important to ensure complementarity between the activities in the field of customs, as financed under the Customs 2013 Programme, and activities in the field of control of people at the external borders including those of the External Border Agency.

Counterfeiting and piracy causes huge economic damage and, since customs is the major interceptor of such goods, it is essential that this is combated in an efficient way. This will include improvements to risk indicators in the field.

In order to follow these priority issues, and recognising the trend towards e-government, it is necessary to modernise customs legislation and to radically simplify it. Legislation alone will not be sufficient and there is a pressing need to develop new integrated systems or reshape existing ones. The programme will be the only way to make the electronic customs initiative fully operational. From an IT point of view, it will allow the transmission of customs declarations between customs offices in different Member States, together with the possibility of the interchange of information with existing databases. This will not only improve the risk management of imported and exported goods, but also customs clearance where the customs office of entry or exit is in a Member State other than that of the customs office of import or export.

3.2. Taxation

The Commission believes that the main priority for tax policy is addressing the concerns of individuals and businesses operating within the Internal Market by focusing on the elimination of tax obstacles to all forms of cross-border economic activity . In addition it has been evident that other issues that adversely affect the functioning of the market also need to be addressed, in particular the fight against harmful tax competition and tax fraud.

In recent times all of the legal instruments for cooperation in the fields of VAT, excise and direct taxation and recovery have been reinforced. These legal instruments have further strengthened the consolidation of a well developed and efficient administrative cooperation structure which is underpinned by the Fiscalis programme. The successor programme should build upon the work of the current programmes and aim at better understanding and implementation of Community law, improved cooperation, continued improvement of administrative procedures for administrations and taxpayers, dissemination of good administrative practice and the fight against fraud.

The exchange of information between administrations plays an important role in solving a number of difficult issues, such as enabling the effective taxation of savings income. Similarly, in the VAT and excise fields, the exchange of information solution is being seen as almost a precondition for further progress. Examples of this philosophy in the VAT field include the Commission proposal for a one-stop shop for businesses trading in more than one Member State and the proposal to change the place of supply of services. In the future, it is more and more likely that an IT solution will be seen as a first resort.

The growing need to improve transparency and the effective exchange of information is not limited to the Member States or the immediate neighbours of the EU . In the active promotion of sound practices, as outlined in the Commission's Communication on preventing and combating corporate and financial malpractice, the Fiscalis programme could also prove to be a useful tool in support of reform in the so-called cooperative tax havens and, more generally, EU partners. The lessons which have been learned from recent high-profile fraud cases have convinced the Commission that a more widespread use of administrative cooperation is necessary so as to avoid the manipulation of the rules by unscrupulous businesses.

4. IMPLEMENTATION CHALLENGES FOR THE SUCCESSOR PROGRAMMES

4.1. Trans European computerised networks

During the last years, the Trans-European computerised networks became of strategic importance for the operational activities of European customs and tax administrations. The huge success of CCN/CSI and the tax and customs IT systems has resulted in a tremendous increase in use of these systems, which has caused a doubling of capacity on an annual basis. The traffic generated by the 10 new Member States is only part of the reason for this increase, since the surge is primarily the result of more intensive use of the systems to facilitate trade, to control the main bulk of cross-border transactions and to fight fraud. It is expected that tax and customs officials will make even greater use of the systems in the coming years.

The more intensive use of the systems will require further upgrading of the CCN system and it is expected that security arrangements will need to be reviewed and improved in the very near future.

The progressive build-up of centralised operations and management of these trans-European computerised networks will also be of major importance and impact. As well as the increased efficiency which would result from the use of a single system rather than the multiplication of national systems which exist today, this would result in major savings at a national level.

4.2. The strategic importance of the trans-European computerised networks

If the European computerised customs network were unavailable, the old paper system would have to be used. This would provoke serious delays in the movement of goods, which economic operators are no longer willing to accept. The unavailability or malfunctioning of these systems would also have a considerable adverse impact on business through the incorrect application of the tariff and the customs code, and traffic blockages at the borders, quickly leading to damaging consequences to trade.

Similarly, the unavailability or malfunctioning of the VIES system would jeopardise VAT controls and pave the way for large-scale fraud such as carousel fraud.

4.3. Joint Actions

The Lisbon Strategy emphasises that the work on the Internal Market is shifting from law making towards practical implementation by Member States of the different measures on a daily basis. Joint actions addressed this issue from the start and have become a key instrument of the Commission and Member States to foster a unique cooperation culture between the Member States. There is a need to ensure the active participation of Member States because of the knowledge and the expertise they have in many areas, to further strengthen mutual assistance and to expand cooperation to officials working outside headquarters.

In order to make efficient use of the resources available in the Community, a range of possibilities will need to be explored, including sharing equipment between Member States, exchanging know-how on the deployment and use of equipment and financial support for the purchase of equipment.

4.4. Common Training Tools

Common training is an essential element in ensuring a uniform approach to Member States' actions. The work on the development of common training tools and the use of e-learning tools must continue and a new impetus must be given to the distribution of the outcomes and results of activities. In addition to these, and especially in the field of customs, further consideration must be given to the provision of common training in core areas at European level.

4.5. Candidate countries, Western Balkan Countries, European Neighbourhood Policy and Third Countries

In both the Customs 2013 and Fiscalis 2013 programmes, there will be an external component financed by the Pre-Accession Instrument under heading 4 of the Financial Perspectives 2007-2013. Specific arrangements will be agreed with the RELEX Directorates-General for the programming and implementation of the funds involved.

With regard to security, international cooperation based on common standards and mutual recognition of control results is the only way to efficiently reduce the burden on legitimate traders. Such cooperation is therefore a priority task under a new programme.

The programmes will provide assistance to candidate countries and may provide assistance to the partner countries of the European Neighbourhood Policy and other third countries. In the field of customs, it is important to take initiatives that will align the working practices of our neighbours and trading partners with Community legislation and strengthen their administrative and operational capacity, for example in terms of controls on prohibited, dangerous and illegal goods. Within the tax field it is important to help these countries strengthen their administrative capacity to be able to cooperate in particular to fight cross-border tax frauds. Interconnectivity with our computerised systems has to be established for customs and tax administrations of candidate countries before the date of accession. Interconnectivity may also be envisaged for customs and tax administrations of other neighbouring countries, on a case by case basis according to the needs.

5. BUDGET

The budgets proposed for the programmes show a significant increase over a six year period, namely from EUR 157,435 million to EUR 323,8 million for the Customs programme and from EUR 67,25 million to EUR 175,30 million for the Fiscalis programme. The rise is mainly due to the development of new computerised systems to support the new business and legislative initiatives in the customs and taxation area that are expected in the near future.

In the customs area it is envisaged that EUR 77 million is required to operate and evolve the existing TRANSIT and Tariff systems. The Customs 2013 budget includes EUR 104,5 million over six years to carry out the electronic customs project which is currently being drafted. Systems required for managing initiatives related to the security aspects of customs policy, are estimated to require EUR 38,7 million.

In the Customs 2013 programme an amount of EUR 46 million is budgeted to finance joint actions. The budget has been increased from 2007 to 2008 as it is expected that the external border policy will result in a surge of activities with non-EU countries, especially neighbouring countries. Finally the Customs programme foresees an amount of EUR 11,4 million over six years to support the development of common training tools in support of the customs policy objectives mentioned earlier. The common training initiatives will continue the initiatives developed under the current programme.

In the tax area EUR 30,3 million will be required to operate and evolve the VIES system. As from 2009, the Fiscalis 2013 programme will incorporate the EMCS system. It is estimated that over six years EUR 19,5 million is needed for EMCS. Finally, an amount of EUR 37 million has been budgeted to support new policy initiatives in the tax area like the VIES II system, the one-stop shop facility for traders and new initiatives for the exchange of information. The joint actions on taxation are budgeted at EUR 39 million. The Fiscalis programme will also support the development of common training tools. This initiative is new and is expected to start at the beginning of the new programme in connection with the new legal initiatives. An amount of EUR 3,3 million is budgeted.

Finally, both successor programmes include a significant higher amount for the CCN system: EUR 46,2 million for each programme as compared to EUR 18,5 million in each of the present programmes. This sharp increase has been budgeted to support the current trend of doubling capacity every year. This reality is confirmed by the continuous need for interoperability and the level of availability required. Indeed, the IT systems financed by the programmes need to be available increasingly on a permanent basis, 24 hours a day and 7 days a week. To attain this level of availability an exponential increase in the budget is required as this involves setting up fall-back architectures and associated services.

Currently, the Customs programme only finances first-pillar activities. As it is impossible to confine customs actions to a specific pillar activity, the future programme should allow for co-financing from first and third pillar programmes.

6. CONCLUSION

The Customs and Fiscalis programmes 2007 are improving cooperation between customs and tax administrations and their officials and are establishing trans-European computerised networks required to meet the customs control obligations within the internal market and to maintain taxation of goods and services in accordance with national and Community tax legislation within this market. The programmes play a key role in the smooth functioning of the internal market and the management of the EU's external border, and as such contribute to the realisation of the Commission's 2005–2009 objectives and the Lisbon Strategy. Therefore, the Commission proposes to have two successor programmes, Fiscalis 2013 and Customs 2013 inserted in the Financial Perspectives 2007–2013 and to finance the EMCS project from Fiscalis 2013 as from 2009.

The renewal of the programmes is essential for the competitiveness of European trade, the collection and protection of Community revenues and the safety and security of the EU citizens. The enormous volume of customs declarations, coupled with the demands for facilitation of legitimate commerce and the expectations of stakeholders regarding the protection of their interests, can only be met with the actions which are supported by the Customs programme. The Community element of the IT systems is crucial: improving controls and increasing trade facilitation requires electronic exchange of data between economic operators and customs, the rapid provision of high-risk information to customs posts and the key actors having access to up-to-the-minute customs information. The single market demands equivalent treatment throughout the Community and the Customs programme make an essential contribution to the prevention of divergent practice by customs in their application of Community legislation. Furthermore, without the programme customs would find it much more difficult to apply effective controls with reasonable compliance costs for business. The discontinuation of the Customs programme would put at risk European competitiveness, security and employment and adversely impact on the perception of the EU as a single entity in international discussions.

If the current Fiscalis programme were to be interrupted, the functioning of the single market would be put in jeopardy, because of the role of the programme in financing the VAT Information Exchange System (VIES) as well as several key excise systems. The VIES system currently provides information to Member States so that they can undertake control of intra-Community tax transactions in an EU without internal borders and at the same time it makes it easier for business to trade in the internal market. Without this electronic exchange of information, Member States would have to find another methodology for VAT controls, and this would be a step backward in terms of burdens on businesses. Furthermore, it is essential to foster and develop administrative cooperation between tax administrations, and the Fiscalis programme is ideally placed to do this.

SUPPLEMENTS

FREE TRADE AGREEMENTS IN FORCE

The EU is a party to trade agreements and other agreements with a trade component both in the WTO context and bilaterally with certain countries and regions.

WTO AGREEMENTS

The WTO agreements cover goods, services and intellectual property. They spell out the principles of liberalization, and the permitted exceptions. They include individual countries' commitments to lower customs tariffs and other trade barriers, and to open and keep open services markets. They set procedures for settling disputes. They prescribe special treatment for developing countries. They require governments to make their trade policies transparent by notifying the WTO about laws in force and measures adopted, and through regular reports by the secretariat on countries' trade policies.

Umbrella	AGREEMENT ESTABLISHING WTO		
	Goods	Services	Intellectual property
Basic principles	GATT	GATS	TRIPS
Additional details	Other goods agreements and annexes	Services annexes	
Market access commitments	Countries' schedules of commitments	Countries' schedules of commitments(and MFN exemptions)	
Dispute settlement	DISPUTE SETTLEMENT		
Transparency	TRADE POLICY REVIEWS		

ADDITIONAL AGREEMENTS

Another group of agreements not included in the diagram is also important: the two "plurilateral" agreements not signed by all members: civil aircraft and government procurement.

THE DOHA AGENDA

These agreements are not static; they are renegotiated from time to time and new agreements can be added to the package. Many are now being negotiated under the Doha Development Agenda, launched by WTO trade ministers in Doha, Qatar, in November 2001.

THE URUGUAY ROUND AGREEMENTS

The "Final Act" signed in Marrakesh in 1994 is like a cover note. Everything else is attached to this. Foremost is the Agreement Establishing the WTO (or the WTO Agreement), which serves as an umbrella agreement. Annexed are the agreements on goods, services and intellectual property, dispute settlement, trade policy review mechanism and the plurilateral agreements. The schedules of commitments also form part of the Uruguay Round agreements.

MARRAKESH DECLARATION OF 15 APRIL 1994

Final Act

Agreement Establishing the World Trade Organization

MULTILATERAL AGREEMENTS ON TRADE IN GOODS

GATT 1994 - Must be read with **GATT 1947**,

Other duties and charges (GATT Art.II:l(b)),

State trading enterprises (GATT Art.XVII),

Balance-of-payments,

Regional trade agreements (GATT Art.XXIV)

aivers of Obligations, Understanding

Concession withdrawal (GATT Art.XXVIII), Understanding

Marrakesh Protocol to the GATT 1994

Agriculture

Sanitary and Phytosanitary Measures

Textiles and Clothing

Note: this Agreement was terminated on 1 January 2005. See Textiles

Technical Barriers to Trade

Trade-Related Investment Measures (TRIMs)

Anti-dumping (Article VI of GATT 1994)

Customs valuation (Article VII of GATT 1994)

Preshipment Inspection

Rules of Origin

Import Licensing

Subsidies and Countervailing Measuresinterpretation

Safeguards

Annex 1B General Agreement on Trade in Services (GATS)

Annex 1C Trade-Related Aspects of Intellectual Property Rights (TRIPS)

Annex 2 Dispute Settlement Understanding

Annex 3 Trade Policy Review Mechanism

Annex 4 Plurilateral Trade Agreements

Annex 4(a) Agreement on Trade in Civil Aircraft

Annex 4(b) Agreement on Government Procurement

Annex 4(c) International Dairy Agreement
Note: this Agreement was terminated end 1997. See document IDA/8

Annex 4(d) International Bovine Meat Agreement
Note: this Agreement was terminated end 1997

URUGUAY ROUND MINISTERIAL DECISIONS AND DECLARATIONS

Decisions adopted by the Trade Negotiations Committee on 15 December 1993 and 14 April 1994

Measures **in favour of least-developed countries** > browse text > MS Word > pdf

Notification procedures

Agriculture: measures concerning the possible negative effects of the reform programme on **least-developed and net food-importing developing countries**

Textiles and clothing: **notification of first integration under Article 2.6**

Technical barriers to trade:

Proposed Understanding on WTO-ISO Standards Information System

Review of the ISO/IEC Information Centre Publication

Customs valuation (GATT Article VII):
Cases where **customs administrations have reasons to doubt the truth or accuracy of the declared value**

Minimum values and **imports by sole agents, sole distributors and sole concessionaires**

Services:

Institutional arrangements for the GATS

Certain **dispute settlement procedures** for the GATS

Trade in **services and the environment**

Negotiations on movement of natural persons

Financial services

Negotiations on maritime transport services

Negotiations on basic telecommunications

Government procurement: **accession to the agreement**

Dispute settlement: **application and review of the Dispute Settlement Understanding**

Agreement Establishing the WTO: **acceptance of and accession to the agreement**

Trade and environment

Organization and financial consequences flowing from implementation of the Agreement Establishing the WTO

Establishment of the **Preparatory Committee for the WTO** > browse text > MS Word > pdf

Declarations adopted by the Trade Negotiations Committee on 15 December 1993

Contribution of the WTO to achieving **greater coherence in global economic policymaking**

Relationship of **the WTO with the International Monetary Fund**

Decisions and declarations on **anti-dumping** (GATT Article VI) and **subsidies and countervailing measures** adopted by the Trade Negotiations Committee on 15 December 1993

Decision on **anti-circumvention**

Decision on **review of Article 17.6 of the Anti-Dumping Agreement** > browse text > MS Word > pdf

Declaration on **dispute settlement** pursuant to the Anti-Dumping and Subsidies and Countervailing Measures agreements > browse text > MS Word > pdf;

GATT 1947

The original agreement dealing with trade in goods, now incorporated into GATT 1994

Post-1994 goods agreement (Information Technology Agreement)

Post-1994 GATS protocols

These are additional agreements negotiated after the Uruguay Round and attached to the General Agreement on Trade in Services. There is no “First Protocol”.

Second protocol: financial services

Third protocol: movement of natural persons

Fourth protocol: basic telecommunications

Fifth protocol: financial services

Post-1994 accession protocols

These are the negotiated terms of membership for countries joining the WTO after it was created on 1 January 1995. They include each new member's schedules of commitments.
Countries' schedules of commitments

These schedules contain the commitments made by individual WTO members allowing specific foreign products or service-providers access to their markets. The schedules are integral parts of the agreements. In the print version these schedules comprise about 30,000 pages for all WTO Members.

Goods

For goods in general: binding commitments on tariffs. For agriculture: tariffs, combinations of tariffs and quotas, export subsidies and some types of domestic support.

Goods schedules gateway: gives links to individual member governments' goods schedules agreed during the Uruguay Round.

Post-1994 **Information Technology Agreement schedules**

Protocols of accession, for countries that have negotiated and become WTO members after 1995.

Paper versions: available from the WTO on-line bookshop (Volumes 3-32 of the Legal Instruments embodying the Results of the Uruguay Round. You can select the countries which interest you from the titles and order online.)

Services

Binding commitments on how much access foreign service providers are allowed for specific sectors. Includes lists types of services where individual countries say they are not applying the "most-favoured-nation" principle of non-discrimination.

TRATE AGREEMENTS EUROPE

EU EUROPEAN COUNTRIES

Faroe Islands - 01 January 1997

Norway - 01 July 1973

Iceland - 01 April 1973

Switzerland - 01 January 1973

The former Yugoslav Republic of Macedonia - Stabilisation and Association Agreement, 01 May 2004

Croatia - Stabilisation and Association Agreement, 01 February 2005

Albania - Stabilisation and Association Agreement, 01 April 2009

Montenegro - Stabilisation and Association Agreement, 01 May 2010

Bosnia and Herzegovina - Interim Agreement on trade and trade related matters, 01 July 2008

Serbia - Interim Agreement on trade and trade related matters, 01 February 2010

EU MEDITERRANEAN COUNTRIES

Algeria - Association Agreement, 01 September 2005

Egypt - Association Agreement, 01 June 2004

Israel - Association Agreement, 01 June 2000

Jordan - Association Agreement, 01 May 2002

Lebanon - Interim Agreement, 01 March 2003

Morocco - Association Agreement, 01 March 2000

Palestinian Authority - Association Agreement, 01 July 1997

Syria - Co-operation Agreement, 01 July 1977

Tunisia - Association Agreement, 01 March 1998

OTHER COUNTRIES

Mexico - Economic Partnership, Political Coordination and Cooperation Agreement, 01 July 2000

South Africa - Trade, Development and Co-operation Agreement, 01 January 2000

CARIFORUM States - Economic Partnership Agreement, Provisionally applied

Chile - Association Agreement and Additional Protocol, 01 February 2003 (trade) / 01 March 2005 (full agreement)

Madagascar, Mauritius, the Seychelles, and Zimbabwe Interim Partnership Agreement signed in August 2009

Korea - New Generation Free Trade Agreement, signed 06 October 2010

Papua New Guinea and Fiji - Interim Partnership Agreement ratified by Papua New Guinea in May 2011

EU-Iraq - Partnership and Cooperation Agreement, signed on 11 May 2012

EU CUSTOMS UNIONS

Andorra - 01 July 1991

Turkey - 31 December 1995

San Marino - 01 December 1992

GLOSSARY

A

accession criteria
See Copenhagen criteria (accession criteria)

accountability
The legal and political obligation of an independent institution to properly explain and justify its decisions to the citizens and their elected representatives, thereby making it responsible for fulfilling its objectives. The ECB is accountable to the European citizens and, more formally, to the European Parliament.

ACH
See automated clearing house (ACH)

actual/360
The day-count convention applied for the calculation of interest on a credit, implying that the interest is calculated over the actual number of calendar days over which the credit is extended, on the basis of a 360-day year. This day-count convention is applied in Eurosystem monetary policy operations. See also day-count convention

aggregated balance sheet of the MFI sector
See aggregated MFI balance sheet

aggregated MFI balance sheet
A balance sheet comprising the sums total of the data included in the harmonised balance sheets of all the MFIs resident in the euro area (inter-MFI positions on gross basis). The legal basis for the collection of harmonised balance sheet statistics is laid down in Regulation ECB/2001/13, as amended. This Regulation is complemented by Guideline ECB/2003/2, as amended, which sets out the procedures to be followed by NCBs when reporting data relating to money and banking statistics to the ECB.

American auction
See multiple rate auction (American auction)

amortisation
The systematic reduction in the accounts of the value of assets over a period of time or of the value of a premium/discount.

ASLP

See automated security lending programme (ASLP)

asset
A resource controlled by an enterprise as a result of past events and from which future economic benefits are expected to flow to the enterprise.

ATM
See automated teller machine (ATM)

automated clearing house (ACH)
An electronic clearing system in which payment orders are exchanged among financial institutions, primarily using magnetic media or via telecommunication networks, and handled by a data-processing centre. See also clearing

automated security lending programme (ASLP)
A financial operation combining repo and reverse repo transactions where specific collateral is lent against general collateral. As a result of these lending and borrowing transactions, income is generated through the different repo rates of the two transactions (i.e. the margin received). The operation may be conducted under a principal-based programme, i.e. the bank offering this programme is considered the final counterparty, or under an agency-based programme, i.e. the bank offering this programme acts only as agent, and the final counterparty is the institution with which the security lending transactions are effectively conducted.

automated teller machine (ATM)
An electromechanical device which permits authorised users, typically using machine-readable plastic cards, to withdraw cash from their accounts and/or perform additional banking operations such as making balance enquiries, transferring funds or making deposits. ATMs may be operated either online with real-time access to an authorisation database or offline.

autonomous liquidity factors
Liquidity factors that do not normally stem from the use of monetary policy instruments. They include, for example, banknotes in circulation, government deposits with the central bank and net foreign assets of the central bank.

availability
The criterion used to evaluate a payment or securities settlement system on the basis of its backup facilities and the possibility of switching over to them.

average cost
The continued (or weighted) average method, by which the cost of every purchase is added to the existing book value to produce a new weighted average cost.
averaging provision
A provision allowing counterparties to fulfil their reserve requirements on the basis of their average reserve holdings over the maintenance period. The averaging provision contributes to the stabilisation of money market interest rates by giving institutions an incentive to smooth the effects of temporary liquidity fluctuations. The Eurosystem's minimum reserve system allows for averaging.

B

b.o.p.
See balance of payments (b.o.p.)

balance of payments (b.o.p.)

A statistical statement that summarises, for a specific period of time, the economic transactions of an economy with the rest of the world. The transactions considered are those involving goods, services and income, those involving financial claims on, and liabilities to, the rest of the world and those that are classified as transfers (such as debt forgiveness).

bank identifier code (BIC)
A universal means of identifying financial institutions in order to facilitate the automated processing of telecommunication messages in financial environments.

base money (monetary base)
Currency (banknotes and coins) in circulation plus the minimum reserves credit institutions are required to hold with the Eurosystem and any excess reserves they may voluntarily hold in the Eurosystem's deposit facility, all of which are liabilities on the Eurosystem's balance sheet. Base money is sometimes also referred to as the "monetary base".

batch processing
The transmission or processing of a group of payment orders and/or securities transfer instructions in batches at discrete intervals of time. See also real-time processing

BEPGs
See Broad Economic Policy Guidelines (BEPGs)

BIC
See bank identifier code (BIC)

bilateral procedure
A procedure whereby the central bank deals directly with only one counterparty or a few counterparties on a one-to-one basis, without making use of tender procedures. Bilateral procedures include operations executed through stock exchanges or market agents.

bond market
The market for interest-bearing securities (with either a fixed or a floating rate and with a maturity of at least one year) that companies and governments issue to raise capital for investment. Fixed-rate bonds account for the largest share of this market.

book-entry system
An accounting system that permits the transfer of securities and other financial assets without the physical movement of paper documents or certificates (e.g. the electronic transfer of securities). See also dematerialisation

Broad Economic Policy Guidelines (BEPGs)
Guidelines adopted by the EU Council to provide the framework for defining the economic policy objectives and orientations of the Member States and the European Community.

business continuity
A payment system or securities settlement system arrangement which aims to ensure that the system meets agreed service levels even if one or more components fail or if it is affected by another abnormal event. This includes both preventive measures and arrangements to deal with these events.

C

capital account (in a b.o.p. context)

A b.o.p. account that covers all capital transfers and acquisitions/disposals of non-produced, non-financial assets between residents and non-residents.

capital accounts
Part of the system of national (or euro area) accounts consisting of the change in the net worth that is due to net saving, net capital transfers and net acquisitions of non-financial assets.

caps
Quantitative limits on the funds transfer activity of individual participants in a system; limits may be set by each individual participant or may be imposed by the body managing the system. Limits can be placed on the net debit position and the net credit position of participants in the system.

cash card
A card for use only in ATMs or cash dispensers. (Other cards often have a cash function which permits the holder to withdraw cash.)

cash/settlement approach
An accounting approach under which accounting events are recorded at the settlement date.

CCBM
See Correspondent central banking model (CCBM)

central bank
An institution which - by way of a legal act - has been given responsibility for conducting the monetary policy for a specific area.

central bank credit (liquidity) facility
A standing credit facility which can be drawn upon by certain designated account holders (e.g. banks) at a central bank. The facility can be used automatically at the initiative of the account holder. The loans typically take the form of either advances or overdrafts on an account holder's current account which may be secured by a pledge of securities or by repurchase agreements.
See also daylight credit (or daylight overdraft, daylight exposure, intraday credit)
repurchase agreement

central bank independence
The legal provision which guarantees that a central bank can carry out its tasks and duties without political interference. Article 108 of the Treaty establishes the principle of central bank independence for the euro area.

central counterparty
An entity which interposes itself as the buyer to every seller and as the seller to every buyer of a specified set of contracts.

central government
The government as defined in the ESA 95, but excluding regional and local governments. It includes all administrative departments of the (central) state and other central agencies whose competence extends over the entire economic territory, except for the administration of social security funds. See also general government

central parity
The exchange rate vis-à-vis the euro of currencies of member countries of ERM II, around which the ERM II fluctuation margins are defined.

central securities depository (CSD)

An entity which holds and administers securities or other financial assets, holds issuance accounts and enables transactions to be processed by book entry. Assets may exist either physically (but immobilised within the CSD) or in a dematerialised form (i.e. only as electronic records).

cheque
A written order from one party (the drawer) to another (the drawee, normally a bank) requiring the drawee to pay a specified sum on demand to the drawer or to a third party specified by the drawer. Cheques may be used for settling debts and withdrawing money from banks.

clean price
The transaction price excluding any rebate/accrued interest, but including any transaction costs that form part of the price.

clearing
The process of transmitting, reconciling and, in some cases, confirming payment orders or security transfer instructions prior to settlement, possibly including the netting of instructions and the establishment of final positions for settlement. Sometimes the term is used (imprecisely) to include settlement.

clearing and settling institution
An institution which transmits information and funds through a payment system network. It may operate as an agent or a principal.

clearing house
A department of an exchange or a separate legal entity which provides a range of services related to the clearing and settlement of transactions and payments, and the management of risks associated with the resulting contracts. In many cases the clearing house acts as central counterparty. See also central counterparty
clearing

close link
A situation in which, according to Article 1 (26) of Directive 2000/12/EC, "two or more natural or legal persons are linked by (a) participation, which shall mean the ownership, direct or by way of control, of 20% or more of the voting rights or capital of an undertaking, or (b) control, which shall mean the relationship between a parent undertaking and a subsidiary, in all the cases referred to in Article 1 (1) and (2) of Directive 83/349/EEC, or a similar relationship between any natural or legal person and an undertaking; any subsidiary undertaking of a subsidiary undertaking shall also be considered a subsidiary of the parent undertaking which is at the head of those undertakings. A situation in which two or more natural or legal persons are permanently linked to one and the same person by a control relationship shall also be regarded as constituting a close link between such persons."

CLS Bank (CLSB)
CLS stands for Continuous Linked Settlement. The CLS Bank provides global multi-currency settlement services for foreign exchange transactions, using a payment versus payment (PvP) mechanism (meaning that a foreign exchange operation is settled only if both counterparties simultaneously have a sufficient position in the currency they are selling).

CLSB
See CLS Bank (CLSB)

collateral

Assets pledged (e.g. by credit institutions with central banks) as a guarantee for the repayment of loans, as well as assets sold (e.g. to central banks by credit institutions) as part of repurchase agreements (repos).

collateral pool
A pool account on which a pooling system's participant holds securities pledged in favour of the central bank in charge of the system when obtaining credit (for intraday, overnight or monetary policy operations). See also collateral pooling system

collateral pooling system
A central bank system for managing collateral, in which counterparties open a pool account to deposit assets in order to collateralise their transactions with the central bank. A pooling system differs from an earmarking system in that the underlying assets are not earmarked for individual transactions. See also collateral pool

collection of fixed-term deposits
A monetary policy instrument available to the Eurosystem for fine-tuning purposes. The Eurosystem offers remuneration on counterparties' fixed-term deposits on accounts with the national central banks in order to absorb liquidity from the market.

Commission of the European Communities
See European Commission (Commission of the European Communities)

compensation of employees
The total remuneration, including gross wages and salaries as well as bonuses, overtime payments and employers' social security contributions, that is payable, in cash or in kind, by employers to employees in return for work done by the latter during the accounting period (definition according to the ESA 95).

compensation per employee
The sum total of the compensation of employees divided by the total number of employees.

consolidated balance sheet of the MFI sector
See consolidated MFI balance sheet

consolidated MFI balance sheet
This is obtained by netting out inter-MFI positions (e.g. inter-MFI loans and deposits) on the aggregated MFI balance sheet. It provides statistical information on the MFI sector's assets and liabilities vis-à-vis residents of the euro area not belonging to this sector (i.e. general government and other euro area residents) and vis-à-vis non-euro area residents. This consolidated balance sheet is the main statistical source for the calculation of monetary aggregates and it provides the basis for the regular analysis of the counterparts of M3.

consumer credit
Loans granted to households for personal use in the consumption of goods and services.

consumer price index (CPI)
A measure of changes over time in prices of consumption goods and services acquired or used by households.

convergence criteria
The four criteria set out in Article 121(1) of the Treaty that must be fulfilled by each EU Member State before it can adopt the euro, namely a stable price level, sound public finances (a deficit and a level of debt that are both limited in terms of GDP), a stable exchange rate and low and

stable long-term interest rates. In addition, each EU Member State must ensure the compatibility of its national legislation, including the statutes of the national central bank, with both the Treaty and the Statute of the European System of Central Banks and of the European Central Bank.

Copenhagen criteria (accession criteria)
The criteria defined by the Copenhagen European Council in June 1993 (and confirmed by the Madrid European Council in December 1995) that must be fulfilled by any country wishing to join the European Union. Included are political criteria (stable institutions guaranteeing democracy, the rule of law, human rights and respect for minorities), economic criteria (a functioning market economy) and the incorporation into national law of the acquis communautaire (the EU's body of law).

Core principles for systemically important payment systems
Ten minimum standards for the design and operation of such systems, namely (i) a sound legal basis under all relevant jurisdictions, (ii) rules and procedures that ensure a clear understanding of the risks involved, (iii) clear procedures for the management of credit and liquidity risk by both operator and participants, (iv) provision for prompt final settlement on the day of value, (v) the capability, in the case of multilateral netting, of ensuring a timely completion of daily settlement if the participant with the largest single settlement obligation cannot settle, (vi) the use of assets for settlement that constitute claims on the central bank or carry little or no credit and liquidity risk, (vii) a high degree of security and operational reliability, (viii) practical and efficient means of making payments, (ix) objective and publicly disclosed participation criteria for open access, and (x) an effective, accountable and transparent governance.

correspondent banking
An arrangement under which one credit institution provides payment and other services to another credit institution. Payments through correspondents are often executed through reciprocal accounts (nostro and loro accounts), to which standing credit lines may be attached. Correspondent banking services are primarily provided across international boundaries, but are also known as agency relationships in some domestic contexts. A loro account is the term used by a correspondent to describe an account held on behalf of a foreign credit institution; the foreign credit institution would in turn regard this account as its nostro account.

Correspondent central banking model (CCBM)
A mechanism established by the European System of Central Banks with the aim of enabling counterparties to use underlying assets in a cross-border context. In the CCBM, national central banks act as custodians for one another. This means that each national central bank has a securities account in its securities administration for each of the other national central banks (and for the ECB).

Council
See EU Council (Council of Ministers)

Council of Ministers
See EU Council (Council of Ministers)

counterparty
The opposite party in a financial transaction (e.g. any party transacting with a central bank).

Court of Justice
See Court of Justice of the European Communities (Court of Justice)

Court of Justice of the European Communities (Court of Justice)

The EU institution that rules on the interpretation and application both of the Treaty and of the legal acts laid down by other EU institutions.

CPI
See consumer price index (CPI)

credit card
A card indicating that the holder has been granted a line of credit. It enables the holder to make purchases and/or withdraw cash up to a prearranged ceiling; the credit granted can be settled in full by the end of a specified period or can be settled in part, with the balance taken as extended credit. Interest is charged on the amount of any extended credit and the holder is sometimes charged an annual fee.

credit institution
Any institution covered by the definition contained in Article 1(1) of Directive 2000/12/EC, as amended. Accordingly, a credit institution is "(i) an undertaking whose business is to receive deposits or other repayable funds from the public and to grant credits for its own account; or (ii) an undertaking or any other legal person, other than those under (i), which issues means of payment in the form of electronic money." The most common types of credit institutions are banks and savings banks. See also electronic money (e-money)

credit limit
The limit on the credit exposure which a payment system participant incurs vis-à-vis another participant (bilateral credit limit) or vis-à-vis all other participants (multilateral credit limit) as a result of receiving payments which have not yet been settled.

credit risk/exposure
The risk that a counterparty will not settle an obligation in full, either when due or at any time thereafter. In exchange-for-value systems, the credit risk is generally defined as including replacement cost risk and principal risk.

credit to euro area residents
A broad measure of the financing of non-monetary financial institution (MFI) euro area residents (including general government and the private sector) provided by the MFI sector. It is defined as including MFI loans to euro area residents and MFI holdings of securities issued by euro area residents. The latter include shares, other equity and debt securities. As securities can be seen as an alternative source of funds to loans, and as some loans can be securitised, this definition provides more accurate information on the total amount of financing provided by the MFI sector to the economy than a narrow definition comprising loans only.

credit transfer
A payment order or sometimes a sequence of payment orders made for the purpose of placing funds at the disposal of the beneficiary. Both the payment instructions and the funds described therein move from the bank of the payer/originator to the bank of the beneficiary, possibly via several other banks as intermediaries and/or via more than one credit transfer system.

credit transfer system
A funds transfer system through which payment orders move from (the bank of) the originator of the transfer message or payer to (the bank of) the receiver of the message or beneficiary.

cross-border payment
A payment between counterparties located in different countries.

cross-border position

For the purposes of monetary statistics, the stock of financial claims and financial liabilities of MFIs residing in the euro area vis-à-vis MFIs and non-MFIs residing (i) in the euro area, (ii) in non-euro area EU Member States and (iii) in countries outside the EU.

cross-border settlement
A settlement which takes place in a country other than the country or countries in which one or both of the parties to the trade are located.

CSD
See central securities depository (CSD)

currency in circulation
Banknotes and coins in circulation that are commonly used to make payments. Since 1 January 2002, currency in circulation in the euro area has included banknotes issued by the Eurosystem and other monetary financial institutions (MFIs) as well as coins issued by euro area central governments, denominated in both euro and legacy currencies, even though the euro became sole legal tender in all euro area countries on 1 March 2002. Legacy currency banknotes and coins ceased to be included in currency in circulation as from 1 January 2003, both for Eurosystem financial reporting and for statistical purposes. Currency in circulation as included in M3 is a net concept, meaning that it refers only to banknotes and coins in circulation that are held outside the MFI sector (i.e. currency held by MFIs or "vault cash" has been subtracted). Excluded are central banks' stocks of own banknotes (as they have not been put into circulation) and commemorative coins (as they are not commonly used to make payments).

current account
A b.o.p. account that covers all transactions in goods and services, income and current transfers between residents and non-residents.

custodian
An entity which undertakes the safekeeping and administration of securities and other financial assets on behalf of others. See also global custodian

custody
The holding and administration of securities and other financial instruments on behalf of others.

custody risk
The risk of loss of securities held in custody occasioned by the insolvency, negligence or fraudulent action of the custodian or subcustodian. Even if an appropriate legal framework is in place, which eliminates the risk of loss of value of the securities held by the custodian in the event of its failure, the ability of participants to transfer the securities might be temporarily impaired. See also custodian
custody

customer payment
A payment where the originator or the final beneficiary, or both, are not financial institutions.

D

daily processing
In a payment or securities settlement system, the complete cycle of processing tasks which needs to be completed in a typical business day, from start-of-day procedures to end-of-day procedures, including the backing-up of data.
daily settlement
The completion of settlement on the day of value of all payments accepted for settlement.

day-count convention
The convention regulating the number of days included in the calculation of interest on credits. The Eurosystem applies the day-count convention actual/360 in its monetary policy operations.

daylight credit (or daylight overdraft, daylight exposure, intraday credit)
Credit extended for a period of less than one business day. Daylight credit may be extended by central banks to even out mismatches in payment settlements. In a credit transfer system with end-of-day final settlement, daylight credit is, in effect, extended by a receiving institution if it accepts and acts on a payment order even though it will not receive final funds until the end of the business day.

daylight exposure
See daylight credit (or daylight overdraft, daylight exposure, intraday credit)

daylight overdraft
See daylight credit (or daylight overdraft, daylight exposure, intraday credit)

debit card
A card enabling the holder to have his/her purchases directly charged to funds on his/her account at a deposit-taking institution. (This may sometimes be combined with another function, e.g. that of a cash card or cheque guarantee card.)

debit transfer system
A funds transfer system in which debit collection orders made or authorised by the payer move from (the bank of) the payee to (the bank of) the payer and result in a charge (debit) to the account of the payer; for example, cheque-based systems are typical debit transfer systems. Also called debit collection system.

debt (in the context of the financial accounts)
Loans, deposit liabilities, debt securities issued and pension fund reserves of non-financial corporations (created through direct pension commitments of employers on behalf of their employees), valued at market value at the end of the period. However, due to data limitations, the debt given in the quarterly financial accounts does not include loans granted by non-financial sectors (e.g., inter-company loans) or by banks outside the euro area, whereas these components are included in the annual financial accounts.

debt market
The market in which the debt instruments are issued and traded. Securitised debt has to be repaid by the issuer at maturity. See also debt security
equities
equity market

debt ratio
The subject of one of the fiscal criteria used to define the existence of an excessive deficit, as laid down in Article 104 (2) of the Treaty. It is defined as the ratio of government debt to gross domestic product at current market prices, while government debt is defined in Protocol No 20 (on the excessive deficit procedure) as the total gross debt at nominal value outstanding at the end of the year and consolidated between and within the sectors of general government.

debt security
A promise on the part of the issuer (the borrower) to make one or more payment(s) to the holder (the lender) on a specified future date or dates. Such securities usually carry a specific rate of interest (the coupon) and/or are sold at a discount to the amount that will be repaid at maturity. Debt securities issued with an original maturity of more than one year are classified as long-term.

Money market paper and, in principle, private placements are included in the debt securities statistics of the ECB.

default
The failure to complete a funds or securities transfer according to its terms for reasons which are not technical or temporary, usually as a result of bankruptcy. Default is usually distinguished from a "failed transaction".

deficit ratio
The subject of one of the fiscal criteria used to define the existence of an excessive deficit, as laid down in Article 104 (2) of the Treaty. It is defined as the ratio of the planned or actual government deficit to gross domestic product at current market prices. The government deficit is defined in Protocol No 20 (on the excessive deficit procedure) as net borrowing of the general government.

deflation
A decline in the general price level, e.g. in the consumer price index. See also inflation

degree of openness
A measure of the extent to which an economy depends on trade with other countries or regions, e.g. the ratio of the sum of total imports and exports to GDP.

delayed debit card
A card issued by banks indicating that the holder may charge his/her account up to an authorised limit. It allows holders to make purchases but does not offer extended credit, the full amount of the debt incurred having to be settled at the end of a specified period. The holder is usually charged an annual fee.

delivery
Final transfer of a security, another financial instrument or a commodity.

delivery against payment system
See delivery versus payment (DVP) system

delivery versus payment (DVP) system
A mechanism in an exchange-for-value settlement system which ensures that the final transfer of assets (securities or other financial instruments) occurs if, and only if, the final transfer of another asset (or other assets) occurs.

Delors Committee
A committee mandated by the European Council in June 1988 to study and propose concrete stages leading to economic and monetary union. The committee, which takes its name from that of its chairman, Jacques Delors (then President of the European Commission) had the following members: the governors of the central banks of the Member States of the then European Community (EC), Alexandre Lamfalussy (then General Manager of the Bank for International Settlements (BIS)), Niels Thygesen (Professor of economics, Denmark) and Miguel Boyer (then President of Banco Exterior de España). The conclusions reached by the committee, published in the so-called Delors Report, were that economic and monetary union should be achieved in three stages.

dematerialisation
The elimination of physical certificates or documents of title which represent ownership of financial assets so that the financial assets exist only as accounting records.

deposit facility

A standing facility of the Eurosystem which counterparties may use to make overnight deposits at a national central bank, which are remunerated at a pre-specified interest rate.

deposit rate
The interest rate paid on the surplus liquidity that credit institutions may deposit overnight in an account with a national central bank that is part of the Eurosystem.

depository
An agent with the primary role of recording securities either physically or electronically and keeping records of the ownership of these securities.

deposits redeemable at notice
Savings deposits for which the holder must respect a fixed period of notice before withdrawing the funds. In some cases there is the possibility of withdrawing on demand a certain fixed amount in a specified period or of early withdrawal subject to the payment of a penalty. Deposits redeemable at a period of notice of up to three months are included in M2 (and hence in M3), while those with a longer period of notice are part of the (non-monetary) longer-term financial liabilities of the MFI sector.

deposits with an agreed maturity
Mainly time deposits with a given maturity that, depending on national practices, may be subject to the payment of a penalty in the event of early withdrawal. Some non-marketable debt instruments, such as non-transferable (retail) certificates of deposit, are also included. Deposits with an agreed maturity of up to two years are included in M2 (and hence in M3), while those with an agreed maturity of over two years are included in the (non-monetary) longer-term financial liabilities of the MFI sector.

derivative
A financial contract, the value of which depends on the value of one or more underlying reference assets, rates or indices. The basic classes of derivatives are futures contracts, options, swaps and forward rate agreements.

direct debit
A pre-authorised debit on the payer's bank account initiated by the payee.

direct investment
Cross-border investment for the purpose of obtaining a lasting interest in an enterprise resident in another economy (assumed, in practice, for ownership of at least 10% of the ordinary shares or voting power). Included are equity capital, reinvested earnings and other capital associated with inter-company loans.

direct investment account
A b.o.p. account that records net acquisitions of assets abroad by euro area residents (as “direct investment abroad”) and net acquisitions of euro area assets by non-residents (as “direct investment in the euro area”).

direct participant in an IFTS
A participant in an Interbank Funds Transfer System (IFTS) which is responsible to the settlement agent (or to all other direct participants) for the settlement of its own payments, those of its customers, and those of the indirect participants on whose behalf it is settling. See also indirect participant/member
interbank funds transfer system (IFTS)

discount

The difference between the par value of a security and its price when such price is lower than par.

discount security
An asset which does not pay coupon interest, and the return on which is achieved by capital appreciation because the asset is issued or bought at a discount.

domestic payment
A payment between counterparties located in the same country.

Dutch auction
See single rate auction (Dutch auction)

DVP
See delivery versus payment (DVP) system

DVP schemes as defined by the G10
Three schemes or models can be distinguished: in Model 1, transfer instructions for both securities and funds are settled on a trade-by-trade basis, with final transfer of the securities from the seller to the buyer (delivery) occurring at the same time as final transfer of the funds from the buyer to the seller (payment); in Model 2, securities transfer instructions are settled on a gross basis with final transfer of securities from the seller to the buyer (delivery) occurring throughout the processing cycle, but funds transfer instructions are settled on a net basis, with final transfer of funds from the buyer to the seller (payment) occurring at the end of the processing cycle; and in Model 3, transfer instructions for both securities and funds are settled on a net basis, with final transfers of both securities and funds occurring at the end of the processing cycle. See delivery versus payment (DVP) system

E

e-money
See electronic money (e-money)

earmarking system
A system for central banks' collateral management where liquidity is provided against assets earmarked for each individual transaction.

ECB
See European Central Bank (ECB)

ECB payment mechanism (EPM)
The payment arrangements organised within the ECB and connected to TARGET for the purpose of effecting: (i) payments between accounts held at the ECB; and (ii) payments through TARGET between accounts held at the ECB and at the national central banks.

ECB time
The time of the place in which the ECB is located.

ECOFIN
See EU Council (Council of Ministers)

Ecofin Council
See EU Council (Council of Ministers)

Economic and Financial Committee (EFC)

A consultative Community body set up at the start of Stage Three of Economic and Monetary Union (EMU). The Member States, the European Commission and the ECB each appoint no more than two members of the Committee. Each Member State selects one member from among the senior officials of its national administration, and the second member from among the senior officials of its national central bank. However, the national central bank members only participate in EFC meetings when issues of their institution's particular expertise or competence are being discussed. Article 114 (2) of the Treaty contains a list of the tasks of the Economic and Financial Committee.

Economic and Monetary Union (EMU)
The outcome of the (partly) still ongoing process set out in the Treaty for the harmonisation by EU Member States of their economic and monetary policies and for the introduction of a single currency. Three stages were provided for: Stage One (1 July 1990 to 31 December 1993) saw the removal of all barriers to the free movement of capital within the European Union as well as a better coordination of economic policies and closer cooperation between the central banks, Stage Two (1 January 1994 to 31 December 1998) began with the establishment of the European Monetary Institute (EMI) and was dedicated to technical preparations for the introduction of the single currency, the avoidance of excessive deficits and an enhanced convergence of economic and monetary policies (to ensure stable prices and sound public finances) and Stage Three (since 1 January 1999) began with the irrevocable fixing of exchange rates, the transfer of monetary competence to the ECB and the introduction of the euro as the single currency.

economic approach
The accounting approach under which deals are recorded on the transaction date.

ECU
See European Currency Unit (ECU)

EEA countries
See European Economic Area (EEA) countries

EERs
See effective exchange rates (EERs) (nominal/real)

EFC
See Economic and Financial Committee (EFC)

effective exchange rates (EERs) (nominal/real)
See euro effective exchange rates (EERs) (nominal/real)

electronic money (e-money)
An electronic store of monetary value on a technical device that may be widely used as a prepaid bearer instrument for making payments to undertakings other than the issuer without necessarily involving bank accounts in the transactions. In order to be considered e-money, such devices must operate as general-purpose payment instruments.

electronic purse
A reloadable multi-purpose prepaid card which may be used for small retail or other payments instead of banknotes and coins. See also multi-purpose prepaid card

EMI
See European Monetary Institute (EMI)

EMS

See European Monetary System (EMS)

EMU
See Economic and Monetary Union (EMU)

end-of-day
The time of the business day (after the TARGET system has closed) at which the payments processed in the TARGET system are finalised for the day.

EONIA
See euro overnight index average (EONIA)

EPM
See ECB payment mechanism (EPM)

equities
Securities representing ownership of a stake in a corporation, i.e. shares traded on a stock exchange (quoted or listed shares), unquoted or unlisted shares and other forms of equity. Equities usually produce income in the form of dividends.

equity instruments
Dividend-bearing securities (corporate shares, and securities evidencing an investment in an equity fund).

equity market
The market in which equities are issued and traded. See also equities
equity instruments

equity price risk
The risk of loss arising from movements in equity prices. The Eurosystem is exposed to equity price risk in its monetary policy operations to the extent that equities are considered to be eligible as tier two assets.

ERM II
See exchange rate mechanism II (ERM II)

errors and omissions
An item in b.o.p. statements used to offset the overstatement or understatement of the other b.o.p. components.

ESA 95
See European System of Accounts 1995 (ESA 95)

ESCB
See European System of Central Banks (ESCB)

EU Council (Council of Ministers)
An EU institution made up of representatives of the governments of the Member States, normally the ministers responsible for the matters under consideration (so that it is often referred to as the "Council of Ministers"). The EU Council meeting in the composition of the ministers of economics and finance is often referred to as the "Ecofin Council". In addition, for decisions of particular importance, the EU Council meets in the composition of the Heads of State or Government (but should not be confused with the "European Council"). See also European Council

EU enlargement
In 2003 a total of 13 countries in central and eastern Europe and the Mediterranean were recognised by the European Council as candidates for accession to the European Union (EU). The following ten countries signed the Accession Treaty with a view to joining the EU on 1 May 2004: the Czech Republic, Estonia, Cyprus, Latvia, Lithuania, Hungary, Malta, Poland, Slovenia and Slovakia, and on 1 January 2007: Bulgaria and Romania. Turkey is another official candidate for accession.

EU Member State
See Member State

EURIBOR
See euro interbank offered rate (EURIBOR)

euro
The name of the European single currency adopted by the European Council at its meeting in Madrid on 15 and 16 December 1995.

euro area
The area encompassing those EU Member States in which the euro has been adopted as the single currency in accordance with the Treaty and in which a single monetary policy is conducted under the responsibility of the Governing Council of the ECB. It currently comprises Belgium, Germany, Greece, Spain, France, Ireland, Italy, Luxembourg, the Netherlands, Austria, Portugal, Finland and Slovenia.

euro effective exchange rates (EERs) (nominal/real)
Nominal euro EERs are weighted averages of bilateral euro exchange rates against the currencies of the euro area"s main trading partners. The ECB publishes nominal EER indices for the euro against the currencies of a narrow and a broad group of trading partners. The weights used reflect the share of each partner country in euro area trade. Real EERs are nominal EERs deflated by a weighted average of foreign, relative to domestic, prices or costs. They are, thus, measures of price and cost competitiveness.

euro interbank offered rate (EURIBOR)
The rate at which a prime bank is willing to lend funds in euro to another prime bank. The EURIBOR is calculated daily for interbank deposits with a maturity of one week and one to 12 months as the average of the daily offer rates of a representative panel of prime banks, rounded to three decimal places.

euro overnight index average (EONIA)
A measure of the effective interest rate prevailing in the euro interbank overnight market. It is calculated as a weighted average of the interest rates on unsecured overnight lending transactions denominated in euro, as reported by a panel of contributing banks.

Eurogroup
An informal gathering of the ministers of economics and finance of the euro area member countries, at which they discuss issues connected with their shared responsibilities in respect of the single currency. The European Commission and the ECB are invited to take part in the meetings. The Eurogroup usually meets immediately before an Ecofin Council meeting.

European Central Bank (ECB)
The EU body established on 1 June 1998 in Frankfurt am Main that lies at the centre of the European System of Central Banks (ESCB) and the Eurosystem. Together with the national central banks of those EU Member States that have adopted the euro, the ECB defines and

implements the monetary policy for the euro area. See also euro area
European System of Central Banks (ESCB)
Eurosystem
national central bank (NCB)

European Commission
See European Commission (Commission of the European Communities)

European Commission (Commission of the European Communities)
The EU institution established in 1967 (for the then three European Communities) that drafts proposals for new EU legislation (which it presents to the European Parliament and the EU Council for adoption), makes sure that EU decisions are properly implemented and supervises the way EU funds are spent. Together with the Court of Justice of the European Communities, it ensures that legislation applying to all EU Member States is properly implemented and that the provisions of the Treaty are applied in full. See also Court of Justice of the European Communities (Court of Justice)

European Commission surveys
Harmonised surveys of business and consumer opinion conducted on behalf of the European Commission in each of the EU Member States. Questions are addressed to managers in manufacturing, construction, retail and services industries as well as to consumers. From each monthly European Commission survey, composite indicators are calculated that summarise the replies to a number of different questions in a single indicator (confidence indicators).

European Council
An EU body that brings together the Heads of State or Government of the EU Member States and the President of the European Commission to provide the European Union with the necessary impetus for its development and to define the general political guidelines thereof. See also EU Council (Council of Ministers)

European Currency Unit (ECU)
Prior to Stage Three of EMU, the ECU was a basket currency made up of the sum of fixed amounts of 12 out of the then 15 currencies of the EU Member States. The value of the ECU was calculated as a weighted average of the value of its component currencies. The ECU was replaced by the euro on a one-for-one basis on 1 January 1999.

European Economic Area (EEA) countries
The EU Member States and Iceland, Liechtenstein and Norway.

European Monetary Institute (EMI)
A temporary EU body established on 1 January 1994 to strengthen central bank cooperation and monetary policy coordination in Stage Two of Economic and Monetary Union (EMU) and to carry out the preparations required for the establishment of the European System of Central Banks (ESCB), for the conduct of the single monetary policy and for the introduction of a single currency in Stage Three. It was replaced by the ECB on 1 June 1998.

European Monetary System (EMS)
An exchange rate regime established in 1979 to foster closer monetary policy cooperation between the central banks of the Member States of the European Economic Community (EEC) so as to lead to a zone of monetary stability in Europe. The main components of the EMS were the ECU (a basket currency made up of the sum of fixed amounts of currencies of EEC Member States), the exchange rate and intervention mechanism (ERM) and various credit mechanisms. It was replaced by ERM II (exchange rate mechanism II) at the start of Stage Three of Economic and Monetary Union (EMU) on 1 January 1999. See also European Currency Unit (ECU)

exchange rate mechanism II (ERM II)

European Parliament
An EU institution that currently consists of 732 directly elected representatives of the citizens of the Member States. It plays a role in the EU's legislative process, although with differing prerogatives that depend on the procedures through which the respective EU legislation is to be enacted. Where monetary policy and the ESCB are concerned, the powers of the European Parliament are mainly consultative in character, although the Treaty provides for certain procedures with respect to the democratic accountability of the ECB vis-à-vis the Parliament (presentation of the ECB's Annual Report, including a general debate on monetary policy, and hearings before the competent parliamentary committees).

European System of Accounts 1995 (ESA 95)
A system of uniform statistical definitions and classifications aimed at achieving a harmonised quantitative description of the economies of the EU Member States. The ESA 95, implementation of which began in accordance with Council Regulation (EC) No 2223/96 in the course of 1999, is the Community's current version of the internationally used System of National Accounts (SNA 93).

European System of Central Banks (ESCB)
The central banking system of the European Union. It comprises the ECB and the national central banks of all EU Member States (but the national central banks of EU Member States that have not yet adopted the euro are not involved in the conduct of the Eurosystem's monetary policy for the euro area because they retain responsible for monetary policy under national law). See also
euro area
European Central Bank (ECB)
Eurosystem
national central bank (NCB)

Eurostat
The Statistical Office of the European Communities. It is part of the European Commission and responsible for the production of Community statistics.

Eurosystem
The central banking system of the euro area. It comprises the ECB and the national central banks of those EU Member States that have adopted the euro. See also euro area
European Central Bank (ECB)
European System of Central Banks (ESCB)
national central bank (NCB)

Eurosystem business day
Any day on which the ECB and at least one national central bank are open for the purpose of conducting Eurosystem monetary policy operations.

Eurosystem staff projections
The results of exercises conducted by Eurosystem staff to project possible future macroeconomic developments in the euro area as part of the economic analysis.

Eurozone Purchasing Managers' Surveys
Surveys of business conditions in manufacturing and in services industries that are conducted for a number of countries in the euro area and used to compile indices. The Eurozone Manufacturing Purchasing Managers' Index (PMI) is a weighted indicator calculated from indices of output, new orders, employment, suppliers' delivery times and stocks of purchases. The service sector survey asks questions on business activity, expectations of future business activity, the amount of

business outstanding, incoming new business, employment, input prices and prices charged. The Eurozone Composite Index is calculated combining the results from the manufacturing and services sector surveys.

excessive deficit procedure
The provision set out in Article 104 of the Treaty and specified in Protocol No 20 on the excessive deficit procedure requires EU Member States to maintain budgetary discipline, defines the criteria for a budgetary position to be considered an excessive deficit and regulates steps to be taken following the observation that the requirements for the budgetary balance or government debt have not been fulfilled. This is supplemented by an EU Council Regulation on speeding up and clarifying the implementation of the excessive deficit procedure, which is one element of the Stability and Growth Pact.

exchange rate mechanism II (ERM II)
The exchange rate arrangement established on 1 January 1999 that provides a framework for exchange rate policy cooperation between the Eurosystem and EU Member States that have not yet adopted the euro. Although membership in ERM II is voluntary, Member States with a derogation are expected to join. This involves establishing both a central rate for their respective currency's exchange rate against the euro and a band for its fluctuation around that central rate. The standard fluctuation band is ±15%, but a narrower band may be agreed on request. Foreign exchange intervention and financing at the margins of the standard or narrower fluctuation bands are, in principle, automatic and unlimited, with very short-term financing available. However, the ECB and the non-euro area national central banks participating in ERM II could suspend automatic intervention if such intervention were to conflict with their primary objective of maintaining price stability.

exchange rate targeting
A monetary policy strategy aiming for a given (usually a stable or even fixed) exchange rate against another currency or group of currencies.

exchange-for-value settlement system
A system which involves the exchange of assets, such as money, foreign exchange, securities or other financial instruments, in order to discharge settlement obligations. These systems may use one or more funds transfer systems in order to satisfy the payment obligations which are generated. The links between the exchange of assets and the payment system(s) may be manual or electronic. See also delivery versus payment (DVP) system

Executive Board
One of the decision-making bodies of the ECB. It comprises the President and the Vice-President of the ECB and four other members, all of whom are appointed by common accord by the Heads of State or Government of the EU Member States that have adopted the euro. See also General Council of the ECB
Governing Council

exemption threshold
The cut-off point below which respondents are not required to report the data required.

experimental data
A subset of data collected and compiled by the ECB, the quality of which is somewhat poorer than that of other ECB statistics, but sufficiently reliable for policy analysis and other purposes. They include data that are insufficiently harmonised, of incomplete coverage, sub-optimal in terms of statistical concepts and methodologies and/or based on estimation techniques.

external debt

The gross amount, at any given time, of disbursed and outstanding contractual liabilities of residents of a country for the repayment of principal (with or without interest) or the payment of interest (with or without principal) to non-residents.

external statistics
Statistics comprising the euro area b.o.p. (transactions), the euro area i.i.p. (outstanding positions) and the Eurosystem's template on international reserves and foreign currency liquidity.

external trade in goods
Exports and imports of goods with countries outside the euro area, measured in terms of value and as volume and unit value indices. External trade statistics are not comparable with the exports and imports recorded in the national accounts as the latter include both intra-euro area and extra-euro area transactions, and also combine goods and services. Nor are they fully comparable, with the goods item in b.o.p. statistics. Besides methodological adjustments, the main difference is to be found in the fact that imports in external trade statistics are recorded including insurance and freight services, whereas they are recorded free on board in the goods item in the b.o.p. statistics.

extra-euro area trade
The exchange of (i.e. trade in) goods and services between euro area countries and other countries.

F

failed transaction
A securities transaction which does not settle on the contractual settlement date.
fair value accounting (FVA)
A valuation principle that stipulates the use of either a market price, where it exists, or an estimation of a market price as the present value of expected cash flows to establish the balance sheet value of financial instruments.

FIN
See financial application (FIN)

final (finality)
Irrevocable and unconditional (settlement).

final settlement
Settlement which is irrevocable and unconditional.

final transfer
An irrevocable and unconditional transfer which effects a discharge of the obligation to make the transfer.

finality
See final (finality)

financial account (in a b.o.p. context)
A b.o.p. account that covers all transactions in direct investment, portfolio investment, other investment, financial derivatives and reserve assets, between residents and non-residents.

financial accounts
Part of the system of national (or euro area) accounts showing the financial positions (stocks) and financial transactions of the different institutional sectors of an economy by type of financial

instrument.

financial application (FIN)
The SWIFT application enabling financial institutions to exchange structured message-based financial data worldwide in a secure and reliable manner.

financial asset
Any asset that is (i) cash; or (ii) a contractual right to receive cash or another financial instrument from another enterprise; or (iii) a contractual right to exchange financial instruments with another enterprise under conditions that are potentially favourable; or (iv) an equity instrument of another enterprise.

financial auxiliary
A corporation or quasi-corporation that is engaged primarily in auxiliary financial activities, e.g. insurance brokers, investment advisors and corporations providing infrastructure for financial markets.

financial corporations engaged in lending
Corporations and quasi-corporations, classified as OFIs, specialising mainly in asset financing for households and non-financial corporations. Included are also firms specialising in financial leasing, factoring, mortgage lending and consumer lending.

financial intermediary
A commercial entity that serves as an interface between lenders and borrowers, e.g. by collecting deposits from the general public and extending loans to households and businesses.

financial liability
Any liability that is a legal obligation to deliver cash or another financial instrument to another enterprise or to exchange financial instruments with another enterprise under conditions that are potentially unfavourable.

financial markets
Markets in which those who have a surplus of funds lend to those who have a shortage.

financial risk
A term used to describe a range of risks incurred in financial transactions - both liquidity and credit risks. See also credit risk/exposure
liquidity risk

fine-tuning operation
A non-regular open market operation executed by the Eurosystem mainly to deal with unexpected liquidity fluctuations in the market.

fixed rate bond
A debt security with a nominal coupon payment that does not change during the life of the issue.

fixed rate instrument
A financial instrument for which the coupon is fixed throughout the life of the instrument.

fixed rate tender
A tender procedure, in which the interest rate is specified in advance by the central bank and in which participating counterparties bid the amount of money they want to transact at that interest rate.

floating rate instrument
A financial instrument for which the coupon is periodically reset relative to a reference index to reflect changes in short or medium-term market interest rates. Floating rate instruments have either pre-fixed coupons or post-fixed coupons.

flow (transactions)
The creation, transformation, exchange, transfer or extinction of economic value involving a change in the ownership of goods and/or financial assets, the provision of services or the provision of labour and capital. Flows can be calculated as differences in stocks adjusted to remove the effect of reclassifications, exchange rate variations, other revaluations and any other changes that do not arise from transactions.

foreign currency holding
The net position in the respective currency. For the purpose of this definition special drawing rights (SDRs) shall be considered as a separate currency.

foreign exchange forward
A contract in which the outright purchase or sale of a certain amount denominated in a foreign currency against another currency, usually the domestic currency, is agreed on one day and the amount is to be delivered at a specified future date, more than two working days after the date of the contract, at a given price. This forward rate of exchange consists of the prevailing spot rate plus/minus an agreed premium/discount.

foreign exchange operations
The buying or selling of foreign exchange. In the context of the Eurosystem, this means buying or selling other currencies against euro.

foreign exchange revaluation
An adjustment to remove from flow data the effects of any change in the euro value of balance sheet items originally denominated in foreign currency that arises from changes in the relevant exchange rates against the euro.

foreign exchange settlement risk
The risk that one party to a foreign exchange transaction will pay the currency it sold but not receive the currency it bought. This is also called cross-currency settlement risk or principal risk.
See also principal risk

foreign exchange swap
Simultaneous spot and forward transactions exchanging one currency against another. The Eurosystem can execute open market monetary policy operations in the form of foreign exchange swaps, where the national central banks (or the ECB) buy or sell euro spot against a foreign currency and at the same time sell or buy them back in a forward transaction.

forward rate agreement (FRA)
An agreement whereby one party undertakes to pay another party a certain interest rate on a certain principal amount for a certain period of time beginning at some point in the future.

forward transactions in securities
Over-the-counter contracts in which the purchase or sale of an interest rate instrument (usually a bond or note) is agreed on the contract date, for delivery at a future date, at a given price.

FRA
See forward rate agreement (FRA)

free-of-payment delivery
The delivery of securities with no corresponding payment of funds.

futures contract
A contract to buy or sell securities or a commodity at a predetermined price on a specified future date.

FVA
See fair value accounting (FVA)

G

GDP
See gross domestic product (GDP)

General Council of the ECB
One of the decision-making bodies of the ECB. It comprises the President and the Vice-President of the ECB and the governors of the national central banks of all EU Member States. See also
Executive Board
Governing Council

general government
A sector defined in the ESA 95 as comprising resident entities that are engaged primarily in the production of non-market goods and services intended for individual and collective consumption and/or in the redistribution of national income and wealth. Included are central, regional and local government authorities as well as social security funds. Excluded are government-owned entities that conduct commercial operations, such as public enterprises. See also central government
state government

GESMES
A United Nations standard (EDIFACT message) designed by Expert Group 6 (Statistics) of the e-Business Board for European Standardisation that allows partner institutions to exchange multi-dimensional statistical arrays in a generic but standardised way.

GESMES/TS
A message (a GESMES profile, previously called GESMES/CB) used to exchange statistical time series, related attributes and structural metadata in a standardised format.

global custodian
A custodian which provides its customers with custody services in respect of securities traded and settled not only in the country in which the custodian is located but also in numerous other countries throughout the world.

Governing Council
The supreme decision-making body of the ECB. It comprises the President and the Vice-President of the ECB plus the other members of the Executive Board and the governors of the national central banks of those EU Member States that have adopted the euro. See also
Executive Board
General Council of the ECB

government deficit/surplus
Net borrowing/lending by the general government sector.

government expenditure

The set of non-financial transactions defined in the ESA 95 as decreasing general government net lending or increasing general government net borrowing, i.e. transactions that decrease the general government sector's net worth.

government revenue
The set of non-financial transactions defined in the ESA 95 as increasing general government net lending or decreasing general government net borrowing, i.e. transactions that increase the general government sector's net worth.

gridlock
A situation which can arise in a funds or securities transfer system when the failure of some transfer instructions to be executed (because the necessary funds or securities balances are unavailable) prevents a substantial number of other instructions from other participants being executed. See also failed transaction
queuing
systemic risk

gross domestic product (GDP)
A measure of economic activity, namely the value of an economy's total output of goods and services, less intermediate consumption, plus net taxes on products and imports, in a specified period. GDP can be broken down by output, expenditure or income components. The main expenditure aggregates that make up GDP are household final consumption, government final consumption, gross fixed capital formation, changes in inventories, and imports and exports of goods and services (including intra-euro area trade).

gross monthly earnings
The gross monthly wages and salaries of employees, including employees' social security contributions.

gross settlement system
A transfer system in which the settlement of funds or the transfer of securities occurs on an instruction-by-instruction basis. See also net settlement system
transfer system

H

haircut
See valuation haircut

Harmonised Index of Consumer Prices (HICP)
The index of consumer prices calculated and published by Eurostat, the Statistical Office of the European Union, on the basis of a statistical methodology that has been harmonised across all EU Member States. The HICP is the measure of prices used by the Governing Council to define and assess price stability in the euro area as a whole in quantitative terms.

HICP
See Harmonised Index of Consumer Prices (HICP)

hourly labour cost
Labour costs, including gross wages and salaries (as well as bonuses of all kinds), employers' social security contributions and other labour costs (e.g. vocational training costs, recruitment costs and employment-related taxes), net of subsidies, per hour actually worked. Hourly costs may be obtained by dividing the sum total of these costs for all employees by the sum total of all hours worked by them (including overtime).

households
One of the institutional sectors in the European System of Accounts 1995 (ESA 95). The household sector covers individuals or groups of individuals as consumers, but also as entrepreneurs (i.e. sole proprietorships and partnerships). Non-profit institutions serving households are a separate institutional sector according to the ESA 95, although they are often reported together with households.

hybrid system
A payment system which combines characteristics of RTGS systems and netting systems. See also gross settlement system
net settlement system
transfer system

I

i.i.p.
See international investment position (i.i.p.)
IBAN
See International Bank Account Number (IBAN)

ICSD
See international central securities depository (ICSD)

IFTS
See interbank funds transfer system (IFTS)

IMF
See International Monetary Fund (IMF)

IMF Balance of Payments Manual
A manual of international standards issued by the IMF to provide guidance for compilers of b.o.p. and i.i.p. statistics (the fifth edition of 1993 is the latest update).

immobilisation
Placement of certificated securities and financial instruments in a central securities depository to facilitate book-entry transfers. See also central securities depository (CSD)

implied volatility
A measure of expected volatility (standard deviation in terms of annualised percentage changes) in the prices of, for example, bonds and stocks (or of corresponding futures contracts), which can be extracted from option prices.

incident
A situation which prevents a system from functioning normally or causes substantial delays.

index of industrial producer prices
See industrial producer price

indicator of negotiated wages
A measure of the changes over time in the direct outcome of collective bargaining in terms of basic pay (i.e. wages and salaries excluding bonuses) at the euro area level. It refers to the implied average change in monthly wages and salaries.

indirect participant/member

A type of participant in a funds or securities transfer system in which there is a tiering arrangement. Indirect participants are distinguished from direct participants by their inability to perform some of the system activities (e.g. inputting of transfer orders, settlement) performed by direct participants. Indirect participants thus require the services of direct participants to perform those activities on their behalf. In an EU context the term refers more specifically to participants in a transfer system which are responsible only to their direct participants for settling the payments input into the system. See also direct participant in an IFTS

industrial producer price
The factory-gate price (transportation costs are not included) of any product, excluding imports, sold by industry excluding construction on the domestic markets of the euro area countries.

industrial production
The gross value added created by industry at constant prices.

inflation
An increase in the general price level, e.g. in the consumer price index. See also deflation

inflation risk premium
Compensation of investors for the risks associated with holding assets (denominated in nominal terms) over the longer term.

inflation targeting
A monetary policy strategy aimed at maintaining price stability by focusing on deviations in published inflation forecasts from an announced inflation target.

inflation-indexed government bond
A debt security issued by the general government, the coupon payments and principal of which are linked to a specific CPI.

initial margin
A risk control measure that may be applied by the Eurosystem in reverse transactions, implying that the collateral required for a transaction is equal to the credit extended to the counterparty plus the value of the initial margin. See also margin call
variation margin (marking to market)

insurance corporations and pension funds
A sector defined in the ESA 95 as comprising all financial corporations and quasi-corporations that are engaged primarily in financial intermediation as the consequence of the pooling of risks.

interbank funds transfer system (IFTS)
A funds transfer system in which most (or all) direct participants are financial institutions, particularly banks and other credit institutions. See also direct participant in an IFTS

interbank money market
The market for short-term lending between banks, usually involving the trading of funds with a maturity of between one day (overnight or even shorter) and one year.

interbank payment
A payment where both the originator and the final beneficiary are financial institutions.

interest rate
The ratio, usually expressed as a percentage per annum, of the amount that a debtor has to pay to the creditor over a given period of time to the amount of the principal of the loan, deposit or

debt security.

interest rate future
An exchange-traded forward contract. In such a contract, the purchase or sale of an interest rate instrument, e.g. a bond, is agreed on the contract date to be delivered at a future date, at a given price. Usually no actual delivery takes place; the contract is normally closed out before the agreed maturity.

interest rate swap (cross-currency)
A contractual agreement to exchange cash flows representing streams of periodic interest payments with a counterparty either in one currency or in two different currencies.

interest-bearing claim
Any financial asset that gives its owner the right to receive interest payments from the debtor who issued the asset.

interlinking
The technical infrastructures, design features and procedures which are put in place within or constitute adaptations of each national RTGS system and the ECB payment mechanism (EPM) for the purpose of processing cross-border payments in the TARGET system. See also RTGS system
TARGET (Trans-European Automated Real-time Gross settlement Express Transfer system)

interlinking mechanism
Within the TARGET system, the interlinking mechanism provides common procedures and an infrastructure which allow payment orders to move from one domestic RTGS system to another.

internal rate of return (IRR)
A rate at which the accounting value of a security is equal to the present value of the future cash flow.

International Bank Account Number (IBAN)
The IBAN concept was developed by ECBS and by the International Organization for Standardisation (ISO) and is an internationally agreed standard. It was created as an international bank identifier, used to uniquely identify the account of a customer at a financial institution, to assist error-free cross-border customer payments, and to improve the potential for straight-through processing (STP), with a minimum amount of change within domestic schemes.

international central securities depository (ICSD)
A securities settlement system which clears and settles international securities or cross-border transactions in domestic securities. At present, there are two ICSDs located in EU countries: Clearstream Luxembourg and Euroclear Bank.

international investment position (i.i.p.)
The value and composition of an economy's outstanding net financial claims on (or financial liabilities to) the rest of the world.

International Monetary Fund (IMF)
An international organisation, based in Washington, D.C., with a membership of 184 countries (2002). It was established in 1946 to promote international monetary cooperation and exchange rate stability, to foster economic growth and high levels of employment and to help member countries to correct balance of payments imbalances.

international reserves template

A statistical statement used to report the stock of reserve assets, other foreign currency assets and reserve-related liabilities of the Eurosystem on a specific reference date.

International Securities Identification Number (ISIN)
An international identification code assigned to securities issued in financial markets.

intra-euro area trade
The exchange of (i.e. trade in) goods and services between individual euro area countries.

intraday credit
See daylight credit (or daylight overdraft, daylight exposure, intraday credit)

intraday liquidity
Funds which can be accessed during the business day, usually to enable financial institutions to make payments in real time. See also daylight credit (or daylight overdraft, daylight exposure, intraday credit)

inverse floating rate instrument
A structured note where the rate of interest paid to the holder of the note varies inversely with changes in a certain reference interest rate.

IRR
See internal rate of return (IRR)

irrevocable and unconditional transfer
A transfer in a payment or securities settlement system which cannot be revoked by the transferor and is unconditional (and therefore final).

ISIN
See International Securities Identification Number (ISIN)

issuer
The entity which is obligated on a security or other financial instrument.

H

haircut
See valuation haircut

Harmonised Index of Consumer Prices (HICP)
The index of consumer prices calculated and published by Eurostat, the Statistical Office of the European Union, on the basis of a statistical methodology that has been harmonised across all EU Member States. The HICP is the measure of prices used by the Governing Council to define and assess price stability in the euro area as a whole in quantitative terms.

HICP
See Harmonised Index of Consumer Prices (HICP)

hourly labour cost
Labour costs, including gross wages and salaries (as well as bonuses of all kinds), employers' social security contributions and other labour costs (e.g. vocational training costs, recruitment costs and employment-related taxes), net of subsidies, per hour actually worked. Hourly costs may be obtained by dividing the sum total of these costs for all employees by the sum total of all hours worked by them (including overtime).

households
One of the institutional sectors in the European System of Accounts 1995 (ESA 95). The household sector covers individuals or groups of individuals as consumers, but also as entrepreneurs (i.e. sole proprietorships and partnerships). Non-profit institutions serving households are a separate institutional sector according to the ESA 95, although they are often reported together with households.

hybrid system
A payment system which combines characteristics of RTGS systems and netting systems. See also gross settlement system
net settlement system
transfer system

J

job vacancies
A collective term covering newly created positions, unfilled positions or positions about to become vacant, for which an employer has recently taken active steps to find a suitable candidate.

K

key ECB interest rates
The interest rates that reflect the stance of the monetary policy of the ECB and that are set by the Governing Council. The key ECB interest rates are: the interest rate on the main refinancing operations (the fixed rate in fixed rate tenders and the minimum bid rate in variable rate tenders); the interest rate on the marginal lending facility; and the interest rate on the deposit facility.

L

labour force
The sum total of persons in employment and the number of unemployed.

labour force participation rate
The labour force as a proportion of the total working age population. The working age population is normally defined as the population aged between 15 and 64 years of age. The labour force comprises both employed and unemployed persons.

labour productivity
The output that can be produced with a given input of labour. It can be measured in several ways, but is commonly measured as GDP at constant prices divided by either total employment or total hours worked.

Lamfalussy standards
See minimum standards of the Lamfalussy report (Lamfalussy standards)

large-value funds transfer system
A funds transfer system through which large-value and high-priority funds transfers are made between participants in the system for their own account or on behalf of their customers. Although, as a rule, no minimum value is set for the payments they carry, the average size of payments passed through such systems is usually relatively large. Large-value funds transfer systems are sometimes known as wholesale funds transfer systems.

large-value payments
Payments, generally of very large amounts, which are mainly exchanged between banks or between participants in the financial markets and usually require urgent and timely settlement.

leading indicators
Economic variables which anticipate or contain useful information for predicting future developments in other variables.

legal risk
The risk of loss because of the unexpected application of a law or regulation or because a contract cannot be enforced.

liability
A present obligation of the enterprise arising from past events, the settlement of which is expected to result in an outflow from the enterprise of resources embodying economic benefits.

link between securities settlement systems
A link consists of all the procedures and arrangements which exist between two securities settlement systems (SSSs) for the transfer of securities between the two SSSs concerned through a book-entry process. See also Securities Settlement System (SSS)

liquidity
The ease and speed with which a financial asset can be converted into cash or used to settle a liability. Cash is thus a highly liquid asset. Bank deposits are less liquid, the longer their maturities. The term "liquidity" is also often used as a synonym for money.

liquidity risk
The risk that a counterparty or a participant in a payment or settlement system will not settle an obligation at its full value when due. Liquidity risk does not imply that the counterparty is insolvent, since it may be able to settle the required debt obligations at some unspecified time thereafter.

loans for house purchase
Credit extended to households for the purpose of investment in housing, including building and home improvements. Included are loans secured by residential property (i.e. mortgage loans) that are used for house purchase and, where identifiable, other loans for house purchase provided on a personal basis or secured by other types of asset.

loans to euro area residents
Funds lent by monetary financial institutions (MFIs) to borrowers and not evidenced by negotiable documents or represented by one single document (if it has become negotiable). This description includes loans granted to households, non-financial corporations and government. Loans to households can take the form of consumer credit (loans granted for personal use in the consumption of goods and services), lending for house purchases (credit extended for the purpose of investing in housing, including building and home improvements) and other lending (loans granted for purposes such as debt consolidation, education, etc.). See also credit to euro area residents

local government
A sector defined in the ESA 95 as comprising public authorities and/or bodies, excluding social security funds' local agencies, whose competence extends only to a local area of the country's economic territory.

longer-term interest rates
The rates of interest or the yield on interest-bearing financial assets with a relatively long period to maturity, for which the yield on government bonds with a maturity of ten years are often used as a benchmark.

longer-term refinancing operation
A regular open market operation executed by the Eurosystem in the form of a reverse transaction. Longer-term refinancing operations are carried out through monthly standard tenders and normally have a maturity of three months. See also reverse transaction

loss-sharing agreement
An agreement among participants in a clearing or settlement system regarding the allocation of any losses arising from the default of a participant in the system or of the system itself.

lump-sum allowance
A fixed amount which an institution deducts in the calculation of its reserve requirement within the minimum reserve framework of the Eurosystem. See also Eurosystem
minimum reserve requirement

M

M1
A “narrow” monetary aggregate that comprises currency in circulation and overnight deposits.
M2
An "intermediate" monetary aggregate that comprises M1 plus deposits with an agreed maturity of up to two years and deposits redeemable at notice of up to three months.

M3
A “broad” monetary aggregate that comprises M2 plus repurchase agreements, money market fund shares and units as well as debt securities with a maturity of up to two years.

Maastricht criteria
See convergence criteria

MAC
See Message Authentication Code (MAC)

main refinancing operation
A regular open market operation executed by the Eurosystem (in the form of a reverse transaction) for the purpose of providing the banking system with the amount of liquidity that the former deems to be appropriate. Main refinancing operations are conducted through weekly standard tenders (in which banks can bid for liquidity) and normally have a maturity of one week. See also open market operation
reverse transaction

maintenance period
The period over which compliance with reserve requirements is calculated. The ECB publishes a calendar of the reserve maintenance periods at least three months before the start of each year. The maintenance period begins on the settlement day of the first main refinancing operation following the meeting of the Governing Council at which the monthly assessment of the monetary policy stance is pre-scheduled. Under special circumstances, the published calendar may be amended, depending, among other things, on changes in the schedule of Governing Council meetings. See also reserve requirements

margin call
A procedure related to the application of variation margins, implying that if the value, as regularly measured, of the underlying assets falls below a certain level, the central bank requires counterparties to supply additional assets (or cash). Similarly, if the value of the underlying assets, following their revaluation, were to exceed the amount owed by the counterparties plus the variation margin, the counterparty may ask the central bank to return the excess assets (or

cash) to the counterparty. See also repurchase agreement
variation margin (marking to market)

marginal interest rate
The interest rate at which the total tender allotment is exhausted.

marginal lending facility
A standing facility of the Eurosystem which counterparties may use to receive overnight credit from a national central bank at a pre-specified interest rate against eligible assets.

marginal lending rate
The interest rate on the Eurosystem's marginal lending facility which banks may use for overnight credit from a national central bank that is part of the Eurosystem.

marginal swap point quotation
The swap point quotation at which the total tender allotment is exhausted. See also swap point

market price
The price that is quoted for a gold, foreign exchange or securities instrument usually excluding accrued or rebate interest either on an organised market e.g. a stock exchange, or a non-organised market, e.g. an over-the-counter market.

marking to market
See variation margin (marking to market)

matching
In a payment or settlement system, the process used for comparing the trade or settlement details provided by counterparties in order to ensure that they agree on the terms of the transaction. Also called comparison checking.

maturity at issue (original maturity)
The period of life of a financial instrument that is fixed at the time it is issued. A redemption of that financial instrument is not possible before that period has expired (in the case of debt securities, for instance) or is possible earlier only if some form of penalty is paid (in the case of some types of deposit). Financial instruments are classified according to the period of notice only when there is no agreed maturity.

maturity bucket
A class of debt instruments within a liquidity category of tier one assets or within a liquidity category of tier two assets, the residual maturity of which is within a certain range of values, e.g. the three to five-year maturity bucket.

maturity date
The date on which a monetary policy operation expires. In the case of a repurchase agreement or swap, the maturity date corresponds to the repurchase date.

maximum bid limit
The limit on the largest acceptable bid from an individual counterparty in a tender operation. The Eurosystem may impose maximum bid limits in order to avoid disproportionately large bids from individual counterparties. See also tender procedure

maximum bid rate
The upper limit to the interest rate at which counterparties may submit bids in variable rate tenders. Bids at a rate above the maximum bid rate announced by the ECB are discarded. See

also tender procedure

Member State
A country that is a member of the European Union.

Member State with a derogation
A Member State that is, as set out in Article 122 of the Treaty, preparing to adopt the euro, but has not yet done so. There are currently 11 Member States with this status (Sweden and the new Member States): rights and obligations relating to the introduction of the euro as a single currency do not apply to them. The cases of Denmark and the United Kingdom are different in that these two Member States have been granted an exemption from participating in the third stage of Economic and Monetary Union.

Message Authentication Code (MAC)
A hash algorithm parameterised with a key to generate a number which is attached to the message and used to authenticate it and guarantee the integrity of the data transmitted.

metadata
Any kind of statistical information that defines or describes other data (e.g. attributes, structures, code lists, etc.).

MFI
See monetary financial institution (MFI)

MFI credit to euro area residents
MFI loans granted to non-MFI euro area residents (including the general government and the private sector) and MFI holdings of securities (shares, other equity and debt securities) issued by non-MFI euro area residents.

MFI interest rates
The interest rates that are applied by resident credit institutions and other MFIs, excluding central banks and money market funds, to euro-denominated deposits and loans vis-à-vis households and non-financial corporations resident in the euro area.

MFI longer-term financial liabilities
Liabilities that are not included in M3 and that comprise deposits with an agreed maturity of over two years, deposits redeemable at a period of notice of over three months, debt securities issued by euro area MFIs with an original maturity of more than two years and the capital and reserves of the euro area MFI sector.

MFI net external assets
The external assets of the euro area MFI sector (e.g. MFI holdings of cash in non-euro area currencies, MFI holdings of securities issued by non-euro area residents,and MFI loans granted to non-euro area residents, as well as gold and SDRs held by the Eurosystem) minus the external liabilities of the euro area MFI sector (e.g. non-euro area residents' holdings of deposits, repurchase agreements, money market fund shares/units and debt securities issued by MFIs with a maturity of up to and including two years).

mid-market price
The mid-point between the bid price and the offer price for a security based on quotations for transactions of normal market size by recognised market-makers or recognised trading exchanges. The mid-market price is used for the year-end revaluation procedure.

mid-market rate

The ECB daily concertation rate at 2.15 p.m., which is used for the year-end revaluation procedure.

minimum allotment amount
The lower limit of the amount to be allotted to individual counterparties in a tender operation. The Eurosystem may decide to allot a minimum amount to each counterparty in its tender operations. See also tender procedure

minimum allotment ratio
The lower limit, expressed in percentage terms, of the ratio of bids at the marginal interest rate to be allotted in a tender operation. The Eurosystem may decide to apply a minimum allotment ratio in its tender operations. See also tender procedure

minimum bid rate
The lower limit to the interest rates at which counterparties may submit bids in variable rate tenders. See also tender procedure

minimum reserve requirement
The minimum amount of reserves a credit institution is required to hold with a central bank. In the minimum reserve framework of the Eurosystem, the reserve requirement of a credit institution is calculated by multiplying the reserve ratio for each category of items in the reserve base by the amount of those items on the institution's balance sheet. In addition, institutions are allowed to deduct a lump-sum allowance from their reserve requirement. See also reserve base
reserve ratio

minimum standards of the Lamfalussy report (Lamfalussy standards)
Six minimum standards for the design and operation of cross-border, multi-currency netting schemes or systems, namely (i) a well-founded legal basis under all relevant jurisdictions, (ii) rules and procedures that ensure a clear understanding of the impact of the particular scheme on the financial risks involved in netting, (iii) clearly defined procedures for the management of credit and liquidity risk by both the netting provider and participants, including both incentives for doing so and limits on the maximum level of credit exposure which can be produced by each participant, (iv) the capability, as a minimum, of ensuring the timely completion of daily settlements in the event of an inability to settle by the participant with the largest single net debit position, (v) objective and publicly disclosed admission criteria that permit fair and open access and (vi) an operational reliability of technical systems, as well as backup facilities, that is capable of completing daily processing requirements.

monetary aggregate
Currency in circulation plus outstanding amounts of certain liabilities of monetary financial institutions (MFIs) that have a relatively high degree of liquidity and are held by non-MFI euro area residents outside the central government sector. The Governing Council has announced a reference value for the growth of M3. See also M1
M2
M3
reference value for monetary growth

monetary base
See base money (monetary base)

monetary financial institution (MFI)
Financial institutions which together form the money-issuing sector of the euro area. These include the Eurosystem, resident credit institutions (as defined in Community law) and all other resident financial institutions whose business is to receive deposits and/or close substitutes for

deposits from entities other than MFIs and, for their own account (at least in economic terms), to grant credit and/or invest in securities. The latter group consists predominantly of money market funds.

monetary income
Income accruing to the euro area NCBs in the performance of the Eurosystem's monetary policy function, derived from assets earmarked in accordance with guidelines established by the Governing Council and held against banknotes in circulation and deposit liabilities to credit institutions. See also earmarking system

monetary policy
Action undertaken by a central bank using the instruments at its disposal in order to achieve its objectives (e.g. maintaining price stability).

monetary policy strategy
The general approach to the conduct of monetary policy. The monetary policy strategy of the ECB comprises a quantitative definition of the primary objective of price stability and an analytical framework based on two pillars - economic analysis and monetary analysis - which forms the basis of the Governing Council's overall assessment of the risks to price stability and of its monetary policy decisions. It also provides the framework for explaining monetary policy decisions to the public.

monetary policy transmission mechanism
The process through which monetary policy decisions, e.g. the interest rate decisions taken by the Governing Council in the case of the euro area, affect the economy in general and the price level in particular.

monetary presentation of the b.o.p.
A presentation that distinguishes the external transactions of the MFI sector from those of the non-MFI sector. The analysis of the external counterpart of M3 contributes, together with that of the domestic counterparts, to the assessment of M3 developments.

monetary targeting
A monetary policy strategy aimed at maintaining price stability by focusing on the deviations of money growth from a pre-announced target.

money
An asset accepted by general consent as a medium of exchange. It may take, for example, the form of coins or banknotes or units stored on a prepaid electronic chip-card. Short-term deposits with credit institutions also serve the purposes of money. In economic theory, money performs three different functions: (1) a unit of account; (2) a means of payment; and (3) a store of value. A central bank bears the responsibility for the optimum performance of these functions and does so by ensuring that price stability is maintained.

money demand
A key economic relationship that represents the demand for money balances by non-monetary financial institutions (non-MFIs). The demand for money is often expressed as a function of prices and economic activity, which serves as a proxy for the level of transactions in the economy, and certain interest rate variables, which measure the opportunity costs of holding money.

money market
The market in which short-term funds are raised, invested and traded, using instruments which generally have an original maturity of up to one year.

money market fund
A collective investment undertaking that primarily invests in money market instruments and/or other transferable debt instruments with a residual maturity of up to one year, and/or that pursues a rate of return that approaches the interest rates on money market instruments.

money order
An instrument used to remit money to the named payee, often used by persons who do not have a current account with a financial institution, to pay bills or to transfer money to another person or to a company. There are three parties to a money order: the remitter (payer), the payee and the drawee. Drawees are usually financial institutions or post offices. Payees can either cash their money orders or present them to their bank for collection.

multi-purpose prepaid card
A prepaid card which can be used at the outlets of several service providers for a wide range of purposes and which has the potential to be used on a national or international level, but which may sometimes be limited to a certain area. A reloadable multi-purpose prepaid card is also known as an electronic purse. See also electronic money (e-money)

multilateral net settlement position
The sum of the value of all the transfers a participant in a net settlement system has received during a certain period of time less the value of the transfers made by the participant to all other participants. If the sum is positive, the participant is in a multilateral net credit position; if the sum is negative, the participant is in a multilateral net debit position.

multilateral net settlement system
A settlement system in which each settling participant settles (typically by means of a single payment or receipt) the multilateral net settlement position which results from the transfers made and received by it, for its own account and on behalf of its customers or non-settling participants for which it is acting. See also direct participant in an IFTS
multilateral net settlement position
multilateral netting

multilateral netting
An arrangement among three or more parties to net their obligations. The obligations covered by the arrangement may arise from financial contracts, transfers or both. The multilateral netting of payment obligations normally takes place in the context of a multilateral net settlement system. Such netting is conducted through a central counterparty. The multilateral net position is also the bilateral net position between each participant and the central counterparty. See also multilateral net settlement position
multilateral net settlement system

multiple rate auction (American auction)
An auction at which the allotment interest rate (or price/swap point) equals the interest rate offered in each individual bid.

N

national central bank (NCB)
A central bank of an EU Member State that has adopted the single currency in accordance with the Treaty.

NCB
See national central bank (NCB)

NCB business day

Any day on which the national central bank of a specific Member State is open for the purpose of conducting Eurosystem monetary policy operations. In some Member States, branches of the national central bank may be closed on NCB business days owing to local or regional bank holidays. In such cases, the relevant national central bank is responsible for informing the counterparties in advance of the arrangements to be made for transactions involving those branches.

net credit (or net debit) position
A participant's net credit or net debit position in a netting system is the sum of the value of all the transfers it has received up to a particular point in time less the value of all transfers it has sent. If the difference is positive, the participant is in a net credit position; if the difference is negative, the participant is in a net debit position. The net credit or net debit position at settlement time is called the net settlement position. These net positions may be calculated on a bilateral or multilateral basis. See also net settlement
net settlement system

net settlement
The settlement of a number of obligations or transfers between or among counterparties on a net basis. See also netting

net settlement system
A funds transfer or securities settlement system whose settlement operations are completed on a bilateral or multilateral net basis. See also multilateral net settlement system

netting
An agreed offsetting of positions or obligations by trading partners or participants. The netting reduces a large number of individual positions or obligations to a smaller number of obligations or positions. Netting may take several forms which have varying degrees of legal enforceability in the event of the default of one of the parties. See also multilateral netting
novation
position netting
substitution (of party)

neutrality of money
A basic economic principle stating that in the long run changes in the money supply only lead to changes in nominal variables but not in real variables. Changes in the money supply will therefore have no long-term effect on variables such as real output, unemployment or real interest rates.

new business
An aggregate in MFI interest rate statistics that comprises any new agreement between a household or non-financial corporation and a credit or other institution, i.e. all financial contracts, the terms and conditions of which specify for the first time the interest rate on the deposit or loan, and all new negotiations of existing deposits and loans. Tacit renewals of existing deposit and loan contracts, i.e. renewals without any active involvement of the household or non-financial corporation concerned and not involving any renegotiating of the terms and conditions of the contracts, including the interest rate, are not considered new business.

nominal effective exchange rates
See effective exchange rates (EERs) (nominal/real)

nominee
A person or entity named by another to act on his/her behalf. A nominee is commonly used in a securities transaction to obtain registration and legal ownership of a security.

non-financial corporation
A corporation or quasi-corporation that is not engaged in financial intermediation but is active primarily in the production of market goods and non-financial services.

novation
Satisfaction and discharge of existing contractual obligations by means of their replacement by new obligations (whose effect, for example, is to replace gross with net payment obligations). The parties to the new obligations may be the same as to the existing obligations or, in the context of some clearing house arrangements, there may additionally be substitution of parties.

O

obligation
A duty imposed by contract or law.

OECD
See Organisation for Economic Co-operation and Development (OECD)

OFI
See other financial intermediary (OFI)

OFI sector
A sub-sector defined in the ESA 95 as comprising the OFIs (excluding insurance corporations and pension funds).

open market operation
An operation executed on the initiative of the central bank in the financial market. With regard to their aims, regularity and procedures, Eurosystem open market operations can be divided into four categories: main refinancing operations; longer-term refinancing operations; fine-tuning operations; and structural operations. As for the instruments used, reverse transactions are the main open market instrument of the Eurosystem and can be employed in all four categories of operations. In addition, the issuance of debt certificates and outright transactions are available for structural operations, while outright transactions, foreign exchange swaps and the collection of fixed-term deposits are available for the conduct of fine-tuning operations.

operational risk
The risk of human error or a breakdown of some component of the hardware, software or communications systems which is crucial to settlement.

opportunity cost
Measure of the costs of holding an asset, typically measured as the spread between its own return and the return on an alternative asset.

option
A financial instrument that gives the owner the right, but not the obligation, to buy or sell specific assets (e.g. a bond or a stock) at a predetermined price (the strike or exercise price) at or up to a certain future date (the exercise or maturity date). A call option gives the holder the right to purchase the underlying assets at an agreed exercise price, whereas a put option gives the holder the right to sell them at an agreed price.

Organisation for Economic Co-operation and Development (OECD)
The OECD (based in Paris) was founded in 1961 as the successor to the Organisation for European Economic Co-operation (OEEC). It brings together 29 member countries (2001) in an organisation that, most importantly, provides governments with a setting in which to discuss,

develop and perfect economic and social policy.

original maturity
See maturity at issue (original maturity)

other financial intermediary (OFI)
A corporation or quasi-corporation other than an insurance corporation and pension fund that is engaged mainly in financial intermediation by incurring liabilities in forms other than currency, deposits and/or close substitutes for deposits from institutional entities other than MFIs, in particular those engaged primarily in long-term financing, such as corporations engaged in financial leasing, financial vehicle corporations created to be holders of securitised assets, financial holding corporations, dealers in securities and derivatives (when dealing for their own account), venture capital corporations and development capital companies.

other lending
Credit other than consumer credit and loans for house purchase that is extended to households for special purposes such as business needs, the procurement of office equipment, debt consolidation, education, the purchase of securities, etc.

other revaluations
An aggregate in monetary statistics that comprises changes in the MFI balance sheet that are due to a change in the market price of negotiable securities held, sold or issued and/or to the (partial) removal from the balance sheet of loans that are subject to write-offs or write-downs. A change in the market value of securities held, sold or issued by MFIs affects the outstanding stock of securities, in addition to actual transactions in these securities. A write-off or write-down of loans has an impact on the reported value of the outstanding amount of loans, but is not related to a change in the amount of MFI lending to the economy.

output gap
The difference between the actual and potential levels of output of an economy, expressed as a percentage of potential output. Potential output is the level of output that can be achieved when the factors of production are utilised at non-inflationary levels.

outright transaction
A transaction whereby assets are bought or sold outright in the market (spot or forward).

overnight deposits
Deposits with next-day maturity. This instrument category comprises mainly those sight/demand deposits that are fully transferable (by cheque or similar instrument). It also includes non-transferable deposits that are convertible on demand or by close of business the following day. Overnight deposits are included in M1 (and hence in M2 and M3).

oversight of payment systems
A central bank task, principally intended to promote the smooth functioning of payment systems and to protect the financial system from possible "domino effects" which may occur when one or more participants in the payment system incur credit or liquidity problems. Payment systems oversight aims at a given system (e.g. a funds transfer system) rather than individual participants.

oversight of securities settlement systems
A task, principally intended to promote the smooth functioning of securities settlement systems and to protect the financial system from possible "domino effects" which may occur when one or more participants in the securities settlement system incur credit or liquidity problems. The oversight of securities settlement systems aims at a given system (e.g. a securities transfer

system) rather than individual participants. It is performed by the dedicated financial authority/authorities and/or the central bank in accordance with the local legal framework.

P

payment
The payer's transfer of a monetary claim on a party acceptable to the payee. Typically, claims take the form of banknotes or deposit balances held at a financial institution or at a central bank.

payment instrument
Any instrument enabling the holder/user to transfer funds.

payment message/instruction/order
An order or message to transfer funds (in the form of a monetary claim on a party) to the account of the beneficiary. The order may relate either to a credit transfer or to a debit transfer. See also
credit transfer
debit transfer system
payment

Payment Settlement Message Notification (PSMN)
The response to a PSMR, which can be either positive or negative. A PSMN is normally positive (indicating that the beneficiary's settlement account in the receiving NCB/the ECB's books has been successfully credited). It may be negative, in which case it is returned to the sending central bank with an error code. See also Payment Settlement Message Request (PSMR)

Payment Settlement Message Request (PSMR)
The settlement of TARGET cross-border payments involves the exchange of PSMRs from the sending NCB/the ECB and PSMNs from the receiving NCB/the ECB. The sender of the PSMR requests the receiver to process a payment; this message requires a positive or negative response from the receiver (PSMN). See also Payment Settlement Message Notification (PSMN)

payment system
A payment system consists of a set of instruments, banking procedures and, typically, interbank funds transfer systems which facilitate the circulation of money.

payment versus payment (PVP)
A mechanism in a foreign exchange settlement system which ensures that a final transfer of one currency occurs if, and only if, a final transfer of the other currency or currencies takes place.

pension fund
Provision or similar fund set aside by non-financial corporations to pay for their employees' pensions.

percentage balance
The form in which the results of European Commission surveys are usually presented, namely as the difference between the percentage of respondents giving positive and that of those giving negative replies.

personal identification number (PIN)
A numeric code which the cardholder may need to quote for verification of identity. In electronic transactions, it is seen as the equivalent of a signature.

PIN

See personal identification number (PIN)

point of sale (POS)
This term refers to the use of payment cards at a retail location (point of sale). The payment information is captured either on paper vouchers or by electronic terminals, which, in some cases, are designed to also transmit the information (in which case the arrangement may be referred to as "electronic funds transfer at point of sale" (EFTPOS)).

portfolio investment account
A b.o.p. account which records cross-border investment in equities (quoted and unquoted shares) and debt securities (bonds and notes, and money market instruments), excluding amounts recorded in direct investment or reserve assets.

POS
See point of sale (POS)

position netting
A netting of instructions in respect of obligations between two or more parties which neither satisfies nor discharges those original individual obligations. Also referred to as payment netting, in the case of payment instructions, or advisory netting.

post-fixed coupon
A coupon on floating rate instruments which is determined on the basis of the values taken by the reference index at a certain date (or dates) during the coupon accrual period.

PPP
See purchasing power parity (PPP)

pre-fixed coupon
A coupon on floating rate instruments which is determined on the basis of the values taken by the reference index at a certain date (or dates) before the start of the coupon accrual period.

premium
The difference between the par value of a security and its price when such price is higher than par.

prepaid card
A card on which value is stored, and for which the holder has paid the issuer in advance. See also electronic purse
multi-purpose prepaid card

price stability
The primary objective of the Eurosystem, which has been defined by the Governing Council as a year-on-year increase in consumer prices (as measured by the HICP) for the euro area that is below but close to 2% over the medium term.

primary balance
The general government sector's net borrowing or net lending excluding interest payments on consolidated government liabilities.

principal risk
The risk that a party will lose the full value involved in a transaction (credit risk). In the settlement process, this term is typically associated with exchange-for-value transactions when there is a lag between the final settlement of the various legs of a transaction (i.e. the absence of delivery

versus payment). The principal risk which arises from the settlement of foreign exchange transactions (foreign exchange settlement risk) is sometimes called cross-currency settlement risk or Herstatt risk. See also credit risk/exposure
delivery versus payment (DVP) system

projections
See Eurosystem staff projections

provisional transfer
A conditional transfer in which one or more parties retain the right by law or agreement to rescind the transfer.

provisions
Amounts set aside before arriving at the profit and loss figure in order to provide for any known or expected liability or risk, the cost of which cannot be accurately determined.

PSMN
See Payment Settlement Message Notification (PSMN)

PSMR
See Payment Settlement Message Request (PSMR)

purchasing power parity (PPP)
The rate used for the conversion of one currency into another that equalises the purchasing power of the two currencies by eliminating the differences in the price levels prevailing in the countries concerned. In their simplest form, PPPs show the ratio of the prices in national currency of the same good or service in different countries.

PVP
See payment versus payment (PVP)

Q

queuing
An arrangement whereby transfer orders are held pending by the originator/deliverer or by the system until sufficient cover is available in the originator's/deliverer's clearing account or under the limits set against the payer; in some cases, cover may include unused credit lines or available collateral. See also caps

quick tender
The tender procedure used by the Eurosystem for fine-tuning operations when it is deemed desirable to have a rapid impact on the liquidity situation in the market. Quick tenders are executed within a time frame of one hour and are restricted to a limited set of counterparties.

R

real effective exchange rates
See effective exchange rates (EERs) (nominal/real)
real-time gross settlement (RTGS) system
A settlement system in which processing and settlement take place on an order-by-order basis (without netting) in real time (continuously). See also gross settlement system
net settlement system
TARGET (Trans-European Automated Real-time Gross settlement Express Transfer system)

real-time processing

The processing of instructions at the time they are received rather than at some later time. See also batch processing

realised gains or losses
Gains/losses arising from the difference between the sale price of a balance sheet item and its (adjusted) cost.

reclassifications
An aggregate in monetary statistics that comprises changes in the MFI balance sheet that are due to a change in the MFI reporting population, to corporate restructuring, to a reclassification of assets and liabilities and to the correction of reporting errors (whenever the reporting error can be totally removed from the series, no specific reclassification needs to be reported). The occurrence of these factors gives rise to breaks in the series and, hence, affects the comparability of successive end-of-period levels.

reference value for monetary growth
In order to assess monetary developments, the Governing Council has announced a reference value for the growth of the broad monetary aggregate M3. This reference value refers to the rate of M3 growth that is deemed to be compatible with price stability over the medium term. The reference value is derived in a manner that is consistent with and serves the achievement of the Governing Council's definition of price stability on the basis of medium-term assumptions regarding trend real GDP growth and the trend in the velocity of circulation of M3. Substantial or prolonged deviations of M3 growth from the reference value would, under normal circumstances, signal risks to price stability over the medium term. However, monetary policy does not react mechanically to deviations of M3 growth from the reference value. At present, this reference value is 4½%.

reference value for the fiscal position
Treaty Protocol No 20 on the excessive deficit procedure sets explicit reference values for the general government deficit ratio (3% of GDP) and the debt ratio (60% of GDP). See also Stability and Growth Pact

registration
The listing of ownership of securities in the records of the issuer or its transfer agent/registrar.

remote access to an SSS
The facility enabling a securities settlement system (SSS) in one country ("home country") to become a direct participant in an SSS established in another country ("host country") and, for that purpose, to have a securities account in its own name with the SSS in the host country. See also securities settlement system (SSS)

remote access to TARGET
The possibility for an institution established in one country in the EEA to become a direct participant in the RTGS system of another country and, for this purpose, to have a settlement account in euro in its own name with the central bank of the second country without necessarily having established a branch or subsidiary in that country.

remote participant
A participant in a system which has neither its head office nor any of its branches located in the country where the system is based.

replacement cost risk
The risk that a counterparty to an outstanding transaction for completion at a future date will fail to perform on the settlement date. This failure may leave the solvent party with an unhedged or

open market position or deny the solvent party unrealised gains on the position. The resulting exposure is the cost of replacing, at current market prices, the original transaction. See also credit risk/exposure

repo
See repurchase agreement
repurchase operation

repo operation
See repurchase operation

repurchase agreement
An arrangement to sell an asset and to repurchase it at a specified price on a predetermined future date or on demand. Such an agreement is similar to collateralised borrowing, except that in this case ownership of the securities is not retained by the seller. The Eurosystem uses repurchase agreements with a fixed maturity in its reverse transactions.

repurchase date
The date on which the buyer is obliged to sell back assets to the seller in relation to a transaction under a repurchase agreement. See also repurchase agreement

repurchase operation
A liquidity-providing reverse transaction based on a repurchase agreement.

repurchase price
The price at which the buyer is obliged to sell back assets to the seller in relation to a transaction under a repurchase agreement. The repurchase price equals the sum of the purchase price and the price differential corresponding to the interest on the extended liquidity over the maturity of the operation. See also repurchase agreement

reserve account
An account with the national central bank on which a counterparty's reserve holdings are maintained. The counterparties' settlement accounts with the national central banks may be used as reserve accounts.

reserve base
The sum of the eligible balance sheet items (in particular liabilities) that constitute the basis for calculating the reserve requirement of a credit institution. See also reserve requirements

reserve holdings
Counterparties' holdings on their reserve accounts which serve to fulfil reserve requirements. See also reserve requirements

reserve ratio
The ratio defined by the central bank for each category of eligible balance sheet items included in the reserve base. The ratios are used to calculate reserve requirements. See also reserve requirements

reserve requirements
See minimum reserve requirement

reserve-related liabilities

Predetermined and contingent short-term net drains on the Eurosystem, similar to reserve assets and other foreign currency assets of the Eurosystem.

reserves
An amount set aside out of distributable profits, which is not intended to meet any specific liability, contingency or expected diminution in value of assets known to exist at the balance sheet date.

residence
The location (dwelling, place of production or other premises) within the economic territory of a country, from which an institutional entity engages and intends to continue engaging (indefinitely or for a finite period of, as a rule, one year or more) in economic activities and transactions on a significant scale. See also resident

resident
An individual or entity defined in Council Regulation No 2533 of 23 November 1998 concerning the collection of statistical information by the European Central Bank, and in line with the ESA 95, as having a centre of economic interest in the economic territory of a country, i.e. the euro area in the case of Eurosystem statistics. See also residence

residential property price indicator
A measure of the average changes over time in prices of residential dwellings (including both new and second-hand houses and flats). There is no harmonised methodology, and euro area aggregates are currently based on heterogeneous national indicators.

residual maturity
Time remaining until the maturity date of a debt instrument.

responsibilities of a central bank when applying the Core Principles
(A) The central bank should define clearly its payment system objectives and should disclose publicly its role and major policies with respect to systemically important payment systems. (B) The central bank should ensure that the systems it operates comply with the Core Principles. (C) The central bank should oversee compliance with the Core Principles by systems it does not operate and it should have the ability to carry out this oversight. (D) The central bank, in promoting payment system safety and efficiency through the Core Principles, should cooperate with other central banks and with any other relevant domestic or foreign authority. See also Core principles for systemically important payment systems

retail bank interest rates
See MFI interest rates

retail funds transfer system
A funds transfer system which handles a large volume of payments of relatively low value in such forms as cheques, credit transfers, direct debits, and ATM and EFTPOS transactions.

retail payments
This term describes all payments which are not included in the definition of large-value payments. Retail payments are mainly consumer payments of relatively low value and urgency.

retail sales
The turnover in the retail trade (excluding sales of motor vehicles and motorcycles and excluding repairs) invoiced during the reference period; all duties and taxes, with the exception of VAT, are included.

revaluation accounts

Balance sheet accounts for registration of the difference in the value of an asset or liability between the adjusted cost of its acquisition and its valuation at an end-of-period market price, when the latter is higher than the former in the case of assets, and when the latter is lower than the former in the case of liabilities. They include differences in both price quotation and/or market exchange rates.

reverse repo
See reverse sale and repurchase agreement ("reverse repo")

reverse sale and repurchase agreement ("reverse repo")
A contract under which a holder of cash agrees to the purchase of an asset and, simultaneously, agrees to re-sell the asset for an agreed price on demand, or after a stated time, or in the event of a particular contingency. Sometimes a repo transaction is agreed via a third party ("triparty repo"). See also repurchase agreement

reverse transaction
An operation whereby the central bank buys or sells assets under a repurchase agreement or conducts credit operations against collateral.

RTGS system
See real-time gross settlement (RTGS) system

S

S.W.I.F.T. s.c.r.l
See SWIFT (S.W.I.F.T. s.c.r.l.) (Society for Worldwide Interbank Financial Telecommunication)

safe custody account
A securities account managed by the central bank on which credit institutions can place securities deemed suitable to back central bank operations.

SDR
See special drawing right (SDR)

Securities Settlement System (SSS)
A system which permits the holding and transfer of securities or other financial assets, either free of payment (FOP) or against payment (delivery versus payment). See also delivery versus payment (DVP) system

security-by-security data collection
The collection of data broken down into individual securities.

settlement
An act which discharges obligations in respect of funds or securities transfers between two or more parties. A settlement may be final or provisional. See also final settlement
gross settlement system
net settlement
net settlement system

settlement account
An account held by a direct participant in a national RTGS system with the central bank for the purpose of processing payments. See also gross settlement system

settlement agent

An institution which manages the settlement process (e.g. the determination of settlement positions, the monitoring of payment exchanges, etc.) for transfer systems or other arrangements requiring settlement.

settlement date
The date on which a transaction is settled. The settlement might take place on the same day as the trade (same-day settlement) or one or several days after the trade (the settlement date is specified as the trade date (T) + the settlement lag). See also trade date (T)

settlement risk
A general term used to designate the risk that settlement in a transfer system will not take place as expected. This risk may comprise both credit and liquidity risks. See also credit risk/exposure liquidity risk

settlement unwind
See unwinding (or settlement unwind)

single rate auction (Dutch auction)
An auction in which the allotment interest rate (or price/swap point) applied for all satisfied bids is equal to the marginal interest rate. See also variable rate tender

social security funds
A sector defined in the ESA 95 as comprising all central, state and local institutional units, the principal activity of which is to provide social security benefits and which fulfil both of the following two criteria: (i) certain groups of the population are required by law or by regulation to participate in the scheme or to pay contributions; and (ii) the general government is responsible for the management of the scheme.

Society for Worldwide Interbank Financial Telecommunication
See SWIFT (S.W.I.F.T. s.c.r.l.) (Society for Worldwide Interbank Financial Telecommunication)

solvency risk
The risk of loss owing to the failure (bankruptcy) of an issuer of a financial asset or to the insolvency of the counterparty.

special drawing right (SDR)
An international reserve asset created by the IMF to supplement other reserve assets that are periodically allocated to IMF members in proportion to their respective quotas. SDRs are not considered liabilities of the Fund, and IMF members to whom SDRs are allocated do not incur actual (unconditional) liabilities to repay SDRs allocated.

SSS
See Securities Settlement System (SSS)

Stability and Growth Pact
The Stability and Growth Pact consists of two EU Council Regulations, on "the strengthening of the surveillance of budgetary positions and the surveillance and coordination of economic policies" and on "speeding up and clarifying the implementation of the excessive deficit procedure", and of a European Council Resolution on the Stability and Growth Pact adopted at the Amsterdam summit on 17 June 1997. More specifically, budgetary positions close to balance or in surplus are required as the medium-term objective for Member States since this would allow them to deal with normal cyclical fluctuations while keeping their government deficit below the reference value of 3% of GDP. In accordance with the Stability and Growth Pact, countries participating in EMU will submit annual stability programmes, while non-participating countries will

continue to provide annual convergence programmes.

stability programmes
These are medium-term government plans and assumptions provided by euro area countries regarding the development of key economic variables with a view to the achievement of the medium-term objective of a budgetary position close to balance or in surplus as referred to in the Stability and Growth Pact. These programmes present measures for the consolidation of fiscal balances as well as the underlying economic scenarios. Stability programmes must be updated annually. They are examined by the European Commission and the Economic and Financial Committee (EFC). Their reports serve as the basis for an assessment by the ECOFIN Council, focusing in particular on whether the medium-term budgetary objective in the programme is in line with a budgetary position close to balance or in surplus, providing for an adequate safety margin to ensure that an excessive deficit is avoided. Countries that have not yet adopted the euro must submit annual convergence programmes, in accordance with the Stability and Growth Pact. See
Economic and Financial Committee (EFC)
EU Council (Council of Ministers)
Stability and Growth Pact

Stage One
See Economic and Monetary Union (EMU)

Stage Three
See Economic and Monetary Union (EMU)

Stage Two
See Economic and Monetary Union (EMU)

standard tender
A tender procedure used by the Eurosystem in its regular open market operations. Standard tenders are carried out within 24 hours. All counterparties fulfilling the general eligibility criteria are entitled to submit bids.

standardised deduction
The fixed percentage of the amount outstanding of debt securities with an agreed maturity of up to two years (including money market paper) which can be deducted from the reserve base by issuers that cannot present evidence that such outstanding amount is held by other institutions subject to the minimum reserve system of the Eurosystem, by the ECB or by a national central bank. See also reserve base
reserve requirements

standing facility
A central bank facility available to specified credit institutions on their own initiative. The Eurosystem offers two overnight standing facilities, the marginal lending facility and the deposit facility.

standing order
An instruction from a customer to his bank to make a regular payment of a fixed amount to a named recipient.

start date
The date on which the first leg of a monetary policy operation is settled. The start date corresponds to the purchase date for operations based on repurchase agreements and foreign exchange swaps.

state government
A sector defined in the ESA 95 as comprising separate institutional units exercising some of the functions of government (excluding the administration of social security funds) at a level below that of the central government and above that of local government.

stock market
See equity market

STP
See straight-through processing (STP)

straight line depreciation/amortisation
Depreciation/amortisation over a given period is determined by dividing the cost of the asset, less its estimated residual value, by the estimated useful life of the asset pro rata temporis.

straight-through processing (STP)
The automated end-to-end processing of trades/payment transfers including the automated completion of confirmation, generation, clearing and settlement of instructions.

strip (separate trading of interest and principal)
A zero-coupon bond created in order to trade separately the claims on particular cash flows of a security and the principal of the same instrument.

structural operation
An open market operation executed by the Eurosystem mainly in order to adjust the structural liquidity position of the financial sector vis-à-vis the Eurosystem.

substitution (of party)
The substitution of one party for another in respect of an obligation. In a netting and settlement context the term typically refers to the process of amending a contract between two parties so that a third party is interposed as counterparty to each of the two parties and the original contract between the two parties is satisfied and discharged. See also net settlement
novation

supervision of financial institutions
The assessment and enforcement of compliance by financial institutions with laws, regulations or other rules intended to ensure that they operate in a safe and sound manner and that they hold capital and reserves sufficient to support the risks which arise in connection with their business operations.

swap
An agreement to exchange future cash flows according to a prearranged formula. See also
foreign exchange swap

swap point
The difference between the exchange rate of the forward transaction and the exchange rate of the spot transaction in a foreign exchange swap.

SWIFT (S.W.I.F.T. s.c.r.l.) (Society for Worldwide Interbank Financial Telecommunication)
The cooperative organisation created and owned by banks which operates a network to facilitate the exchange of payment and other financial messages between financial institutions (including broker-dealers and securities companies) throughout the world. A SWIFT payment message is an instruction to transfer funds; the exchange of funds (settlement) subsequently takes place over a

payment system or through correspondent banking relationships.

systemic disruption
An event or events whose impact has the potential to threaten the stability of the financial system through transmission from one financial institution to another, including through the payment system. See also systemic risk

systemic risk
The risk that the failure of one participant in a transfer system, or in financial markets generally, to meet its required obligations will cause other participants or financial institutions to be unable to meet their obligations (including settlement obligations in a transfer system) when due. Such a failure may cause significant liquidity or credit problems and, as a result, might threaten the stability of financial markets.

systemically important payment system
A payment system is systemically important where, if the system were insufficiently protected against risk, disruption within it could trigger or transmit further disruptions amongst participants or systemic disruptions in the financial area more widely. See also systemic risk

T

TARGET (Trans-European Automated Real-time Gross settlement Express Transfer system)
A payment system comprising 15 national real-time gross settlement (RTGS) systems and the ECB payment mechanism (EPM). The national RTGS systems and the EPM are interconnected by common procedures (interlinking), so that TARGET gives access to almost 1,100 direct participants and more than 48,000 credit institutions (including branches and subsidiaries) for the real-time processing of cross-border transfers throughout the European Union. See also ECB payment mechanism (EPM)
gross settlement system
real-time gross settlement (RTGS) system

TARGET availability
The ratio of time when TARGET is fully operational to TARGET operating time.

TARGET business continuity
The ability of each national TARGET component to switch to a remote secondary site in the event of a failure at the primary site, to enable operations to continue normally within the shortest time possible.

TARGET contingency measures
Arrangements in TARGET which aim to ensure that it meets agreed service levels during abnormal events even if the use of an alternative site would not be possible or would require too much time.

TARGET market share
The percentage processed by TARGET of the large-value payments in euro exchanged via all euro large-value payment systems. The other systems are Euro 1 (EBA), PNS (Paris Net Settlement), SPI (Servicio de Pagos Interbancarios), and Pankkien On-line Pikasiirrot ja Sekit-järjestelmä (POPS).

TCP/IP (Transmission Control Protocol/Internet Protocol)
A set of commonly used communications and addressing protocols; TCP/IP is the de facto set of communications standards used for the internet.

tender procedure

A procedure in which the central bank provides liquidity to or withdraws liquidity from the market on the basis of bids submitted by counterparties in competition with each other. The most competitive bids are satisfied with priority until the total amount of liquidity to be provided or withdrawn by the central bank is exhausted. See also variable rate tender

tier one asset
A marketable asset fulfilling certain uniform euro area-wide eligibility criteria specified by the ECB.

tier two asset
A marketable or non-marketable asset for which specific eligibility criteria are established by the national central banks, subject to ECB approval.

trade date (T)
The date on which a trade (i.e. an agreement on a financial transaction between two counterparties) is struck. The trade date might coincide with the settlement date for the transaction (same-day settlement) or precede the settlement date by a specified number of business days (the settlement date is specified as T + the settlement lag). See also settlement date

trading
Trading is the process whereby two counterparties reach an agreement with regard to buying and selling securities. Each trade can be considered as a contractual agreement between a buyer and a seller, who agree to exchange a certain amount of securities for a certain amount of cash. Trading can take place on regulated markets (an example would be a stock exchange), or it can take place outside regulated markets, in multilateral trading facilities or over the counter (OTC).

Trans-European Automated Real-time Gross settlement Express Transfer system
See TARGET (Trans-European Automated Real-time Gross settlement Express Transfer system)

transaction
An economic flow that reflects the creation, transformation, exchange, transfer or extinction of economic value and involves changes in ownership of goods and/or financial assets, the provision of services, or the provision of labour and capital.

transaction cost
Costs that are identifiable as related to the specific transaction.

transaction price
The price agreed between the parties when a contract is made.

transfer
Operationally, the sending (or movement) of funds or securities or of rights relating to funds or securities from one party to another party by (i) the conveyance of physical instruments/money; (ii) accounting entries on the books of a financial intermediary; or (iii) accounting entries processed through a funds and/or securities transfer system. The act of transfer affects the legal rights of the transferor, the transferee and possibly third parties with regard to the money, security or other financial instrument being transferred.

transfer system
A generic term covering interbank funds transfer systems and exchange-for-value systems.

Transmission Control Protocol/Internet Protocol

See TCP/IP (Transmission Control Protocol/Internet Protocol)

transmission mechanism
See monetary policy transmission mechanism

Treaty
The short form generally used to refer to the Treaty establishing the European Community, the original version of which - the Treaty often referred to the as the "Treaty of Rome" because it was signed there on 25 March 1957 - entered into force on 1 January 1958 to establish the European Economic Community (EEC). The Treaty establishing the European Community was subsequently amended by the Treaty on European Union (often referred to as the "Maastricht Treaty") that was signed on 7 February 1992 and entered into force on 1 November 1993, thereby establishing the EU. Thereafter, both the Treaty establishing the European Community and the Treaty on European Union were amended by, first, the "Treaty of Amsterdam", which was signed in Amsterdam on 2 October 1997 and entered into force on 1 May 1999, and then, most recently, by the "Treaty of Nice", which was signed on 26 February 2001 (in conclusion of the Intergovernmental Conference of 2000) and entered into force on 1 February 2003.

trigger point
A pre-specified level of the value of the liquidity provided at which a margin call is executed.

U

unemployed
Any person, according to the EU definition, aged 15 to 74 who is (i) without work during the reference week, (ii) currently available for work and (iii) actively seeking work.

unemployment rate
The number of unemployed persons as a percentage of the labour force.

unit labour costs
Total labour costs per unit of output calculated for the euro area as the ratio of total compensation per employee to GDP at constant prices per person employed.

unrealised gains or losses
Gains/losses arising from the revaluation of assets compared with their adjusted cost of acquisition.

unwinding (or settlement unwind)
A procedure followed in certain clearing and settlement systems in which transfers of securities or funds are settled on a net basis, at the end of the processing cycle, with all transfers being provisional until all participants have discharged their settlement obligations. If a participant fails to settle, some or all of the provisional transfers involving that participant are deleted from the system and the settlement obligations from the remaining transfers are then recalculated. Such a procedure has the effect of transferring liquidity pressures and possible losses arising from the failure to settle to other participants, and may, in an extreme case, result in significant and unpredictable systemic risks. Also called settlement unwind. See also net settlement

W

write-down
An adjustment to the value of loans recorded in the balance sheets of MFIs. A loan is written down when it is recognised as having become partly unrecoverable, and its value in the balance sheet is reduced accordingly. See also write-off

write-off
An adjustment to the value of loans recorded in the balance sheets of MFIs. A loan is written off when it is considered to be totally unrecoverable, and is removed from the balance sheet. See also write-down

X

XML
The acronym used for “Extensible Markup Language”, a computer metalanguage used to simplify the transmission of formatted data

Y

yield curve
A curve describing the relationship between the interest rate or yield and the maturity at a given point in time for debt securities with the same credit risk but different maturity dates. The slope of the yield curve can be measured as the difference between the interest rates at two selected maturities.

TITLE
EU Defense Strategy and Armed Forces Handbook
EU Emission Trading Laws, Regulations and Programs Handbook
EU Healthcare Sector Organization, Management and Payment Systems Handbook - Strategic Information, Programs and Regulations
EU Intelligence and Security Policy and Cooperation Handbook
EU Intelligence and Security Policy and Cooperation Handbook
EU Mediterranean Partnership Handbook
EU Military and Special Forces Handbook
EU Military and Special Forces Handbook
EU Monetary Financial Institutions Handbook
EU Money Laundering Prevention Regulations Handbook
EU National Cyber Security Strategy and Programs Handbook - Strategic Information and Developments
EU Nuclear Energy Policy Handbook
EU Pacific Region Countries Economic and Political Cooperation Handbook
EU Pacific Region Countries Economic and Political Cooperation Handbook
EU Pharmaceutical Legislation Handbook. Vol. 1. Legislation on Medicinal Products for Human Use
EU Pharmaceutical Legislation Handbook. Vol. 1. Legislation on Medicinal Products for Human Use
EU Pharmaceutical Legislation Handbook. Vol. 3 Legislation on Gene and Cell Therapy: see in particular Part IV of Annex I (Advanced therapy medicinal products)
EU Pharmaceutical Legislation Handbook. Vol. 3 Legislation on Gene and Cell Therapy: see in particular Part IV of Annex I (Advanced therapy medicinal products)
EU Pharmaceutical Legislation Handbook. Vol. 4 Legislation on Medical Devices
EU Pharmaceutical Legislation Handbook. Vol. 4 Legislation on Medical Devices
EU Pharmaceutical Legislation Handbook. Vol. 5 Legislation on the Quality and Safety of human tissues and cells
EU Pharmaceutical Legislation Handbook. Vol. 5 Legislation on the Quality and Safety of human tissues and cells
EU Postal Service Handbook
EU Postal Service Handbook
EU Privatization Yearbook: Major Programs and Projects
EU Security Strategy and Cooperation Handbook
EU Security Strategy and Cooperation Handbook
EU Shipbuilding Industry Handbook
EU Shipbuilding Industry Handbook
EU Shipbuilding Industry Investment and Business Guide - Strategic and Practical Information
EU Shipbuilding Industry Investment and Business Guide - Strategic and Practical Information
EU Shipbuilding Industry Law and Regulations Handbook
EU Shipbuilding Industry Law and Regulations Handbook
EU Terrorism Prevention Regulations Handbook
EU Western European Armaments Organization Handbook
EU Western European Armaments Organization Handbook
EU-China Political and Economic Relations Handbook
EU-China Political and Economic Relations Handbook

TITLE
EU-Mexico Political and Economic Relations Handbook
Eurasian Economic Union Trade and Investment Agreements Handbook - Strategic Information and Basic Agreements
Euro-Mediterranean Free Trade Area Business Opportunities Handbook
Europe E-commerce Business Handbook
Europe E-commerce Business Handbook
Europe Financial and Economic Development Handbook
Europe Financial and Economic Development Handbook
European Airlines Handbook
European Airlines Handbook
European Association For Aviation Psychology (EAAP) Handbook
European Aviation Safety Agency (EASA) Handbook
European Aviation Safety Handbook
European Bank for Reconstruction and Development (EBRD) Handbook
European Bank for Reconstruction and Development (EBRD) Handbook
European Banking System Handbook Vol. 1 History and Functions
European Banking System Handbook Vol. 2 Banking, Financial System and Regulations
European Countries Antiterrorism Programs and Operations Handbook
European Countries Antiterrorism Programs and Operations Handbook
European Defense Agency Handbook: Strategy, Activities Contacts
European Defense Agency Handbook: Strategy, Activities Contacts
European Defense Policy Handbook: Strategy & Cooperation
European Defense Policy Handbook: Strategy & Cooperation
European Flight Regulations Handbook: System and Procedures
European Flight Regulations Handbook: System and Procedures
European Free Trade Association (EFTA) Handbook
European Free Trade Association (EFTA) Handbook
European Investment Bank (EIB) Handbook
European Investment Bank (EIB) Handbook
European Investment Fund (EIF) Handbook
European Investment Fund (EIF) Handbook
European Police Office - EUROPOL Handbook
European Police Office-EUROPOL Handbook
European Police System Organization Handbook
European Publishers Directory
European Publishers Directory
European Space Agency Handbook - Strategic Information, Programs, Contacts
European Space Agency Handbook - International Agreements and Regulations
European Space Policy and Programs Handbook
European Space Policy and Programs Handbook
European System for Security and Cooperation Handbook
European System for Security and Cooperation Handbook
European Union (EU) Government and Business Contacts Handbook
European Union (EU) Government and Business Contacts Handbook
European Union Airport Handbook

TITLE
European Union Airports Handbook
European Union at the United Nations Handbook
European Union at the United Nations Handbook
European Union Aviation & Aerospace Industry Handbook
European Union Aviation & Aerospace Industry Handbook
European Union Banking & Financial Market Handbook
European Union Banking & Financial Market Handbook
European Union Business Law Handbook - Strategic Information and Basic Laws
European Union Business Law Handbook - Strategic Information and Basic Laws
European Union Company Laws and Regulations Handbook - Strategic Information and Basic Laws
European Union Cosmetics Industry Handbook
European Union Cosmetics Industry Handbook
European Union HANDBOOK Volume 1 Strategic and Practical Information
European Union Insolvency (Bankruptcy) Laws and Regulations Handbook - Strategic Information and Basic Laws
European Union Investment and Business Guide - Strategic and Practical Information
European Union Investment and Business Guide - Strategic and Practical Information
European Union Pharmaceutical Industry Handbook
European Union Pharmaceutical Industry Handbook
European Union Pharmaceutical Legislation Handbook
European Union Pharmaceutical Legislation Handbook
European Union Privatization Programs and Regulations Handbook
European Union Privatization Programs and Regulations Handbook
European Union, The (EC) Handbook
EUROPOL û European Police Office Handbook
EU-Russia Political and Economic Relations Handbook
EU-Russia Political and Economic Relations Handbook

GLOBAL
WORLD INTERNATIONAL ORGANIZATIONS BUSINESS AND DEVELOPMENT LIBRARY

PRICE - $149.95 EACH

1. Abu Dhabi Fund for Development Handbook
2. African Development Bank Group(AfDB) Handbook
3. African Development Fund (AfDF) Handbook
4. Nigeria Trust Fund (NTF) Handbook
5. African Export-Import Bank (AFREXIMBANK) Handbook
6. Andean Community General Secretariat Handbook
7. Andean Development Corporation (CAF) Handbook
8. Arab Authority for Agricultural Investment and Development (AAAID) Handbook
9. Arab Bank for Economic Development in Africa (BADEA) Handbook
10. Arab Fund for Economic and Social Development (AFESD) Handbook
11. Arab Gulf Programme for United Nations Development Organizations (AGFUND) Handbook
12. Arab Maghreb Union (AMU) Handbook
13. Arab Monetary Fund (AMF) Handbook
14. Arab Organization for Agricultural Development (AOAD) Handbook
15. Arab Planning Institute - Kuwait Handbook
16. Arab Trade Financing Program (ATFP) Handbook
17. Asia-Pacific Economic Cooperation (APEC) Handbook
18. Asian and Pacific Coconut Community (APCC) Handbook
19. Asian Clearing Union (ACU) Handbook
20. Asian Development Bank (AsDB) Handbook
21. Association of Natural Rubber Producing Countries (ANRPC) Handbook
22. Association of South East Asian Nations (ASEAN) Handbook
23. Baltic Council of Ministers Handbook
24. Bank for International Settlements (BIS) Handbook
25. Bank of Central African States (BEAC) Handbook
26. Black Sea Trade and Development Bank (BSTDB) Handbook
27. Caribbean Centre for Monetary Studies (CCMS) Handbook
28. Caribbean Community (CARICOM) Handbook
29. Caribbean Development Bank (CDB) Handbook
30. Caribbean Regional Technical Assistance Centre (CARTAC) Handbook
31. Center for Latin American Monetary Studies (CEMLA) Handbook
32. Center for Marketing Information and Advisory Services for Fishery Products in Latin America and the Caribbean (INFOPESCA) Handbook
33. Central American Bank for Economic Integration (CABEI) Handbook
34. Central American Monetary Council (CAMC) Handbook
35. Central Bank of West African States (BCEAO) Handbook
36. Colombo Plan for Co-operative Economic and Social Development in Asia and the Pacific Handbook
37. Colombo Plan Staff College for Technician Education Handbook

38. Common Fund for Commodities Handbook
39. Common Market for Eastern and Southern Africa (COMESA) Handbook
40. Cooperation Council for the Arab States of the Gulf (GCC) Handbook
41. Council of the Baltic Sea States (CBSS) Handbook
42. Council of Europe Development Bank (CEB) Handbook
43. East African Development Bank (EADB) Handbook
44. Eastern Caribbean Central Bank (ECCB) Handbook
45. Economic Community of West African States (ECOWAS) Handbook
46. Economic Cooperation Organization (ECO) Handbook
47. European Bank for Reconstruction and Development (EBRD) Handbook
48. European Central Bank (ECB) Handbook
49. European Free Trade Association (EFTA) Handbook
50. European Investment Bank (EIB) Handbook
51. European Investment Fund (EIF) Handbook
52. European Union, The (EC) Handbook
53. Financial Fund for the Development of the River Plate Basin (FONPLATA) Handbook
54. Food and Agriculture Organization of the United Nations (FAO) Handbook
55. Fund for Co-operation, Compensation and Development (ECOWAS Fund) Handbook
56. Inter-American Development Bank (IDB) Handbook
57. Inter-American Institute for Cooperation on Agriculture (IICA) Handbook
58. Inter-Arab Investment Guarantee Corporation (IAIGC) Handbook
59. International Atomic Energy Regulations Handbook
60. International Civil Aviation Regulations Handbook
61. International Cocoa Production and Trade Regulations Handbook
62. International Coffee Production and Trade Regulations Handbook
63. International Confederation of Free Trade Unions (ICFTU) Handbook
64. International Cotton Advisory Committee (ICAC) Handbook
65. International Fund for Agricultural Development (IFAD) Handbook
66. International Grains Council Handbook
67. International Labour Organization (ILO) Handbook
68. International Lead and Zinc Study Group Handbook
69. International Monetary Fund (IMF) Handbook
70. International Olive Oil Council (IOOC) Handbook
71. International Rubber Study Group Handbook
72. International Sugar Organization (ISO) Handbook
73. International Telecommunications Union (ITU) Handbook
74. International Tropical Timber Organization (ITTO) Handbook
75. Islamic Development Bank Group (IsDB) Handbook
76. Islamic Research and Training Institute (IRTI) Handbook
77. Joint Vienna Institute (JVI) Handbook
78. Kuwait Fund for Arab Economic Development Handbook
79. Lake Chad Basin Commission (LCBC) Handbook
80. Latin American Association of Development Financing Institutions (ALIDE) Handbook
81. Latin American Economic System (SELA) Handbook
82. Latin American Energy Organization (OLADE) Handbook
83. Latin American Export Bank (BLADEX) Handbook
84. Latin American Integration Association (ALADI) Handbook
85. Latin American Reserve Fund (LARF) Handbook
86. League of Arab States Handbook
87. Mekong River Commission (MRC) Handbook
88. Nordic Development Fund (NDF) Handbook

---

89. Nordic Investment Bank (NIB) Handbook
90. OPEC Fund for International Development Handbook
91. Organisation for Economic Co-operation and Development (OECD) Handbook
92. Organisation of Eastern Caribbean States (OECS) Handbook
93. Organization of American States (OAS) Handbook
94. Organization of Arab Petroleum Exporting Countries (OAPEC) Handbook
95. Organization of the Petroleum Exporting Countries (OPEC) Handbook
96. Pacific Financial Technical Assistance Centre Handbook
97. Pacific Islands Forum Secretariat Handbook
98. Pan American Health Organization (PAHO) Handbook
99. Regional Association of Oil and Natural Gas Companies in Latin America and the Caribbean (ARPEL) Handbook
100. Regional Electrical Integration Commission (CIER) Handbook
101. Saudi Fund for Development (SFD) Handbook
102. Secretariat for Central American Economic Integration (SIECA) Handbook
103. Secretariat of the Pacific Community Handbook
104. Sectorial Commission for the Common Market of the South (MERCOSUR) - Uruguay Handbook
105. South Asian Association for Regional Cooperation (SAARC) Handbook
106. South-East Asian Central Banks (SEACEN) Research and Training Centre Handbook
107. Training Centre for Regional Integration (CEFIR) Handbook
108. United Nations African Institute for Economic Development and Planning (IDEP) Handbook
109. United Nations Conference on Trade and Development (UNCTAD) Handbook
110. United Nations Development Program (UNDP) Handbook
111. United Nations Economic and Social Commission for Asia and the Pacific (ESCAP) Handbook
112. Asian and Pacific Centre for Transfer of Technology (APCTT) Handbook
113. Regional Coordination Centre for Research and Development of Coarse Grains, Pulses, Roots and Tuber Crops in the Humid Tropics of Asia and the Pacific (ESCAP CGPRT Centre) Handbook
114. Statistical Institute for Asia and the Pacific (SIAP) Handbook
115. United Nations Economic and Social Commission for Western Asia (ESCWA) Handbook
116. United Nations Economic Commission for Africa (UNECA) Handbook
117. United Nations Economic Commission for Europe (UN/ECE) Handbook
118. United Nations Economic Commission for Latin America and the Caribbean (ECLAC) Handbook
119. United Nations Educational, Scientific and Cultural Organization (UNESCO) Handbook
120. United Nations Industrial Development Organization (UNIDO) Handbook
121. United Nations Latin American and Caribbean Institute for Economic and Social Planning (ILPES) Handbook
122. World Postal Service Handbook: Volume 1 Strategic information and basic regulations
123. West African Development Bank (BOAD) Handbook
124. West Africa Economic and Monetary Union Handbook
125. World Bank Group Handbook
126. World Food Program (WFP) Handbook
127. World Health Organization (WHO) Handbook
128. World Trade Organization (WTO) Handbook